THE
BEERS
OF
FRANCE

By

JOHN WOODS
and
KEITH RIGLEY

DEDICATIONS

To my mother – from whom I get my love of books, if not my love of beer.

John Woods

Thanks to those who give support, encouragement and understanding. You know who you are.

Also to Tim Duquénoy and Dick Palmer for the company on the long days and nights of research trips.

Keith Rigley

ACKNOWLEDGEMENTS

The authors would like to thank the following for permission to use the illustrations listed below:

Brasseries Fischer & Adelshoffen – p. 132
Brasseries Kronenbourg – p. 172
Musée Français de la Brasserie – pp. 22, 23 (top)
Phil Toms, Charlbury, Oxon – p. 58

The authors gratefully acknowledge the translation services of Valérie Zitoun of VZ Translations, Charlbury, Oxon; Sue Harmes of Charlbury, Oxon; Stephen Pearson of Munich, Germany; and Philippe Rubrecht. Also the proof reading services of Richard Palmer of Straitext, Charlbury, Oxon, and the research assistance of Ben Henry, John White, Simon van Tromp, Allen Worsfold and Colin Heapy.

ISBN 0 9529238 3 1

© 1998 The Artisan Press

A CIP catalogue record for this book is available from the British Library.

All research, photography (except as stated), editorial, design and typesetting by the authors.
Printed and bound by Information Press, Eynsham, Oxford

The Artisan Press
PO Box 1098, Winscombe, Bristol BS25 1DT, UK

Contents

INTRODUCTION

France is a country of contrasts. It is large and diverse enough to be considered many countries in one. The south basks in the warmth of the Mediterranean while the maritime climate of the north and west ensures cooler summers and less harsh winters than those of the interior. Drawing a line from Biarritz to Metz, to the west are the basins, plains and low hills, while to the east the topography is of the plateaux of the Massif Central, dramatic valleys and high hills, culminating in the highlands of the Vosges, Jura, Alps and Pyrénées.

The lifestyles of the people are just as varied. There is little in common between the Parisiens seen in the chic, pavement cafés of the Champs Elysées and the almost peasant-like existence of the small farmers in the Cévennes. Even the cultural identities of the people of the various regions display many differences – the Flemish of the far north, the German-speaking Alsacians and the Catalans of Roussillon are some of the legacies of acquisitions by the country over the years; the Bretons of Brittany and Basques of the extreme south-west are evidence of migrations of persecuted people centuries ago. The old language of Occitanian (*langue d'oc*, once spoken throughout lower central and southern France, similar to Catalan) still shows in the odd word spoken by the Provençal people. Around 750,000 Jews (the largest community in Europe) live in France. There have been many more recent waves of immigrants, most notably when the country was picking up the pieces after the Second World War, when many North African and Portuguese came to supplement the workforce.

Accounting for one-fifth of the total area of the European Union, France is the largest country in Western Europe and over a quarter of it is forested (the highest proportion of any European country after Sweden and Finland). The country is no stranger to revolution, but it was revolution of a more peaceful kind which has shaped it since the 1950s. A series of radical social and industrial policies laid the foundations for the modern France we see today – the fourth economic power of the world in terms of GDP and fourth largest exporter of goods. The once-rural backwater employing 33% of its inhabitants in farming before the Second World War now has only 4% working the land. As late as 1954 only 10% of French homes possessed a bath or shower and only 27% had a flushing toilet – but a programme of public housing addressed this problem by building up to half a million new homes per year, many of which were accounted for by the ubiquitous apartment blocks in the suburbs of the major towns.

The French people are fierce supporters of their republic and can be very quick to fly in the face of any over-ambitious policy or ruling which they interpret as an infringement of their rights. Generally, they take the attitude that they want to be left to get on with their lives and resist any intrusions by a potential 'nanny' government. The Gallic pride in their country and its traditional products has given rise to a reputation for being somewhat insular, yet this has meant that, perhaps more than any other country in Western Europe, they have retained so many of their old ways and have not, until recently, been losing their national identity like so many of their neighbours. It is this 'quaint' but very genuine adherence to the old ways which attracts the vast amount of tourists – bringing in over 40 billion Francs per year – who spend time there not expecting the French to change their customs to suit the holidaymaker, but rather to absorb themselves in a truly different culture. By contrast, the Spanish tend to create a home-from-home atmosphere for their tourists, and the English have re-invented olde-worlde tourist conventions such as the obligatory 'Cotswold cream tea'.

In spite of the adoption of English as the official (or in many cases the unofficial but 'popular') second language throughout Europe, France is not an easy place to visit if you don't attempt to master the basics of the French language. There is no doubt that the French and the British both have some way to go, in comparison to most other Western European countries, to become even remotely bi-lingual. It is this reluctance by many to speak each other's languages (despite having the other's as their official second tongue in the State education system) which has accounted for the almost xenophobic attitudes between some of the British and some of the French in the past. Thankfully, with both countries moving towards a united Europe, and with a more cosmopolitan attitude developing through the younger generations, this barrier seems gradually to be receding.

To understand France, you need to get to grips with its history, the events of which explain the reasons for its many cultures, minority languages and regional variations in food and drink. A resumé of a country's history will always be flawed but this is, after all, a guide to French beer and not a history book, so please treat the following as the fleeting overview it necessarily needs to be.

A brief history of France
Pre-historic people left their mark in many places throughout France – like the 17,000-year-old Cro-Magnon cave paintings at Lascaux in Périgord and the 3,000 megaliths which make up the site at Carnac in Brittany, erected between 5500 and 1000 BC. The Celts began to appear in central Europe in the 7th Century BC and migrated outwards eventually to settle an area from the whole of France in the west to the Black Sea in the east, although the Greeks had already founded colonies (such as Marseilles) on the Mediterranean coast.

Julius Caesar found the disorganised Celtic tribes easy prey to his divide-and-rule techniques and had consolidated Roman control over the whole of what the Celts called Gaul within seven years (by 50 BC). This conquest brought a long period of peace to the region as the Celts benefited from the Roman defence of its border country with the war-like Germanic tribes to the north and east. As the Roman Empire showed signs of decline in the 5th Century, various Germanic tribes invaded Gaul, some settling, some passing through to Spain. The Romanised Celts of Britain were suffering similar invasions from the Angles and Saxons, and many took refuge in north-western Gaul – so many that these 'Britons' became the modern-day Bretons.

The name France comes from its next group of invaders – another Germanic tribe – the Franks, who had originally lived along the Rhine. The Frankish Kingdom laid the foundations for modern French history. Their leader, Clovis, quickly conquered the area south from the Low Countries down to the Loire Valley, but as the Roman Empire crumbled he conquered the whole country. Under Charlemagne (768–814), the Frankish empire ranged from Denmark to Rome and the Pyrénées, but Brittany remained unconquered. After the parting of the churches of Rome and Constantinople, the papal authorities crowned Charlemagne (the dominant Western power of the time) as

Emperor of the Romans in AD 800 – the start of the Holy Roman Empire, which later moved to Germany.

The Frankish tradition of dividing land amongst heirs ushered in a period of instability in France, allowing the Norsemen (Normans) to settle in what is now Normandy while Magyars and Saracens sacked the country. This left a disjointed collection of petty barons to defend the land, while the monarchy set about modernising France through a system of feudalism. Following William the Conqueror's invasion of England in 1066, France was split between the Anglo-Norman (English) Angevin in the west and French control in the east. By 1214, however, only Gascony (now corresponding to the area from Charente-Maritime to Pyrénées-Atlantique) was in English hands. Religious wars, particularly against the Cathars – an heretical sect in the central south – resulted in the demise of the Languedoc culture. The papacy moved to Avignon in 1305 after unrest in the Rome area.

Disputed claims to the throne led to an English bid for Flanders and the Hundred Years War in the 14th Century, while the Black Death was wiping out a third of the population. In 1453 Bordeaux fell, leaving Calais as the sole English territory. The Duchy of Burgundy was incorporated into France in the reign of Louis XI and Brittany, the last independent principality, joined the royal domain in 1491 following the marriage of Charles VIII to Anne, Duchess of Britanny.

The Catholic hold on Europe suffered greatly in the 16th century when almost 40 per cent of the population 'reformed' to Protestantism. Originating in Germany and Switzerland, France followed later, adopting the Calvinist form. This process tore France apart and led to another period of religious conflict which even saw the assasination of Henry III (a Huguenot whose son converted to Catholicism).

The 17th century saw the major European powers conquering territories overseas and France sent colonists to Canada, Africa and the West Indies. Closer to home the Habsburg Dynasty introduced a Spanish influence in Germany and the Low Countries, but the Thirty Years War was raging throughout the area and when France joined the fray it managed to gain most of Alsace and later the provinces of Artois (Pas de Calais) and Roussillon.

French monarchy reached its height under Louis XIV and XV but wars and epidemics weakened the country to the point of financial crisis. The resentment of the people eventually brought about the French Revolution of 1789 and the formation of the First Republic in 1792. As monarchs, nobles, priests and many commoners were sent to the guillotine in a frenzy of reform, many abbeys and monasteries were razed to the ground, forcing monks and nuns to take refuge in Belgium – although even there they were not free from persecution. The Trappist brewing monasteries (some of which later restarted) were all closed at this dangerous time and many were destroyed.

This period of instability and upheaval came to an abrupt end (as did the First Republic) when Napoleon Bonaparte staged a successful coup in 1799, creating the French Empire of which he crowned himself Emperor. It was Napoleon who gave the French the Franc as a unit of currency and introduced an administrative and legislative structure, much of which is still in place today. But for most, he will be remembered as the man who spread French control over much of Europe before the disastrous campaign in Russia and his abdication and exile to the island of Elba. His exile was short-lived, however, as he later deposed the re-introduced monarchy, before finally conceding defeat at Waterloo after which Louis XVIII was restored to power.

The Revolution of 1830 came after dissent against Charles X which led to the reign of Louis Philippe as the state imposed strict limits on the power of the monarchy. This prosperous time of industrial growth was cut short by another revolution, in 1848, which ushered in the Second Republic but which was itself short-lived as Louis-Napoleon Bonaparte (nephew of Napoleon), after being voted in as President, took power through a coup in 1851, becoming Emperor of the Second Empire as Napoleon III. A war against Austria in support of Italian independence resulted in Nice and Savoy being gained by France.

In 1870 the Franco-Prussian war raged across France with Prussia (the united German states) defeating the armies of Napoleon III, leading to the establishment of the Third Republic after Bismarck granted the country an armistice for new elections. Peace was negotiated at a price – it cost 5 billion francs and the loss of Alsace and one-third of Lorraine (with Metz in Prussian control and Nancy in French hands).

Civil war followed in 1871, during which time the Commune of Paris held out against government troops for two months, but the country settled eventually into decades of an uneasy peace and relative prosperity. Bismarck encouraged France to expand its colonial influence throughout Africa and Asia and, by the 1890s, it ruled a land area second only to the British Empire.

Prussia, now Germany, posed a constant threat so France was forced to enter into an alliance with its old foes Russia and Britain in the Triple Entente, while Germany forged links with Austria-Hungary and Italy. The decades of uncertainty finally exploded in 1914 into what became the First World War, when the heir to the Austrian throne was assassinated by a Serbian and a chain-reaction of countries backing their allies thrust almost the whole of Europe into full-blown war.

The main area of France affected was along a front extending from Lens and Lille, through the Champagne region, Verdun and over to the Vosges in the east. Flanders, the Somme and Verdun will always be remembered as the main areas of prolonged conflict as the armies tried to bleed each other dry from their entrenched positions. By September 1918 Germany was in retreat and was eager to end the war, which it did in November. Through the Treaty of Versailles, France regained Alsace and Lorraine amongst its many reparations for war damage. A quarter of all French men between 18 and 30 had been killed in the war and much of the north was levelled.

The inter-war years were marked by economic instability and a devaluation of the Franc, compounding the problems caused by the Great Depression. Fascism raged throughout Europe and France did not escape the political conflicts of the Left and Right. Hitler's rise to power in Germany and the subsequent invasions of allied countries led France into war again in 1939. Unlike in the First World War it quickly capitulated – six weeks after the Germans blasted their way through the Ardennes – and, in June 1940, France signed an armistice putting two-thirds of the country under German occupation.

Liberation of Paris came in August 1944 after which Charles de Gaulle, leader of the Free French Army, formed a provisional government. He stood down in 1946 and a new constitution was drawn up to start the Fourth Republic, which saw France through its post-war recovery amid the colonial strife which was to bring the regime down. Abandoning its territory in Indochina in 1955, after a costly 9-year struggle, France found itself fighting a war of independence against Algerian nationalists. A coup by the French military siezed control of Algiers to stop the civilian government in Paris negotiating with the

Algerian rebels and, fearful of a spread of the coup to France itself, the National Assembly brought de Gaulle out of political retirement to defuse the situation. He was given six months to govern the country and prepare a new constitution, and in September 1958 he was voted in by a huge majority of French people to lead the Fifth Republic – the constitution of which applies today.

In his 11-year period as President, de Gaulle took major steps towards the concept of a united Europe while distancing France from American and Nato influence. The European Economic Community (EEC) flourished, prompting peace across Europe while the domestic scene was one of prosperity and growth. De Gaulle's regime came to an end in 1968 after violent student riots and a general strike forced him to seek a vote of confidence from the electorate. His gamble failed, leading to his resignation and the election of Pompidou as president in 1969.

The expansion of the EEC and the programme of harmonisation to bring France in line with the rest of Europe (to allow entry into full monetary union) has continued through the terms of presidency of Pompidou (1969–1981), Mitterand (1981–1995) and Chirac (elected 1995).

As a convenient link from the history section to the more relevant business of beer, it is worth mentioning here that there is only one other place in the world to retain its historical connections with the Frankish Kingdom by name – and that is the legendary beer region of Franconia in northern Bavaria.

FOOD & DRINK AND THE FRENCH
For over a century now France has rightly had the reputation for being the gastronomic centre of the world, but to keep itself at the top has meant having to adapt, innovate and move with the trends. It can still boast the highest number of quality eating places and – with the Gallic pride in its national cuisine and the fact that its people, especially the city-dwellers, eat out far more often than in other countries – it's going to be a hard act to beat.

Rural France is still the preserve of the home-made food culture – such as terrines, potages, quiches and soufflés – where wholesome ingredients and traditional recipes handed down from generations before are standard household practice. The dedication of time and the philosophy of self-sufficiency have ensured that age-old recipes and practices have survived to this day, and show few signs of receding. Often very isolated, these communities can sometimes be so far from the nearest bar or restaurant that the kitchen has become the scene of their entertainment and socialising.

There has, however, been a major sea-change in the last couple of decades. The time of only seeing traditional French food on menus is on the wane, and it is now not unusual to see 'foreign' dishes offered by even upmarket restaurants and hotels throughout the country.

Vietnamese oriental-style and North African cous-cous restaurants have been around for quite some time, but these have now been joined in the main streets of towns by Mexican, Italian, Greek, Japanese and other restaurants, while the American-style grills and fast food outlets seem to pop up on the out-of-town malls almost daily. A drive around a French town once revealed a total absence of pizza/pasta and other foreign-influenced restaurants, yet today they seem often to outnumber the traditional French ones. It is undoubtedly the younger generations – with their more cosmopolitan attitudes and predilection for trends, especially those from America – who have brought about this change.

There is no escaping the fact that eating at home has also undergone something of a revolution – a quick glance at a supermarket trolley will show that, especially for those families with children, even the French now stock up with frozen and branded, packaged food. The once-uncommon barbecue is now very fashionable and butchery departments of hypermarkets now offer pre-packed selections of chorizo (Spanish), andouillette (chitterling) and the obligatory merguez (North African) sausages for the barbie fans.

The arrival of the huge hypermarkets could be one of the reasons for the differing habits of the French shopper. Prior to the one-stop shopping experience, they had to buy much of their produce from small, individual stores such as bakers, butchers, charcuteries and patisseries. With limited shelf space these family-run shops could not offer anything like the variety of products on sale in today's hypermarkets, and they have suffered a sharp decline, bringing about the introduction of a moratorium on new hypermarket developments.

There was a time, in the 60s, when the average French household spent 40% of their budget on food – the figure is now around 20% which is probably due to the population buying more luxury goods such as dishwashers, TVs, etc. and spending more on leisure pursuits. Nevertheless, it represents a major shift in the French lifestyle.

One thing which doesn't look set for imminent change is the French institution of the two-hour lunchbreak (sometimes longer in the far south in summer) which is still alive and kicking, but one wonders just how long this luxury will hold out against pressures from business and commerce for a more flexible attitude to midday stoppages. As much of the world is moving toward seven-day opening and shorter lunch-breaks it can often seem ludicrous (and sometimes infuriating) that French business stops dead from noon until 2pm, with the obvious exception of the restaurant and bar trade.

Most of the traditional French alcoholic drinks revolve around the obsession for food and all seem to have their place before, during or after a meal – aperitifs before a meal, wine with the food itself (often a particular wine matched to the course) and digestifs afterwards would be the usual convention. There is little place for beer on the table to accompany a traditional French meal except for the Flemish and Alsacians, both of whom have regional dishes just made to be eaten with beer – amongst others, mussels or potjeflesch for the Flemish and choucroute (sauerkraut) for the Alsacians.

The most famous drink of France has to be wine. Although it is not the largest producer in Europe, it is certainly at the top for quality wines – with its quality assurance helped along by very strict appellation controls. There is a wine to suit just about any budget – from the Grand Cru Classé Bordeaux to the plastic capped 'vin de table' in a returnable bottle. However, it is increasingly rare to see the French people drinking wine in bars without food, with the exception of the cheap 'rouge' (favoured as always by the older men), and chilled dry white – often taken, with the addition of crème de cassis, as 'kir'.

BEER DRINKING IN FRANCE

As recently as the mid-1970s, beer outside the major towns was mainly a bottled product. On entering a bar you would rarely see more than a serving bar and an order for 'une bière' would mean taking a bottle out of one of the numerous fridges behind or underneath the bar

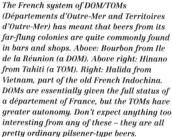

The French system of DOM/TOMs (Départements d'Outre-Mer and Territoires d'Outre-Mer) has meant that beers from its far-flung colonies are quite commonly found in bars and shops. Above: Bourbon from Ile de la Réunion (a DOM). Above right: Hinano from Tahiti (a TOM). Right: Halida from Vietnam, part of the old French Indochina. DOMs are essentially given the full status of a département of France, but the TOMs have greater autonomy. Don't expect anything too interesting from any of these – they are all pretty ordinary pilsener-type beers.

itself and pouring it into a dry glass (none of the glass fountains in those days). Looking around the bar, most of the youth and a good number of the young adults would be drinking beer (as long as it wasn't the pre-lunch or pre-dinner visit when they would be partaking in the obligatory pastis) but the middle-aged and older clients would generally be sipping one of the wide variety of drinks unique to France (and often even to the region) or wine by the glass.

Just as in the towns, the main bar of a large village (such as the PMUs, which double as betting shops) may have possessed one of the new 'pression' founts – in those days a chromed, single- or twin-tapped affair rising above the stainless steel drainers with the push-down-squirt-up glass-wetting fountain. In a very few years just about every bar in every village had one, but for a few years it was still the done thing to specifically order a 'pression' for a draught beer and just a 'bière' for a bottle. These founts were invariably supplied by the brewery, or a subsidised loan was offered, in exchange for a contract to serve only that particular brewery's beer (usually just the one beer) – and few bar owners could afford to say no to the offer.

Bars these days are just as full of colourful characters, but it is obvious that things have changed. In all but the very rural or the very local watering hole, French bars will usually offer at least two beers from multiple taps built into the founts, and most will have a range of bottled beers, albeit often just foreign lagers. The selection of bottled beers will probably be displayed via a row of bottles somewhere on a shelf behind the bar. In towns there will almost certainly be at least one bar which sells four or five draught beers – though closer inspection will probably reveal all of them to be from the same brewery or perhaps one or two from another in which it has a major stake, due again to the brewery loan system. A pattern starts to emerge, and once you get accustomed to it you find that although there really is more variety, it is essentially one of only three varieties in all but the true speciality beer bars and independent locals which have usually started up without the brewery tie restrictions.

This speciality beer bar phenomenon is no stranger to Belgium (and, of late, the UK and the Netherlands) but in France the concept is in its infancy but for a handful of trail-blazers in Paris. Many breweries listed in the main section of this book would dearly love to have the opportunity to sell their beers to all bars in France – but it is a sad fact that most bars are only allowed to sell small quantities of bottled beer from other companies without running into problems with their contractual obligations to their tied brewery.

The speciality beer bar scene has a good following in the major cities, especially in Paris. Lille has surprisingly few non-tied bars considering its proximity to so many good quality, small, local breweries. Unfortunately, for many owners the term 'speciality beer bar' means 'Belgian beer bar' and you will find a pitiful amount of French beer on sale – and of that minority you may find few surprises. Another habit of the more unscrupulous speciality bars is to fill its beer list with indifferent, so-called 'international' brands (from, say, New Zealand, Australia, Spain, Poland, etc.), leaving you flicking through dozens of pages to sift out the few genuine classics from the dross. On the whole, though, these bars should be supported as they offer the smaller breweries a higher profile and a good shop window.

One problem with many of the speciality bars is that they serve all their beers from the fridge. If you have strong feelings about the temperature your beer is served at (as we do) then don't be afraid to ask for one less cold – they may not have one, but at least they will get the message that not everyone likes everything chilled.

Unfortunately, there can often be a very hefty cost premium for a special beer. Before ordering that rare beer you have spent years searching for, check the price – it can sometimes be staggeringly high – and consider how long it may have been on the shelf. Don't be afraid to ask to see the bottle before parting with a fortune for something a year (or more) past its BBE date.

Because many of the beers in this book will be so difficult to find we have listed outlets at the end of each brewery section (if they were supplied) which should stock the products of that particular brewery. The vast majority of these recommended bars have not been visited by ourselves, so we point out that we list them purely as an outlet for their beer. Again, please support these bars as a lack of demand may one day mean they may not be able to justify the shelf space.

The authors – John Woods (left) and Keith Rigley.

THE DECLINE AND RISE
OF FRENCH BREWING

**French beer culture has been marred by the years of
big brewery domination – but now that's changing**

France has always been considered (and to many, always will be)
a wine nation, but there was once a thriving local beer tradition
all over the country although, like today, it was more prevalent in the
industrial areas of the north and north-east. Evidence of the farm
breweries which must have existed in the rural areas has long been
lost, but it is likely that farmworkers would have been given beer as
part of their pay – wine being far less quenching and too strong in
alcohol to have been a suitable restorative for those working in the
fields of the hot interior and the south. As in the rest of Europe, beer
was a far safer drink than the often-contaminated local water supply
due to the purifying effects of the long boil in the brewing process
and the need for cleanliness in the bottling or barrelling operation.

The industrial age was a time of major change in the towns and
cities of France. Steam-powered breweries started to appear even in
the provinces and, with the arrival of the railways, breweries were
able to brew on a far larger scale than before due to the larger market they could reach. This was the period in which breweries proudly
portrayed themselves on publicity posters as huge industrial, factory-
like establishments with more than just a little artistic licence on the
scale and proportions of the buildings and their plot of land.

The last decades of the 19th century were probably the heyday of
the independent brewers, but as the turn of the century came, the
closures started coming thick and fast. Depopulation of the countryside became a major concern in the provinces as the rush for jobs in
the burgeoning urban areas began. This exodus to the cities was good
news for the urban brewers but spelt disaster for the rural brewers
as the working men were the core of their clientele.

A display board on the wall inside Brasserie St-Martial makes very
interesting reading, listing every brewery to have closed this century
in the large region of Limousin in central France. Altogether it lists
61 breweries, although it only states the closing date and not when
they opened, so it is impossible to work out exactly how many were
operational at any one time. One thing which does stand out, however, is the sheer number of closures between 1900 and 1910 – 39 in
all. Although the board is essentially a way of promoting St-Martial
as the only Limousin brewery left today, it offers a good insight into
the plight of the industry in an area of rural France often assumed to
have had little or no beer history.

The decades before the First World War were a growth time for
heavy industry when Nord/Pas-de-Calais and Alsace-Lorraine were
littered with breweries in the urbanised areas around the mining
and steel towns of both regions. Other areas of industry also relied on
their local breweries to supply the workers with their daily restorative, but without the concentration of the expanding conurbations of
the north they were obviously thinner on the ground.

In 1914 the call to arms of the French people to stave off the threat
of the German invasion had a devastating effect on industry. Much of
the productive north was in German hands and output from the rest

of the country was concentrated on supplying food and munitions for the war effort. When the war was over, circumstances led to the gradual demise of beer production in the provinces.

In the north, previously successful breweries whose buildings were damaged, demolished or had been stripped of valuable materials (such as copper) had to decide whether it was worth rebuilding on their own or whether to join forces with others in a similar predicament – and many chose the latter. It was a time of reparation negotiations, and companies which had merged had a better chance to recover sufficient funds to build a new brewery and also take advantage of each other's pre-war client base along with, in some instances, estates of tied bars. It was in this scenario that many hundreds of northern breweries disappeared altogether or were swallowed up in merger deals. The surviving breweries were often far larger than those of previous years and enjoyed something of a boom in a market place with less competition than before. This period had seen development of many new techniques and inventions in machinery and plant, so breweries receiving a major injection of capital from war reparations benefited from up-to-date, efficient brewplant while many also invested in a fleet of motorised dray-trucks.

The breweries of the provinces were spared the destruction and the horror of war on their doorsteps, but this meant they did not have the chance to start all over again and most limped through the difficult times of economic recovery with ancient plant and brewing techniques. With 25% of their client base being lost in the battlefields, many had little choice but to close their doors and find alternative work. Each time a brewery closed in the provinces, the gap in the market would be filled by a larger northern brewery taking advantage of the vastly expanded national railway network built after the war.

Another nail in the coffins of struggling local breweries was the Second World War. Under occupation, the brewers had to make beer with inferior ingredients and, as the tide of war turned against the Germans, the raw materials for munitions became harder to find, resulting in breweries being stripped of their useful materials again – leaving many with no option but to close for good.

It is hardly surprising, therefore, that very few independent breweries survived into the 1950s. Those which did, found themselves in a highly-competitively world where consumers could be sold a brand

Signs of the times. Some of the recent closures leaving their evidence behind. Top left: Brasserie Amiel in St-Girons, Ariège (now a Kronenbourg depot). Top right: Brasserie Rinckenberger in Bischwiller. Left: Saint Rémi – a new wave northern brewery which didn't make it. Right: Brasserie Schneider from Salies-de-Béarn in the south-west – its coppers now make up the decor of Brasserie St -Poloise.

image and the 1960s saw the start of the truly international beers. Family-owned, and often family-operated, breweries simply couldn't promote their beers outside the very local area and certainly didn't have the funds to invest in full-blown advertising campaigns. The mergers and closures continued even at this late stage.

The terms 'de luxe' and 'spéciale' were used in conjunction with many of the big brewers' beers to indicate they were stronger (usually 5%) and of a more consistent quality than those from the local breweries. Like elsewhere in Europe, the fickle consumer was convinced that modern and consistent meant it was better.

Another trend which made it possible for the big brewers to grow even larger was the brewery-loan system, whereby a bar owner could obtain a subsidised loan if they signed up to buy only the beers of that particular brewery. The logistics of this system and the fact that only companies with major financial clout could underwrite such a deal meant that local breweries were not allowed to sell their products to bars in the same village (a barrier which, infuriatingly, is still alive and well to this day).

Many of the smaller provincial breweries were just about holding their own by supplying basic, and relatively uninteresting, bocks and table beers, mostly by direct sale from the brewery or on a door-to-door basis – a service the giants of the brewing world could never do as successfully or as personably.

In the 1970s the disposable glass bottle was being vaunted as something of a revolution and soon became the norm. Throughout Europe the smaller breweries needed their old screen-printed bottles to be returned and most would be of the swing-top, ceramic-stoppered type which were filled by the old-style labour-intensive bottling methods. To offer their beer in crown-corked and labelled bottles required a totally new bottling line – something many small breweries even today find impossible to justify on cost grounds.

Fortunately, many brewers obstinately refused to concede to these financial pressures and, eventually, the tide began to turn. There were two saving graces for the small brewer – firstly, the love by the French for anything 'artisanal' and, secondly, the growth of interest in speciality beers – initially from Belgium, but then from France itself. More than any other country, an artisan of any trade – be it pottery, cheesemaking or painting – can be assured of a reasonable living due to the French obsession for hand-made, individual products which have the character and appeal lacking in mass-produced items.

Jenlain had the good fortune to become the trendy drink of the students of Lille – a large market and one which established the brand on a national level when the students returned (doubtless with their qualifications) back to the provinces. It was the beer which gave us the first glimmer of hope that France could offer the beer drinker more than just bière blonde if you bothered to ask at the bar.

It was in the late 1970s and early 1980s that the revival in brewing special beers took off in a big way with Castelain, La Choulette and Gayant blazing the trail. Although we may be perhaps a little dubious about the claims that many were revived recipes and beer styles, it was a brave step to take at the time and these breweries should be commended for their part in the revival of French special beer.

It is no surprise that most of these innovations were taking place in the Nord/Pas-de-Calais area. Along with Alsace-Lorraine (which had long had a tradition of drinking German-style lagers), Nord/Pas-de-Calais enjoyed the highest beer consumption per head of any region in France, and its proximity to the richly-varied products of the Belgian provinces of East and West Flanders ensured the locals had a far more diverse palate than their eastern France compatriots.

An organisation called 'Les Amis de la Bière' (the friends of the beer) formed in 1986 in Nord/Pas-de-Calais to promote the beers and breweries of the region and to help make sure they survived. It must be said that Les Amis has done an excellent job and we would like to see it expand its influence to cover the entire country. At present, the breweries of Nord/Pas-de-Calais have a distinct advantage over those in the rest of France because Les Amis is there to bring every new beer or brewery to the world's attention. One of the affiliated organisations of the European Beer Consumers Union (such as CAMRA in the UK and the OBP in Belgium), it prefers to concentrate more on supplying information and organising social events like brewery tours and seminars, rather than campaigning for beer drinkers' rights by lobbying national government and the EC.

There should be special mention of the role played by the national chains of hypermarkets – all of whom did a great service for the promotion of speciality beer, even though most bars and cafes chose not to stock them. They should be congratulated for their innovative and adventurous attitude which has given many small breweries by far their largest outlets. If was, however, very frustrating for us to see dozens of special beers on the hypermarket shelves, while not being able to order them in anything but the very specialist beer bars.

By the late-1980s there was a great rise in interest for special beers, even if it initially took time for the provincial French to accept that brewers from their country could compete against the classics of the established beer countries of Belgium, Germany and the UK.

The Bretons, through their Celtic connection, had long been avid fans of Guinness and other Irish ales and it was only a matter of time before Brittany would become effectively the third beer region of France. It currently boasts five breweries.

Concerns about fertilisers, herbicides and insecticides has led to a recent trend toward the virtues of all things 'organic' – and this has been a blessing for some of the very rural microbreweries. There are regular organic food fairs throughout France, and specialist distributors offer a wide market to those brewers who obtain the necessary certification from the organic validation organisations.

The brewpub revolution, which is currently running rampant around the country, has brought characterful local beer back to the provinces and raised the profile of the brewer's art through the spectacle of watching its actual production in the bar. Although many of these brewpubs offer pretty ordinary beer, just about all of them are very popular – and bear in mind that the concept is still in its infancy, so we may see more adventurous beers being offered one day.

Our impression is that we have yet to witness the peak of this flurry of new brewing activity in France.

The newsletter of Les Amis de la Bière, La Gazette des Eswards, *which offers all the latest news of the Nord/Pas-de-Calais region. To join Les Amis, contact M. Louis Peugniez, 5 Route de Mametz, 62120 Aire Sur La Lys. Tel/Fax: 03 21 39 14 52.*

BIÈRE DE GARDE & NORD/PAS-DE-CALAIS

Focus on France's most prolific brewing region and its speciality brew

Many countries lay claims to various 'beer styles' – and France is no exception with its bières de garde. However, just as we found while researching *The Beers of Wallonia*, trying to define a particularly style (in Wallonia it is saison) creates all sorts of difficulties as the ingredients and processes vary so wildly from one brew to another. This huge variation usually makes the term 'beer style' virtually worthless and bière de garde is another example of this.

Having read the various tomes in the English language on French beer, it is almost without exception that bière de garde has been described as 'beer for keeping' or 'beer to be laid down'. Our experience has shown this to be anything but the case. Our interpretation is that bière de garde is simply 'beer which has been kept' or, more technically correct, 'beer which has been garded (lagered)'.

Authors and brewers often wax lyrical about how beer was made in the cooler months of autumn to early spring and laid down for consumption in the summer months when brewing was difficult due to the increased chances of infection. There is no doubt that, before refrigeration and other developments we now take for granted, such a practice did occur – but it was certainly not unique to France. This practice was widespread throughout Europe and such a beer would probably have been unfiltered, bottle conditioned, very hoppy and having a reasonably high alcohol content. If there is a such a tradition left in Europe, then we believe the saisons of Wallonia and the genuine Märzenbiers of Germany would be truer to form than most.

Certainly the present day bières de garde, virtually all of which are products recently re-introduced (or rather re-invented), have little or no similarity to the beers that were once layed down for summer drinking. The current logic is that the style is typified by a filtered, unpasteurised, top fermenting beer with a rich, fruity malt character and which usually comes out at around 5% to 8.5% alc/vol. Typify is perhaps an overstatement, as by no means the vast majority of bières de garde are actually top fermenting – for instance all of the well-respected Castelain (Ch'ti) beers and Terken's Septante 5 are bottom fermenting. Also, we have to consider that the ranges from Bécu and Bailleux are unfiltered and bottle refermented. And with numerous distinctly pale-coloured bières de garde now on sale (like Duyck's Sebourg and Choulette's Blonde) we cannot even state that an amber hue is typical. All in all, the term is best used to describe a beer from the départements of Nord and Pas-de-Calais (though some would add the two Picardie breweries) which has undergone a reasonably long garding period at cold temperature. To our knowledge there is just one brewery which calls some of its products bière de garde yet doesn't fit this criteria, and that is Brasserie Bailleux which tends to make distinctly Belgian-type beer.

The process of garding beer (also known as lagering) has its origins in southern Bavaria. It was found that by storing fresh beer in barrels in very cold cellars or mountain caves for many weeks or months, a cleaner taste would develop while the beer itself absorbed the carbon dioxide (a by-product of yeast converting sugar to alcohol), into solution as a long and slow secondary fermentation took place. At a temperature of around 0°C the yeast was found to produce a beer very different from what had been made before. It wasn't until science (with the help of Louis Pasteur – the man who also gave the world pasteurisation) found out what made yeast tick that the development of specific yeasts occurred, resulting in two very different types – top and bottom fermenting – and single cultures which, when carefully chosen, could be made to work well in specific processes and impart distinctive characteristics to a beer's taste.

Before such scientific intervention, garding beer was a long process as non-specific yeasts struggled to perform their duty in near-zero temperatures. These days, yeasts can be cultured to complete the garding cycle in far less time, though most beer purists would argue that the longer the garde the better the beer should be. With some breweries having to store thousands of hectolitres at any one time it is perhaps inevitable that many of the cheap lagers have pitifully short garding periods. Garding replaces the need for beer to be bottle conditioned although some Nord/Pas-de-Calais brewers (such as Bécu) still choose to do so, effectively giving their products a triple fermentation.

It is possible to draw comparisons between the top-fermenting bières de garde and German 'altbier' in that they are both lagered and have a strong malt character yet display a far cleaner overall taste to most varieties of ale. But it is very difficult to find anything in the beer world to compare to the bottom-fermenting bières de garde which are often fuller and fruitier than just about any other 'bottom' beer probably because many use ale yeast fermented at low temperature.

Although true 'bières de garde' are only made in the two départements of Nord and Pas-de-Calais, it should not be assumed that all special beers made there are necessarily defined as such. A good example is Trois Monts, from Brasserie St-Sylvestre, which has no mention of the term anywhere on the label (and the brewery defines it as a 'bière spéciale') yet it is considered by most as one of the classics of the style. Likewise, Castelain uses the term on the labels of all the Ch'ti range (with the strange exception of its Bière de Mars) but Jade, St-Patron and the St-Pol beers have no such tag. Brasserie La Choulette describes its Bière de Noël as a bière de garde, but not its Bière de Mars, and certainly not its raspberry beer. Confused? We certainly are. But this is, as mentioned earlier, the problem with being too obsessed with blindly putting beers into 'style' pigeon-holes.

Looking through reference material of old labels and posters you will see no mention of the term bière de garde, so it must be a relatively recent trend which was quickly picked up on by the brewers of Nord/Pas-de-Calais. It nevertheless serves as a useful and well-deserved regional identity for the collective products of the smaller breweries of northern France.

The official region of Nord/Pas-de-Calais has had a history punctuated by

Now you see it, then you didn't. Bière de garde is featured on the current Jenlain label (top), but it wasn't in the 1980s (bottom).

times of boom and bust, wildly changing frontiers and being in one of the central arenas of two World Wars. The area is not blessed with a particularly interesting topography. Starting at the Channel coast with its maritime plain and the flat farmland bordering Belgium the far north displays its Flemish ancestry through town/village names (like Hazebrouck) and the surnames of its people. Even today the locals of French Flanders proudly keep their links with their historical brethren across the Belgian border.

The south-west of the region has a landscape of rolling hills and was the scene of many a French–English battle in medieval times (Azincourt is the site of the Battle of Agincourt and, further south, is Crécy), but surprisingly, although well-visited by tourists in comparison to the urban areas to the east, it remains a relative beer desert.

Taking the A26 from Calais and bypassing St-Omer the view changes from one of sleepy farming country to the beginning of a wide band of dense urban development starting with Béthune and Bruay, taking in Lens and Lille, then Douai, Denain and Valenciennes before crossing the Belgian border to continue again around Mons. Beneath this swathe of high population lies the Nord/Pas-de-Calais coalfield, the western extremes of Belgium's Sambre-Meuse coalfield. With the coal came the heavy industry and the workforce needed to turn the area into a major coalmining and metalworking centre. This concentration of people and industry brought about the need for breweries to slake the thirst of the workers. The same process was happening in the Lorraine coalfield area, centred around the town of Metz in north-eastern France which accounts for the glut of breweries which sprung up there in the early years of this century but which have now closed.

In the mid-1950s there began a series of pit closures throughout France as, particularly in Nord/Pas-de-Calais, the economic viability of extracting coal from the thin seams with many faults began to make imported coal more attractive. Although the region is still a major manufacturing area, the coal mines have dwindled to the point that Lorraine is probably going to be the only coal-producing area in France by the year 2000.

The legacy of spoil-heaps litter the landscape as a poignant reminder of its mining past, but as the memory fades and the harsh reality of facing up to a new future sinks in, so too comes the sad demise of the

A poignant snapshot in time of the social history of Nord/Pas-de-Calais – the miner's face which originally featured strongly on Castelain's labels but has since vanished.

The explanation offered was that the image obscured the wording. We prefer the theory that the miner has outlived his usefulness and has little place as the main identity for a successful brewery looking to expand and export beyond its old, local mining area base. Early-90s (above left), mid-90s (above right) and current (right) labels show his gradual demise.

Castelain was not the only brewery to use a mining theme on its labels – these are from across the border in Wallonia (the French-speaking, southern half of Belgium) where the coal industry has suffered as much as in France. Left: A beer brewed by Du Bocq for distributor Paul Maton. Right: La Gueule Noire (literally Black Mouth, patois for miner) brewed by Silly for Corman-Collins.

image of the wizened face of the Ch'ti miner. His portrait was once portrayed on all publicity from the then Brasserie Bénifontaine (now Castelain) but underwent a gradual phasing out throughout the 90s and now has vanished altogether. As a snapshot in time of the social history of Nord/Pas-de-Calais, the miner served the brewery well in terms of giving its products a strong and loyal local identity. It would be nice to see his image return one day, maybe on a celebration beer label, to acknowledge the part he played in Castelain's success.

Wherever there is a severe pit-closure programme there is the inevitable problems of unemployment and a downturn in the local economy. As recently as 1993 a group of people in the film industry felt moved enough by the plight of the people of the Nord/Pas-de-Calais area to launch 'Germinal, L'Association' (see Brasserie Des Amis Réunis in the brewery section) which helps new enterprises to start up and gives funds for children's projects. The idea to form the association came while making a film of a book by Emile Zola, called *Germinal* (written in 1885), which centred on the conflicts between miners and pit-owners.

The two World Wars took an awesome toll in property and trade in the region, especially during the First World War when the front-line ran right through the heart of Nord/Pas-de-Calais (see map on following page). The German army tore westwards through Belgium in what is now called the 'Race to the Sea' – the theory being that once the Channel ports had been taken, the Western Front would be won. Although huge gains were achieved, the onslaught ground to a halt in October 1914 and both sides dug in to begin the long period of trench warfare which lasted with little change to this front-line until the First Battle of the Somme in July 1916. Massive artillery bombardments prior to attacks devastated the landscape either side of the front-line with many towns and villages effectively flattened.

Mines and factories were strategically important to the war effort and the coalfield was virtually split between the two sides. Many businesses, including breweries, were requisitioned by the armies and many were stripped of their useful materials.

The Nord/Pas-de-Calais area was squeezed between two major battlegrounds – the Somme to the south and the Ypres (Ieper) salient to the north, but with much conflict around Armentières and Vimy (for the strategic high ground of Vimy Ridge) it saw a fair amount of sporadic action. The south of the region suffered from the scorched earth tactic prior to the Germans' planned withdrawal to the fortified Hindenburg line in 1917, when wells were poisoned, buildings levelled and booby traps laid to slow the advance of the Allied troops.

With the capitulation of the Russians on the Eastern Front, the Ger-

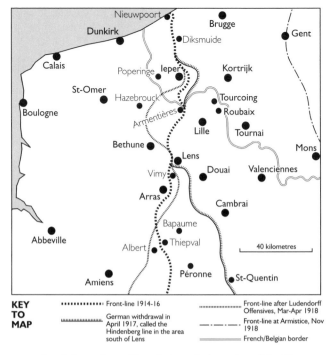

mans found themselves able to bolster their armies of the Western Front and two major offensives – 'Michael' in the Somme and 'Georgette' in Nord/Pas-de-Calais – were instigated in March and April 1918 respectively. The latter's main objective was the important railway junction at Hazebrouck and cost over 100,000 casualties on each side before the offensive stalled short of its target.

With the Allied force being strengthened by the American army in 1918 the disheartened and depleted German army was pushed back throughout the summer before the horror and bloodshed of the war ended with the armistice in November. This left France, especially in the north, with a battle-torn landscape and its infrastructure in tatters. In an effort to resurrect the local economy, with the aid of German reparations, a massive rebuilding programme started, but with a high percentage of the workforce killed in the war many businesses were lost forever while others became 'unions' or 'co-operatives' to attract enough investment for new plant.

With the First World War still fresh in the memories of the people of Nord/Pas-de-Calais, the relatively prosperous years following the war came to an abrupt end when the Second World War began with another race to the sea. Having learnt from the bloody consequences of trench warfare, Hitler's armies – now highly mobile with tanks and trucks – launched 'Operation Sickle-Cut' on 10 May 1940. Within three weeks the Panzers and shock-troops had penetrated deep into France with the speed of the invasion preventing any concerted resistance. Pouring across the Belgian border south-east of Lille and looping up, the Germans had effectively trapped close to half a million Allied troops in an enclave around Dunkirk, bringing about the famous evacuation with a flotilla of ships and small boats. The town of Dunkirk suffered terribly as the Germans were kept at bay long enough for over 338,000 troops to be picked up before it finally surrendered on 4 June 1940.

Ten days later, the German army marched into Paris and the Maginot Line in the north-east was breached – France had been forced to surrender, starting a 4-year period of occupation which would last until soon after the D-Day landings in Normandy in June 1944.

The initially slow progress of the Allied invasion soon became a rout and, by August, the Germans had been forced to retreat back into Belgium. Although Nord/Pas-de-Calais did not suffer the same devastation as in the First World War, the railways, roads and bridges were destroyed and, to ensure local industry was of no use to the Allies, many of the factories and other strategic plants were sabotaged. Another major redevelopment programme began once the war was over, a year later.

Much of the reinvestment in the region was in heavy industry and mining, which was essentially returning the area to its previous state. However, by the 1970s, the changing world economy enabled the cheap importation of coal, steel and other manufactured goods, leaving the domestic heavy industries struggling to compete.

Nord/Pas-de-Calais is now opening up to tourism and business, helped by the TGV (Train à Grande Vitesse) linking the Channel Tunnel with Lille on its way to Brussels. More than ever before the area is successfully promoting itself as a tourist destination and visitors are often surprised at just how much it has to offer.

Cosmopolitan Lille is the undisputed capital of the north – home to a huge amount of students and the birthplace of Charles de Gaulle. It boasts a large old citadel, a characterful old town and plenty of interest for the beer enthusiast. It is quite central to the breweries of the region and is gaining a reputation as being the French capital of beer, though we believe it still has a little way to go to better Paris.

The ancient textile town of Arras offers much to the tourist, especially its beautiful galleried squares in the town centre (which were heavily damaged in the bombardments of the First World War and were sympathetically rebuilt soon after) and the vast network of underground chambers which were used to billet troops.

Douai, at first glance a bad example of modern town planning, has many old buildings in its centre (including a C14th gothic belfry) and possesses a long, interesting history. Being the centre of the Nord/Pas-de-Calais coal industry it is fitting that there is a major mining museum a few kilometres to the east at Lewarde.

Despite its involvement in the First World War, the area from Vimy to the Belgian border attracts far fewer battlefield visitors than Ieper (Ypres) and the main areas of conflict in the Somme. Vimy Ridge (with the Canadian Memorial crowning Hill 145), Arras and Bapaume were at the northern extreme of the Somme campaign where it extended into Pas-de-Calais and are on most war tourists' itineraries, unlike towns such as Armentières, Lens, Douai and Cambrai, where there are many cemeteries, memorials, bunkers and other such reminders.

The region has always been, and always will be, a major brewing and beer-drinking area. Today it has by far the highest concentration of breweries in France, although many of the breweries are quite new or, like La Choulette and Bécu, have started up again. With the larger breweries concentrating on mass-market bières blondes, a healthy market has emerged which the smaller, artisanal breweries have managed successfully to exploit. Each year sees the opening of at least one new brewery and there is an underlying feeling that the interest in beer is still on the up. We are confident that the brewing scene of the region will continue to prosper.

THE MUSEUMS OF LORRAINE

A look at the brewery museums on the tourist trail in the once-major brewing region of Lorraine

The north-eastern region of France known as Lorraine is often overlooked by holidaymakers, but should not be ignored by the beer enthusiast. The region, which takes in the departments of Moselle, Meurthe-et-Moselle, Vosges and Meuse, could be considered medium-sized when compared to other regions yet contains a higher percentage of woodland than any other (much of it state-owned) and has a greater amount of surface water than most. Three large rivers drain the region – the Moselle, the Meurthe and the Meuse – and it also has a number of major canals and many lakes, particularly on the eastern side. Despite the presence of the major cities of Nancy and Metz, this abundance of natural countryside has helped Lorraine maintain much of its rural charm and it has managed to preserve many of its older buildings and traditions. Perhaps this is why there is a higher concentration of brewing museums here than elsewhere.

Lorraine has had its fair share of breweries over the years (over 200 in 1890) and many of them were of considerable size. Today, however, there are just two 'proper' breweries, the massive Kronenbourg plant at Champigneulles and the tiny Brasserie Henry. There is also the Institut Français des Boissons et de la Brasserie Malterie (IFBM), which is more of a brewing school and research centre, though it does supply beers on a commercial basis. There are also two brewpubs – La Cabane des Brasseurs in Nancy and La Taverne du Brasseur in Amnéville – and last but not least a museum which also brews and has been treated as a brewery in this book – the Musée de la Brasserie at Ville-sur-Illon. From a volume viewpoint that is not a very impressive list but if one considers the variety represented it has to be said that it has something for every taste and preference.

When considering the museums the picture is similar. There are four museums, two of which are in old breweries, one in an old malt-house and the other on a farm. There is also variety in what they are showing and the way in which they achieve it; so, if you have been to one, do not simply dismiss the others as more of the same.

Starting in the north there is the grandly named **Musée Européen de la Bière** in Stenay situated way up in the north-western extremity of the region. Stenay is on the Meuse, close to the Belgian border, in fact just 23 kilometres from the Abbaye d'Orval (source of the Trappist beer Orval). Though not really comparable with the abbey the initial sight of the museum is very impressive. Walking down to the entrance the first thing you notice is the tower of the old malt-house which, like Orval, is constructed from a mellow yellowish stone and topped with a contrasting grey slate roof. This is approached through a pair of impressive wrought iron gates which once graced the old Brasserie Vézelise. The museum is housed, over three floors, in an old malt-house and most of the buildings date from the beginning of the 17th century, though the malt-house tower is actually from the end of that century. It opened its doors as a museum in 1986.

The museum, in addition to being extremely well stocked, is well laid out and takes you through the world of beer in a reasonably

The entrance to the Musée Européen de la Bière at Stenay

logical sequence. From the entrance you go up to the first floor where you find out about the history of beer from its naissance in Mesopotamia, through its development in the abbeys. Then you need to know what goes into it and this is well illustrated with displays covering water, barley, hops and malting techniques. From there you move onto brewing techniques which are illustrated by, among other things, some discarded brew-plant from La Choulette and Duyck. Moving upstairs you pass through displays of advertising posters, glasses, bottles, ashtrays and the like, all of which give an insight into the art of beer and its place in popular culture. The sociology of beer is presented via more displays of photos, bottle labels, publicity material and general symbolism such as Gambrinus, Saint Arnould and the brewer's star before you move back to the large displays of brewing kit. This brewing kit includes brew kettles from Duyck and the com-

Stenay's brewing copper exhibition.

The bottling and barrel filling display at Stenay.

plete brew-house, dating from 1921, from the now defunct brewery at Clavy-Warby, just the other side of Charleville-Mezieres. From here one moves on to the conditioning of the beer, via a reconstruction of a laboratory, downstairs to the ground floor and the final displays. Here are various old and new fermentation vessels (wood and metal), bottle fillers, label applicators, barrel filling and even old drays, both horse-drawn and motorised.

You will pass many superb exhibits on your trip around Stenay and if we were to pick a few which merit a closer look on the grounds of rarity, novelty or just the way they are presented it could be the series of twelve amusing posters showing 'the gentle art of making Guinness' or the 30 beer mats from Cantillon showing the process of making gueuze.

The good collection of beer mugs and glasses is augmented by a collection of glass moulds and a static display of glassblowing. They also have what must be the first automatic beer dispenser. It was invented in 1889 for the l'Exposition Universalle de Paris and works by allowing a lever to be moved once a coin is inserted, thereby releasing a measured quantity of beer into the glass you have hopefully positioned under the spout. Finally, an Orval connection

Brewery drays – old and older in Stenay's vaulted cellars.

materialises via a hop press and a yeast egg (the latter once used for storage and dispensing of yeast). If you can take your eyes off the exhibits it is well worth giving your attention to the building itself, which is a work of art, from the stone-built cavern-like rooms at ground level through the two wooden storeys above.

Having sated your appetite for history and culture it is time to satisfy the thirst. This is easily done by visiting the well-stocked bar at ground level. The museum has its own beer in the form of Stenay Blonde and Bière de Stenay, both of which are supplied by La Choulette. In addition to these there is a good selection of other French beers. Two novel, edible items – both worth trying – are beer sausage and beer chocolates. In addition to the usual souvenirs there is also a good stock of beer-related books.

Moving further south through Lorraine you can find the small **Maison de la Polyculture** at Lucey, just north-west of Toul. Located in an old farm this museum is not devoted exclusively to brewing but concentrates more on agriculture and presents such diverse subjects as bee-keeping, vine growing and hop growing. It is the hop element which merits its inclusion here, especially as it is not just the growing but also the drying and conservation which are covered.

Having found out something about the raw materials a visit to **Musée Français de la Brasserie** in St-Nicolas-de-Port on the south-east edge of Nancy will give an injection of culture to the tour. The city of Nancy is the origin of the Nancy School of Art Nouveau and the influences are to be widely seen within the city. Musée Français de la Brasserie also displays influences from this period.

The museum is in what used to be the Brasserie Vézelise and is easy to find as it is well signposted. The museum is in two parts – the larger part being the restored and maintained original brewery building which is virtually intact and a good example of art deco styling. The brewery was built in 1907 and is now declared as a National Monument. In the old administration building there are static dis-

The art deco-styled Brasserie Vézelise in its heyday – now the Musée Français de la Brasserie.

The stained glass windows at Musée Français de la Brasserie are a literal highlight.

plays, many of which celebrate the art deco and other general artistic influences. There are some very attractive stained glass windows amongst the exhibits in one room whilst another room manages to display some impressive works of art along with many old bottles and other breweriana.

Next door to this display is what looks like a small laboratory but is in fact a small home-brew outfit. An impressive feature of this museum is that it not only celebrates the past through displays such as each year's class photos from the Nancy School of Brewing (now the IFBM) but also acts as a centre of excellence for home-brewing. It hosts its own home-brewing club and, in 1997, ran a week-long course in brewing and organised the second National Home-Brew Competition.

Returning to the purely visual aspects of the museum, a visit to the old brewery is a rewarding experience. The main brewing hall, on the first floor, is a sight to behold – acres of polished copper gleaming in the sunlight which streams through the massive panelled windows. These coppers are original to the Vézelise brewery but the immense hop press that you have to walk round to get to the coppers is not –

The original Vézelise steam engine still in place at Musée Français de la Brasserie.

that arrived just a couple of years ago from the Adelshoffen brewery where it was still in use in 1992 (it dates from 1930). Getting it into the museum was not particularly easy as it required a crane, the brewhouse windows to be removed, and a lot of care to avoid damaging the coppers as it was manoeuvred past. A piece of equipment you may not immediately identify is in the next room and turns out to be a sort of washing machine. It was supplied with the hop press and is for cleaning the enormous filter cloths.

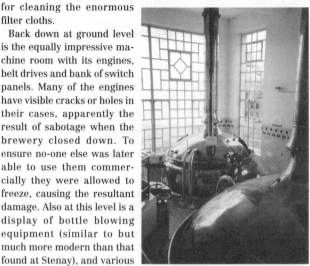

Gleaming copper and plenty of light at Musée Français de la Brasserie.

Back down at ground level is the equally impressive machine room with its engines, belt drives and bank of switch panels. Many of the engines have visible cracks or holes in their cases, apparently the result of sabotage when the brewery closed down. To ensure no-one else was later able to use them commercially they were allowed to freeze, causing the resultant damage. Also at this level is a display of bottle blowing equipment (similar to but much more modern than that found at Stenay), and various bottle- and barrel-filling equipment as well as labelling plant. The display of the diverse forms of packaging includes a bottle from Britain – unfortunately to demonstrate two-litre plastic bottles. Compared to Stenay the collection of exhibits, though still growing, is small and the majority are more modern. However, this fits in with one of the museum's aims which is to become the most important brewery museum in Europe for mass-produced beer, whereas Stenay has become the most important for small-scale beer production.

Back in the other building and down to the basement you find a pleasant little bar which usually offers beers supplied by the Institute Français des Boissons et de la Brasserie Malterie in Nancy. Although they would like to offer the fruits of the home-brew club the volume is not really enough to warrant such a supply.

The final museum is located in another old brewery and malt-house – the **Musée de la Brasserie Vosgienne** at Ville-sur-Illon which is south from Nancy and to the west of Épinal. Brasserie Vosgienne ceased brewing in 1956 and stopped its malting operations ten years later. It then suffered the indignity of being a source of soft drinks until finally closing completely in 1975. A decade later it was resurrected as a brewing museum and opened its doors to visitors in 1987. It is run by the very enthusiastic Bernard Saunier who retired from a high-powered job only to find that he works even harder now.

Being based in an old brewery it is very easy to create the right atmosphere, especially as much of the major equipment is still in place. Sadly many of the smaller items disappeared over the years so to enhance the displays extra exhibits have been borrowed from other places. These, added to the main features, re-create the scene and tell the complete brewing story. A tour of the museum should last

More stained glass and copper – this time at the Musée de la Brasserie Vosgienne.

about 75 minutes after which you end up in the tasting room/bar for the appropriate refreshment supplied by the 'home-brewers' who produce the draught beers available. There is also a reasonable choice of other bottled beers.

The museum covers a surprisingly large area of the old brewery and is certainly worth a visit even if a lot of the exhibits are still in need of some tender loving care. The focal point, as it would be for the working brewery, is the brew-house. This one is described as in the art nouveau style after the Nancy School, possibly because of the large stained-glass window set into the back wall. However, it was originally designed in the Bavarian style, producing bottom fermenting beers, and houses some impressive brick-clad copper vessels.

As it is a relatively new museum, many of the exhibits have been borrowed from various (mostly Alsacian) breweries but this does not detract from its overall interest. Two of the larger exhibits are an interesting-looking machine for filling two barrels at a time and a

The Musée de la Brasserie Vosgienne's old malt mill complete with dust socks.

*Two-barrel filling equipment at
Musée de la Brasserie
Vosgienne.*

malt grinder. The latter is possibly the most impressive piece in the exhibition. It is made of varnished wood and has an imposing filter of dust socks in an effort (probably unsuccessfully) to keep the air breathable. It is belt-driven with the power originally supplied by a steam engine and is apparently in working order.

Towards the end of the tour you will pass through a large hall containing a number of vehicles in need of restoration. One day there could well be a good display of brewery vehicles, but at the moment they look more as though they are still where they were left when the brewery closed.

A number of the breweries featured in this book are creating small museum-style exhibitions on their premises, so the interest in the history of brewing appears to be growing, as is the interest in beer itself. The ones most worthy of a visit are at Bécu, Castelain and La Choulette. Perhaps it is this growing interest that has prompted the region to support its brewing institutions with the well-publicised 'La Route Lorraine de la Bière'. This features not only the museums and breweries mentioned here but focuses on the region's brewing heritage by locating many of the closed breweries.

MUSEUM CONTACT DETAILS & OPENING TIMES

Musée Européen de la Bière, rue de la Citadelle, 55700 Stenay.
Tel. 03 29 80 68 78.
1 May to 30 November – Daily 1000–1200 & 1400–1800.

Maison de la Polyculture, 94 Grande Rue, 54200 Lucey.
Tel. 03 83 63 85 21.
1 May to 15 October – Thur to Sun 1400–1800.

Musée Français de la Brasserie, 62 rue Charles Coutois,
54210 St-Nicolas-de-Port.
Tel. 03 83 46 95 52.
15 June to 15 September – Daily.
16 September to 14 June – Weekends 1430–1830.

Musée de la Brasserie Vosgienne, 88270 Ville-sur-Illon.
Tel. 03 29 36 53 18.
15 June to 30 September – Tue to Sun 1430–1800.

*Opening details should be valid for 1998 but please telephone to
confirm and to arrange for group visits.*

POPULAR SYMBOLOGY IN FRENCH BREWING

If you want a successful brew every time, it pays to have 'someone from above' watching over its production

Many trades have their associated superstitions, symbology, lucky charms and patron saints. Needless to say, brewing is no exception. Over the centuries, and throughout various countries, a number of saints have been associated with beer and brewing though some have a stronger claim than others.

Amongst the more dubious claimants are Saint Columbanus who, when he was serving as a missionary priest, prevented the sacrifice of a barrel of ale to the pagan god Wodan when he caused it to explode merely by breathing on it. Apparently ale was only good when drunk in the name of the true God. Saint Florian is said to have prevented the German city of Nürnberg from burning down in the 8th century by extinguishing the flames with beer. Saint Brigid gave beer to lepers and even possessed the ability to turn used bathwater into beer when the supplies ran dry.

Saint Hildegard is one of the more laudable claimants. She was abbess of Diessenberg and her writings on herbalism include the earliest known references to adding hops to beer.

The other two are often confused with one another as both are referred to with various spellings of their names. Saint Arnold is the one revered in Belgium and northern France. Born in 1040 at Tiegem in Flanders, he spent time at St-Médard abbey near Soissons before returning to Flanders and founding a monastery at Oudenburg. He died in 1087 and was canonised in 1120. Chief amongst the justifications for canonisation was saving the people of Soissons from the plague by plunging his crucifix into a vat of beer, encouraging them to drink that in preference to the water.

Saint Arnold on Castelain's St-Patron.

Doubtless the boiling in the brewing process had a lot to do with the beer being a safer drink than the water, but it was considered a miracle nevertheless. There are many references to Saint Arnold (or Arnoldus) in French brewing. His icon can be seen in many breweries and there are even beers named after him, such as Castelain's St-Patron.

The final saint is Saint Arnould (or Arnou) who is favoured by the brewers of Lorraine. He was born in 580 and became bishop of Metz in 612 before becoming a hermit in the forests of the Vosges and finally dying in 640. His beery miracle came

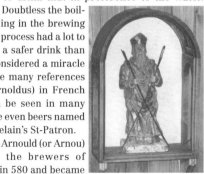

Saint Arnould depicted in a sculpture by Philippe Ravaille in the Musée Européen de la Bière in Stenay.

after his death, when his body was being transported back to Metz for a ceremonial burial. The porters were tired and thirsty but had nothing to drink. They prayed to Arnould, and miraculously their jugs were filled with vast quantities of good tasting beer.

Another character figuring large in brewing mythology, both in Belgium and France, is Gambrinus or Jean (sometimes Jan) Primus. He is generally considered to be the patron of brewers and is popularly believed to be the real Jean Primus, who became Jean I, Duke of Brabant in 1268. His influence in the brewing industry stems from the laws he enacted in 1292 that were aimed at creating the foundations of a more stable social order. Amongst those laws was one that made it an offence for anyone to 'willingly adulterate wine, ale or any other beverage'. In an age when all manner of things were regularly added to ale this law was warmly welcomed by local drinkers.

A symbol which was once very common in French breweries is the Brewers' Star which has, since the alchemists of the Middle Ages, been used to represent the four elements of the universe – air, water, fire and earth.

It was considered a protective symbol, but was also used to denote areas of the brewery where only certain people were allowed to enter. For instance, it was often found on the doors of the brewing hall which not only lent protection to the vulnerable processes going on within but also kept out the likes of the drayman who could tramp around with wild yeasts on his clothing, thereby infecting the next batch of beer. A good place to see this usage is at the Musée de la Brasserie Vosgienne at Ville-sur-Illon.

A statue of Gambrinus on display at Musée Français de la Brasserie

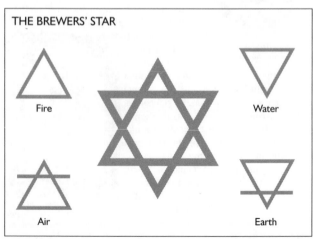

THE BREWERS' STAR

Fire

Water

Air

Earth

A LITTLE SOMETHING IN YOUR BEER, SIR/MADAM?

The French have a predilection for adding flavours to their drinks – and beer is no exception

The French have always liked the idea of adding things to a drink to make it different. It doesn't really matter what the drink is, even well-known international brands of soft drinks don't escape the treatment – for instance a common tipple of French café youth is 'coca-menthe', which, as you've probably guessed, is Coca-Cola with the addition of sirop de menthe (mint syrup). This begs the question – if it is so popular why don't Coca-Cola sell Mint Coke themselves?

Any visit to a bar in France will reveal the awesome selection of bottles of sirop (pronounced see-ro) and it is bewildering to see just how many drinks the population wish to adulterate with them. Sirops have few comparable substitutes outside Continental Europe – fruit squashes and juices being very different.

A pleasant change to a straight pastis is a 'moresque' – a pastis (usually a Ricard or a Pastis 51) with a shot of sirop d'orgeat (an almond-flavoured barley water syrup, pronounced orzhah) which gives a certain fullness and a greater depth to an otherwise thin, quite one-dimensional drink. If you haven't tried a moresque, why not give it a try – even better, order one with syrup and one without so you can compare – you may be pleasantly surprised. And before any francophiles throw their hands up in horror when someone suggests adding something to their favourite sunshine accompaniment to a game of boules, it is worth reminding them that absinthe, the until-recently-banned precursor to pastis, was often served by adding water poured over sugar on its way into the glass, just as some of the specialist brands of pastis are even today.

Adding sugary-sweet syrup to a spirit – or, as is usually the case in France, to a bottle of water like Vittel or Perrier – is one thing, but adding it to beer is another thing altogether. One of the last drinks we would ever order personally is a beer with syrup of grenadine, yet it is the singularly most popular adulteration in France after lemonade. Shandy (panaché in French) is shandy the world over and will always be the best way to drink weak beer (albeit horribly sweetened) in a bar without paying the premium for the low-alcohol or alcohol-free beers. A 'grenache' (beer with grenadine, topped up with lemonade) may seem a bizarre concept but it is no more absurd than the popular British habit of adding lime cordial to lager.

In a trendy cafe it is possible to see just about any obscure syrup being added to a beer – almost always using a 'pression', the cheapest bière blonde on draught. The new variety of French brewpub and speciality beer bar often list what they call 'beer cocktails' which inevitably means perfectly good beer with something sweet and sickly thrown in, usually one of the house syrups. It seems a suitably exotic name for the 'cocktail' is enough for it to sell in droves.

When the adulteration is forced upon a common-or-garden bière blonde it is, perhaps, not so bad. Perhaps the customer just wants their beer to actually taste of *something* even if that something is a fruit syrup. But occasionally, and somewhat less understandably, we have seen people paying vast sums of money for a quality artisanal beer cocktail. Some of the bars in Belgium (yes, it happens there as well) are offering drinks such as a 'Chouffe Royale' – based on the expensive but very rewarding La Chouffe beer – which is essentially one of the best beers in Belgium – with a shot of crème de cassis and served with a multi-coloured mixing stick. Sorry, but some trends can occasionally make your blood boil.

Enough of syrups. Another 'trendy' habit of the French, and again down to the Gallic habit of wanting to spice up an already reasonable beer list, is what is termed a 'bière flambée' (something we have also seen offered in Belgium). This is done by adding a shot of spirit – usually a volatile, flammable variety such as Sambuca – and serving it at the table with the inevitable blue flame. This has less to do with tradition and more to do with the visual experience of the cocktail bar. No matter how much of the spirit is burnt off, the residual ingredients will change the flavour of your drink quite dramatically. The actual process of the flambée can give a toasty, biscuity edge to your beer which you may or may not like. For those who are inclined to try it, we won't attempt to deprive you of your first time – but having had one, we don't believe many beer lovers would order another out of preference. There seems to be a belief throughout France that drinkers in Franconia (the northern part of Bavaria in Germany), like to flambée their Rauchenfels Steinbier and Steinweizen as an age-old tradition (even though the beer was only re-invented in 1982), and quite a few specialist beer bars stock these wonderful beers just to set alight to them. In one case we were actually refused a Steinbier because they needed all their bottles for the weekend flambée-fest of young trendies. Oh well, everyone to their own.

Occasionally you may come across a beerlist which gives a selection of various beer to which a spirit or liqueur has been added. To our knowledge there are no universal terms for any of these (with the exception of an 'amer bière', see later) – the bar owners or their clientele appear to give them different names even in the same town but all are suitably exotic or butch.

As a sample of what can be done to a beer, we list the beer cocktails on sale at two French brewpubs. St-Martial in Limoges offers a 'Blanche parfumée framboise' (raspberry-scented, presumably with the addition of raspberry syrup), a 'Douceur' (a brune with almond liqueur and strawberry syrup), a 'Pêcher Mignon' (brune with gin and strawberry syrup), a 'Russian' (blonde with gin and lemon juice) and a 'Blanche Pêche' (with added peach syrup). Les 3 Brasseurs in Strasbourg suggests an 'El Mexicano' (blonde with tequila), a 'Créole' (ambrée with dark rum), a 'Russian Bière' (blonde with vodka and lemon juice), a 'Monaco' (blonde with lemonade and grenadine syrup), and a 'Nord Express' (blonde with blackcurrant liqueur and lemon juice). And if you want to mix solids with liquid, why not try the latter's 'Délice du Brasseur' – a glass of blonde with a scoop of vanilla ice-cream floating in it and flavoured with 'fleur de bière' (a spirit made with hops).

Before we get on to France's singularly acceptable 'beer additive', we must broach the subject of serving beer with slices of fruit in it. A good bar will make a point of asking you if you want a slice of lemon with your bière blanche or one of the new wave of tequila-laced drinks, but the vast majority (probably following the brewery's or bar owner's instructions) will serve it 'avec citron'. This is one of our particular pet hates as there is no need whatsoever to have a slice of lemon in a white beer, and all spirit-flavoured drinks tend to be so citric already that the drink becomes more of a spirit-laced lemon drink with occasional wafts of beer character. If you are sitting at the bar it is possible to stop them reaching for the bowl of lemon slices, but if you order at the table it is invariably too late to do anything about it. And contrary to common belief, tossing the slice into the ashtray as soon as you receive your glass still means your drink is spoiled. By all means the bar should offer the choice, but in no way should it be obligatory.

Finally, we come to the French beer adulteration which really does have a tradition – Picon Bière. This nationally-famous beer additive has been around since 1837, being invented by someone called Gaëtan Picon. Many believe it was previously most popular in the north-east of France but it has now become something of a national institution. Just about every bar will have a bottle of it although, like many French bars, if it is not particularly popular in their bar it will be at the back with a good few years' worth of dust covering it.

Picon is essentially a bittering agent with a base of that bitterest of ingredients – gentian (not the violet type, but from the herb) – with bitter orange peel and quinine. In the bottle it has a rich, orangey colour and gives a blonde beer a distinct ruddy hue with a strong bitter orange nose. It can make even the cheapest of dumpy-bottled beer actually taste of something. It may not make it the most complex drink you've ever tasted, but it changes the character of a 'pression' completely – thereby breaking up the monotony of a whole night out with just the one bland beer on sale. Another French drink which uses gentian to add bitterness to its taste is the once-ubiquitous Suze, an aperitif, the popularity of which appears to have waned to the point that its identity may one day be restricted to the faded, peeling paintwork on rendered house walls beside the routes nationale.

Picon is surprisingly strong – 21% alc/vol. – and the label on the back recommends mixing it at a ratio of 3cl of Picon to a 25cl glass of bière blonde. A true 'Picon bière' – sometimes called an 'amer bière' (amer is French for bitter) – according to the French should be made with a shot of 'sirop de citron' (lemon syrup) which adds fullness to the flavour but also adds the usual Gallic sweetness they don't seem to be able to do without. If you prefer it not to be too sweet, then we suggest you try it without the syrup. You may also like to experiment with the ratio of Picon to beer, as its recommended dosage can be a little too bitter for many.

If you are looking around a hypermarket to buy a bottle of Picon to bring home, be warned – Picon also make an aperitif which has a very similar label. Look for the words 'Picon Bière'. There are also

other brands of 'amer' on sale and France is not the only country to like amer beer (the Walloons of French-speaking Belgium also have their own brands) but none will ever achieve the fame of the original.

Why don't you try it, you may be pleasantly surprised.

Left: Something of a French institution. If you really must add something to your beer, this would be our preference.

THE SPECIALITY BEER BARS OF PARIS

John White, a British beer buff living on the Continent, lists the favourite bars he has found on his travels around the capital

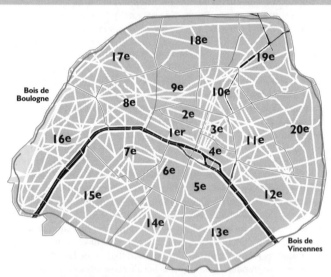

Map of Paris showing Arrondissements, main streets, River Seine and Périphérique (outer thick grey line)

The growing interest in speciality beer in France has spawned an increasing number of bars which offer a large selection of beers – and nowhere is this more evident than in the capital where 'cartes de bières' listing over 400 beers can be found. However, it should be pointed out that just because a bar has a very large beer list, it does not necessarily mean there will be a good selection of interesting beers. One recurring feature is that of trying to squeeze in offerings from as many different countries as possible, many of which have no great brewing tradition.

Belgian beers are well represented throughout Paris (as in most other major cities in France), although it is often the case that the genuine classics are mixed together with the commercial brews such as the Leffe and Mort Subite ranges, so it pays to have done a little research to know which ones to avoid.

In addition to the selection of the better-known French beers, you may also come across beers such as Pietra, the chestnut beer from Corsica. This is typical of the fairly rare, but not particularly special, beers which feature on some of the large beer lists these days. Beers from the DOM-TOMs (Départements d'Outre Mer and Territoires d'Outre Mer), such as Bourbon from Réunion, are often listed along with those from former colonies and where France was once a major foreign influence, like Vietnam.

Thankfully, in some bars, there are also classic rarities from Nord/ Pas-de-Calais, and even from the Paris region itself!

Being France, most of the bars also serve very good food – often typical 'brasserie' fayre, such as mussels, sauerkraut (choucroute) and onion soup. Andouillettes, which look like superb sausages, are very common – but avoid them if you don't like chitterlings. It is, however, quite in order just to drink a glass of beer or two in most of the bars listed.

With Paris being such a large city, I have listed bars by their official arrondissement number to break the city up into logical, and easily-located geographical areas. All Paris postcodes begin with 75 (the département number of Paris) and the last three figures denote its arrondissement within the city – for instance a bar in the 17th Arrondissement will have a postcode of 75017. Note the numbers are abbreviated to the French language – e.g. 5th is 5e (cinquième). The arrondissement numbers are very prominent on maps and street signs, but at times it can happen that the same street or square can have different numbers depending on where the boundary goes. One bar listed goes beyond the Périphérique and is actually in another département, so there is no arrondissement number applicable.

When a beer has been mentioned (e.g. Jenlain at Le Dieu Gambrinus) it does not necessarily mean that it is the only draught beer available – the named beers are simply the ones of particular interest to the beer fan. Gambrinus has in fact 30 draught beers, including Belgian beers like Hoegaarden and Pauwel Kwak plus French beers such as the rum-flavoured Kingston.

1er Arrondissement

LE DIEU GAMBRINUS, 62 rue des Lombards – Beamed ground floor bar with three paintings of drunken debauchery, one involving monks. The attractive 13th century vaulted cellar (Chapelle des Templiers) features live rock and country & western music. Jenlain, like the other draught beers on offer, is served from a lovely patterned ceramic fount. (Métro: Châtelet)

LA TAVERNE DES HALLES, 12 rue de la Cossonerie – In the same group and with a similar beer range to the excellent, well-established La Taverne de St-Germain des Prés in the 6th Arrondissement. (Métro: Châtelet-les-Halles (RER))

LA TAVERNE DE RUBENS (CHEZ GAËTAN), 12 rue St-Denis – The Belgian classic La Chouffe is on draught. The draught beer of the month is usually something interesting from France. (Métro: Châtelet)

AU TRAPPISTE, 4 rue St-Denis – Worth having a look in if you are on the rue St-Denis pub crawl, as opposed to the rue St-Denis sex show crawl! (Métro: Châtelet)

HALL'S BEER TAVERN, 68 rue St-Denis. (Métro: Châtelet-les-Halles (RER))

THE FROG & ROSBIF, 112 rue St-Denis – See *Paris Real Ale Brewery* article in brewery section. (Métro: Etienne Marcel)

LE SOUS-BOCK TAVERN, 49 rue St-Honoré (open 24 hours) – Close to being the best speciality beer bar in Paris. As befits its name, beer mats decorate the walls of the 'Beer Mat Tavern', which has a superbly adorned, long bar. Its list of 400 beers has far less duds than most of its size, all fully described in the excellent carte de bières. An excellent selection of French speciality beers. Typical brasserie cuisine, plus pub food from around the world. Nearly 200 different whiskys. Large darts area downstairs. The beer shop next door (number 51) is open from 11.30 am to 8 pm. (Métro: Châtelet)

2e Arrondissement

MANNEKEN-PIS, 4 rue Daunou – Limited beer range (Pauvel Kwak on draught, 3 Monts in bottles) but worth a visit. Pleasant inside and out. Good display of jazz photos, though the piped music is not restricted to jazz. Naturally it has a Manneken-Pis statue (the original in Brussels being probably the world's most boring tourist attraction). (Métro: Opéra)

3e Arrondissement

LA TAVERNE RÉPUBLIQUE, 5 Place République – In the same group and has a similar beer range as La Taverne de St-Germain des Prés in the 6th Arrondissement (Métro: République)

4e Arrondissement

L'ABBAYE, 1 Place de la Bastille – After a drink here you can visit the nearby Brasserie Bofinger, a classic Alsacian restaurant decorated in the belle époque style (Métro: Bastille)

5e Arrondissement

L'ACADEMIE DE LA BIÈRE, 88 Boulevard de Port-Royal. (Métro: Port Royal (RER))

LA GUEUZE, 19 rue Soufflot – A most friendly speciality beer hall which attracts students from the nearby Sorbonne. Although commercial gueuzes such as Bécasse dominate, this is probably the only outlet in central Paris for the classic gueuze, kriek and framboise from the Cantillon brewery in Brussels. Interesting French beers include the St-Landelin range from Gayant, with one often on draught. Sauerkraut is also available cooked in gueuze. (Métro: Luxembourg (RER))

LE TANGO DU CHAT, 6 rue St-Séverin – Small, very old, bar in the Latin Quarter. Beer list is not massive but includes some quality beers.

6e Arrondissement

LE MAZET, 61 rue St-André-des-Arts – Not a big selection (Belgian Riva Blanche and Pauwel Kwak on draught, the Ch'ti range and a couple of other French specialities in the bottle), but very friendly – a real don't-miss. It is superbly located; the second entrance around the corner is in the oldest alley in Paris. Food is good and inexpensive, and menus are translated into English. (Métro: Odéon)

LA TAVERNE DE NESLE, 32 rue Dauphine – Best bar in Paris for French speciality beers, along with such rare Belgian beers as Abbaye des Rocs. Note that it does not open until 8 pm – this is a good time to come for a quiet drink (from 10 pm until closing time, around 4 am, it can be quite a raucous place in a nice sort of way). Not to be missed. (Métro: Odéon)

LA TAVERNE DE ST-GERMAIN DES PRÉS, 155 Boulevard St-Germain – The Belgian La Chouffe on draught. Excellent selection of bottled French beers, including the wonderful Cuvée des Jonquilles from Au Baron – a beer surprisingly absent from some otherwise good beer lists elsewhere. Eating area surrounds the atmospheric raised bar area. Another don't-miss. (Métro: St-Germain des Prés)

PUB ST-GERMAIN DES PRÉS, 17 rue de l'Ancienne Comédie – Not to be confused with the previous entry. On entering one gets an initial impression of a fairly small, pleasant conventional bar and eating place featuring pannelled cubicles. However, this leads to a trendy, surprisingly large, drinking/live-music area downstairs – one of eight air conditioned rooms collectively seating up to 750 people. The 500-strong beer list includes such rarities as Bière des Volcans from Cerf. The beer of the month is chosen by Les Compagnons de Gambrinus. 24-hour opening. 'The Greatest Pub in France' is prominently displayed – and I have to say that it is far from the worst, a visit being obligatory when in Paris, and it is in a great part of the capital. (Métro: Odéon)

O'NEIL, 20 rue des Canettes – Brewpub in the same chain as Les 3 Brasseurs (*see Bars de France in brewery section*). Very nice place and very popular. (Métro: St-Germain des Prés)

THE FROG & PRINCESS, 9 rue Princesse – As if one 'Frog' brewpub in Paris was not enough, this one on the rive gauche appeared in 1997 (see *Paris Real Ale Brewery* article in brewery section). It is on a road parallel to O'Neil. (Métro: Mabillon)

LA MARINE, 59 Boulevard du Montparnasse. (Métro: Montparnasse Bienvenüe)

8e Arrondissement

THE CRICKETERS, 41 rue des Mathurins – Owned by Adnams (a UK real ale brewery) where the handpumped Bitter, Extra and Broadside are as good as in most places you will get them in the UK (Broadside was 35FF per pint in October 1997). Excellent decor with outstanding cricket memorabilia. Each December it holds the Paris Beer Festival – an English pub festival style occasion with English ales served straight from the barrel. It does offer the French Wel Scotch (a rival to Adelscott) on draught. Open 11 am to 2 am every day. (Métro: St-Augustin)

THE BOWLERS, 13 rue d'Artois – Another Adnams pub (see previous entry), and clearly continuing the cricket theme. Although in the same arrondissement, they are a good 20 minutes walk apart. Same opening times and prices as The Cricketers but by buying a 4-pint jug at 100FF you get a considerable saving. Happy hour at varying times on different days. (Métro: St-Philippe du Roule)

9e Arrondissement

AU GENERAL LA FAYETTE, 52 rue La Fayette – Truly superb. One of the speciality beer bars before they became fashionable, yet still retaining its classic Parisian bar atmosphere with locals just as likely to order a pastis or vin rouge as a beer. Marvellous art nouveau interior, especially the ceiling. A limited range of excellent food, cheap by Parisian standards. Not the most extensive beer list, but enough Belgian classics to keep the beer buff interested. If you only have time for one speciality beer bar in Paris, this has to be the one. (Métro: Chaussée D'Antin)

LE GRAND ZINC, 5 rue du Faubourg Montmartre – A nice restaurant with some good beers, including Jenlain, and a zinc-topped bar (on the right, near the entrance). For amazingly good value, simple food, pop next door to Chartier – a Parisien institution (Métro: Rue Montmartre)

10e Arrondissement

LA BRASSERIE DE L'EST, 78 Boulevard de Strasbourg. (Métro: Gare de l'Est)

CAFÉ-CONCERT FALSTAFF, 15 rue de Dunkerque – A don't-miss if in the Gare du Nord area – a great place to kill time waiting for your Eurostar train home. The music is blues, rock and pop. Usually has a speciality French beer, such as one from the Ch'ti range, on draught. Bottles include a couple from the Dutch La Trappe range and 3 Monts. A good place to eat, in an area with way over its fair share of junk food establishments, but some good Indian restaurants. (Métro: Gare du Nord (RER))

11e Arrondissment

LA JUVENTUS, 10 Place de la Bastille – Pizza place with some interesting beers. (Métro: Bastille)

L'OISEAU DE FEU, 12 Place de la Bastille. (Métro: Bastille)

14e Arrondissement

CAFÉ-CONCERT FALSTAFF, 42 rue de Montparnasse – Similar to the entry of the same name in the 10e Arrondissement. (Métro: Montparnasse Bienvenüe)

17e Arrondissement

LE BAR BELGE, 75 avenue de St-Ouen. (Métro: Guy Môquet)

Département 93 (Seine-St-Denis)

PUB MALKEHR, 147 avenue Gallieni, 93170 Bagnolet – (See article in brewery section). In a scruffy street in an area of secondhand shops, but don't let this put you off, as it is very interesting and its two beers – brewed on the premises – are in a different league to the ones made in other Parisien brewpubs. 14FF per glass for the Blonde or Ambrée (March 1998), an extra 3FF to drink on the terrace. The brewery itself is a sensation, with the mash tun and copper being built into the actual serving bar (ask for a house card which has a good photo of the set-up). Good and cheap food for menus or plat du jour. Well worth a visit, let's hope it survives its location. (Métro: Gallieni – or the stop before, Porte de Bagnolet, if you only want to use a Zone 1 ticket)

BEER SHOP

14e Arrondissement

BOOTLEGGER, 82 rue de l'Ouest, 75014 Paris – From the outside, and the hanging De Koninck sign, this looks like a rather scruffy Belgian locals' bar (befitting the area in which it is located), but in fact is an excellent beer shop. Open Tuesday to Saturday, 10.30 am – 1 pm and 4 pm – 9 pm. A far better selection than that offered by the hypermarkets, such as Au Baron's Cuvée des Jonquilles and Theillier's La Bavaisienne. Also a good selection of glasses and Belgian beers, including a 9-litre St. Feuillien bottle for 585FF! (Métro: Pernety)

SEE THE ARTISAN PRESS WEBSITE FOR LATEST DETAILS OF BARS IN PARIS – www.artisanpress.com

---

BUYING FRENCH BEER IN THE HYPERMARKETS

It's not all Eurofizz! There are some great French beers on sale in hypermarkets – and some are real bargains

There is no doubt about it, France is a very cheap place to buy beer in supermarkets compared to Britain and many other countries in mainland Europe – and it will remain that way until there is a little more parity in excise duty across the European Economic Community. For the foreseeable future the hordes of British shoppers piling their trolleys full of wine and beer will be a feature of the hypermarkets of Dunkerque, Calais, Boulogne and Dieppe, and to a lesser extent those of Le Havre and Cherbourg.

The reason the British will travel miles to do their shopping, even after taking into account the petrol, wear and tear of the vehicle and the ferry/tunnel fare is simply down to the fact that the British government imposes a duty on beer far in excess of that of France and Belgium. Campaigns are still in progress to force the powers-that-be to address this imbalance, but in the meantime the sheer volume of beer imported (and in many cases reimported, as British beer is also far cheaper when bought in France) will continue to infuriate the UK brewers and publicans alike.

The vast majority of beer bought in French hypermarkets is the 'pile-'em-high-and-sell-'em-cheap' type of 'bière blonde' which probably appeals most to the British canned lager home-drinker but is often blamed for the downturn in the UK pub trade in the late 1990s. The bière blonde market is very cut-throat in its pricing, which has resulted in dozens of very similar products with, we suspect, a certain amount of re-labelling going on. Many of the cheapest beers will be supermarket own-brands, but whichever one you go for it will make little difference – they will all be bland imitations of the pilsener style. If you buy bière blonde in a channel port hypermarket, there is a good chance it will have been made by either Brasserie St-Omer or Terken – two of the major players in budget beer brewing in the Nord/Pas-de-Calais region – although it may be very difficult to tell who made it from the pack. The best way to check is to find the small print stating 'EMB' (for embouteillage, meaning bottled by) and the postcode following should correspond to one of the breweries in this book. Some of the Alsacian breweries seem to be muscling in on the act more each year, but this is little more than a side-show – after all, it is impossible to tell the difference between a 'bière des Flandres' and a 'bière d'Alsace' because essentially there isn't any, other than the geographical location of its production.

If price is the main criteria when choosing your French beer, then it is impossible to beat the value for money of bière blonde when comparing alcohol by volume with unit price. Unfortunately, it will almost certainly be a very bland and characterless product because it has to appeal to such a wide market where any amount of character will be a positive disadvantage. However, by spending a little more – but still far less than an equivalent special beer in the UK – you can then start to look at many of the better French products, some of which offer excellent quality and character for a very reasonable price.

Priced slightly above the bières blonde are what the French call the 'de Luxe' brands – such as Export 33, Kronenbourg 1664, Kanterbrau Gold, Mützig Old Lager, etc. – which will normally be between 5% and 6% alc/vol., compared to the bières blonde ranging from 3.5% to 5% (although the latter seem to get stronger every year, fudging this distinction). The Luxe beers are fuller tasting as they are usually pure malt brews which vary enough in character to at least be able to distinguish one from another. As most of the Luxe beers are well-known, internationally-exported brands there is no point giving too much space for them here. Instead the intent is to concentrate on what are termed 'spéciale' beers – priced well above the Luxe beers and more often than not being top fermenting.

This section is not meant to be a recommended list of all the beers of France – it attempts to assess the availability and the price you can expect to pay. Obviously the rarer, more artisanal beers you will read about in this book will need to be bought nearer to their source, but because many people will first come across French beer through a visit to a hypermarket or a trip to the Nord/Pas-de-Calais region, we believe this will be a useful pointer in helping beer enthusiasts to make an informed choice. The prices following are for 75cl bottles unless otherwise stated.

Perhaps the most easily obtainable range of good beers comes from the Brasseurs de Gayant. Goudale (sold in screen-printed 75cl corked bottles) makes a great introduction to French beer and can be found in many hypermarkets at a very good price (as cheap as FF8.50), along with its stablemates La Bière du Désert (from FF9.95) and the palate-warming 12% Bière du Démon (from FF10.30 for 33cl). Gayant also offer a range of beers under the St-Landelin name – all of which make good buys. The relatively new Amadeus Bière Blanche is also now widely available (around FF7.90) but would not be our choice.

The classic Jenlain (perhaps best known of all the bières de garde) from Brasserie Duyck and its often-overlooked blonde counterpart Sebourg offer great value, saving you loads of money in comparison to a typical bar price in France (from FF9.30 and FF9.45 respectively).

The breweries of Castelain (Ch'ti) and La Choulette have excellent ranges of bières de garde, most of which we would have no problems with recommending – as long as you bear in mind our comments regarding drinking them while they are young (Ch'ti Blonde from FF11.45, Choulette Blonde from FF12.95).

If you can handle the fruity tanginess and warmth of Trois Monts you will find it a relative bargain on the hypermarket shelves (from FF11.80), but the only other St-Sylvestre beer we have seen has been the newly-introduced Gavroche. A real pity that its excellent Bière Nouvelle and Bière de Noël are not often seen.

The characterful Annœullin range is another hypermarket regular. The wonderful L'Angélus (from FF14.50) may not be cheap but is one of those beers you just have to try.

Another of the more characterful breweries represented, especially in the Nord/Pas-de-Calais region, is the range from Brasserie Jeanne d'Arc. Its Ambrée des Flandres and Grain d'Orge (from FF12.30 and FF13.50 respectively) are quite easy to find and have recently been joined by the 15% sipping beer Belzebuth (thankfully only sold in 25cl bottles from FF6.90).

The breweries of St-Omer and Terken will have the vast majority of their presence in the cheap bière blonde section, but if you want to try their better beers have a go at Terken's Septante Cinq (from FF7.70) and La Millionième and L'Épi de Facon from St-Omer. Even these won't be particularly challenging but are cheap and tasty enough to make people look a little harder at the choice on offer.

Various Alsacian breweries will be represented, although most will be there to appeal to the cheap bière blonde drinkers. Adelshoffen makes its fair share of Euro-fizz but it also makes the whisky malt Adelscott beers (in normal and brune versions) which are now sold in just about every supermarket in France since it was bought by Heineken. Likewise, Fischer's better-than-most pilsner-type offerings such as Tradition (from FF7.05 for 65cl) are easily obtainable even at the Channel ports. Sadly, with the sole exception of Mortimer (which we consider the best of France's whisky malt beers), we found it difficult to find any of Meteor's beers on the hypermarket shelves.

There does appear to be a regional variation in which smaller breweries' products are stocked – for instance Lupus Ale and Loup Garou (both from FF13.90) and others from Brasserie Chant du Loup, near Rouen, were only found in the shops around Le Havre. Cherbourg, or better still St. Malo, will be the best places to go to find the Breton specialities like Lancelot and Deux Rivières.

At the colossal Auchan store in Grande Synthe (near Dunkerque) it is good to see their policy of stocking local micro's beer is coming on stream. It is now possible to buy Blonde d'Esquelbecq (FF16.50) and other brews from the tiny Brasserie Thiriez. Although major retail chains in rural France often stock the products of local micros, it has yet to be a major feature in the Channel port hypermarkets.

The British-owned stores like East Enders continue to sate the appetite of cheap-beer-loving Brits, while on the same trading estate is the French-owned Pidou which has an excellent range of French and Belgian beers, albeit at a higher price than the hypermarkets.

It can be a mistake to believe that the bigger the shop the cheaper it will be. There are many bargains to be had at the smaller supermarkets along the streets in and out of town, like GB and Casino. For instance if you take the East Enders turn-off from the ring-road at Calais, but turn towards the 'centre ville' instead of the trading estate, you will find the Intermarché supermarket on the left-hand side which is worth a visit if only to stock up on the beers of Brasserie de Clerck.

Many stores stock a variety of Belgian beers, although most of them will probably be those of Interbrew (which has a major presence in northern France as Brasseries Stella Artois) such as the Mort Subite fruit beers and gueuze, Hoegaarden, Leffe, etc. Duvel, Pauwel Kwak and the Trappist beers from Chimay and Orval are usually present – all of which are worth stocking up on.

A newer oddity on sale at many French hypermarkets these days is the range of beers from Canada made by Quebec brewer Unibroue. Best of the bunch is the excellent, dark Maudite, but also available are Fin du Monde, Raftman and Blanche de Chambéry.

BARGAIN FRENCH BEER AWARD
has to go to Gayant's Goudale – a superb beer at a ludicrously low price. Widely available and often in boxes of six. Buy it, you won't be disappointed.

BEST SUPERMARKET AWARD
goes to Intermarché in Calais for its consistently good range and usually being amongst the lowest in price.
Watch the website for new awards.

PLEASE NOTE: This survey of prices and availability was carried out at Easter 1998 and could have changed considerably by the time you are reading it. For more current information, please refer to our website at www.artisanpress.com.

	BOULOGNE					CALAIS						DUNKERQUE			LE HAVRE	
	E.Leclerc	Intermarche	Auchan	Carrefour	Auchan	P.G.	Pidou	Continent	Match	Intermarche	Auchan	Cora	Carrefour	Auchan	E.Leclerc	Marché U
Des Amis Réunis																
Bière de St-Amand									13.80							
Annœullin																
L'Angélus	14.50	15.95	14.50	16.45	17.00	15.50			16.90	14.95				16.95		
Rijsel									14.80			18.20				
Bécu																
Atrébate Ambrée								16.10								
Atrébate Blonde								15.10								
Castelain																
Ch'ti Ambrée		14.45	12.95	11.95	13.25				13.90	14.95		14.45	14.90			
Ch'ti Blonde		14.45	12.45	16.05	11.45					14.95				13.70	14.70	
Ch'ti Triple			15.10			13.45	17.20	14.95			13.70				16.45	
Jade												17.90				
Korma												10.90				
St-Léonard	10.70															
St-Patron													21.90			

The Beers of France

	1	2	3	4	5	6	7	8	9	10	11	12	13	14
Chant du Loup														
Cervoise Lupulix												16.50	13.90	17.95
Loup-Garou											13.90	13.90	17.95	
Lupus Ale											13.90	13.90	17.95	
Viking Wolf												13.90	13.90	17.95
La Choulette														
Choulette Ambrée		15.40		15.65		12.95			12.95			16.95		
Choulette Blonde		13.50		15.65		12.95			12.95			13.95	18.50	
De Clerck														
La Belle Siska				12.95				12.90						
Colvert						12.95		12.90						
La Fanette								12.90				16.95		
Réserve du Caveau		12.35						12.35						
Duyck														
Jenlain	9.90	9.55	9.65	9.40		9.40	9.65	9.30	10.25	8.45	9.40	10.25	11.60	11.10
Sebourg		9.90	9.90	9.95			9.30		7.70			8.95		
Fischer/Adelshoffen														
Fischer Tradition (65cl)	7.60	7.05	8.15		7.45		8.90	7.05	7.20	7.05	7.30			

	BOULOGNE				CALAIS						DUNKERQUE			LE HAVRE		
	E.Leclerc	Intermarche	Auchan	Carrefour	Auchan	P.G.	Pidou	Continent	Match	Intermarche	Auchan	Cora	Carrefour	Auchan	E.Leclerc	Marché U
Brasseurs de Gayant																
Bière du Démon (33cl)			12.95					10.30		13.20						
Bière du Désert		12.95					15.55			12.95				10.95		
Blanche d'Amadéus			8.15	8.95	9.95	8.95	9.75	8.90	9.20	9.30	8.15			7.75		
Goudale	8.50	10.25	8.80	9.40	8.90	10.75			9.85	10.25	9.40	9.70	9.50			
Lutèce	11.30	12.75			9.55	9.95	11.50			12.10		9.90	9.80			
Jeanne d'Arc																
Ambrée des Flandres	12.50								13.50	12.30	13.45			15.95		
Grain d'Orge								16.95		13.85	17.80		17.80	16.10	16.10	
Belzébuth (25cl)	7.70	8.25		11.65					6.90	8.25				12.50		
Meteor																
Mortimer	12.95		13.00		13.50						14.50					
St-Sylvestre																
3 Monts	11.80	14.65	11.95	16.00		11.95	19.35	14.75	13.80	13.95	11.95	13.50		16.20	16.40	17.95
Terken																
Septante 5	8.80		8.75		10.25	9.95			9.30		7.70			8.95		
Thiriez																
L'Esquelbecq Ambrée											16.50					
L'Esquelbecq Blonde											16.50					

Beer Label Interpretation

Some basic translations to help you understand the label

French beer labels convey a fair bit of information, sometimes in English, but always in French. To make deciphering this information a little easier we have included here a list of the more common phrases and symbols used along with an explanation of their meaning.

A consommer de préférence avant fin ...	Best before end date.
Aromatisée à ...	Flavoured with ...
Aucun (or) Sans additives	Without additives.
Bière artisanale	A handcrafted beer.
Biologique	Organic.
Brassée et embouteillée a ...	Brewed and bottled at ...
Consigné (or) Verre Consigné	Returnable bottle. Sometimes used in conjunction with a value
Embouteillée le ...	Bottled date.
Fermentation haute	Top fermented.
Fermentation basse	Bottom fermented.
Mis en bouteille ... Embouteillée (or) EMB ...	Bottled by ... *(useful for checking out the brewer of label beers – the postcode will be the same, or similar, to the brewery)*
Non Filtrée	Unfiltered.
Non Pasteurisée	Unpasteurised.
Pur Malt	Pure malt. Uses no other grain.
Refermentée en bouteille (or) Bière sur lie (or) Sur levure	Refermented in the bottle. (Literally, beer on yeast) (ditto)
Servir frais/Servir à ... Servir entre ... à ...	Serve cool / Serve at ... (temperature) Serve between ... and ... (temperature)
Tenir au frais et à l'abri de la lumière	Store in a cool and dark place
Triple fermentation	Has undergone a primary fermentation, a garde and a bottle refermentation.

SOME COMMON INGREDIENTS

Avoine	Oats.	*Gingembre*	Ginger.
Châtaigne	Chestnut.	*Houblon*	Hops.
Citron / Citron Vert	Lemon / Lime.	*Levure*	Yeast.
Coriandre	Coriander.	*Mäis*	Maize.
Épice / Épicée	Spice / Spiced.	*Orge*	Barley.
Farine	Flour.	*Réglisse*	Liquorice.
Froment	Wheat.	*Riz*	Rice.
Genévrier	Juniper.	*Seigle*	Rye.

ACCREDITATION SYMBOLS

All organic beers should have at least one of these logos on the label to state that the ingredients have been certified organic with Ecocert (left) and Nature & Progres.

Some Départements allow official badges for products which meet certain criteria. This one can only be used if over 50% of the ingredients used in a product are from the Nord/Pas-de-Calais region.

THE BREWERIES OF FRANCE

The list below is in alphabetical order (as logically as we can make it). The numbers correspond to those shown on the following maps. In brackets is the nearest large town/village and the grid reference (those marked with *N/PdC* are on the detailed map of Nord/Pas-de-Calais, while those without are on the national map).

1 Les 3 Brasseurs/O'Neil. *Four different locations – a: Angers (D3), b: Lille (N/PdC C6), c: Paris (C5), d: Strasbourg (C9)*

2 Brasserie d'Alauna *(Valognes, B3)*

3 Brasserie des Amis Réunis *(Saint-Amand-Les-Eaux, N/PdC D7)*

4 Brasserie Annœullin *(Carvin, N/PdC D5)*

5 Petite Brasserie Ardennaise *(Charleville-Mézières, B7)*

6 Brasserie Bailleux *(Bavay, N/PdC D8)*

7 Ferme-Brasserie Beck *(Bailleul, N/PdC B5)*

8 Brasserie Bécu *(Arras, N/PdC E5)*

9 Brasserie de Bernoville *(Guise, B6)*

10 Brasserie Bobtail *(Aubeterre-sur-Dronne, F4)*

11 La Cabane des Brasseurs *(Nancy, C8)*

12 Brasserie Artisanale du Cambier *(Cambrai, N/PdC E6)*

13 Brasserie du Caroux *(Bédarieux, H6)*

14 Brasserie Castelain *(Lens, N/PdC D5)*

15 Les Caves de la Brasserie *(Mulhouse, D9)*

16 Brasserie du Cerf *(Combronde, E6)*

17 La Cervoiserie (Chez Nino) *(Nice, H9)*

18 Brasserie des Champs *(Sens, C6)*

19 Brasserie du Chant du Loup *(Rouen, B4)*

20 Café Le Chantecler *(Lyon, F7)*

21 Brasserie La Choulette *(Cambrai, N/PdC D6)*

22 Brasserie de Clerck *(Péronne, B6)*

23 Brasserie des Deux-Rivières *(Morlaix, C1)*

24 Micro-Brasserie des Diaouligs *(Plancoët, C2)*

25 Brasserie Duyck *(Valenciennes, N/PdC D7)*

26 Entre-Temps *(Valenciennes, N/PdC D7)*

27 Brasseries Fischer & Adelshoffen *(Strasbourg, C9)*

28 Ferme-Brasserie Garland *(Toulouse, H5)*

29 Les Brasseurs de Gayant *(Douai, N/PdC D6)*

30 Brasserie de Granges-sur-Baume *(Poligny, E8)*

31 Brasseries Heineken. *Three different locations – a: Mons-en-Baroeul (N/PdC C6), b: Marseille (H8), c: Strasbourg (C9)*

32 Brasserie Henry *(Bar-le-Duc, C7)*

33 Institut Français des Boissons et de la Brasserie Malterie *(Nancy, C8)*

34 Brasserie Jeanne d'Arc *(Lille, N/PdC C6)*

35 Brasseries Kronenbourg. *Four different locations – a: Champigneulles (C8), b: Obernai (C9), c: Rennes (C3), d: Strasbourg (C9)*

36 Brasserie Lampée-Baumgartner *(Ile de Ré, E3)*

37 Brasserie Lancelot *(Ploërmel, D2)*

㊳ **Pub-Brasserie Malkehr** *(Paris, C5)*
㊴ **Brasserie Meteor** *(Hochfelden, C9)*
㊵ **Brasserie Métreau** *(Montguyon, F4)*
㊶ **Le Moulin à Bière** *(Calais, N/PdC A2)*
㊷ **Brasserie des Naufrageurs** *(Ile d'Oléron, E3)*
㊸ **Brasserie L'Olanier** *(Aubenas, G7)*
㊹ **Paris Real Ale Brewery** *(Two locations in Paris, C5)*
㊺ **Brasserie Pietra** *(Bastia, H9)*
㊻ **Brasserie Piste-Rouge** *(Les Eyzies-de-Tayac, F4)*
㊼ **Café de la Poste** *(Saint-Pol-sur-Ternoise, N/PdC D3)*
㊽ **Brasserie Ste-Colombe** *(Retiers, D3)*
㊾ **Brasserie Artisanale St-Martial** *(Limoges, F5)*
㊿ **Brasserie de St-Omer** *(St-Omer, N/PdC B3)*
(51) **Brasserie St-Poloise** *(St-Pol-sur-Ternoise, N/PdC D3)*
(52) **Brasserie de St-Sylvestre** *(Cassel, N/PdC B4)*
(53) **Brasserie de Saverne** *(Saverne, C9)*
(54) **Brasserie Schutzenberger** *(Strasbourg, C9)*
(55) **Brasserie de Séverac** *(Redon, D2)*
(56) **Spirit of Factory** *(Angers, D3)*
(57) **Brasseries Stella Artois** *(Armentières, N/PdC C5)*
(58) **Taverne du Brasseur** *(Metz, B8)*
(59) **Taverne de l'Écu** *(Lille, N/PdC C6)*
(60) **Brasserie Terken** *(Roubaix, N/PdC C6)*
(61) **Brasserie Theillier** *(Bavay, N/PdC E8)*
(62) **Brasserie Thiriez** *(Wormhout, N/PdC B4)*
(63) **Brasserie de Ville-sur-Illon** *(Epinal, C8)*

THE DÉPARTEMENTS OF FRANCE

1. Ain
2. Aisne
3. Allier
4. Alpes-de-Haute-Provence
5. Hautes-Alpes
6. Alpes-Maritimes
7. Ardèche
8. Ardennes
9. Ariège
10. Aube
11. Aude
12. Aveyron
13. Bouches-du-Rhône
14. Calvados
15. Cantal
16. Charente
17. Charente-Maritime
18. Cher
19. Corrèze
2A. Corse-du-Sud
2B. Haute-Corse
21. Côte-dOr
22. Côtes-d'Armor
23. Creuse
24. Dordogne
25. Doubs
26. Drôme
27. Eure
28. Eure-et-Loir
29. Finistère
30. Gard
31. Haute-Garonne
32. Gers
33. Gironde
34. Hérault
35. Ille-et-Vilaine
36. Indre
37. Indre-et-Loire
38. Isère
39. Jura
40. Landes
41. Loir-et-Cher
42. Loire
43. Haute-Loire
44. Loire-Atlantique
45. Loiret
46. Lot
47. Lot-et-Garonne
48. Lozère
49. Maine-et-Loire
50. Manche
51. Marne
52. Haute-Marne
53. Mayenne
54. Meurthe-et-Moselle
55. Meuse
56. Morbihan
57. Moselle
58. Nièvre
59. Nord
60. Oise
61. Orne
62. Pas-de-Calais
63. Puy-de-Dôme
64. Pyrénées-Atlantiques
65. Hautes-Pyrénées
66. Pyrénées-Orientales
67. Bas-Rhin
68. Haut-Rhin
69. Rhône
70. Haute-Saône
71. Saône-et-Loire
72. Sarthe
73. Savoie
74. Haute-Savoie
75. Paris
76. Seine-Maritime
77. Seine-et-Marne
78. Yvelines
79. Deux-Sèvres
80. Somme
81. Tarn
82. Tarn-et-Garonne
83. Var
84. Vaucluse
85. Vendée
86. Vienne
87. Haute-Vienne
88. Vosges
89. Yonne
90. Territoire-de-Belfort
91. Essonne
92. Hauts-de-Seine
93. Seine-St.-Denis
94. Val-de-Marne
95. Val-d'Oise

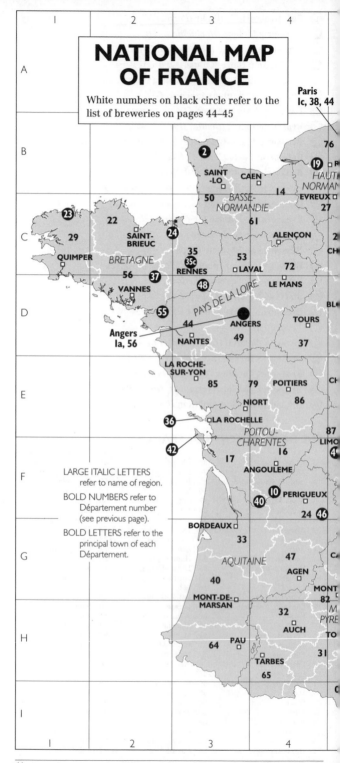

NATIONAL MAP OF FRANCE

White numbers on black circle refer to the list of breweries on pages 44–45

Paris
lc, 38, 44

2

SAINT-LO □   CAEN □

BASSE-NORMANDIE

50   61

76

19 □ R

HAUTE NORMANDIE

EVREUX □   27

ALENÇON □   2

CH

23

22

SAINT-BRIEUC □

24

BRETAGNE

QUIMPER □

29

56   **37**

VANNES □

35
35c
RENNES □

48

53
LAVAL □   72

LE MANS □

BL

55

PAYS DE LA LOIRE

Angers
la, 56

44
NANTES □   ANGERS ●   49

TOURS □

37

LA ROCHE-SUR-YON □
85   79   POITIERS □   86

NIORT □

36   □ LA ROCHELLE

42

17   *POITOU-CHARENTES*   16

ANGOULEME □

CH

87   LIMO
4

40   **10** PERIGUEUX □

24   **46**

LARGE ITALIC LETTERS refer to name of region.

BOLD NUMBERS refer to Département number (see previous page).

BOLD LETTERS refer to the principal town of each Département.

BORDEAUX □

33

AQUITAINE

40

MONT-DE-MARSAN □

47
AGEN □

CA

MONT
82

M
PYRE

32
AUCH □

TO

64   PAU □

TARBES □
65

31

0

For Nord/Pas-de-Calais – see separate map on page following pages

Nancy
11, 33, 35a

Strasbourg
1d, 27,
31c, 35d,
54

Map legend (grid references)

| | | | |
| 1 | 2 | 3 | 4 |

A
DUNKERQUE
Gravelines
CALAIS
41

B
Guînes
Ardres
Marquise
BOULOGNE-SUR-MER
SAINT-OMER
50
Arques
Bergues
Hondschoote
62 Wormhout
Cassel
Steenvoorde
52
Hazebrouck
7 Bailleu

C
Desvres
Lumbres
Aire-sur-la-Lys
62 – PAS-DE-CALAIS
Le Touquet
Lillers
BETHUNE
Win

D
MONTREUIL
Berck
Hesdin
51 **47**
Saint-Pol-sur-Ternoise
Bruay-en-Artois
Houdain
Nœux-les-Mines
Bully-les-Mines
Wim
Li
Vi
ARRAS

E
Auxi-le-Château
Avesnes-le-Comte
Beaumetz-lès-Loges
Pas-en-Artois
Cro
Bapa

F

| 1 | 2 | 3 | 4 |

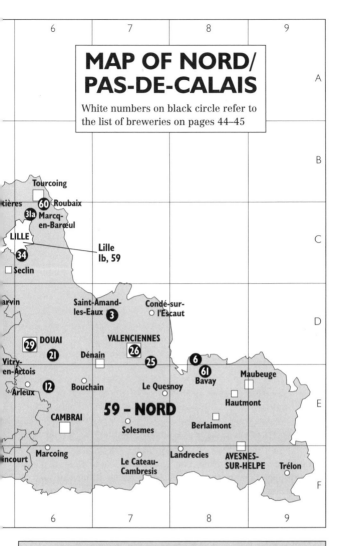

MAP OF NORD/ PAS-DE-CALAIS

White numbers on black circle refer to the list of breweries on pages 44–45

Tourcoing
tières
60 Roubaix
31a Marcq-en-Barœul
LILLE
Lille
1b, 59
34
Seclin

arvin
Saint-Amand-les-Eaux **3**
Condé-sur-l'Escaut

29 DOUAI
VALENCIENNES
26
21
Dénain
25
6
Vitry-en-Artois
61 Bavay
Maubeuge
12
Bouchain
Le Quesnoy
Hautmont
Arleux

59 – NORD

CAMBRAI
Solesmes
Berlaimont

incourt
Marcoing
Landrecies
AVESNES-SUR-HELPE
Trélon
Le Cateau-Cambresis

READER REGISTRATION FORM

STAY UP TO DATE WITH INFORMATION ON FRENCH BREWERIES AND THEIR BEERS

Please photocopy this page, complete the details, and send it to: **The Artisan Press, PO Box 1098, Winscombe, Bristol BS25 1SN, UK.**

I would like my name and address to be placed on your database in order to receive free updates and to be notified of the publication date of a second edition (along with any pre-publication discounts available). *Please print clearly in capital letters*

Mr / Mrs / Miss / Ms   *(please delete as appropriate)*

First Name ....

Surname ....

Address ....

Town ....

County/State ....

Country ....

Post/ZIP Code ....

Email Address ....

Signature ....

BAR/SHOP RECOMMENDATION FORM

If you have any recommendations you would like to pass on, please copy this page as many times as necessary (or use a separate piece of paper), complete the details and send it to **The Artisan Press, PO Box 1098, Winscombe, Bristol, BS25 1SN, UK.** It would help if you can include a business card or leaflet from the bar or shop.

☐ BAR   ☐ SHOP   *(please tick as appropriate)*

Bar/Shop Name ....

Address ....

....

Opening times ....

What beers do they stock? ....

....

....

Why do you recommend it ? ....

....

....

The
BREWERIES
and their
BEERS

See overleaf for How To Use This Guide

How To Use This Guide

BREWERY INFORMATION

The amount of information forthcoming from the breweries varied, but we have reproduced the relevant information, such as ingredients and annual production, about the beers where it was available. Understandably the brewers were often guarded when it came to giving full details of ingredients. We have listed everything they told us.

General information about the breweries is contained in the start of each section and is identified by the following symbols:

⊠ Address.

☎ Telephone number (plus fax if appropriate).

🕘 Brewery opening times.

🏃 Tour availability, notice required, languages spoken on the tour, charge (if any).

🍺 What can be bought – cases, individual bottles, glasses.

🍺 Annual production in hectolitres (hl). 1hl = 100 litres (approx. 22 UK gal.).

➔ Directions to the brewery.

Information common to the range of beers is recorded in the brewery text.

THE BEERS

Regular beers, seasonal or otherwise, are listed with full details after the brewery text. Under 'Other Beers' we list and briefly describe those beers brewed under contract for distributors, fêtes, etc., and those which are not considered to be part of the brewery's prime portfolio. Many breweries were reluctant for us to feature their bock beers in this book, so these generally appear here. The names of relabelled beers (including those marketed under a different name for export) and one-off, special occasion beers appear in bold type in the text.

BEER TASTING NOTES

Almost all the beers have been tasted independently on more than one occasion by both authors, generally in a controlled atmosphere at home. The tasting notes reflect a joint opinion, though where they differ greatly this is recorded by using the initials of the relevant author.

HOW THE BEERS WERE MARKED

Each beer was marked out of four by each author and represents the appeal the beer had for the author. To quantify the ratings, no ticks means the author would not like to have the beer again, one represents an acceptable drink, two are given to a beer which has plenty to offer and is well worth drinking, and three ticks indicates a beer which should definitely be sampled if the opportunity arises.

RECOMMENDED BARS/CAFES AND BEER SHOPS

Whilst researching this book we frequently had problems finding many of the beers without going to the brewery. To ease this situation we asked the breweries to recommend bars and cafes which store and serve their beers in the correct way, along with shops where their beers can be bought should the brewery be closed (most close over the weekend). These recommendations (where given) appear at the end of the appropriate brewery section, and the full collated list (sorted by town/village) can be found in the Recommended Outlets section, with additional recommendations from the authors.

Les 3 Brasseurs/O'Neil

A company called Bars de France started a minor brewpub revolution in France. Running their business a little like a franchise, the company sells the name, along with the expertise and technical support, to other companies which own and run brewpubs called Les 3 Brasseurs and O'Neil (however, any subsequent bars will all be called the former name). All are very similar in style and all have the same beers on offer so we have put them all together here. Bars de France can be contacted at 146 rue de Paris, 59800 Lille, tel: 03 20 74 66 66, fax: 03 20 74 66 67, website at www.bars-de-france.fr.

The furniture and decoration of the buildings is quite basic, as is the beer and food on offer. Each site sells only its own beer on draught and generally has blonde, amber, brown and white beers on offer, with Bière de Mars and La 'Haute' du Père Noël at Easter and Christmas respectively. Despite being brewed to the same recipes they can vary from site to site (thankfully the brewpub in Mulhouse, which we found to be producing the worst beer by far, has now closed). Their food is simple but good with flammekueches being the house speciality; otherwise there is a range of salads, grills and popular dishes.

All the beers are top fermented, unfiltered, unpasteurised and served direct from the storage tanks, and are available in various quantities – 25cl, 33cl, 50cl or a 1.8 litre jug. If you want to taste them all you can have a tray with a 15cl glass of each beer. If you want to try them at home you can usually buy 5 litre mini-kegs and 75cl bottles.

A useful and impressive part of the image is provided by *'La Gazette'* a news-sheet style menu and information sheet which, although it hardly ever changes, seems to be very popular as a souvenir.

In addition to the Les Brasseurs and O'Neil bars, the company also installed the equipment for the Moulin à Bière at Coquelles and St. Martial in Limoges (see individual sections for full details).

Les 3 Brasseurs, 22 Place de la Gare, 59800 Lille.
Tel: 03 20 06 46 25

This is where it all started back in 1986 – and what a location; directly opposite the pedestrian entrance to the main station in Lille. Like Angers it makes extensive use of wooden barrels in decorating the façade, which is below the Hotel Chagnot. Although not a particularly large frontage it is a good size inside with much use of wood in the construction and decoration. The seating is partly open and partly more private. The brewing kit is plainly visible and the current and recent brews are clearly marked on blackboards.

Les 3 Brasseurs, 22 rue des Veaux, 67000 Strasbourg.
Tel: 03 88 36 12 13

This is not the easiest of places to find. From the square in front of the cathedral head down the right hand side of the cathedral and diagonally across the little square then do not turn down towards the river but go past the front of a couple of restaurants. At the end of this short road take a right and then an immediate left. This is rue des Veaux and the bar is right at the far end of it. Approaching from this route will take you in via the bierstub entrance; the larger frontage is around the corner.

Once through the door you are in a fairly dark building with a low ceiling. The woodwork, a major feature of the interior, is predominantly dark, as is the paintwork. The main room is dominated by the bar which is L-shaped around the centrally placed brewkit and liberally strewn with hop bines. This takes up a substantial area but leaves room around each side for tables, chairs and bar-stools. The arrangement contributes to the atmosphere as it avoids large areas with few people. On our midweek evening visits we found it to be full and buzzing, more so than other bars visited on the same evenings. To cater for those who want more space, and doubling as the overflow from the main bar, there is a large cellar off to one side which has substantial seating capacity.

The brewkit is well laid out with everything visible and customers are encouraged to be inquisitive by suitable placing of descriptive labels. There is plenty to be inquisitive about. The site itself has a significant history. 22 rue des Veaux was where Jean Hatt founded Brasserie de l'Esperance in 1746, though the operation moved to Schiltigheim in 1854 (and was later absorbed into Heineken). Bars de France prides itself in having brought brewing back to such an historical site after more than 130 years.

Les 3 Brasseurs, Centre Commercial Les Halles,
Place Mondain Chanlouineau, 49100 Angers. Tel: 02 41 87 93 30
At the time of going to press we were told that Les 3 Brasseurs in Angers was due to close at any time. Just in case it gets a reprieve or is delayed for many months we have included it here anyway.

It is in a prominent city centre position in the Les Halles shopping centre, close to the cathedral. Stand with your back to the main doors of the cathedral, turn right and go down the hill. The square in front of you is Les Halles. There are two heavily decorated entrances to the distinctive building, both of which take you up steps into the brewpub.

From the front, one corner of which is constructed of glass, you can see a massive brick-clad brewing kettle which appears to almost take up two storeys. Once inside, both entrances lead to the same place, you are in a very large high-ceilinged drinking area arranged on different levels with plush, mainly stall type, seating. This was a Saturday evening visit and the clientele were almost entirely young and created a good atmosphere in the packed bar. We found the beers here to be less dry and chalky than in the other outlets.

O'Neil, 20 rue des Canettes, 75006 Paris.
Tel: 01 46 33 36 66

Opened in August 1991 in a quiet side street on the south bank this is now a well established brewpub conveniently close to the Frog & Princess (the next street in fact). From the Mabillon metro station on Boulevard St-Germain head south-west down rue du Four and rue des Canettes is the third left. O'Neil is on the right after about 100 metres. It has a big glass window with the copper brewing kit clearly visible behind it. Once inside it is essentially a long, narrowish bar which widens at the back due to a raised seating area above the rest of the brewing kit which is behind glass and at a lower level than the main bar floor. The interior is a pleasant building with an oldish feel thanks to the brick and stone walls and the beamed ceiling.

LATE NEWS – A new Les 3 Brasseurs opened in March 1998 on the site of the Kinépolis cinema complex at **Lomme** on the western outskirts of Lille. Unfortunately there was no time to visit prior to the publication of the book. See The Artisan Press website for details.

AMBRÉE

6.2% alc/vol.   Draught.

DECLARED INGREDIENTS: Aroma hops; 2-row spring Pilsener, Carapils and Caravienne malts.

APPEARANCE: Hazy amber colour.

NOSE: Neutral with just a faint hint of malt.

PALATE: Initially such a harsh dryness you notice nothing else, but once the mouth grows accustomed a crystal like malt gradually builds.

FINISH: Starts dry with nothing else until a slightly tangy, faintly bitter malt develops. There is an odd coating on the roof of the mouth and it is quite saliva inducing.

OVERALL: Most definitely an uncompromising beer that unfortunately is almost one-dimensional – dry. Untypically of French beers, there is almost no sweetness coming through and the malt in the palate never gets to balance the dryness.

GENERAL: First brewed 1986. Described by Bars de France as a beer in the pale ale style.   JW:☐☐☐   KR:☐☐☐

BLANCHE

4.6% alc/vol.   Draught.

DECLARED INGREDIENTS: Aroma hops; 2-row spring Pilsener malt and wheat.

APPEARANCE: A very cloudy wheat colour.

NOSE: Very floral with coriander and citric notes.

PALATE: Through a sweet fragrant, soapy, lactic wheatiness, many elements attack the tastebuds – wheat, coriander, orange, lemon, lime and other floral elements. Very sweet with a tanginess from the hops.

FINISH: A dry wheaty and hoppy tang that gets drier with time and seems to react with the teeth.

OVERALL: A stronger hop element than in Belgian white beers and a good, very full palate which has a distinct delineation from the finish though a lactic tartness detracts from the appeal.

GENERAL: First brewed 1987. Usually labelled as **Blanche de Lille**.

JW:☑☐☐   KR:☑☐☐

BLONDE

5.2% alc/vol.   Draught.

DECLARED INGREDIENTS: Aroma hops; 2-row spring Pilsener malt.

APPEARANCE: Pale gold.

NOSE: A very light nose, a little yeasty and milky with just a touch of hops. The yeastiness dies down with the head.

PALATE: A full mouth of taste which starts sweet and is followed by plenty of pale malt with a distinctive hop element.

FINISH: Very dry with a milky, gently tangy bitterness. KR: Unpleasantly dry.

OVERALL: A bizarre beer for a Blonde. It has a very nice soft and creamy texture cut through by a fair bit of fizz. There is an interesting use of hop giving a surprisingly light bitterness for the amount of dryness. A very interesting but ultimately unsatisfying beer.

GENERAL: First brewed 1986. Described by Bars de France as a top fermenting lager.

JW: ☐☐☐   KR: ☐☐☐

BRUNE

6.3% alc/vol.   Draught.

DECLARED INGREDIENTS: Aroma hops; 2-row spring Pilsener, Carapils and Caravienne malts.

APPEARANCE: Deep dark chestnut.

NOSE: Minimal until it starts warming then a gently roasted chocolate malt with winey notes develops.

PALATE: A mellow sweet roast malt and chocolate just about overpowers the resiny hop that is in the background.

FINISH: A harsh tangy hop dryness with a lingering fruity chocolatey malt.

OVERALL: Has an excellent creamy texture and a fairly well balanced palate. Unlike the Blonde and Ambrée, this has enough dark malt character to help balance the dryness.

GENERAL: First brewed 1986. Described by Bars de France as being in a Scotch ale style.

JW: ☐☐☐   KR: ☑☐☐

LA 'HAUTE' DU PÈRE NOËL

6.2% alc/vol.   Draught only in the Christmas period.

DECLARED INGREDIENTS: Aroma hops; 2-row spring Pilsener, Carapils and Caravienne malts.

APPEARANCE: Mid-brown colour.

NOSE: Just a sweetish malt.

PALATE: The sweet malt develops a strong resiny, tangy, sharp bitterness that grows into the finish.

FINISH: Strong tangy bitterness dies down to a lingering caramel. A bit cloying and with an unpleasant hairspray sensation.

OVERALL: The unpleasant hairspray and resiny bitterness in the finish destroy any credibility engendered by the palate that has quite a range from the initial sweetness through to the final bitterness.

GENERAL: First brewed 1994.

JW: ☐☐☐   KR: ☐☐☐

OTHER BEERS BREWED ————————————————————————

Bière de Mars (6.3% alc/vol) – Served only around Easter time.

Brasserie d'Alauna

- ✉ Le Bas Castelet, 50700 Valognes
- ☎ 02 33 95 14 98
- 🕐 Ring in advance, especially at weekends
- ♨ Phone for latest tour availability
- 🏭 Bottles and cases
- 🍺 100hl (projected for 1998, 200hl projected for 1999)
- ➡ From Cherbourg follow directions for Valognes, go through the town until you come out on the other side but, before rejoining the main road towards Caen, turn left onto a minor road by a water tower. After approximately 800 metres there is a sign for the brewery and, further down, two buildings on the right hand side of the road. The one with the slate roof is the brewery.

The Contentin peninsula is well known to many British due to the frequent ferry crossings to Cherbourg and to Americans as the site of Utah Beach, one of the objectives of the D-Day Landings of June 1944. Near the top of the peninsula is Valognes where the tiny brewery of Alauna operates in a rural location just south-east of the town.

Started in June 1996 by Luc Léonard, the operation is run from a converted barn attached to the house and is operated by Luc and his wife. The name Alauna comes from the nearby Gallo-Roman site of the same name where archaeological surveys have found the remains of a substantial settlement.

Luc originally started brewing as a hobby but was encouraged to consider going commercial by his friends who were keen samplers of his wares. The publicity of the brewery makes a big play of thanking them for all their support and advice.

At present there is just one product made here, called Korma d'Alauna. Korma is the name given to the ancient brews of the Gauls (also sometimes called cervoise). All of the modern equivalents are now hopped whereas before they were unhopped (or very lightly hopped) and heavily spiced with herbs. Alauna's Korma is hopped and spiced (but the brewery is keeping the identity of the spices secret) and also has honey amongst its ingredients which is introduced at the boil.

The design of the brewkit makes good use of gravity in its double-tiered structure

From their self-constructed brewplant, made from secondhand equipment, they usually brew twice per week (usually Tuesdays and Thursdays) to achieve their 800 litres per month turnover. The beer undergoes a three-day fermentation and a one-week garde prior to bottling.

A blanche is being considered in the latter half of 1998.

Luc sells most of his beer direct from the brewery, but also supplies specialist shops and various local bars and restaurants.

KORMA D'ALAUNA

6% alc/vol. 75cl corked bottles.

BREW DETAILS: Unfiltered. Unpasteurised. Top fermentation.

DECLARED INGREDIENTS: Honey

APPEARANCE: Red orange colour.

NOSE: An artisanal aroma of tart red fruit, a distant honeyed note and a herbal hint. JW: A honeyed, tangy, dark malt with a hop note.

PALATE: Tart and sharp start with huge helpings of bittersweet, berry-like fruit. You soon get accustomed to the tartness and the large helping of honey is more apparent giving a bitter-sweetness to the hop character.

FINISH: JW: A slightly tart and tangy red fruit that is quite astringent. KR: A toffee like, lightly bitter, honeyed malt underlies a very salivating red fruit sharpness.

OVERALL: Distinctly tart and fruity, with an abundance of berry-like red fruit. The strong honey element lifts the character but tends to be masked by the amount of fruit, a crystal malt and a good hop.

GENERAL: First brewed 1996. Gets tarter as it ages. The notes are based on beers 2–3 months old – at 18 months a tart element can become overpowering.   JW:☑☐☐   KR:☑☐☐

BARS & CAFES RECOMMENDED BY THE BREWERY

Le Bar Eldorado, 52 rue Françoise la Vieille, Cherbourg
Le Vertigo, 7 pass Digard, Cherbourg
La Renaissance, rue Anglaise, Cherbourg
Le Freedom Café, 9 rue Charles Blondeau, Cherbourg

Brasserie Des Amis Réunis

✉ 2 Avenue du Collège, 59230 St-Amand-les-Eaux

☎ 03 27 48 77 77   Fax: 03 27 48 80 00

🕐 0900-1230 & 1330-1730

🏭 Pre-arranged only. 7 days notice. In French & English. 10FF

🍾 Cases, bottles, glasses

🍺 3,000hl (in 1997)

➔ See article

This brewery is aptly named since the three principal characters are all friends from years ago who have now been reunited with the formation of this brewery. Gérard Félizas and Olivier Forest originally formed Brasserie Steinbeer in the north of France, but after its short term of operation they both went on to Brasserie Brunehaut in Belgium. Bernard Pierre grew up with Gérard in Florenville, Belgium, and then spent 10 years as a brewer in the nearby Orval Abbey. In late 1996 plans were underway to start another new brewery and by the time the operation was truly under way in September 1997 the three friends were all together again.

The story of the brewery is inextricably linked to the name Germinal, originally the title of a book written in 1885 by Emile Zola about the conflicts between miners and mine-owners. In 1993 a film of the book was made in the area by Claude Berri who, along with leading actor Gérard Depardieu and others involved, were shocked by the level of unemployment and poverty still prevalent in the region. Wanting to do something to alleviate the problems, they founded 'Germinal, L'Association' in 1994 which, amongst other aims, gives aid to children with difficulties and helps small enterprises start up. Since its conception, it has created 65 businesses and 120 jobs.

Any charitable association needs a steady influx of money to carry on its work and one early idea was for the Germinal Association to brew beer to raise funds. After buying equipment it soon became apparent that it didn't have the expertise within its ranks to make the project reach fruition. A solution was found by agreeing a deal with the newly-formed Brasserie des Amis Réunis who had all the expertise but were looking for investment. The Association supplied much of the start-up plant in return for 5% of profits from the sale of beers called Germinal, of which there are now two produced.

The brewery's two other beers have both been around for a while as they were previously made at Brasserie Brunehaut. At present there are some legalities to be sorted out and, at the time of publication, both breweries were making versions of L'Écume des Jours and a juniper-flavoured beer called Abbaye de St-Amand (by Brunehaut) and l'Abbatiale de St-Amand (by Amis Réunis). An association in the town previously commissioned Abbaye de St-Amand from Brunehaut but now Des Amis Reunis claim to have negotiated their own deal, with a percentage going to projects in the town. The confusion is further complicated by the fact that some supermarkets even stock both versions – although you can tell which is which because the Brunehaut labels are metallic-embossed. Hopefully this unfortunate situation will be resolved in time.

The site chosen for the brewery is more than a little unusual as it is in the unused portion of the municipal abattoir. This gave the space needed in a suitable location but generated an enormous amount of work getting it clean enough for refurbishment as a brewery. Work is still continuing as it is expanding to offer facilities such as a bar and reception room. The owners consider St-Amand to be lacking a lively night-time bar so are planning to build one onto the side of the brewery which, given the scale of the operation, would create a pretty spectacular brew-pub.

By Easter 1998 there were six people working for the brewery (all of whom are friends, perpetuating the sentiments of the brewery's name), and the maturation facilities were being expanded with the addition of eight 40hl storage tanks. With a three-week garde these additional tanks will allow a threefold increase in production without the need to increase the size of the brew-plant. This has enabled the brewery to plan for an anticipated production for 1998 of 5,000hl which it hopes will rise to 8,000hl in 1999.

The brewery is on the edge of town and is most easily found from the D169 Valenciennes to Tournai road. From Valenciennes ignore the first sign for St-Amand (on a roundabout) and continue towards Tournai. At the second roundabout, take the left to St-Amand. This is Avenue du Collège. Pass the college on your right and take the left-hand lane because the brewery is on the left behind the abattoir just before you reach the bridge.

A look around the inside of the brewery gives some idea of the amount of investment it has acquired in its short life.

L'ABBATIALE DE ST-AMAND

7% alc/vol.   33cl & 75cl bottles.

BREW DETAILS: Filtered. Unpasteurised. Top fermentation. Bottle re-fermentation.

DECLARED INGREDIENTS: Styrian & Saaz hops; 2-row spring Pilsener & Munich malts; spiced with coriander, ginger & juniper berries.

APPEARANCE: Pale golden colour with a massive head and good lacework.

NOSE: Very fragrant, yet light, herbal aroma with juniper berries and fresh hops. Inviting. KR: Quite sweet and citric.

PALATE: Fresh and invigorating with plenty of lightly citric hop and a strongly herbal element that is light and fragrant. Behind this is some gentle pale malt

with a gentle hop bitterness. Throughout there is a sharp note, possibly alcohol-generated. KR: Lots going on in the taste department. The citric element is strong enough to give a light sharpness.

FINISH: Surprisingly light. A lingering bitterness and a gentle juniper induced herbal taste. KR: Quite creamy with a lingering citric hop.

OVERALL: JW: Excellent, fairly complex, light herbal tasting beer with plenty of juniper character. A very pleasant taste although the lingering bitterness in the finish gets a bit much eventually. KR: Very satisfying beer with great depth, yet light and refreshing enough to drink year round. Thankfully the juniper is not overdone, but the taste will be too sharp for many people.

GENERAL: First brewed 1997. Lighter and fresher than the Brunehaut version.

JW: ☑☑☐ KR: ☑☑☐

GERMINAL AMBRÉE

6.5% alc/vol. 33cl crown corked & 75cl corked bottles and draught.

BREW DETAILS: Filtered. Unpasteurised. Top fermentation.

DECLARED INGREDIENTS: Saaz, Styrian & Kent Goldings hops; 2-row spring Pilsener & Munich malts; spiced with coriander & liquorice.

APPEARANCE: Rich amber with a large creamy head.

NOSE: JW: Very unusual earthy, yeasty, fruity aroma with a disturbing vegetable note. KR: Rich and fruity with a light coriander hint.

PALATE: A strongly resinous palate that is also bitter though there is a good fruity malt underlying the resin tastes. A slightly spicy suggestion adds interest. KR: Light and spritzy with an underlying, quite vinous, fruit.

FINISH: Particularly resinous and bitter with a drying hoppiness and some leftover fruit.

OVERALL: JW: The disappointing nose leads into a very distinctive beer which is very tangy and resinous with a moderate bitterness. The mouthfeel is particularly smooth and full. KR: Impressively full and fruitily bitter beer with a somewhat harsh resin note which some may find disagreeable.

GENERAL: First brewed 1997.

JW: ☑☐☐ KR: ☑☑☐

GERMINAL BLONDE

6.5% alc/vol. 33cl crown corked bottles & draught.

BREW DETAILS: Filtered. Unpasteurised. Top fermentation.

DECLARED INGREDIENTS: Styrian & Saaz hops; 2-row spring Pilsener & Munich malts; spiced with coriander, sweet orange and others.

APPEARANCE: Bright orange gold.

NOSE: Full, sweet, pale malt with a little hop trying to impose itself. Promises a grainy fruitiness.

PALATE: Very full taste with lots of pale malt and a good, slightly resiny, hop. A fair degree of malt sweetness but very little of the promised fruit. The resiny hop imparts a growing bitterness and a distinctly tangy element.

FINISH: Resiny gentle bitterness lingers after the initial sweetish pale malt has gone. The obviously high hop content generates little bitterness but an unusual resiny dryness.

OVERALL: A full tasting malt produces plenty of sweetness but the high level of resinous hop takes over, producing a beer that is very tangy but only gently bitter.

GENERAL: First brewed 1997.   JW: ☑☑☐   KR: ☑☑☐

L'ÉCUME DES JOURS

7% alc/vol. 33cl crown corked & 75cl corked bottles.

BREW DETAILS: Filtered. Unpasteurised. Top fermentation. Bottle refermentation.

DECLARED INGREDIENTS: Styrian, Saaz & Brewers Gold hops; 2-row spring Pilsener & Munich malts; spiced with coriander.

APPEARANCE: Golden with a massive head.

NOSE: Good blend of pale malt

and a strongly aromatic hop. Suggests a distinctly hoppy palate with citricity. KR: A quite soapy pale malt.

PALATE: Very hoppy initially. A light lemony hop which builds to a bitter resiny hoppiness with a tangy fruity malt.

FINISH: Gently hoppy yet drying, very resiny and quite bitter. Pretty astringent as well.

OVERALL: A powerfully hoppy beer with plenty of lemon throughout. The finish becomes very resiny with some fruit – almost tangy.

GENERAL: First brewed in 1994, by Brasserie Brunehaut in Belgium and both versions are still widely available in France. Also sold as **La Bière du Chamane de la Grande Braderie de Lille**.

JW: ☑☑☐   KR: ☑☐☐

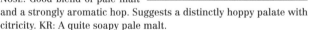

BEER SHOPS RECOMMENDED BY THE BREWERY

E. Leclerc, 59230 St-Amand

Brasserie Annœullin

- ✉ 5 Grand Place, 59112 Annœullin
- ☎ 03 20 86 83 60   Fax: 03 20 86 69 27
- ⏱ Phone brewery for details
- Rarely possible
- Cases only
- 4,000hl (in 1996)
- ➔ In the Grand Place at Annœullin

Looking around the main square of the large village of Annœullin it is not immediately obvious that a brewery is lurking behind the distinctly residential façade of Number 5. The only tell-tale sign is a very discrete pub-like sign suspended from a post protruding from the front wall of the house. To the left is an alley which leads to a group of buildings arranged around a yard with the white-washed walls giving it a mediterranean feel.

The Grand Place (which is easily dismissed as just any other square) is at the northern end of Annœullin which is itself located roughly half-way between Lille and Lens. The brewery prefers to be called after the village rather that its more official title of Brasserie Lepers, which has the obvious connotation to English speakers. Many local people also refer to it simply as L'Angélus, after its flagship brand.

The salle de brassage is on the first floor (approached by an external staircase) which contains two brewing coppers – one of which is a kettle which doubles as the mash tun. Most of the 50-hectolitre plant dates back to 1945 when the brewing industry was making huge investments to rebuild its trade after the Second World War, but some other parts are original installations from when the brewery started. It currently brews twice per week and the beers undergo a week's fermentation and four to five weeks of garding prior to bottling.

At the turn of the century Auguste Maille was dabbling with brewing at his farm on the present site when, in 1905, he decided to go commercial. Now, after five generations, the brewery is still owned by the same family despite a chequered history through two world wars. Being close to the front line in the First World War, the building was taken over by the Germans, fortified with large amounts of concrete and used as a base.

After the war Auguste undertook the task of rebuilding the brewery and recommenced operations soon after. This proved to be a brief respite from its troubles, however, when the region was again under occupation in the Second World War. Auguste's grandson (also called Auguste), son of the original Auguste's eldest daughter Cécile, spent most of the war as a prisoner, leaving the day-to-day running of the business to the women of the family. The second Auguste's daughter, Bertrande, married Bernard Lepers in 1950 and they continued the operation before handing over to their son, Bertrand, and his wife Yolande – thus bringing us up to date on the Annœullin family tree.

Bertrand and Yolande are passionate about their brewery and they intend to keep their beers as traditional as possible. The quality and

consistency of their beer has attracted many contract brews, some of which are widely available, along with the now ubiquitous L'Angélus in major supermarket chains.

All the Annœullin beers are filtered but unpasteurised and undergo a top fermentation.

The entrance, viewed from the Grand Place.

L'ANGÉLUS

7% alc/vol   75cl corked bottles and draught.

DECLARED INGREDIENTS: Flanders & Brewers Gold hops; 2-row spring, Escourgeon malt and wheat.

APPEARANCE: Pale gold with a lovely, creamy head.

NOSE: Very aromatic and very inviting. Sweetish creamy pale malt and wheat with a pleasant flowery lemony hop. An overtly perfumed aroma. KR: Wafts of meadow flowers.

PALATE: A full, rounded, soft palate of pale malt with masses of wheat and a good helping of hop character. Quite complex with some citric notes and a light malt fruitiness. JW: A slightly perfumed taste that is both sweet and bitter with the bitterness developing and becoming resiny. KR: Strongly perfumed with tantalisingly fleeting herbal notes.

FINISH: Daintily complex. A little perfumed and mouthwateringly citric. JW: Long lasting dry bitterness with a touch of fruit. KR: A lingering creamy wheat turning lightly bitter.

OVERALL: Excellent beer which has quality and roundness written all over it. An impressive aroma leads into a palate that has lots of pale malt and wheat but still lets the hops come out on top. There is also the wonderfully smooth and creamy texture throughout. KR: Can tend to be a little over-sweet for some occasions.

GENERAL: First brewed 1988. The attractive design for the label (and the origins of its name) was inspired by a painting by Millet of peasants giving thanks while working in the fields of northern France. The image is also used on their glasses. JW: ☑☑☐ KR: ☑☑☑

L'ANGELUS DE MARS

5.5% alc/vol. 75cl corked bottles and draught.

APPEARANCE: Golden amber in colour with a nice, but short-lived, pillowy head.

NOSE: An interestingly aromatic nose that is a little perfumed. Slightly sweet with plenty of hop and a few fruity hints. JW: Some vanilla and pale malt. KR: Appley/citric hop with a toffee hint.

PALATE: A degree of wateriness impacts an otherwise very full taste. There is a wheaty element and some slightly citric hops plus an intriguing dark malt character. JW: Lightly bitter with a touch of vanilla. KR: A few apple hints and a sweet, toffeeish, darker fruit element.

FINISH: Dry, wheaty and a growing bitterness with a few tired citric hints. KR: Quite watery and creamy with an underlying bittersweet note.

OVERALL: A distinctly wheaty ale that is easy to drink. It has an excellent yet strangely indefinable nose, followed by a good full palate but is let down by a finish which tends to grate after a while.

GENERAL: First brewed 1992. A very ordinary label for a reasonably good beer – a shame the Millet painting theme didn't make it onto this label. JW: ☑☐☐ KR: ☑☐☐

L'ANGELUS DE NOËL

7.5% alc/vol. 75cl corked & 25cl crown corked bottles and draught.

APPEARANCE: Amber with a short-lived head.

NOSE: Sweetish fruity malt with a few yeasty notes.

PALATE: Full, sweet and malty with a moderate hop character enhanced by a light alcohol note. Hints of caramel become apparent towards the end.

FINISH: A fair caramel element in a lingering, slightly hoppy malt with a lingering alcohol note.

OVERALL: A Christmas beer that is pleasantly malty with an interesting hop character and a touch of alcohol. An element of caramel gives it a somewhat different taste.

JW: ☑☑☐ KR: ☑☑☐

PASTOR ALE

6.5% alc/vol. 75cl corked bottles.

DECLARED INGREDIENTS: Flanders & Brewers Gold hops; 2-row spring, Escourgeon malt.

APPEARANCE: Honey gold with a massive but short-lived head.

NOSE: An odd apple note, that is strong when first opened, overlays a strong pale malt which is lightly fruity. Also an interesting and pleasant hop element. KR: A powerful but uninspiring hoppiness.

Pastor Ale

Grande bière Artisanale brassée à Annœullin

Brasserie Lepers

Alcool 6,5% vol.

59112 Annœullin France

5 400133 534963

75 cl ℮

PALATE: Full mouth of unusual fruity hops and malt that is distinctly hoppy and bitter. Starts a little sweet but this is rapidly lost to a resiny hop. There is a nearly hidden fruit present in the malt that is itself almost overpowered by the hops. KR: An unusual apple/hop bite with some herbal and caramel hints.

FINISH: Dry and tangy malt and hop bitterness with a light fruit. It has a powerful oily/resiny bitterness which builds to give a formidable hoppiness which, luckily, is well balanced by the body and depth of the malt fruitiness.

OVERALL: A superbly smooth texture adds to the appeal of an immensely tasty beer which has a surprisingly strong orchard fruit character, and is distinctly hoppy.

GENERAL: First brewed 1975. The name is apparently a play on words – not, as one might imagine, the beer of the pastor but 'pastorale' which translates as 'rural'.

JW: ☑☑☐ KR: ☑☑☐

OTHER BEERS BREWED ────────────────────

Le Rince Cochon (6.4% alc/vol.) – Contract brew which seems to be only sporadically available in some supermarket chains.

La Nuit Parisienne (7.6% alc/vol.) – Contract brew which is again only available occasionally in supermarkets. Peculiarly pale bière de garde character with a strong malty sweetness and a well defined alcohol note.

Rijsel (8.2% alc/vol.) – Contract brew widely available in the north of France. Rijsel is the Flemish name for the city of Lille. Full tasting malty brew with a distinctly buttery taste.

Vita Pils (4.7% alc/vol.) – Locally sold pilsener which is light yet has an interesting taste, with a strong hop character making it very dry and bitter.

BARS & CAFES RECOMMENDED BY THE BREWERY

Café Bellevue, n'guillomet, Grand Place, 62 Carvin
Tiphany's, Place du Marché, 59112 Annœullin

BEER SHOPS RECOMMENDED BY THE BREWERY

Aux Caves d'Annœullin, 1 Grand Place, 59112 Annœullin

Petite Brasserie Ardennaise

✉ 15 Quai Arthur Rimbaud, 08000 Charleville-Mézières

☎ 03 24 37 53 53   Fax: 03 24 33 12 42

🕐 Tue-Sat: 1600-0100, Sun: 1600-2000

🏚 Pre-arranged only. 14 days notice. In French & English. No charge

🍺 Glasses

🍶 150hl (projected for 1998)

➔ See article

René Bertrand made a bold move on 14th January 1998 when he opened a tiny brew-pub which uses English brewing kit, to brew English style ales dispensed by hand-pump. Three years were spent in planning and the chosen location seems well situated on the banks of the Meuse opposite the municipal campsite, reached via an adjacent footbridge. From Place Ducale, leave in the direction of Musée Rimbaud and turn left when you reach the Museum and river, the brew-pub is 150 yards on the left – next to the entrance of Restaurant Venezia. The sign above the door is, however, very difficult to read.

Space inside is quite limited but they have created a cosy drinking area in the front and still managed to cram in the brewery to the rear. The contract to supply and install the brewkit went to Total Brewing International of Worcester, UK, who did a good job to shoe-horn the equipment into such a small area. The capacity is just 250 litres but due to the lack of space the malt has to be milled at home and brought in for use in the brewery. René does, however, manage to find space in the cellar to allow the beer to mature for a month before serving. In summer the space constraints will be alleviated by the provision of outside seating. His lease allows for the parking spaces outside to be replaced by tables and chairs from June to the end of September.

The beers are pumped through swan-necks and sparklers ('because they were delivered with the brewing kit') but a new fount will be installed soon to have a gas dispense as well. On our visit the beers were served in superb condition and the sparkler did not have the detrimental effect as is so often the case with many British beers.

René is a self-taught brewer who puts a lot of thought into his brewing and is prepared to experiment in order to improve the results. He uses dried yeast for his current beers and has settled on a British one for the stout and a Canadian one for the ale – they produce better results that way around. He has been developing a wheat beer for the summer of 1998 and has settled on a live yeast from Belgium for that one, although the intention is to brew a German weizenbier – one of Renée's favoured beer styles. Two bars stock the Ardennaise beers – Caraïbes in Sedan takes the stout and Le Mawhot takes the ale as the owner already supplies Guinness. Le Mawhot is a tastefully converted barge moored close by, stocking a small but well chosen beerlist from Belgium, Germany and France, along with some rare pastis brands. Numerous local folklore paintings adorn the walls inside – including one of a Mawhot, a local river monster. It is closed on Tuesdays.

OUBLIETTE

5.3% alc/vol.   Draught only.

BREW DETAILS: Unfiltered. Unpasteurised. Top fermentation.

DECLARED INGREDIENTS: Saaz & Styrian hops; Pale, Crystal, Munich & Wheat malts.

APPEARANCE: Hazy amber with a good creamy head. Great lacework.

NOSE: Light fruity hops.

PALATE: Slight tart edge to a strongly hopped pale malt. The hops do not provide much bitterness but impart a strong green hop flower taste. Lightly fruity.

FINISH: Stronger than expected with a fruity, faintly tart, start which dies leaving a lingering resiny green fruit and some dryness.

OVERALL: Very interesting variation on an English ale. Strongly hopped but not bitter. Served in perfect condition. KR: A light tartness, though unusual in an English-style ale, gives an almost summery quality.

GENERAL: First brewed 1998. The name derives from the word 'oublier' (to forget).   JW: ☑☑☐   KR: ☑☑☐

STOUTBLIETTE

4.3% alc/vol.   Draught only.

BREW DETAILS: Unfiltered. Unpasteurised. Top fermentation.

DECLARED INGREDIENTS: Fuggles & Styrian hops; Chocolate malt.

APPEARANCE: Pitch black with a lovely tight creamy head and excellent lacework.

NOSE: Intense coffee tempered by a little chocolate.

PALATE: Soft but with an extremely full taste. Plenty of chocolate, coffee and malt complexity. It has a surprisingly light texture for such a full taste. KR: A touch lactic.

FINISH: Dry and a little astringent with only a light bitterness that is distinctly fruity. KR: Lingering dryness with a touch of acidity.

OVERALL: Wonderful smooth texture and perfect conditioning plus all the right characteristics in the right proportions make this a truly excellent stout. It has an extremely full taste for a relatively weak beer and a palate strong enough to deter those who do not like stouts, but seriously impress those that do.

GENERAL: First brewed 1998. The French pronounce "stout" as "stoot" so it almost rhymes with "Oubliette".   JW: ☑☑☐   KR: ☑☑☑

BARS & CAFES RECOMMENDED BY THE BREWERY

Caraïbes, 37 avenue Philippoteaux, 08200 Sedan
Le Mawhot, Quai Charcot, 08000 Charleville-Mézières

Brasserie Bailleux

- ✉ Cafe-Restaurant Au Baron, 2 Rue du Piemont, 59570 Gussignies
- ☎ 03 27 66 88 61   Fax: 03 27 39 89 04
- 🕐 Brewery: Mon-Fri: 0800-1200 and 1400-1700.
  Restaurant: Sat-Sun: 1100 until late. Fri: 1500 until late
- 🏃 Pre-arranged only. 7 days notice. In French & English. 15FF
- 🍾 Cases, bottles, glasses
- 📊 750hl (in 1997)
- ➡ See article

Brasserie Bailleux nestles in the river valley at the base of the village of Gussignies, just inside the French border north-north-west of Bavay. On finding the village, just keep heading downwards to the lowest point via the narrow, winding roads. There you will find the Restaurant Au Baron on the far bank of the small river L'Hogneau on the other side of a narrow bridge. The brewery itself is visible at the back of the restaurant. Park on the gravel on the near side.

The story of this impressive little micro-brewery starts back in 1973 when Roger Bailleux started a small café aimed at the tourist traffic in the area. This was successful enough, over time, to allow the construction of a larger restaurant, with seating for sixty, specialising in typical, regional Avesnois cuisine. By 1989 things had progressed and the final part of the dream (owning a brewery-restaurant similar to those found in Germany) came into place with the construction of a micro-brewery in an extension behind the restaurant. Today Roger tends to look after the brewing whilst his son, Alain, and daughter-in-law run the restaurant.

The first beer to be produced was the Saison Saint Médard, named after the patron saint of the village. This appeared in June 1989 and Saint Médard himself obviously looked favourably on the enterprise as a Cuvée de Noël (now called Bière de Noël), also bearing his name, appeared later that year. Keeping up the momentum, March 1990 saw the launch of Cuvée des Jonquilles which took as its inspiration the profusion of daffodils which appear on the steep banks in and around the village in early spring.

The brewery is clearly visible from the restaurant and with three brews a week in the summer could well be operating when you visit. The brew capacity is 10hl and fermentation lasts a week. With each of the beers being refermented in the bottle (using the same yeast as the primary fermentation) this means that a great number of bottles need to be stored somewhere. This happens underneath the brew-house though the refermentation is started off upstairs as this is generally at a more conducive temperature.

Confusingly, the Saison Saint Médard has recently taken on the sub-title "Bière de Garde de l'Avesnois" – we say confusingly because this beer (like the others in the range) exudes far more Walloon saison characteristics than the northern French neighbours it seems to want to associate itself with.

CUVÉE DES JONQUILLES

7% alc/vol. 75cl corked bottles.

BREW DETAILS: Unfiltered. Unpasteurised. Top fermentation. Bottle refermentation.

DECLARED INGREDIENTS: Brewers Gold & Saaz hops; Pilsener malt.

APPEARANCE: Bright pale gold with a massive, fluffy head and nice lacework.

NOSE: Full, fruity fresh hops with hints of lemon over a solid pale malt. A dry and light promise.

PALATE: Clean and full-tasting with a gently bitter malty tang balanced by an abundance of dry, slightly peppery, citric lemon hop.

FINISH: Long lasting with a balanced bitter, citric hop and a lightly fruity pale malt.

OVERALL: Great interest is maintained through many layers of taste with a superb balance. It gets more bitter with age. JW: Considerably better without any sediment in the glass. KR: Better drunk young so you can savour the fresh, citric characteristics lost with age.

GENERAL: First brewed 1990. Inspired by the number of daffodils in the village. Jonquille is French for daffodil.

JW: ☑☑☑   KR: ☑☑☑

SAISON SAINT MÉDARD

7% alc/vol. 75cl corked bottles.

BREW DETAILS: Unfiltered. Unpasteurised. Top fermentation. Bottle refermentation.

DECLARED INGREDIENTS: Brewers Gold hops; Pilsener, Caramel & Biscuit malts.

APPEARANCE: Good amber colour with an excellent head.

NOSE: Deep and interesting blend of yeast, hops, fruit and malt.

JW: The yeast reduces with age and a spicy edge to the hops develops. KR: Lightly aromatic sherry hints in background.

PALATE: The light and creamy start is followed by a mouthful of fruity malt that has a spicy edge to it. Wonderfully balanced by the hops which grow in bitterness to the finish.

FINISH: Long lingering lightly spicy hop bitterness with a little fruity malt.

OVERALL: This characterful beer has an excellent balance to complement its wonderful texture. KR: A deeply interesting amber ale with a wonderful multi-faceted character.

GENERAL: First brewed 1989. Saint Médard is the patron saint of the village. JW: ☑☑☐ KR:☑☑☐

SAISON SAINT MÉDARD BIÈRE DE NOËL

7% alc/vol. 75cl corked bottles.

BREW DETAILS: Unfiltered. Unpasteurised. Top fermentation. Bottle refermentation.

DECLARED INGREDIENTS: Brewers Gold hops; Pilsener, Torrefied & Caramel malts.

APPEARANCE: Rich red brown verging on black with a light but pillowy head.

NOSE: Complex and inviting. Full rich, raisin malt, dark and spicy with liquorice notes and a hint of clove, over which is a wonderfully interesting hop character. JW: An everpresent bitter chocolate element wafts around the glass.

PALATE: Complex right from the start. A strong herbal, spicy, dark malt with liquorice notes, penetrated by a sharply bitter hop. Excellent. KR: A chocolatey dryness. Surprisingly light in the mouth.

FINISH: A lingering finish of lightly roasted chocolate malt with a hop bitterness and some warming fruit. KR: Various dry spicy notes.

OVERALL: Wonderful beer with an understated balance and taste. Although the mouth always feels full of taste the various elements are subtly portrayed resulting in an absolutely gorgeous and deeply rewarding experience. The perfect winter evening beer.

GENERAL: First brewed 1989. Originally a Christmas beer, now seems to be available most of the year. Saint Médard is the patron saint of the village. JW: ☑☑☑ KR: ☑☑☑

Ferme-Brasserie Beck

✉ Rue Eeckelstraete, 59270 Bailleul

☎ 03 28 49 03 90 Fax: 03 28 42 28 32

🕐 Mar-Nov. Sat: 1900-2100. Sun: 1700-2000

🏃 Pre-arranged only. 15 days notice. In French. 30FF

🍾 Cases, bottles, glasses

🍺 150hl (in 1997)

➔ See article

In the expanse of farmland between the A25 Dunkerque to Lille motorway and the Belgian border is the farm of the Beck family. Denis Beck is a great enthusiast for the country way of life, and likes to pass on his infectious passion whenever he can. This was one of his reasons for building two gîtes opposite the family farmhouse.

These are no ordinary gîtes since they can accommodate an awful lot of people when they are put to their intended use of housing school parties who are visiting the farm to learn about farming and life in the country. For these school parties – usually of primary school age – a wide range of things are laid on over the course of a week. These include a visit around the farm, a trip to the rural museum at Steenwerck, a trip around Bailleul by horse and cart, visits by rural craftsmen such as bee-keepers, visits to a goat farm and a mill, a nature trail and of course the hop farm and brewery. The gîtes were built in 1980 and have proved to be very popular.

As this side of the business grew, a barn opposite was converted into a hall and this now houses the brewery and bar. It is a very impressive building with a mixture of Flemish brickwork and wood. The brewery is downstairs with the bar upstairs, complete with the maximum possible number of tables and chairs fitted into the available space. Hops were already being grown on the farm (it is in the heart of the French hop-growing region) and with the turnover of tourists it seemed a natural progression to start brewing to capitalise on the traditional use of hops.

It started in 1994 and even today it is still a low-key affair. The brew plant came from Brasserie St-Amant (via Castelain after it bought the Auvergne brewery). There are two brews a month, each of 5hl and the bar does not open on a commercial basis. Denis is helped around the brewery by his two sons, Thierry and Dany, but it is still considered a labour intensive operation which should not be allowed to get in the way of their 'real' work around the farm, so the lack of available time will constrain any expansion. As you might expect when the hops are grown on site, they are used to good effect in the beer. Most of the beer is filtered and bottled in 75cl bottles but a reasonable proportion is put into barrels unfiltered for serving in the bar and this has a more balanced and definitely more hoppy taste.

Annually in August there is a hop festival based at the farm (the 'Hommelpap' which the beer has been named after) and this is undoubtedly their single most productive day for beer sales. The rest of the year they are open on Saturday and Sunday evenings but it closes completely in December, January and February.

Being particularly close to the French–Belgian border, the hop festival betrays its Flemish origins by being named after the Flemish for hop (hommel) and not the French (houblon).

It is not easy to find but it is well worth the effort. From the centre of Bailleul – the Grand Place – take the rue d'Ypres (next to the post office), first right (rue des Sœurs Noires) then keep going down the Chemin Rural de Bellekindt and you will see signs to the Ferme-Gîte Brasserie Beck.

HOMMELPAP

7% alc/vol.   75cl corked bottles & draught (unfiltered) at the brewery tap.

BREW DETAILS: Filtered. Unpasteurised. Top fermentation.

INGREDIENTS: A mixture of five hops; Roast and unroasted malt.

APPEARANCE: Orange amber with a good head.

NOSE: An absolute nose-full of unusual aromas – earthy, oily hops with a fruity malt background. JW: A sharp, fruity malt. KR: Dry, tannic, fruity crystal malt lies under the hops if you look hard enough, giving a sweet and fruity, as well as hoppy, promise.

PALATE: A full mouth of hop from a balanced blend. An oily bitterness and lots of resiny taste from the hops, with a little lightly caramellised crystal malt in the background. A little fruit. KR: A background of tannic fruitiness.

FINISH: A maltiness is overpowered by a strong, very resiny hop bitterness. JW: A citric element lightens the dry, tangy bitterness. KR: A fruity malt tang tries to develop but loses out against the rich onslaught of powerful hoppiness.

OVERALL: Good blending of hops results in an intensely hoppy beer with an excellent texture that unfortunately doesn't quite reach its potential when in bottles. The unfiltered draught version in the brewery tap is more balanced with an impressive depth. JW: A little too much on the resiny side for me. KR: As one would expect from a hop farm, one to be avoided by those who don't like hoppy beers.

GENERAL: First brewed 1994.

JW: ☑☐☐   KR: ☑☑☐

Brasserie Bécu

- ✉ 10 rue Paul Verlaine, 62118 Fampoux
- ☎ 03 21 55 97 57   Fax: 03 21 48 24 52
- 🕘 0900-1200, 1400-1700. Closed Saturday & Sunday
- 🏛 Pre-arranged only. 15 days notice. In French. 10FF
- 🍺 Cases, bottles, glasses
- 📊 1,000hl (in 1997)
- ➔ The brewery is in Fampoux, which is just east of Arras. Entering Fampoux from the north you pass over one crossroads and then reach another with a café either side of the road to the left. Take a right here and the brewery is about 100 yards on the left.

The imposing group of buildings which once formed a large, industrious brewery provides a striking backdrop for Brasserie Bécu, one of France's recent wave of re-born artisanal beer producers. Set around a cobbled courtyard, the buildings – one of which is the owner's house – conjure up a feeling that there is a story to be told. And there is.

It was originally founded in 1862 by Henri-Joseph Bécu on the present site, but it was unfortunate enough to find itself right on the front line during the First World War, during which time it was completely destroyed. All was not lost, however, as Joseph Bécu managed to secure sufficient finance from the German reparation fund after the war to build a totally new brewery. What is visible today dates from this 1922 rebuilding, the majority of which remains in surprisingly good condition.

The traumatic memories of the First World War were still fresh in the mind when the brewery was faced with a quandary in the Second World War when the occupying German forces gave the owners the choice of either making beer for them or having it razed to the ground. After losing one brewery, it is perhaps not surprising that it reluctantly chose the former – resulting in a complete and working brewery at the end of hostilities.

The brewery is now run by Pierre Bécu and his wife who restarted brewing in 1994 after many years of the family business operating as a drinks distributor. Until it stopped production in 1962, the brewery concentrated on table beers and bocks but today's products are pitched squarely at the quality bière de garde market.

The beers are all unfiltered, unpasteurised, top fermenting and bottle refermented. The brew capacity is 600 litres and they brew three or four times a week. It takes two months to complete the production process, which includes three weeks in a warm room for the bottle refermentation using the same yeast as the primary fermentation.

The brewing is done with modern equipment but the old brewhouse is still intact, complete with original steam engine and all the drive-belts which powered the plant. Pierre plans to renovate it so he can open it as a working, truly authentic brewing museum and visitor centre. If it ever reaches fruition it should be a real 'must visit' on any beer tourist's itinerary.

When the brewery recommenced operations, Pierre wanted to give his beers a strong local identity so chose the name 'Atrébate' as his brand name. Atrébate is an ancient name of the inhabitants of the Artois region in the time of the Gauls.

L'ATRÉBATE AMBRÉE

6% alc/vol. 75cl corked bottles & draught.

DECLARED INGREDIENTS: Magnum hops; 2-row spring, Pilsener malt.

APPEARANCE: Deep copper colour with a good pillowy head.

NOSE: Pungently hoppy. An aromatic, yeasty, hoppy, fruity malt with the pungent hops growing. KR: A tart edge. Has a dry and fruity promise.

PALATE: A strange but impressive hop character, bitter and remarkably dry. A little sweetness fights against, and loses to, the bitterness. JW: A gently fruity malt pervades the palate but it is dominated by the hop character. KR: A tannic fruitiness with a sharp bite but dominated by a formidable grainy dryness.

FINISH: A bone dry hoppy bitterness (which reduces with age) with just a touch of malt. KR: Lingering fruity notes in the background.

OVERALL: Interesting interpretation of an ambrée – intensely dry and hoppy. JW: Reasonably complex and well balanced with some fruity malt and a little sweetness preventing the dry bitterness from being overpowering. KR: When young it is uncompromisingly dry but tends to acquire a better balance with age.

GENERAL: First brewed 1994.   JW: ☑☐☐   KR: ☑☐☐

L'ATRÉBATE BIÈRE DE MARS

6% alc/vol. 75cl corked bottles.

APPEARANCE: Golden colour with a hazy bloom and a good, lasting, creamy head.

NOSE: A heady, hoppy, lemon and yeast aroma with a little pale malt behind. Some hay notes. KR: A touch appley. Very inviting, complex and intriguing.

PALATE: A full whack of mouthwatering lemony hop with a gentle resiny bitterness cuts through a full sweetish pale malt that supports the hops well. Hiding behind the lemon is a little yeastiness. KR: Quite bitter.

FINISH: Dry and gently bitter with a lingering lemon and a bittersweet pale malt. JW: With sediment it is a mellow pale malt and hop with just a hint of lemon. As it ages this becomes more of a lingering oily hoppiness which is increased with the sediment. KR: A pleasant malt fruitiness balances the finish

OVERALL: JW: Totally different with and without sediment. Without it is a lovely refreshing lemony hop beer of immense character and very clean tastes. With sediment it becomes merely an interesting quaffing beer, mellow and yeasty in character. Age also plays a big part in the character, very lemony when young it takes on a more oily, resiny character as it ages. KR: Impressive beer with a pungent hop yet not excessively bitter. Lovely refreshing citric notes, a great thirst quencher. Sold as **St-Elixir** for a fête in Arras.

JW: ☑☑☑   KR: ☑☑☑

L'ATRÉBATE BLONDE

6% alc/vol.   75cl corked bottles & draught.

DECLARED INGREDIENTS: Magnum hops; 2-row spring. Pilsener malt.

APPEARANCE: Golden colour with a massive head and nice lacework.

NOSE: Excellent clean fresh hops with a faint citric element and a touch of yeast. JW: Adding sediment increases the yeast and removes the citric elements though as it ages the yeastiness reduces and the hops mellow. KR: Pungently hoppy with a lightly sulphurous yeastiness.

PALATE: Full palate of well balanced pale malt and slightly sharp, lightly citric hops. There is an interesting honeyed sweetness. JW: Distinctly lemony. KR: A crisp, light fruitiness with a good bitter hop character. Deep and complex.

FINISH: Long lasting, gently bitter, citric hops. KR: Quite dry with fleeting sweeter notes. Very quenching.

OVERALL: A complex beer that is easy to drink and very satisfying with good texture and great balance even though the citric hops dominate. JW: Good clean tastes without sediment added. KR: Extremely refreshing and light on the palate.

GENERAL: First brewed 1994.

JW: ☑☑☑   KR: ☑☑☐

L'ATRÉBATE BRUNE

6% alc/vol.   75cl corked bottles & draught.

DECLARED INGREDIENTS: Magnum hops; 2-row spring, Pilsener malt.

APPEARANCE: Very, very dark brown with a generous, pillowy beige coloured head.

NOSE: Pungent hops are the strongest element though there is a distinct chocolatey mellow dark malt and a fair bit of yeastiness. JW: The interesting hop grows to overcome the malt though a little chocolate remains. KR: A mellow background fruitiness. A little stout-like.

PALATE: Dry and faintly bitter with a distant sweetness and an instant hit of chocolate and cocoa with a bit of coffee thrown in for good measure. JW: The hops display themselves by balancing the chocolate malt and lending a sharpish note. Adding a little sediment seems to make it both sweeter and more bitter. KR: Good, bitter, fruitiness with complex wafts of various tastes.

FINISH: Oddly saliva-inducing and mouth-drying with a powdery dryness. JW: Dry, roast malt with coffee and cocoa notes. KR: Lingering bitter fruit, quite warming, deeply interesting.

OVERALL: There is an odd wateriness to the character but it is an interesting brown ale with lots of lightly chocolate malt and an interesting hop character. JW: A very well presented, and possibly unique, beer but most definitely not what you would expect – especially if you do not like coffee. KR: Quite stout-like in character but with a greater depth of interest.

GENERAL: First brewed 1994.   JW: ☑☐☐   KR: ☑☑☐

L'ATRÉBATE SPÉCIALE NOËL

8% alc/vol.   75cl corked bottles & draught.

DECLARED INGREDIENTS: Magnum hops; three types of malt.

APPEARANCE: Copper amber with a massive head.

NOSE: JW: Initially almost neutral, just a faint hint of crystal malt but develops some interesting red fruit notes later. KR: Earthy but light fruitiness  with a blanket of gentle hoppiness and red fruit. A few rhubarb hints.

PALATE: Sweet, very rich and malty with a distinct presence of red fruit. Hops develop slowly but give it a bitter element. Some alcohol gives a sharp, warming edge to the fruit. KR: A fair amount of sugary sweetness and some marzipan notes.

FINISH: Lingering fruitiness and astringency. KR: Sweetness subsides to leave a dull, but sharp, red fruit with a little tannin.

OVERALL: JW: For a beer with so little in the nose or finish it has a surprisingly full, mellow, fruity, malty palate and an excellent thick smooth texture. Could do with a bit more oomph to be a great Christmas beer. KR: A great dessert beer. The sharp fruitiness will put a lot of people off. Strange but original concept for a Christmas beer.

GENERAL: First brewed 1995.   JW: ☑☑☐   KR: ☑☑☐

BARS & CAFES RECOMMENDED BY THE BREWERY

Les Garçons, 26 rue de Paris, 59000 Lille
La Tête des Trains, 6 rue de la Mairie, 77123 Tousson
l'Estaminet des Arcades, Place des Héros, 62000 Arras

BEER SHOPS RECOMMENDED BY THE BREWERY

Colas Jacqueline, 31 Place des Héros, 6200 Arras
Le Cellier des Bières, 8 rue de la Taillerie, 6200 Arras
Continent, Z.I. de la Vigogne, 62600 Berck-sur-Mer
Le Palais des Terroirs, 161 rue Florent Evrard, 62220 Carvin
Trogneux, 67 rue Nationale, 59000 Lille
Vinothèque Rohart, 66 rue Faidherbe, 59000 Lille
Various P.G. Supermarkets along the Pas-de-Calais coast

Brasserie de Bernoville

- ✉ 34 rue de Pierre-de-Martimprey, 02110 Aisonville
- ☎ 03 23 66 00 40
- ◷ Contact brewery for details
- 🍴 By arrangement only – groups of 15 or more. In French. 15FF
- 🏬 Cases, bottles and glasses
- 🛢 110hl (in 1997)
- ➔ See article

The Picardie landscape to the west of Guise is a rolling one that consists of enormous fields, mostly featuring an arable crop, and barely punctuated by anything as large as a tree. Set in this landscape is the sprawling village of Aisonville-et-Bernoville, just off the D960 between Guise and Bohain-en-Vermandois. Leaving the village on the D67 to Fieulaine you will pass the school and then, set back from the road, you will see a large white painted house with what appears to be a rather incongruous brewery tower tacked on the end of it. The curious heavily-pollarded trees, which form an avenue in the driveway to the neighbouring chateau-like house gives the setting a very traditionally rural French feel. The entrance to the brewery yard and shop is on the right hand side of the white house.

The structure which looks like a brewery tower turns out to be the real thing – which is initially surprising, given the small output of the brewery – but closer inspection reveals that this part of the premises is not actually being used at the moment. This purpose-built brewery was erected in about 1850 and during its working life (around 120 years) was only owned by two families, the last being called Courroub who apparently made a beer without a name. The current owners, M. and Mme Depierre are in the process of restoring this excellent example of the industrial brewing era, which still has the vast majority of the original equipment in it. If the project ever reaches completion it should be well worth a visit.

The brew capacity of the old plant is 40hl, which probably explains why they call their current operation the 'micro-brewery'.

In the yard behind the house, and to one side of the tower is a brick-built, spacious outbuilding housing the new brewplant. This venture started in October 1993 and the equipment has a brew capacity of just 8hl. Unlike the profusion of copper in the old tower, today's brewery uses the ubiquitous stainless steel, in this instance sourced from old dairy equipment, which is quite appropriate for a farmer brewer. There are two brews a month at present, but they claim that production is increasing all the time. Scattered around the yard are various large, stainless steel vessels intended for a major expansion project in the near future.

In the yard, opposite the rear entrance to the house, is a small shop where you can taste and buy the beers.

The Bernoville beers are very characterful and of a high quality, displaying a distinctly Belgian-type taste. All of them undergo 8–10 days fermentation followed by a 10–15 day garde before a three-week bottle refermentation in the warm room prior to sale.

Confusingly, the two stock products, the red- and blue-labelled beers, are not given clearly identifiable names – we have called the red-labelled one La Bernoville and the one with the blue label Bière du Pays de Guise. Although made for the Christmas market, there were many bottles of Bière de Noël still on sale on our visit in April.

It seems a shame that these excellent beers are so difficult to come by – we have not seen any Bernoville product on even the best cartes de bières of speciality beer bars. The brewery tells us that all the production is sold locally to cafés, bars, restaurants and small shops as well as a healthy trade direct from the brewery. Along with Brasserie de Clerck, we hope that the beers of Picardie will one day gain the recognition they justly deserve.

LA BERNOVILLE

7% alc/vol. 25cl & 75cl crown corked bottles and draught.

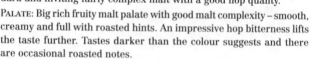

BREW DETAILS: Unfiltered. Unpasteurised. Top fermentation.

APPEARANCE: Deep orange tinged brown with an excellent head.

NOSE: Full, aromatic, fruity, dark and inviting fairly complex malt with a good hop quality.

PALATE: Big rich fruity malt palate with good malt complexity – smooth, creamy and full with roasted hints. An impressive hop bitterness lifts the taste further. Tastes darker than the colour suggests and there are occasional roasted notes.

FINISH: A lasting and satisfying finish full of a tangy, spicy, peppery hop and fruity malt enhanced by a gentle warmth.

GENERAL: Massively malty beer that is impressively complex. There is ample gently spiced fruit suitably tempered by a distinctive hop character that produces enough bitterness to lift any tendency there may have been for it to be cloying. Very satisfying.

JW: ☑☑☑   KR: ☑☑☑

BIÈRE DE NOËL

8% alc/vol. 75cl crown corked bottles.

BREW DETAILS: Unfiltered. Unpasteurised. Top fermentation.

APPEARANCE: Good ruddy colour with a good creamy head.

NOSE: Rich, dark, fruity and spicy. JW: Some coffee and chocolate notes. KR: Lovely dark warming character with a light grassy hop hovering over it all.

PALATE: Really full and rich dark spicy character with multiple malts and strong liquorice hints. Strong, but masked, hoppiness lightens the darkness. Very impressive fullness yet excellent balance. KR: A multi-layered complexity, presumably from the use of many malts. Hops prevent the cloying character expected.

FINISH: Lingering dark spicy fruit with a rich slightly warming glow. Long lingering and very satisfying. KR: Some herbal notes.

OVERALL: Top quality beer which will fit most peoples' idea of a Christmas beer. Rich, smooth and warming with a multi-faceted interest of spicy dark malty fruit and a subdued hop. Gorgeously smooth texture, velvety, dark and rich.

JW: ☑☑☑   KR: ☑☑☑

BIÈRE DU PAYS DE GUISE

5.5% alc/vol. 25cl & 75cl crown corked bottles.

BREW DETAILS: Unfiltered. Unpasteurised. Top fermentation.

APPEARANCE: Rich old gold colour.

NOSE: Artisanal fruity pale malt. Mellow with a pleasant light hop overlaying this. The artisanal quality

is enhanced by a touch of yeast and a greenness that promises a hint of acidity. KR: Beautiful grassy hop. A touch creamy.

PALATE: Light yet full and tasty pale malt with a distinctive green and oily hop generating both a resiny bitterness and a sharpness that verges on tartness. Interesting and relatively complex. KR: Excellent beer with a light, quenching bitterness and a fresh citric-tinged hop. A touch sweet.

FINISH: JW: Mouthdrying, lingering, bitterness, a little resiny and with some acidic remnants. KR: A light malt sweetness turning drier and just a little bitter. A tongue-tingling, lingering hop. Creamy hints.

OVERALL: JW: Unusual artisanal beer which is lightish in texture but full in taste. Moderately complex with an oily green hop threatening a light tartness. KR: Excellent quality beer, light and spritzy in character but not particularly complex. A great stock product which makes a formidable thirst-quencher.

GENERAL: First brewed 1994.

JW: ☑☐☐   KR: ☑☑☐

BARS & CAFES RECOMMENDED BY THE BREWERY

LE CHEVAL NOIR, Vervins
LE ROND D'ALEMBERT, St-Quentin
LE RICHELIEU, St-Quentin

Brasserie Bobtail

✉ Route de St-Séverin, 16390 Laprade

☎ 05 45 98 54 92

🕐 July and August open every day 1200-2100

🎿 48 hours notice out of season. In French and English

🍺 Bottles and cases

📏 10-12hl

➡ From Aubeterre, leave in the direction of the hamlet of Laprade on the D17 where the brewery is on the left on the near side of a left hand junction. Opposite is a built-up gravel parking area. The brewery is on the right-hand side as you pass the house

The village of Aubeterre, 30km south of Angoulême, has been given the official designation *'One of the 100 most beautiful villages in France'* – an accolade hard to achieve. One of its features is a medieval cave church built into the hillside as it slopes down to the main road. Aubeterre is thankfully bypassed nowadays, thereby avoiding the maze of very narrow streets in the pretty centre. Just outside is the tiny hamlet of Laprade, straddling the main road.

The brewery is owned and run by Bruce Hocking, a charismatic French-Canadian ex-archaeologist, who settled in the area after a stint of working in Britain. It was from there he took the inspiration for the brewery name – choosing an Old English Sheepdog (known in France as a bobtail), that most quintessentially English dog, as his logo and easily-remembered identity. He started the brewery in 1985, giving him some rights to his claim that Bobtail was the first microbrewery in France, beating Deux Rivières by a matter of days. His 'real' job is as an estate agent in Aubeterre which has given him a good insight into the vastly changing property market in the area – before the UK property crash of the late 1980s a good proportion of houses in Aubeterre were British-owned, but now few remain. This has meant adapting his range of beers to suit the local market of the time, and he now finds himself dependent on French visitors rather than the earlier English local clientele.

The brewery is open daily during July and August and is run as a tourist attraction, but Bruce will open up out of season if you phone first to book an appointment. There are plans afoot to add a small brewing museum at the site to offer more to his visitors, although this will be a year or two away.

The brewing period is just as limited as the opening period. Apparently the local conditions in October and November are particularly favourable for brewing – especially for fermentation. Being inland and quite far south, the temperatures vary between the sweltering summer highs and the surprisingly cold winter lows. Bruce believes October is ideal for his annual flurry of beer production – although he often brews into November if conditions are right – meaning he doesn't need to heat (or cool) the brewery.

The products of Bobtail are given a particularly artisanal appearance by using bottles of various shapes, sizes and colours (all recycled) and the labels are understated hand-cut photocopies on whatever paper stock can be found locally. Bruce is keen to discuss his recipes which contain many surprises, including packets of Quaker Oats, and is always developing new ones in any year.

What is most unusual about the output from the brewery is the sheer range – 16 different beers were available in 1997 (one year there were 24!) – and the fact that there is something for just about every taste. There are many fruit beers (including pear, Bruce's particular favourite fruit beer), various special beers (such as his honey beer) and the stock range of beers called La Paysanne ('The Peasant Woman') which appear with different-coloured labels.

We have produced full tasting notes on those beers considered to be the premier range and brief descriptions of others which were available in 1997. All Bobtail beers are very original and very artisanal in character, but it is difficult for us to be sure of age and condition of some beers we obtained. More than most other microbreweries, we would recommend a visit to Bobtail to achieve a truly objective assessment of its beers.

MACPHERSON CUVÉE DE NOËL

9% alc/vol. 33cl crown corked bottles.

APPEARANCE: Red amber colour.

NOSE: An aged malt and hop aroma with a little fruit.

PALATE: Very much a full but aged malt with some fruit and lots of aged hop giving a distinctly tangy, oily bitterness. A strong warmth builds as you drink.

FINISH: Lingering tangy, resiny, bitterness follows a fruity malt. KR: Lightly tart bittersweet fruit.

OVERALL: These notes relate to an example one year old with still a year to run to the BBE. JW: Good soft, creamy texture with a lot of malt and a little fruit balanced by a fair whack of oily hop. Shows promise as a warming winter beer. KR: A little strong on the crystal malt but very warming, although an odd version of a Christmas beer.

GENERAL: Described on the label as a barley wine (vin d'orge). Named after a goose – giving it a Scottish identity in keeping with the trend for winter Scotch ales.

JW:☑☐☐   KR:☑☐☐

LA PAYSANNE (CREAM LABEL)

4.9% alc/vol. 75cl crown corked bottles.

APPEARANCE: Golden colour.

NOSE: An artisanal character is engendered by the citric, lemony, hoppy aroma with hints of tropical fruits.

PALATE: Good hop character imparts a strong bitterness. Lots of flowery hop, moderately resiny with a sharp grapefruit citricity building into the finish and helping generate a bittersweet fruit tang.

FINISH: Strong biting, resiny bitterness. Intense oily bitterness. Some grapefruit notes linger.

OVERALL: Light fruity nose belies the intense hoppiness of the rest of the beer. Well hopped but the finish is intensely hoppy and lastingly bitter. Artisanal character, fairly complex yet light and quaffable.

JW: ☐☐☐   KR: ☑☑☐

LA PAYSANNE (ORANGE LABEL)

3.5% alc/vol.   75cl corked bottles.

APPEARANCE: Deep sienna wth a good but short-lived head.

NOSE: Pleasantly mellow yet solid fruity malt with wafts of hop. KR: Some caramel and darker elements (liquorice and molasses).

PALATE: A little watery and thin but starts with plenty of fruit (a little red in character) before a gentle tartness develops, followed by a stronger resiny hoppiness which lifts it from the watery wilderness.

FINISH: Long, lingering, resiny hop bitterness. Quite dry. KR: A peppery edge to the hop.

OVERALL: Essentially not a bad table beer with a wonderful nose that is not quite followed up. For a watery, thin, beer it has a fair bit of taste. Strong on hops but the character builds slowly to a crescendo in the finish.

JW: ☑☐☐   KR: ☑☐☐

LA PAYSANNE (RED LABEL)

4% alc/vol.   75cl crown corked bottles.

APPEARANCE: Copper coloured.

NOSE: Pleasant with a heady spicy hop. JW: A little fruity crystal malt.

PALATE: Bags of slightly washed-out malt with masses of strong oily hop. Quite bitter and fairly tangy. KR: Some pepperiness to the hop.

FINISH: Long lasting very mouthdrying strongly bitter oily hop. KR: Pepperiness gives dryness.

OVERALL: Good texture and pleasant aroma, plus plentiful use of an intensely oily bitter hop give this beer a strong character. Some will find the bitterness, particularly the long lasting bitter finish, a touch too much.

JW: ☐☐☐   KR: ☑☐☐

LA PAYSANNE (YELLOW LABEL)

5.1% alc/vol.   50cl crown corked bottles.

APPEARANCE: Yellow gold with a good fluffy head.

NOSE: Fruity and citric with suggestions of grapefruit.

PALATE: Mellow, moderately bitter with a light hop character and grapefruit notes throughout.

FINISH: Fairly dull and short-lived, just some bitterness.

OVERALL: Fairly nondescript beer with the grapefruit notes to lift it but little else.

JW: ☐☐☐   KR: ☐☐☐

LA RUCHE CERVOISE AU MIEL

8.6% alc/vol.   25cl crown corked bottles.

APPEARANCE: Honey gold colour.

NOSE: Pungent with bags of stale hop and a thick sweetish, fruity, honeyed pale malt.

PALATE: Full, thick, bittersweet, honeyed pale malt. A distinct hoppy taste generates some bitterness. Quite warming.

FINISH: Tangy, bittersweet, honeyed pale malt. Gently spicy with an oily hop bitterness.

OVERALL: Impressively honeyed (almost too much so) and definitely on the sweet side. There is strong level of hopping but few signs of the 8.6% alcohol, though it does generate a satisfying glow.

JW: ☑☑☐   KR: ☑☑☐

OTHER BEERS BREWED ────────────────

Blonde de Neanderthal (7.4% alc/vol.) – Rich golden beer with a full pale malt nose and palate and a good bitter hop edge leading into the lingering finish. Characterful but quaffable.

Cassis du Périgord (5.8% alc/vol.) – As the name suggests, a blackcurrant beer. Pale cherry/orange colour with a strong blackcurrant nose mixed with a distinct hay element. Initially tart, acidic fruit developing a tangy bitterness and a strange cordial quality. A little thin and watery despite its strength.

Granit (5.8% alc/vol.) – Rich orangey brown beer with a complex, fruity nose with hints of toffee, honey and caramel. Lightly roasted maltiness and quite fruity palate leading to a dryish, caramelled, quite tangy finish. The label proclaims it as being the 'Single Stout of Périgord', a good description as the light colour belies the dark character.

Mousse-tic (8.2% alc/vol.) – Quite sweet and fruity with an alcohol glow and a strong, resiny bitterness. KR: A lovely peppery hop character. The name is a play on the word moustique (meaning mosquito).

Old Black Bill (5.5% alc/vol.) – Passable but unexciting beer which has a distinctly farmyardy nose. Despite its name it is orange brown in colour. Rich, malty, but cloying.

Périgord Pale Ale (6.3% alc/vol.) – Golden orange with a surprising amount of sharp red fruit character. A tangy hoppiness.

Poire du Périgord (7.7% alc/vol.) – Made with pears. Very sweet and perfumed nose, not unlike lychees.

La Cabane des Brasseurs

- ✉ 21 Place du Marché Découvert, 54000 Nancy
- ☎ 03 83 32 77 77   Fax: 03 83 35 76 76
- ⏲ 1100-0200 daily except Sundays and public holidays
- 🏃 Pre-arranged only. 14 days notice. In French & English. Visits on the last Monday and Tuesday of every month around 1800
- 🛒 2-litre bottles only and glasses
- 🍺 800hl (in 1997)
- ➡ See article

Another brewpub in a major town, but in spite of that remarkably easy to find. The Marché Centrale, a large covered food market, is signposted from the suburbs of Nancy and the bar is behind it. Finding the Marché may be relatively straightforward, finding somewhere to park will probably not be – in fact Nancy has a reputation for being notoriously difficult to park in. Having found the Marché Centrale, and parked, you need to head up the side street to the Place du Marché which is behind it. If you go up the left hand side you will be in Place Henri Mengin. La Cabane's large frontage takes up a substantial portion of the left-hand side of Place du Marché.

The owner and brewer – Pierre Bisch – learnt to brew with a course at the IFBM in Nancy and then spent quite some time sourcing his brewing kit which he eventually found in Austria.

The installation of the brewplant into the building has been carried out with some forethought since it has been shoehorned in, but very cleverly so. With a ground floor, an upstairs and a cellar area Pierre has been able to spread it over three floors though the bulk of the equipment is on the ground floor. Upstairs are the malt mill and the water treatment and boiling plant. In the cellar are the refrigeration and conditioning tanks, the latter of which uses the modern inner membrane system which contracts and expands with the beer levels to ensure that there is no contact between the beer and the CO_2 in the tank. All in all, the investment in brewing kit appears to have been substantial for a brewpub.

The mashtun has a capacity of 9hl but the fermentation tank can take 16hl, so Pierre normally mashes twice for each fermentation to make the most of the fermentation tank capacity. He generally brews three times a week though this is determined by the malt supply as there is very little storage space.

The pub is really split into a number of functional areas. The eating areas, serving remarkably well-priced food, tend to be upstairs or outside with the ground floor being allocated for serious drinking. Downstairs is that essential feature – a technomusic-playing tapas bar! La Cabane also has a good reputation as a salmon restaurant which explains the fish signs on the external wall.

There are four stock products though normally only two or three are ever on sale at the same time. Others – including the Noël, Mars and various one-offs – also appear on the pumps in season. All the beers are bottom fermented, unfiltered and unpasteurised.

We have been unlucky with our visits since we have only ever found one of his beers on when we have been there. On our first visit there were no beers at all due to a difficulty with the malt supply. Fortunately, Pierre was able to take advantage of his relationship with the IFBM, and also his proximity to them, and get a supply of beer to see him through the problem.

Is it a fishmongers?
Of course not, it's a brewpub

BIÈRE DE NOËL

5% alc/vol. Draught only.

APPEARANCE: Hazy orange brown colour.

NOSE: Fairly neutral, just a hint of malt.

PALATE: Pleasant mellow malt with a good hop character that comes through later. Starts a little sweet but by the time the hops come through it ends distinctly bitter.

FINISH: A lingering bitterness and general hop character.

OVERALL: Well balanced malt and hops with good use of the hops allowing the character to come through slowly.

GENERAL: First brewed 1997. Served ice cold on our visit, to its overall detriment.   JW:☑☑☐   KR:☑☑☐

OTHER BEERS BREWED

La Boréale (4.8% alc/vol.) – Declared ingredients: Brewers Gold and Hallertau hops; Pilsener, Vienne, Cara blond & Munich malts. First brewed 1997. Used to be called La Jennesson but the name was changed to give it a French-Canadian appeal.

La Coup de Grisou (5% alc/vol.) – Declared ingredients: Brewers Gold and Hallertau hops; Pilsener, Vienne, Cara blond & Cara Foncée, Black & Munich malts. First brewed 1997.

L'Illegale (5% alc/vol.) – Declared ingredients: Hallertau and Brewers Gold hops; Pilsener malt. First brewed 1997. The name derives from the idea that it is illegal to make Pils outside of Pilsen, Czech Republic. Also brewed for Bar le Zinc Bleu.

La Moselle

La Sans Nom (4.5% alc/vol.) – Declared ingredients: Hallertau and Brewers Gold hops; Pilsener and Cara malts. First brewed 1997. Also brewed for Bar le Zinc Bleu in Charmes. The name means literally 'The Un-named'.

BARS & CAFES RECOMMENDED BY THE BREWERY

Bar le Zinc Bleu, 88130 Charmes

Brasserie Artisanale du Cambier

- ✉ 18 bis rue Pasteur, 59265 Aubigny-au-Bac
- ☎ 03 27 92 09 95
- 🕐 Ring to book an appointment
- ⚥ By prior arrangement only
- 🏪 Cases or bottles
- 📊 12hl (in 1997)
- ➡ See article

Those who have been drinking beer in France for some time may well find the names Caudrelier and Iris familiar. There was once a brewery called Brasserie Caudrelier, owned and run by Gérard Caudrelier, which used to produce a beer called Iris. Today Gérard is still producing Iris Beer but he now has a small, purpose-built brewery called Brasserie Artisanale du Cambier.

His original brewery was an old established one with a single-brew capacity which far exceeded the local demand for his beer. In those days Gérard found he could satisfy his small market by brewing just four times a year. While this may be considered by some to be a positive advantage, for Gérard it was frustrating as his main interest lay more in the brewing process than in the sales and marketing of the bottled finished product.

To bring the supply and demand elements of the business closer together and to provide himself with more job satisfaction by increasing the brewing frequency, he decided to sell his old brewery and build himself a smaller one.

The chosen location for his new brewery was in the flatlands north of Cambrai. Aubigny-au-Bac is just off the N43 half way between Douai and Cambrai. Approaching from the north, take the first left turn into the village and the brewery is immediately on your left, number 18b, a modern brick construction set back from the road a little.

The barn-like structure has a small office-cum-storeroom at one end and the rest houses the brewery in a single room with a chambre chaud built into it. Apart from the major structural building elements Gérard has done the work himself. In spite of his enterprising skills there was still a substantial outlay and when it came to kitting out the brewery he favoured using various bits and pieces from the drinks industry which he has put together himself to produce his brewery. This approach has also allowed him to be more flexible with regard to what brewing techniques he employs.

Originally trained at the IFBM in Nancy he likes to put this technical training to the test and continues to play with different ways of doing things – something he was unable to do within the confines of the large scale production facility of his previous brewery.

His new plant has a brew capacity of just 600 litres and he brews once or twice a month. One notable feature of the process is the heating of the mash by steam injection. There are other elements of the process that he is experimenting with but these are not employed yet and the beer ends up with a conventional bottle refermentation in the warm room.

Distribution is very limited with most of it being sold locally from small shops like patisseries and boulangeries, but he also does a good trade direct from the brewery. Gérard seems not to have much desire to expand to any great extent, apparently content with his current level of production. However, he did admit to having plans to produce both a blonde and a bière de Noël sometime in the near future.

IRIS BEER

6% alc/vol.   75cl corked bottles

BREW DETAILS: Unfiltered. Unpasteurised. Top fermentation.

INGREDIENTS: Not disclosed.

APPEARANCE: Copper coloured.

NOSE: JW: Interestingly hoppy, fruity amber malt. Deep and with a rich promise. KR: Very fruity (especially red fruit) with

a good, quite tangy, crystal malt facet. Good nose-tingling hoppiness, but mainly a tangy, fruity promise.

PALATE: JW: Massively malty, rich and quite complex. An oily hop provides an interestingly sharp edge to the taste. KR: Very fruity, turning instantly dry and quite acidic. A very bitter, oily hop works on the mouth the whole time adding a building bitterness. Plenty of red fruit with a very full and artisanal character.

FINISH: JW: Rich, dry, tangy and fruity. Verging on being slightly tart. KR: Bitter fruit in abundance with a saliva-inducing acidity which lingers to give a long-lasting fruity dryness.

OVERALL: JW: Impressively fruity amber malt aroma leads into a balanced hop and fruity malt palate. The good, full, hop character has a distinct bite to it. Quite complex. KR: Very full with lashings of red fruit and a great oily hop character. Light acidity enhances the overall taste to give extra depth and interest. Fresh, yet has the qualities of an aged ale. Very impressive.   JW: ☑☑☐   KR: ☑☑☑

Brasserie du Caroux

- ⌧ Imminent change of address – no details at time of publication
- ☎ 04 67 95 72 77   Fax: 04 67 95 73 56 (but subject to change)
- 🕓 Contact brewery for details
- 🏃 No visits available until late summer 1998
- 🍶 Bottles and cases
- 🍺 130hl (in 1997)
- ➡ Colombières-sur-Orb is on the D908, north-west of Béziers. At the time of publication the owners were negotiating new premises. Check the Artisan Press website for latest information.

The River Orb meets the Mediterranean at Valras-Plage after flowing across the plains of Languedoc through Béziers, but it rises high in the southern hills of the Massif Central. Roughly halfway down its course it cuts across the southern edge of a huge rock massif, the highest part of which is called Le Caroux. It is on the sunny, south-facing slopes that Colombières-sur-Orb tumbles down the hillside to the river. On our visit the brewery was at the house of the owners, Jacques Bottemanne and his wife, in the hamlet of Colombières le Haut, where it had been since opening in 1992.

The formidably-steep slopes above the main village was an unlikely place to find a brewery, and the thought of trucks dropping off supplies and collecting beer for delivery was even more unimagineable. On such slopes the houses need to be cut into the hillside, giving residents the facility of a good-sized cellar beneath – an ideal location for a microbrewery, and one which Jacques took advantage of for many years until he outgrew his space. Accessed by steps from the road, it was very cramped by the time of our visit and offered little room for expansion – essentially consisting of two rooms, one for the brewplant and the one behind for bottling and storage.

Like many other smaller rural French micro-breweries, it brews organic beers and the current range consists of three beers – a Cervoise, a Rousse and a Blanche, the Cervoise being flavoured with honey. It does a good trade in the various organic fairs and speciality shops which seem to be opening everywhere in France these days, but doesn't sell to supermarkets.

Although the venture has been successful enough to necessitate the imminent move to new premises, Jacques does not want to become too commercial and is content to keep it as a husband and wife affair.

All the beers undergo a process described as a 'methode Belge' – a 10-day fermentation and a two-week garde prior to bottling.

BLANCHE

7.5% alc/vol.   75cl crown corked bottles.

BREW DETAILS: Unfiltered. Unpasteurised. Bottle refermentation.

APPEARANCE: Hazy, wheaty orange colour.

NOSE: Hoppy with a full and quite fruity wheat/malt base.

PALATE: Some sweet elements run through a resiny, hoppy bitterness.

There is a persistent fruitiness but the hops still manage to give some lemon hints and a little peppery edge.

FINISH: Harsh, bitter fruit with a heavy, very oily hoppiness.

OVERALL: Surprisingly for a Blanche this is far better keeping the sediment well away from the glass – the resiny bitterness becomes intense and overpowering with sediment. Smooth, creamy texture but an unusual bitter fruit tang and far more bitter oily hops than the average blanche. JW: ☑☑☐ KR: ☑☑◓

CAROUSSE

7.5% alc/vol.   75cl crown corked bottles.

BREW DETAILS: Unfiltered. Unpasteurised. Bottle refermentation.

APPEARANCE: Bright orange brown, a good head and excellent lacework.

NOSE: Good, full aroma of a mellow fruity crystal malt with a resiny hop floating over it. KR: A little yeasty.

PALATE: Full mellow crystal malt. Sweet with just a light red fruitiness. A well integrated hop lends a resiny bite. KR: Very bitter in the start.

FINISH: Mellow malt and a gentle red fruitiness are tempered by a resiny/oily bitterness.

OVERALL: JW: Excellent texture and a good full but mellow palate with a well balanced malt and hop, though the hop generates a very strong oily resiny element that builds into the finish. KR: A very bitter beer. Rounded and full with a sticky red fruit character, marred a little by the oily hop. JW: ☑☑☐ KR: ☑☑☐

CERVOISE

7.5% alc/vol.   75cl crown corked bottles.

BREW DETAILS: Unfiltered. Unpasteurised. Bottle refermentation.

DECLARED INGREDIENTS: Honey.

APPEARANCE: Hazy rich orange colour.

NOSE: Starts a little farmyardy but develops into a malty fruitiness behind a pungent, but not very powerful, slightly oily hop. KR: Some red fruit.

PALATE: Full, deep and well balanced with lots of interest. Malty with lots of fruit. A little tartness enhances the fruit and an oily hop adds further character. KR: Quite sweet, with a sticky, bittersweet malt.

FINISH: Fairly complex. Dry but with a strong bittersweet red fruitiness. A resiny hop comes in after the fruit and lingers. KR: Fleeting herbal elements with a certain stickiness.

OVERALL: JW: A good texture, strong fruit element, plenty of malt plus good use of the usual Du Caroux resiny hop add up to a complex beer with plenty of depth. It is easy and very satisfying to drink. KR: Not as oily in the hop department as the other beers but very sticky and fruity. Multi-faceted (sweet, tart, bitter & fruity) with fleeting herbal notes adding to the interest. JW: ☑☑☐ KR: ☑☑☐

Brasserie Castelain

- 13 rue Pasteur, 62410 Bénifontaine, Wingles
- 03 21 08 68 68   Fax: 03 21 08 68 60
  www.francecontacts.com/marche/Castelain/bonjour.htm
- By arrangement in the week (Tue-Fri: 0900-1200, 1400-1800),
  7 days notice. Scheduled tours every Sat (just turn up) at 0900,
  1000 or 1100. In French & English. 20FF
- Just about everything including T-shirts, trays and jam!
- 35,000hl (in 1997)
- See article

Many people know it as Ch'ti after it best selling beer brand, others as Bénifontaine after its location but its correct name is Brasserie Castelain after the family which bought it in 1966.

Founded in 1926 by three brothers of the Delomel family it had always concentrated on making table and bock beers, which it was happy to continue doing even after it was sold. Nothing really changed until Yves (the son of the first Castelain brewer) took an active role in the business in the late 70s. Yves took the decision to make 'special' beers – based mainly around the reintroduction of the once-common bières de garde of the region – and over the years the brewery has tended to concentrate more and more on this style. Out went over 50 years of traditionally making cheap and cheerful beers and in came a more commercial and adventurous approach to the art of brewing. Not all the old traditions were dispensed with, however; it is one of the few breweries still offering door-to-door deliveries, mostly within a 30km radius of the brewery. The principal beer sold in this manner is Renard Pils.

The brewing process saw most of the changes including a move from hop flowers to pellets in an effort to maintain consistency. Most Castelain beers will undergo a primary fermentation of two weeks at 14°C, then a second lasting six to eight weeks at 0°C. For the Noël (originally just a brune but now available in blonde and brune versions) this latter period is extended to between 10 and 12 weeks.

Today Castelain is one of the more commercially aware of the French breweries and has a strong image and market presence. Gratifyingly it has managed to do this whilst remaining a relatively small family concern. A few years after taking over from his parents Yves' sister Annick joined him, making it even more of a family business.

Its products are widely available both within France and abroad, with around 10% of its output being exported (a bar in Tahiti stocks its beers, and it has a strong market presence in Japan). Although most identify the brewery with the Ch'ti range it was the first to introduce a commercially available organic beer in France, in the form of Jade, which is a good example of Castelain's innovative nature.

When the Ch'ti range first appeared the brewery chose to display a picture of a miner's head on the label, giving it an instant local identity, being in the heart of the once hugely productive coal mining area. Although the last of the mines closed some years ago, the legacy of its past will live with the local people for some time in the form of the slagheaps littered prominently around the region. Over the years the label has gradually evolved with the miner having less prominence to the point where, by 1998, he had disappeared altogether (a display cabinet at the brewery clearly shows this evolution through a collection of old bottles). It appears that at the beginning of the 20th century the people of the Nord-Pas de Calais area where given the nickname of Ch'ti because of the way they spoke (they apparently had a tendency to put 'ch' at the beginning of many words). The term is still a way of describing the people of the far north, but rather than mimicking the way they speak, we were told it is now associated with people of the north who like to enjoy life to the full.

Bénifontaine is well located near the Flemish hop growing region with a good source of water, in what is now a predominantly agricultural landscape, though immediately south is a large built-up area in the band from Bethune, through Lens to Douai. The brewery lies just off the N47 Lens to Wingles road, about 4km north of Lens. Approaching from this way you cannot help but see the Ch'ti placards adorning the walls just before leaving the N47 and taking the D165. One feature of interest is the small hop garden used to demonstrate what growing hops look like. Once harvested, the hops bines are destined for the brewery sampling room and Ch'ti Taverns where they are used for decoration.

Once round to the entrance it looks more like a brewery as you glimpse the polished coppers through the glass frontage. It is very geared up to take tour parties with regular tours on the hour on Saturday mornings – you don't even have to book. Around 7,000 visitors were entertained in 1997 and it is expecting even more in 1998 when it celebrates the 20th birthday of Ch'ti on 20 June. All the equipment is kept spotlessly clean and the brewery does a good job in promoting itself to visitors, even though many may just want to get to the excellent tasting room. Included in the tour is a small museum-style room with many artefacts from this and other breweries and there are also videos in a variety of languages.

Castelain boasts a very good shop stocking not only the full range of beers and glasses (with individual bottles and presentation cases), but also lots of other items. These range from the expected items of marketing regalia – T-shirts, umbrellas, bottle openers, playing cards – through some good books, to interesting items of local produce such as jam made with beer, potted chicken in beer and jars of carbonnade.

The brewery has been offering franchises for Tavernes Ch'ti for a while now and there are plans afoot to expand this dramatically by opening another 20 during 1998. The franchise arrangement, like those of the Cafés Leffe and Jenlain Cafés, involves it supplying all the beers, bar equipment and decoration (including tables depicting the principal brands) to the bar owners.

A more impressive venture was undertaken in 1997 when it opened Brasserie St-Poloise in St-Pol-sur-Ternoise. This excellent brewpub produces draught versions of St-Poloise and St-Poloise Grand Cru – both of which are also brewed here but whilst they are offered in their unfiltered form in St-Pol, here they are sold only in a filtered and bottled version. The brewer at St-Poloise is Bertrand Castelain, son of Yves and the latest generation of the family to take up brewing. There is an intention to open some more brewpubs in the future but specific details were not given.

One has to admire Castelain for its meteoric rise from relatively local table beer producer to major player in the French special beer market. Along with La Choulette and Duyck they have proved that a brewery can be successful without have to make 'trendy' spirit-flavoured brews and bland beers which have more marketplace identity than they have character. Thankfully still independent, this is one brewery to watch to see what new innovative developments it introduces in the future.

CH'TI AMBRÉE

5.9% alc/vol. 25cl crown corked, 75cl corked bottles & draught.

BREW DETAILS: Filtered. Unpasteurised. Bottom fermentation.

APPEARANCE: Deep reddish amber with a good creamy head.

NOSE: Moderately sweet, slightly tangy, fruity crystal malt. KR: A touch woody.

PALATE: Rich and warming crystal malt with a somewhat harsh fruity bitterness and a few hops that help balance the taste. JW: Has a slight barley wine edge to the malt. KR: Exceptionally full.

FINISH: Dry and bitter resinous hop with a persistent lingering bitter fruit tang.

OVERALL: A fruity but very malt-oriented beer with a rich, bitter bite from the crystal malt. It has a distinctly warming character more often associated with Bières de Noël. JW: Whilst pleasant in the palate the rich bitter bite gets a bit much in the finish.

GENERAL: First brewed in 1978. Also sold in UK as **Sainsbury's Bière de Garde** and, in 1998, relabelled as **Bière du Carnaval de Dunkerque Ambrée**.

JW:☑☐☐ KR:☑☑☐

CH'TI BIÈRE DE MARS

5.9% alc/vol. 33cl crown corked & 75cl corked bottles.

BREW DETAILS: Filtered. Unpasteurised. Bottom fermentation.

DECLARED INGREDIENTS: Seven different malts.

APPEARANCE: Deep copper brown.

NOSE: An enticing aroma of spicy, herbal, pungent hop with an interesting fruity element. A few fruity esters and a little malt is relegated to the background yet still promises a rich and warming fruity base.

PALATE: A potent, full mouth of spicy and fruity tastes with an ever-present sharp hoppiness. The underlying dark fruity malt base lends it a certain sweetness yet the overall perception is more one of a gentle bitterness. JW: A fair whack of warming alcohol.

FINISH: The palate builds nicely into the finish as a bitter, resiny, lightly spiced dark fruity malt, but is immediately tempered to a lingering fruity hop bitterness. KR: A warmth seems to be induced by the dark, spicy elements.

OVERALL: Very good full, fruity, spicy, malty beer, well tempered by a resiny hop, that seems to be harking back to winter rather than heralding the arrival of spring. The spiciness is unusual for France but very satisfying in a winter beer.

GENERAL: First brewed in 1990. 75cl bottles are screen printed and the figure on the label is Gambrinus.   JW: ☑☑☐   KR: ☑☑☐

CH'TI BLONDE

6.4% alc/vol. 25cl, 33cl crown corked, 75cl corked bottles & draught.

BREW DETAILS: Filtered. Unpasteurised. Bottom fermentation.

APPEARANCE: Honey gold in colour with a beautiful creamy head.

NOSE: Sweet pale malt with plenty of fruit and a distinct, dry hop note with a few esters. KR: Dry, peppery hop with citric hints. Ale-like characteristics despite being bottom fermenting.

PALATE: Full mouth of sweetish fruity pale malt with the hops imparting a little pepperiness and a distinct bitter edge. There are also a few surprising suggestions of roasted malt. JW: Some alcohol notes. Starts sweet but this develops into a strong bitterness. KR: Very strong start of bitter fruit with a very clean taste of well balanced, dry, peppery hop and a sweet maltiness.

FINISH: Lasting dry fruity hop bitterness. KR: Impressively dry.

OVERALL: An accomplished, fairly complex ale with masses of fruit, malt and bitter hops. Quite a range from the initial sweetness of the aroma to the bitterness in the finish. Easy drinking with a smooth almost creamy texture. JW: The elements come out one at a time rather than blending together. KR: Excellent balance from the hops prevent it being over-sweet. Clean, almost clinical, character.

GENERAL: First brewed 1978. Sold as **Minator** in Italy, and **Bière de St-Amand** in USA. In 1998 it was relabelled as **Bière du Carnaval de Dunkerque Blonde**.   JW: ☑☐☐   KR: ☑☐☐

CH'TI BRUNE

6.4% alc/vol. 25cl crown corked, 75cl corked bottles & draught.

BREW DETAILS: Filtered. Unpasteurised. Bottom fermentation.

APPEARANCE: Very dark red brown colour that appears black.

NOSE: Rich fruity dark malt with a slightly roasted dryness. JW: Sometimes very vinous, like a good rich red wine. KR: Very nutty and dry promise.

PALATE: A very full mouth of multi-layered taste. Masses of dark, slightly roasted, fruity malt with hints of liquorice and a slightly astringent dryness and bitterness in spite of suggestions of sweetness. JW: Quite warming.

FINISH: Dry, astringent, bittersweet fruity roast malt with hints of liquorice and a gently warming sensation. It lasts well.

OVERALL: Spectacularly nice version of a brown ale, complex, multi-layered and very fruity yet relatively easy to drink. The roasted, bitter character increases as you drink. KR: Very clean taste.

GENERAL: First brewed in 1978.

JW:☑☑☐   KR:☑☑☑

CH'TI CUVÉE DE NOËL BLONDE

7.5% alc/vol.   33cl crown corked & 75cl corked bottles and draught.

BREW DETAILS: Filtered. Unpasteurised. Bottom fermentation.

APPEARANCE: Old gold colour.

NOSE: Good deep, slightly fruity, malt balanced by a dry, quite pungent English hoppiness. A darker, richer character than expected with a slightly perfumed, sweet confectionery note. KR: A little citric, and with surprising suggestions of melons.

PALATE: Very full rich pale malt with a hop-induced tanginess in addition to the tongue tingling peppery sensation. The sweetness has a perfumed confectionery element. KR: The spicy, bitter and very dry hop offers a perfect balance the light, fruity, vinous malt.

FINISH: JW: Lingering tangy, bittersweet, hoppy, fruity pale malt. KR: Warming, satisfying pale malt – full and rounded with a good depth of complexity. Very, long lasting with an interesting perfumed note lingering.

OVERALL: Very full and rich for a blonde. Interesting and moderately complex but easily accessible beer with an odd perfumed note throughout. JW: Has a distinct oily hop tanginess that detracts a little for me.

GENERAL: First brewed in 1977. Excellent screen printing on the 75cl bottles. Brewed in August.

JW:☑☐☐   KR:☑☑☐

CH'TI CUVÉE DE NOËL BRUNE

7.5% alc/vol.   33cl crown corked & 75cl corked bottles & draught.

BREW DETAILS: Filtered. Unpasteurised. Bottom fermentation.

APPEARANCE: Almost black in colour with some red highlights.

NOSE: A sweetish full dark fruity malt with some roasted notes. KR: Light hop notes with some liquorice.

PALATE: A full fruity dark malt. Fairly sweet though the distinct hop bitterness grows and comes out on top. Some chocolate notes and a gentle roasted element. KR: Not as fruity as the nose suggests.

FINISH: Lingering peppery hop bitterness and gently roasted dark malt with a light fruity dryness.

OVERALL: Full fruity dark malt beer with plenty of taste and a lingering roasted element that builds as you drink more to become quite strong in the finish. Surprising hop character for such a dark beer.

GENERAL: First brewed in 1977. Brewed in August. 75cl bottles are screen printed. JW:☑☐☐ KR:☑☑☐

CH'TI TRIPLE

7.5% alc/vol. 33cl crown corked, 75cl corked bottles & draught.

BREW DETAILS: Filtered. Unpasteurised. Bottom fermentation.

APPEARANCE: Dark gold colour.

NOSE: JW: Rich tangy pale malt with an aged hop adding interest. KR: A heady hop with a strong, very tangy, pale malt and a good whack of alcohol.

PALATE: Full rich pale malt with a growing resiny hop tang. The bitter oily hop character is very strong but lifted a little by some citric notes. You can taste the alcohol and a gentle warmth comes through. KR: Very full and fruity but a touch shallow and one-sided.

FINISH: Dry with a strong resiny, tangy hop and some pale malt. Long lasting with a growing oily resiny bitterness with a peppery edge. Quite warming with a strong alcohol tang.

OVERALL: Masses of tangy pale malt forms the basis of this full tasting beer. Adding to this tanginess is an abundance of oily hop which imparts a resiny bitterness. The whole effect is then exaggerated by warming alcohol. Some citric notes in the palate lift and lighten it a bit but it can become hard work after a while.

GENERAL: First brewed 1997. Has a strong bitterness but is more of a strong blonde than a triple. KR: Oozes quality in terms of ingredients, but too rich and alcoholic for most. JW:☑☐☐ KR:☑☐☐

JADE

4.6% alc/vol. 25cl crown corked & 75cl corked bottles.

BREW DETAILS: Filtered. Unpasteurised. Bottom fermentation.

DECLARED INGREDIENTS: Perle & Aurora hops; Trémois and Volga malts.

APPEARANCE: Paleish gold.

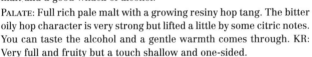

NOSE: A fairly pungent, dry, earthy hop with a pale malt base. KR: Drink young as the nose fades well before the best-before-end date.

PALATE: A very distinctive pale malt and a slight citricity. JW: Faintly biscuity malt and a gentle hoppiness. KR: Quite bland with some forced malt notes.

FINISH: A lingering dry malty tang. JW: A little bitter hop. KR: Suffers from the usual organic malt artificial note.

OVERALL: Interestingly different pale malt-based character, not particularly strong in any department but with enough difference to both the malt and hop to make it outshine the average organic beer in interest and character.

GENERAL: First brewed in 1984. Castelain's first, and so far only, attempt at an organic beer. JW:☑☐☐ KR:☑☐☐

KORMA

5.6% alc/vol. 75cl corked bottles.

BREW DETAILS: Filtered. Unpasteurised. Bottom fermentation.

DECLARED INGREDIENTS: Seven malts.

APPEARANCE: Rich honey gold.

NOSE: JW: Lovely aromatic nose with plenty of malt and a nice green hop over a subdued fruitiness and a faint butteriness. KR: Rich multi-layered maltiness with a full, fruity but rather stale hop. Biscuity and quite buttery.

PALATE: Great balance and depth. Full and rich with an instant mouthful of malt, balanced by a bittering hop with a light pepperiness. JW: Quite fresh and faintly citric. Complex and satisfying with a honeyed note. KR: Bitter, peppery hop keeps the expected clóyness at bay. Seems like it should be sweet but is particularly bitter and even quite dry.

FINISH: A lingering maltiness that is a little buttery. JW: Hoppy with a lingering resiny element. KR: A strong hop alleviates stickiness from the lingering malt. A honeyed note. Turns a little sweet in the end.

OVERALL: Wonderful, quite light beer that is unbelievably full and malty for just 5.6%. Its excellent complex maltiness, well complemented by a fresh greenish hop, gives it a creditable balance and a depth of interest usually associated with beers far stronger. Easy to drink and extremely satisfying. KR: Very clean with an almost perfect balance and excellent malt character – a quality beer.

GENERAL: First brewed by Brasserie de St-Amant, a now-defunct brew-pub in a village just south of Clermont-Ferrand. When the business went under in the early 90s, production switched to Castelain and this has recently become a standard product in its portfolio. The screen printed bottles carry the wording 'Beer born in the Auvergne' in reference to its origins.

JW: ☑☑☑   KR: ☑☑☐

SAINT LÉONARD, BIÈRE DE GARDE DE

5.9% alc/vol. 75cl corked bottles.

BREW DETAILS: Filtered. Unpasteurised. Bottom fermentation.

APPEARANCE: Deep, dark, copper amber.

NOSE: Gentle, full, dark, rich fruity malt with quite a deep hop.

PALATE: A full, rounded, almost totally malt taste which seems to be a blend of pale, amber and dark malts with just a touch of hop to give it an edge and counter the malt sweetness and a dark, quite spicy fruit.

FINISH: JW: Strongly malty with a crystal, almost lightly roasted, character. KR: A hop bitterness comes through to balance the malt.

OVERALL: Lovely texture helps this supremely malty beer get to the higher ranks. It has an excellent full rounded taste and, though almost entirely malt, works very well. For essentially an amber beer it has a surprisingly dark, spiced, winter character. As it ages the slight hop grows in intensity and adds a decidedly tangy element to the palate and finish.

GENERAL: Brewed for Brasseries Stella Artois (previously Interbrew France) and one which has enjoyed a high profile for a number of years, though being brewed quite anonymously. Named after a village in Pas-de-Calais which once had a reputation for making good quality bière de garde. JW: ☑☑☑ KR: ☑☑☐

SAINT PATRON

7.5% alc/vol. 33cl crown corked & 75cl corked bottles.

BREW DETAILS: Filtered. Unpasteurised. Top fermentation. Bottle refermentation.

APPEARANCE: Golden colour with a good creamy head which creates an excellent lacework in the glass.

NOSE: Hoppy with a little fruitiness. JW: A touch sweet with bags of inviting fresh, flowery and citric hops. As it ages this reduces to just being gently fruity, malty and hoppy. KR: A musty hop and apple notes.

PALATE: JW: Bags of hop character over a full pale malt with a slight bitterness and a touch of alcohol. Good clean but mellow tastes. KR: Full and complex. A sweetish malty base is bolstered by a very bitter, appley hoppiness.

FINISH: JW: Very dry, bitter and slightly citric. Very strong hop character. With age it becomes a lingering tangy bitter malt. KR: A strong, lingering and quite warming fruity tang thankfully lifted by a generous hop bitterness.

OVERALL: Surprisingly lightly sedimented for a bottle refermented ale. JW: An excellent hoppy beer with massive hop character throughout. Definitely needs drinking young as the full hop character is lost as it ages. KR: A great beer having a hugely full and quite complex palate, displaying excellent balance and a pronounced alcohol alcohol warmth.

GENERAL: Name refers to Saint Arnold, patron saint of brewers. Comes in an attractive screen-printed bottle. JW: ☑☑☑ KR: ☑☑☑

ST-POLOISE

6.5% alc/vol. 75cl corked bottles.

BREW DETAILS: Filtered. Unpasteurised. Bottom fermentation.

APPEARANCE: Rich, honey tinged gold and a light and fluffy, but short-lived head.

NOSE: Flowery, slightly lemony, hop aroma. Get it quick as it soon goes.

PALATE: Deliciously hoppy. A mouth full of flowery hops and an attendent resiny bitterness. Behind the hops is a gently fruity pale malt. JW: Very citric with loads of lemon. As it ages the citricity reduces and the resiny bitter character increases. KR: Citric but sweet.

FINISH: Huge resiny hop bitterness, both drying and salivating. JW: Citric. With age this reduces to a strong resiny dry hop. KR: Very dry.

OVERALL: This is a serious hop experience. A very distinctive nose is well supported by an equally impressive palate and finish. Very clean and polished beer that is immensely full and moderately complex. Best to drink young as the resiny elements of the hop character takes over with age.

GENERAL: First brewed in 1996. Named after the village of St-Pol-sur-Ternoise where the Castelain-run brewpub opened in 1997. *See Brasserie St-Poloise entry.*

JW: ☑☑☐   KR: ☑☑☐

ST-POLOISE GRAND CRU

7.5% alc/vol.   75cl corked bottles.

BREW DETAILS: Filtered. Unpasteurised. Bottom fermentation.

APPEARANCE: Rich deep old gold with a light, creamy head.

NOSE: Mellow, gently fruity pale malt with an interesting hop. KR: You can smell the alcohol and strong pale malt.

PALATE: Masses of garded pale malt with a definite tanginess. Behind this is a resiny hop which generates some lighter elements and a little lemon. KR: Very strong fruit tang and a warming alcohol note.

FINISH: Tangy pale malt, lots of it, and a tangy resiny hop. KR: Turns quite bitter.

OVERALL: A strongly garded character makes it seem too old in spite of a year of shelf-life left. JW: Tons of pale malt, very tangy. Some hop character but it is overpowered by the tangy malt. KR: Some will love it – a quality product, but just too tangy and alcoholic for me. Very much in the mould of Ch'ti Triple. Chill it to keep the tang down.

GENERAL: First brewed 1997. Named after the village of St-Pol-sur-Ternoise. *See Brasserie St-Poloise entry.*

JW: ☑☐☐   KR: ☑☐☐

OTHER BEERS BREWED

Blanche de Bénifontaine (5% alc/vol.) – Presumably the same recipe as the blanche on sale on draught in Brasserie St-Poloise. A new beer which is still in the development stage.

Blonde de Bénifontaine (5.6% alc/vol.) – Draught only.

Brassin Saint-Yves (4.8% alc/vol.) – Not one that the brewery promotes as a prestige brand, but nevertheless a solid, full and quite interesting beer that is particularly easy-drinking. Bright sparkling gold with an interesting hop aroma and a sweet malt taste tempered by a dry, peppery hop bitterness. Sold in 25cl crown corked bottles.

Renard Pils (4.7% alc/vol.) – Brewed elsewhere under contract. Supplied in 100cl screw-top bottles, it makes up the majority of the door-to-door beer deliveries.

BARS & CAFES RECOMMENDED BY THE BREWERY

TAVERNE DU CH'TI, 253 rue Nationale, 59800 Lille

LA TAVERNE DU CH'TI, place des Héros, 62000 Arras

LA TAVERNE DES CH'TIS, Route de Lille, 62300 Lens

LE DOMAINE DES PINCHONVALLES, rue Gabriel Peri, 62 Eleudit Leauwette

LE RELAIS, rue Principle, 62 Amettes

L'HACIENDA, rue Victor Hugo, 62 Liévin

Les Caves de la Brasserie

✉ 6 rue du Houblon, 68460 Lutterbach

☎ 03 89 57 48 48   Fax: 03 89 57 30 80

🕐 1430-1800

🎟 Pre-arranged only. 8 days notice. In French. 16FF

🛒 Cases, bottles, glasses

🍺 1,000hl (in 1997)

➡ Go through Lutterbach from Mulhouse on the D20. In the centre there is a supermarket (Treff Marché) on the right with a road up the right hand side of it. Take this road and Les Caves is directly in front of you

You will not come across many less likely-looking breweries than Les Caves de la Brasserie in Lutterbach. At first you are confronted by a row of what would euphemistically be described as 'architect-designed' flats, probably dating from the mid-70s. Closer inspection reveals a Restaurant Brasserie sign and coppers in the window but you have to go inside to discover the secret of Les Caves.

These modern flats have been built on what had for a hundred years been the site of Brasserie Lutterbach (a brewery which could trace its origins back to 1648) which had at one time produced 150,000hl per annum. After being taken over and 'rationalised' it closed at the end of 1968 and was demolished in 1971. However, it left a legacy. Under the brewery were extensive corridors and chambers which were used to store 43,000hl of beer. Today the corridors extend back nearly 400 metres, with galleries going off both sides, and have been given a new lease of life – playing host to a modern brewpub.

The first room you enter is modern but well finished and houses the coppers visible from outside which are not just for decoration – they are used by the German brewer, generally on Mondays and Wednesdays. Deeper inside, the restaurant area reveals a room which has a more authentic cellar character and here, behind a glass screen, are the fermenting vessels. Heading toward the toilets you will see the real pièce de résistance – a superb vaulted cellar previously use as a malting floor but now reserved for weddings and parties.

You will need the assistance of the staff to see the old cellars stretching back into the hillside. One gallery off the main corridor has been converted to house the stainless steel beer storage tanks.

The renaissance of brewing in Lutterbach started in June 1994 with a small microbrewery owned by the town. It was not until October 1996 that it was bought by La Société de Restauration Mulhousienne who turned it into what we see today.

The society also owns three other restaurants in the area, at the National Automobile Museum, The French Steam Train Museum, and on top of the Tour de l'Europe. All these are supplied with Lutter'bier Blonde from this brewpub.

All the brewpub's products are unfiltered, unpasteurised and bottom fermented and are brewed using Pilsener malt. All are available in 100cl and 200cl bottles, in 5-litre mini-kegs and on draught.

LA LUTTER'BIER BLONDE

4.8% alc/vol. 100cl, 200cl bottles; 5-litre mini-kegs & draught.

APPEARANCE: More golden brown than blonde.

NOSE: An inviting, fresh hoppy aroma.

PALATE: Very fresh and wonderfully hoppy with a touch of lemon well supported by a slightly sweet creamy pale malt. Moderately bitter.

FINISH: Intensely hoppy, tangy and quite bitter. Very long lasting

OVERALL: A good creamy texture yet still very refreshing, very hoppy blonde beer. Similar to a German pilsner but a little sweeter. The finish grates a little but it is still a satisfying beer.

GENERAL: First brewed 1995.   JW:☑☑☐   KR:☑☑☐

LA LUTTER'BIER NOËL

5.8% alc/vol. 100cl, 200cl bottles; 5-litre mini-kegs & draught.

APPEARANCE: Reddish brown colour.

NOSE: A pleasant mellow darkish malt aroma.

PALATE: Sweet, slightly caramel, malt builds to a more burnt note whilst a slightly bitter hop tries, but does not succeed, to get through.

FINISH: The burnt malt note persists and there is some sweetness but the hops really come to the fore with a long lasting tangy bitterness.

OVERALL: A Christmas beer that displays many of the Blonde's hop characteristics plus the sweetness but with these overpowered by the burnt malt. Could be better balanced.

GENERAL: First brewed 1996.   JW:☑☐☐   KR:☑☐☐

OTHER BEERS BREWED

La Lutter'bier Brune (6% alc/vol.) – First brewed 1995.
La Lutter'bier Fumée (5.6% alc/vol.) – First brewed 1996.
La Lutter'bier Mars (5.6% alc/vol.) – First brewed 1996.
La Lutter'bier Automne (5% alc/vol.).

BARS & CAFES RECOMMENDED BY THE BREWERY

Musée de l'Automobile, 192 avenue de Colmar, 68100 Mulhouse
Musée du Chemin de Fer, 2 rue Alfred de Glehn, 68200 Mulhouse
Restaurant Tour de l'Europe, 3 boulevard de l'Europe, 68100 Mulhouse
Pub le St.Ulrich, 3 place de la République, 68150 Ribeauville

Brasserie Du Cerf

- ✉ 26 bis La Belle Allée, 63460 Combronde
- ☎ 04 73 97 15 03 Fax: 04 73 97 15 03
- 🕐 1400-1800 (but ring in advance if possible). Closed weekends
- 🚹 By appointment only. In French. No charge
- 🛒 Cases, bottles, glasses.
- 🍺 300hl (projected for 1998)
- ➔ Combronde is north of Clermont-Ferrand and is best approached from the A71 motorway and the Riom ring road. Follow signs to Châtelguyon and on to Combronde. In the centre of the town there is a crossroads with traffic lights. Turn right here onto the D223 (signposted St-Myon). 200–300 metres down the road the brewery is on the right hand side (look out for the brown and cream striped doors).

The Auvergne region of France is famous for its extinct volcanoes, one of its highest of which (and possibly the most famous) is the Puy de Dôme which dominates the skyline for miles around. The town of Combronde is some way north of the dramatic volcanic scenery, but the water of the area is celebrated for its purity and mineral content – the source for the bottled Volvic water being very close by.

Brasserie du Cerf (cerf means stag or hart) was started in 1994 by Michel Chalon and Raymond Skrobacz and the operation is run from a large barn which is already becoming more than a little cramped due to a healthy demand for its beer.

As you enter the barn the brewplant is high up on a metal platform to the right, reached by a metal staircase. The brewery likes to brew in large quantities so it can spend more time on the marketing and supply of orders and the 2,000 litre capacity plant is dominated by the huge mash tun which bears testiment to this philosophy. Heat is supplied via an old steam generator.

One of the reasons for the lack of room in the barn is the lengthy production process the beer undergoes – two weeks for the first fermentation, three weeks in garding tanks, then a further month for the refermentation in bottles and kegs.

It hopes to find more outlets for its draught beer which has the advantage of being less labour intensive compared to bottling, but so far it still sells around 70% of the output in bottles.

The local tourist centres promote the brewery as a holiday attraction (the Auvergne is a popular tourist destination) and the brewery prints leaflets for distribution around campsites, etc. The reason it will probably be closed at weekends is so the owners can attend various fairs and shows to sell their beers direct to the public.

Draught Bière des Volcans is very different compared to the bottled version, being distinctly hazy and very, very fruity. The yeast used by the brewery was developed and is regularly supplied by the University of Louvain (Leuven) in Belgium.

LA BIÈRE DES VOLCANS

7% alc/vol. 75cl corked bottles and draught.

DECLARED INGREDIENTS: Belgian hops; French malts.

APPEARANCE: JW: Hazy gold. KR: Cloudy wheat.

NOSE: Intriguing artisanal aroma. JW: A bit farmyardy but light with a suggestion of tartness and a hint of hop. KR: Certain Belgian traits displayed with the addition of a perfumed hop and perhaps coriander. Complex and very inviting.

PALATE: Very sharp in the start with a perfumed, fruity, tart taste which fills the mouth. JW: The fruit is a strong grapefruit. KR: A light coriander note complements the complex citric character.

FINISH: JW: Lingering grapefruit and a little tangy. KR: Lingering sharpness with fleeting herbal notes. Mouthwatering and quenching.

OVERALL: JW: A strongly artisanal, light, tart, refreshing beer with an abundance of grapefruit. KR: Highly original beer which is amazingly full in the mouth yet has a great quenching quality. Commercially though, it may be a little too adventurous for its own good.

GENERAL: First brewed 1995. JW: ☑☐☐ KR: ☑☑☐

VOLCANS XMAS

9% alc/vol. 75cl crown corked bottles.

APPEARANCE: Mid-brown in colour.

NOSE: JW: Intriguing herbal, spicy, fruity, mellow malt. KR: Farmyardy with an understated fruity malt and a light tart note.

PALATE: JW: Strongly spiced mellow fruity malt with a distinct Christmas cake character. A little resiny bitterness lurks behind. KR: Full and deeply interesting but despite a very promising start it stops short in the taste department. It has a rich, Christmasy character with a dried fruit taste but stops tantalisingly short of being satisfying.

FINISH: JW: Dry and spicy, fruity, a touch resiny and a little herbal. KR: Rich and quite warming but in comparison to the fullness of the palate a little disappointing.

OVERALL: JW: Pleasantly complex, full but mellow fruity malt with bags of spice makes this most definitely a beer in the real Christmas spirit. KR: Mightily impressive palate is a big surprise after the nose but let down by the understated, short-lived finish. Great depth of character with a tart edge to the dried fruit and a warming glow in the palate that really needs to be carried over to the finish.

JW: ☑☑☑ KR: ☑☑☐

La Cervoiserie (Chez Nino)

- ✉ 50 rue Trachel, 06000 Nice
- ☎ 04 93 88 07 71
- ⏱ 1200-1400 and 1800-0030. Closed Sundays/Bank Holidays
- 🏨 45hl (in 1997)
- ➡ Close to Gare Nice Ville. Go past the station, keeping it to your left and turn left at the T-junction at the end of the road. The first proper road on the left is Rue Trachel. Park at the first opportunity. The bar is on the right-hand side at the far end of the street

There are many claims to the title 'France's smallest brewery' but in terms of actual size of the brewkit, it must go to La Cervoiserie. The entire operation takes place within the serving counter (even the conditioning). The first brew was made in December 1995.

The bar is owned and run by Ernest Pohl, a long-time beer enthusiast known to his friends as Nino, and his wife Nicole in a busy back street in central Nice. Small and cosy inside, it has a bistro atmosphere and many customers go there to sample Nicole's reasonably-priced meals, one of which will usually be a beer cuisine dish.

Ernest is truly passionate about brewing and just loves to make beer, although he never makes the same brew twice. With such a tiny brew capacity any particular beer is never around for very long, which makes his type of operation a problem for a book of this type. On our visit he was serving a very impressive, spicily-complex blonde ale, but he had a brune made with a champagne yeast (which he hoped would come out at around 15%!) in the next conditioning tank. He uses all types of yeast – ale, blanche, wine and champagne – and varies just about every aspect of a recipe. He revels in the fact that many of his locals come in to drink without having a clue what type or strength of beer he is serving that day.

There is only ever one of his brews being served at any time, but with three conditioning tanks he manages to maintain a constant supply to keep up with demand. He is happy to admit that he has the occasional failure, mainly due to the fact that a small bar is not the ideal brewing environment. He has no qualms about throwing bad beer away as he wants to keep his reputation as a quality brewer.

In addition to the beer he makes, the brewpub has a well-chosen list of around 80 beers, though mostly Belgian.

Brasserie des Champs

- ✉ 8 rue de la Vossière, 89100 Collemiers
- ☎ 03 86 65 19 89   Fax: 03 86 65 12 15
- ◷ Mon-Fri: 0900-1800. Sat: 1400-1800
- Always available when open. In French. No charge
- Cases, bottles and glasses
- 300hl (in 1997)
- → From Sens take the N60 in the direction of Montargis. Just over 5km after crossing the river Yonne, there is a turn-off to the left just before entering the village of Subligny, marked Collemiers. The brewery is signposted.

In the far north of the region of Bourgogne (Burgundy) lies the town of Sens, dominated by its true gothic cathedral on which work commenced in the mid-12th century. Among its famous medieval and renaissance stained-glass windows is one depicting the murder of Thomas à Becket, Archbishop of Canterbury, who had been in exile in Sens from 1166 and 1170.

The reason for this history lesson is to explain the otherwise odd theme of the beer made at the fledgling Brasserie des Champs ('the brewery of the fields') which is found in the sleepy village of Collemiers, a few kilometres south-west of the town. With the French penchant for having patron saints for everything, the brewery believes it very appropriate to name its sole product after an English archbishop who, it states, was the first patron saint of brewers in England and founded the first brewers' guilds.

Though Burgundy is well-known for its wine, it is virtually all made south of Dijon, but the Sens area has had its fair share of breweries in the last couple of centuries – the last one closing down after the Second World War. This new venture opened its doors in November 1996 and is based in a low-level unit in a farming village.

Walking into the reception area, there is a counter where you can partake in a little 'dégustation'. In this large, open-plan room, which makes up the major part of the unit are its numerous fermenters, along with the bottling plant and box-loads of bottles awaiting despatch. It looked a little cramped, and we were told that an extension was being planned. The mash tun and kettle are in another room at the rear of this main section and are both attractive brick-surrounded affairs. Behind this is the office and laboratory equipment.

One of the brewery's claims to fame is that the brewing is done by what we were assured was France's only female 'maître brasseur' (and certainly the only one we have come across), 27-year-old Valérie Gufflet. On our visit, Valérie was on maternity leave which meant that owner Olivier Vanackere had the onerous task of brewing as well as marketing and making deliveries.

Much of the brewplant was the original equipment which Brasserie Lancelot used when it first opened in Brittany, but which it has since outgrown. Coincidentally, Brasserie des Champs also uses the same process as Lancelot in using honey in the bottle refermentation.

It takes the marketing side of the operation very seriously and has spent its money wisely on promoting just the one beer with gusto, rather than rushing into any expansion of its range. It is perhaps surprising that a consistent beer with such a strong identity is not more widely available in speciality beer bars, though with the brewery looking to a wider distribution arrangement, this may change in the near future.

A new beer **Blonde de Bourgogne** was launched in 1998. Another beer product on sale is the 'confiture à la bière' (beer jam), experimental samples of which we bought were very impressive.

THOMAS BECKET

6.5% alc/vol. 33cl crown corked & 75cl corked bottles and draught.

BREW DETAILS: Unfiltered. Unpasteurised. Top fermentation. Bottle refermentation.

DECLARED INGREDIENTS: Not disclosed but honey is used in the bottle refermentation.

APPEARANCE: Rich dark amber colour.

NOSE: Fairly full, aromatic, fruity, crystal malt. JW: A slight nuttiness. KR: Very rich and quite warming promise. A little chicory (vegetable) note with a tired edge, especially as it ages.

PALATE: Full and rich, strong distinctive malt with a little fruit. JW: Grows tangy towards the end and has a distinct sweetish honey element. KR: Very full and rich crystal malt. Some apple skin notes in the background.

FINISH: JW: A bit cloying with a lasting fruity malt and a honeyed tang. KR: Rich and malty with a fleeting honey sweetness. Full and fruity.

OVERALL: A strongly malty beer with plenty of full, fruity, crystal malt and a surprisingly strong honeyed taste. The malt is clean, nutty, fruity and characterful. KR: A good solid beer which will probably go down well with British ale drinkers, but is unfortunately one which has an understated character.

GENERAL: First brewed 1997. The brewery recommends drinking without the sediment, at 8–12°C.   JW: ☑☐☐   KR: ☑☐☐

BARS & CAFES RECOMMENDED BY THE BREWERY

Café de la Gare, place de la Gare, 89100 Sens

Brasserie du Chant du Loup

- ✉ 19 route de Duclair, 76380 Canteleu-Rouen B.P. 87
- ☎ 02 35 36 37 44   Fax: 02 32 83 02 04
- 🕐 Evenings & weekends.
- ⚔ Pre-arranged only. 8 days notice
- ⬛ Cases or bottles
- 🛢 300hl (in 1996)
- ➔ On the D982 between Montigny and Rouen in the small town of Canteleu. From Rouen the brewery is on the left hand side of the main road, where you will see a sign outside a house.

The village of Canteleu, just west of the major city of Rouen, was once known popularly as Chant du Loup (literally 'song of the wolf' or 'wolf howl') and was the name chosen by Patrick Expert when he started brewing commercially in 1988.

The area south of Canteleu is dominated by forests and the deep-cut valley of the meandering River Seine. An alternative approach to the brewery is from the south where you can cross by ferry at La Bouille and travel up the peninsula of one of the Seine's more severe bends through the Forêt de Roumare and turn left onto the D982 where you will find the brewery 100 yards away on the left-hand side. This will give you some idea of what the region was like when it was in the heart of a vast forest, centuries before Rouen's rich started buying property here to escape the city heat in the summer. The names of Patrick's beer range evoke images of the area's wild and dark past.

Patrick once owned a bar nearby, but had never even hobby-brewed. When he decided to take up brewing he went to England to be trained by the Wye Valley Brewery, Hereford, UK. This was essentially to be taught how British real ale is made, but Patrick has adapted his process to make some very original beers. Although others have worked for him at the brewery, he has now made it a family affair with just his wife and daughters helping.

The operation is run from a barn adjoining his house, and the first room you walk into serves as the shop, tasting room and bottle store. At the back is a small room housing a colossal, industrial grist mill which Patrick doesn't use anymore as he now buys his grain ready-milled. To the right of this is a door leading to the brewery itself where he has crammed in a 20 hectolitre capacity brewplant. Most of the equipment was originally used by breweries in the UK, like the stainless steel mash tun and the open brew kettle. On the other side of the room is a fermenter and some garding tanks – he would like to garde it for longer than the current 1–2 weeks but his turnover and lack of space won't permit such a luxury at present. The majority of the equipment is very tall which helps in the limited amount of space available but means he has to work much of the time on a ladder.

Aspects of Patrick's production process go some way to explaining the unique character of his beers. He uses a lager yeast in an open fermenter, and he bottles his beers while they are still actually fermenting, hence doing away with the need to prime the bottles to referment for a good conditioning. All his beers have 10% malted wheat in the mash for head retention and he only uses new bottles, which are bought from the Castelain brewery, as is his yeast which he changes about three times a year.

Patrick recently bought new premises next door (towards Rouen) which were going through the process of being converted on our visit. There is a shop with road frontage, and behind is a series of beautiful, half-timbered, traditional Normandy outbuildings which will make a very characterful brewhouse and tasting room. There will probably be some new brewplant so he can let gravity do more work than it currently does and there will be more garding tanks. The shop will be used as a brewery tap and restaurant. Patrick hopes this new facility will be up and running some time in 1998.

Patrick brews once a fortnight and sells mainly from the brewery, though he has done well to have his beers stocked by Carrefour, Continent and Leclerc supermarkets. Also, he has a trade deal where beers are relabelled and sold as **Calètes Blonde** (Lupus Ale), **Calètes Cervoise**, **Calètes Rousse** (Viking Wolf), **Calètes Brune** (Loup-Garou).

Of the tasting samples we bought at the brewery, there may well have been production problems with the Cervoise Lupulix and Lupus Noël – so we would advise readers to make their own judgements from samples they can find.

CERVOISE LUPULIX

6.5% alc/vol. 75cl corked bottles.

BREW DETAILS: Unfiltered. Unpasteurised.

DECLARED INGREDIENTS: Honey and six herbs.

APPEARANCE: Honey gold in colour.

NOSE: JW: Tart, earthy hop and some musty fruit. KR: Very earthy and yeasty with a tart promise. Quite sulphuric.

PALATE: Very fruity. JW: Orchard fruit with an acidic, musty element. KR: Tart fruity tang with an underlying sweetness, quite sticky and honeyish. Very fruity and a little bitter.

FINISH: JW: Cloying, tangy bitter fruit. KR: Mouthwateringly acidic with some leftover sweet honey, turning more bitter.

OVERALL: Odd, with suspicions of an infection, but drinkable. Through the strongly tart, farmyardy elements you can taste a sweet honey beer with a very artisanal quality. KR: I have sampled this beer in bars where it was very different from our tastings, making us believe the batch we bought as samples was infected. Like the Lupus Noël, we would ask readers to try it for themselves.

GENERAL: First brewed 1991.   JW:☐☐☐   KR:☐☐☐

LOUP-GAROU

6.5% alc/vol.   75cl & 150cl corked bottles.

BREW DETAILS: Unfiltered. Unpasteurised.

APPEARANCE: Light red brown with a ridiculously large head.

NOSE: Fruity. A slightly tart red fruit with occasional musty sour notes. KR: Rich and fruity with blood orange hints.

PALATE: Intensely bitter fruit (almost tangy) which masks a background tartness. There is an unexpected roast/burnt element which adds to the complexity. A full palate. JW: Red fruit and a little caramel.

FINISH: Very long lingering intense distinctive bitterness which is a little astringent and has a slight burnt character. KR: A surprisingly stout-like finish.

OVERALL: A distinctive, intense bitterness overpowers a tart fruity base. Although the brewery describes it as a Brune it is far from a traditional French Brune style. It is surprisingly light yet displays many characteristics of a stout. If you dislike bitter beers this is one best avoided.

GENERAL: First brewed 1989. Loup Garou translates literally as 'werewolf', hence the bizarre 4-eyed wolf label.

JW:☑☐☐   KR:☑☑☐

LUPUS ALE

6.5% alc/vol.   75cl corked bottles.

BREW DETAILS: Unfiltered. Unpasteurised.

DECLARED INGREDIENTS: East Kent Goldings hops; Pale and Lager malts.

APPEARANCE: Golden with a large head and nice lacework.

NOSE: Pleasant, fairly strong hop with a touch of pale malt. JW: A yeasty tartness.

PALATE: Strong resiny hop bite and accompanying bitterness with some pale malt behind. Some tangy honey-like sweetness. Fairly complex array of hop-induced tastes with a touch of tartness lying behind and filling out the taste.

FINISH: A long hoppy, resiny bitterness with a tart edge. KR: Some honeyed notes.

OVERALL: A multitude of unusual hop-induced tastes plus a slight tartness make this quite a complex beer. KR: Deep and interesting with many flavours running through it.

GENERAL: First brewed 1988.   JW:☑☐☐   KR:☑☑☐

LUPUS NOËL

7.5% alc/vol. 75cl corked bottles.

BREW DETAILS: Unfiltered. Unpasteurised.

DECLARED INGREDIENTS: Goldings and Target hops; Pale and Lager malts.

APPEARANCE: Orange amber colour with a large rocky head and excellent lacework.

NOSE: An earthy, musty yeast that gives a farmyardy aroma and a tart promise before eventually developing into an acidic fruitiness. KR: A little sulphuric.

PALATE: A strong resiny hop is to the fore but there is a rich fruitiness behind which is both lightly acidic and fruitily tart. There is a multi-layered promise of complexity but the very green hop comes out on top. KR: The initiated palate would give up here.

FINISH: A light fruity taste does not quite break through the green hop which tries to impart bitterness but settles for a very resiny tang and a distinctly tart astringency. Many fleeting tastes and suggestions throughout.

OVERALL: A very difficult beer to get to grips with. There seems to be a good beer trying to escape many infection-like traits which makes us want to know if it really is supposed to taste like this. Simply too acidic with too many farmyard notes for most drinkers to endure.

GENERAL: First brewed 1996.   JW:☐☐☐   KR:☐☐☐

VIKING WOLF

8% alc/vol. 75cl corked bottles.

BREW DETAILS: Unfiltered. Unpasteurised.

DECLARED INGREDIENTS: Target hops; Pale, Crystal and Lager malts.

APPEARANCE: Red brown in colour with a ridiculously large head.

NOSE: A heady floral hop and an abundance of red fruit. JW: A light mustiness lets it down. KR: A tart promise.

PALATE: Intensely bitter from the first mouthful with the fruity bitterness hiding quite a full crystal malt character. JW: A slight tart edge seems to be imparted by the hops. KR: An annoying crystal malt tang is accentuated by the tart fruit.

FINISH: A bitter, fruity tang lasts for ages. JW: Strong, resiny and a little almondy. KR: Some noticeable alcohol warmth.

OVERALL: An interesting beer with an elusive complexity. Many subtle elements are masked by the intense fruity bitterness. The tendency to tartness also detracts a little. Probably at its best very young.

GENERAL: First brewed 1990. Previously known as Rousse, but the name was changed to avoid conflict with the George Killian's product despite it defying any comparison.   JW:☐☐☐   KR:☑☐☐

Café Le Chantecler

- ✉ 151 Boulevard de la Croix Rousse, 69004 Lyon
- ☎ 04 78 28 13 69 Fax: 04 78 28 45 26
- 🕐 Mon-Sat: 0730-0100. Sun: 0730-2100
- 🍴 Small groups or individuals. Ask at bar at quiet times
- 🍺 Beer available on draught only at brewpub
- 📊 350hl (predicted for 1998)
- ➡ In Lyon's 4th arrondisement in an area known as La Croix Rousse (cafe is a short walk west from Métro La Croix Rousse).

The sprawling, lively city of Lyon is home to Café Le Chantecler, the first of the city's brewpubs, which was opened by Raymond Rushforth and his partner in June 1994. The area of La Croix Rousse is in an elevated position on top of a hill on the western side of the Rhône, under which a major road runs through the Tunnel de la Croix Rousse to link the Rhône and Saône valleys.

It is a very attractive bar, set back from the road with a large sun terrace in front and a conservatory structure to the front and side. Its 8hl brewplant can be seen from the exterior as well as through glass panels in the bar, and was installed by Brewery Design Services from Tring, UK, who also stayed on to develop the adventurous beer range.

Raymond is from Bradford, UK, but has lived in France since around 1975, earning his keep originally by teaching English as a foreign language in university. Since then he went into the bar business and previously ran an English pub called The Albion in Lyon for ten years. An occasional hobby brewer in the past, he was keen to run a brewpub and finally realised his dream soon after taking on Le Chantecler with the same partner he had at The Albion.

There are three regular beers on sale – **Rushforth Blonde** (a 5.4% alc/vol. bière blonde), **Rushforth Rousse** (a 6.4% alc/vol. beer in the rousse style) and **Rushforth Bitter** (4.5% and served on handpump). At any one time there may well be a seasonal beer as well – **Bière de Printemps** (strength varies, served in spring), **Bière Blanche** (a 5.5% alc/vol. Belgian-style blanche made with 30% wheat and spiced with coriander and curaçao, served in summer) and **Winter Warmer** (a 7% alc/vol. porter-style beer). In autumn 1998 Raymond is planning to brew a beer made with chestnut flour from Corsica. Occasionally one-off brews are made for special occasions, such as a Vienna-style lager made for a Viennese festival in Lyon.

The beers undergo a 4–5 day primary fermentation at 20.5°C, followed by around one week's garde in the twelve 40-litre tanks under the bar in the chambre froid at 0°C, and are carbonated prior to being pumped straight from the tank to the bar. The bitter is fined and is kept in the tank under blanket pressure.

Brewing takes place on average every six days, so the brewing day varies each week. Raymond likes people to express an interest in the beer and he will give a short tour to small groups at quiet times.

The city seems to have something of a brewpub culture, with the Ninkasi Ale House opening in August 1997 and another, the Barrel House Irish Pub, which has only recently ceased brewing.

A word of warning. We took the short-cut by foot up a road tunnel from the Palais de la Bière in rue Therme in the city centre to La Croix Rousse. Don't be tempted – it is officially prohibited, potentially dangerous and hard work. Take a cab or use the métro.

Brasserie La Choulette

✉ 16 rue des Écoles, 59111 Hordain

☎ 03 27 35 72 44   Fax: 03 27 25 34 12

🕘 Mon-Fri: 0900-1200, 1400-1700. Sat: 0900-1200

👥 By appointment only (3 weeks notice). In French. 15FF

🏪 Cases, bottles and glasses

📊 4,000hl (projected for 1998)

➡ The brewery is signposted in the village of Hordain

The beers of Brasserie La Choulette have been at the forefront of the bière de garde revival in Nord/Pas-de-Calais for many years. Its success can be measured by the fact that it entertains 2,000–3,000 visitors per year and that its beers are so easily obtainable in most of the major hypermarket chains throughout northern France.

Hordain is a rural community amidst the heavily industrialised mining area of Pas-de-Calais and the brewery building was a farm before becoming Brasserie Bourgeois-Lecerf. It is now fronted by Alain Dhaussy, who bought the business in 1977 and made his first La Choulette beer in 1981. The brewery changed its name to La Choulette (after the ball used in a strange, almost defunct, regional game bearing more than a passing resemblance to golf) in 1986.

In 1983 it introduced Bière des Sans Culottes which, though often amusingly referred to as 'Beer Without Trousers', takes its name from the term for the 'pantalon'-wearing Revolutionaries of 1789 (setting them aside from the 'culotte'-wearing ruling class), a concept taken further by the Republican Guard whose brightly-striped legwear is depicted on the label. The theme continued with a 7.5% alc/vol. special brew of Sans Culottes in 1989 for the bicentennial of the Revolution (though it may also reappear occasionally), called **Brassin Robespierre** after one of the leading figures of the First Republic.

Choulette also brews for the contract market, producing a beer called Abbaye de Vaucelles for an organisation restoring the abbey buildings. Beers are also relabelled for a drinks distributor, La Rondelle, which operates in Senozan in the Burgundy region.

All the brewery's products are filtered, unpasteurised and undergo a top fermentation. The maximum capacity for a single brew is 100hl, but it usually brews 60–70hl at a time. It uses a specially-developed yeast which works well at a temperature of 15–18°C. The fermentation takes 5–8 days after which the beers undergo a 3–6 week garde.

There is a small but interesting museum housed beneath the bar/tasting room which contains many old bottle washers, filtration equipment, etc., along with explanatory notes (in French).

We found that, of all the bières de garde, the Choulette range really do need to be drunk as young as possible – thereby avoiding the strong and rich maltiness which develops within a year of brewing.

ABBAYE DE VAUCELLES

7.5% alc/vol. 75cl corked bottles.

DECLARED INGREDIENTS: Flanders & Hallertau hops; Pale malt.

APPEARANCE: Bright honey gold.

NOSE: Hops dominate but it is slightly citric and a little musty and yeasty. Behind this is a light fruit. KR: A tart fruit promise.

PALATE: Dry and bitter with a strong, tangy and distinctly resiny hop and an ageing fruity malt. JW: A sharp alcohol edge. KR: A touch citric.

FINISH: A few richer, vinous elements liven up a moderately dry, bitter fruit that lingers on and on. KR: Lingering alcohol notes.

OVERALL: Rich, fruity and distinctly bitter bière de garde character but lacking that 'something' needed to lift it above the others.

GENERAL: First brewed 1990.   JW:☑☐☐   KR:☑☐☐

BIÈRE DES SANS CULOTTES

7% alc/vol. 25cl, 33cl crown corked & 75cl corked bottles.

DECLARED INGREDIENTS: Flanders & Hallertau hops; Pale malt.

APPEARANCE: Good, rich gold.

NOSE: Rich and fruity, almost fresh fruit, malt with a winey note. A gently resiny hop lurks in the background and some alcohol notes add to the deeply warming fruity promise. KR: Some apple hints. Very inviting and rich.

PALATE: Very full and quite sweet fruity maltiness. A warming alcohol develops with age. Bags of intriguing earthy malt and a sharp bitterness that helps counteract the sweetness. Distinctly honeyed. With age the fruity malt gets more tangy.

FINISH: A very full and interesting finish. Warming with a strong oily bitterness which almost masks the fruity malt. With age it becomes predominantly a tangy malt.

OVERALL: Has good depth which marks it out as something a little different. A wineyness develops and increases with age as the rest of the palate mellows. JW: For me, the bittersweet earthiness prevents it being a great beer. KR: Multi-layered with an admirably full taste – but drink it young if possible.

GENERAL: First brewed 1983.   JW:☑☑☐   KR:☑☑☑

LA CHOULETTE AMBRÉE

7.5% alc/vol. 25cl, 33cl crown corked, 75cl corked bottles & draught.

DECLARED INGREDIENTS: Flanders & Hallertau hops; Pale & special malts.

APPEARANCE: Rich honey amber in colour.

NOSE: Rich and fruity pale malt with a suggestion of honey. JW: Distinctly earthy, with a hop-soaked malt. KR: Hoppy hints are masked by a rich, jam-like, quite honeyed note. Promises a tangy fruit.

PALATE: Full mouth with lots of rich and tangy malt with a moderately bitter hop. Interestingly bittersweet with some red fruit and a little tartness. KR: Almost honeyed qualities.

FINISH: Bittersweet and a little cloying. JW: Mouthwatering from a citric tartness. KR: Rich, quite sticky fruit lifted by a light hoppiness.

OVERALL: Interesting very full taste that can get a bit much on the second glass.

GENERAL: First brewed 1981.

LA CHOULETTE BIÈRE DE MARS

5.8% alc/vol. 75cl crown corked bottles.

BREW DETAILS: Filtered. Unpasteurised. Top fermentation.

DECLARED INGREDIENTS: Flanders & Hallertau hops; Pale & Vienna malts.

APPEARANCE: Amber in colour.

NOSE: A deep and full, strong, figgy, fruity, hop aroma. JW: An interestingly hoppy malt. KR: A tangy promise with some chicory hints.

PALATE: A full, rich, fig and date fruiti-ness with an underlying candied sweet-ness and plenty of resiny hop bitterness. KR: Some red fruit and appley notes with suggestions of honey. Some sugariness.

FINISH: Fruity with a strong tangy bitterness. KR: Sticky bittersweet fruitiness with just a little hop bitterness

OVERALL: A beer with a very strong fruity character and perhaps a little too sweet and 'sticky' for its own good. This is to a certain extent offset by the resiny hops. Very definitely a different Bière de Mars and one that has to be admired. We think it will probably become difficult to drink as it gets older.

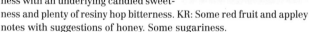

LA CHOULETTE BIÈRE DE NOËL

7% alc/vol. 25 cl crown corked & 75cl bottles and draught.

DECLARED INGREDIENTS: Flanders & Hallertau hops; Pale & special malts.

APPEARANCE: Ruddy amber in colour.

NOSE: Deeply fruity and malty with a pronounced dry promise. JW: Some gentle hoppiness.

PALATE: Lighter and less fruity than the nose suggests. A full, tangy, fruity malt with pleasant layers of interest and a little alcohol warmth. JW: Moderately bitter from a noticeable hop element.

FINISH: Dry and bitter with a warming, tangy fruit.

OVERALL: Interesting, distinctly fruity and malty bière de garde which is barely different enough to merit the Noël tag.

JW:☑☐☐   KR:☑☐☐

LA CHOULETTE BLONDE

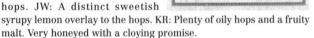

7.5% alc/vol. 25cl, 33cl crown corked, 75cl corked bottles & draught.

DECLARED INGREDIENTS: Flanders & Hallertau hops; Pale malt.

APPEARANCE: Golden honey in colour.

NOSE: Sweet, rich, pale malt and hops. JW: A distinct sweetish syrupy lemon overlay to the hops. KR: Plenty of oily hops and a fruity malt. Very honeyed with a cloying promise.

PALATE: A slightly barley wine character underlines the sweetish, very full, fruity, pale malt that has a slight harsh bitter edge to it. JW: A slight honeyed character with a citric zing on the tongue. Some alcohol notes. KR: Very bitter full mouth of taste. Very honeyed with a sappy character.

FINISH: Very long lasting bittersweet fruity tang. JW: A little citric acidity keeps the mouth on edge. Some alcohol warmth. KR: Very full and multi-layered with bitter honey and some sweet undertones.

OVERALL: A unique and unusual taste highlights the depth and character which has a surprisingly honeyed element. However, it is very thick and rich, making it difficult to drink too much due to the strong taste, and particularly the finish, becoming a little too intense.

GENERAL: First brewed 1991. Much, much better drunk young.

JW:☑☐☐   KR:☑☑☐

LA CHOULETTE FRAMBOISE

7% alc/vol. 25cl, 33cl crown corked & 75cl corked bottles and draught.

DECLARED INGREDIENTS: Hallertau hops; Pale malt; Raspberry juice.

APPEARANCE: Deep cherry brown.

NOSE: Strong raspberry aroma over a fruity malty base. JW: Raspberries give a thick syrupy impression with suggestions of almonds. KR: Interesting and deeply rich.

PALATE: Initially surprising, but actually very pleasant, sharpness and astringency which verges on sourness. Has a good fruity brown malt base with many wafts of taste including a tangy, sharp, hop edge. Not nearly as sweet as the nose suggests.

FINISH: Gently astringent with lingering sharp, sourish red fruit, mostly raspberries and cherries.

OVERALL: Very impressive ale that is far better than the nose suggests. Some Belgian Flemish brown characteristics at the base with a good acidic fruitiness on top. Nice texture.

JW: ☑☑☐   KR: ☑☐☐

LA TOUR D'OSTREVANT

8.3% alc/vol.   75cl corked bottles.

DECLARED INGREDIENTS: Flanders & Hallertau hops; Pale malt.

APPEARANCE: Bright honey gold with a good fluffy head.

NOSE: A gentle complexity is evident in the enticing fresh berry fruit and slightly flowery hop. KR: A little wheaty and honeyed with a sticky promise.

PALATE: Begins sweet but oodles of fruity malt break through. A strong resiny hop edge generates a fair degree of bitterness which grows into the finish though stops short of the expected resinous tang. Throughout it all there is a strong alcohol warmth and distinct honeyed tang over a half-hidden hop character.

FINISH: Complex and warming with many layers of taste around a bitter fruity malt and an equally bitter hoppiness. There is also a lingering honey tang.

OVERALL: A very full fruity malt taste and a distinct honey tang do not overcome the strong hop character that is surprisingly evident only in the resiny bitterness. Unusually for a blonde beer it is rewarding as a late evening relaxer.

GENERAL: First brewed 1996.

JW: ☑☑☐   KR: ☑☑☐

OTHER BEERS BREWED

Bürgersbier (5% alc/vol.) – A pretty uninspiring beer displaying a distinctly sweet pale malt barely balanced by a bland hop. Presumably made to compete in the cheaper beer market and not meant to be a premium brand.

La Gambière (7% alc/vol.) – A reddish/amber-coloured beer which displays a strong crystal malt note on the nose. The palate gives a strong tangy maltiness, an alcohol glow and some apple notes. Somewhat disappointing in the finish with a tired fruity malt and hoppy bitterness. Overall a reasonable beer with a good helping of hops helping to balance the strong crystal malt element.

The brewery also produces (or most probably relabels despite the claim on the labels to be 'sur lie') the following beers for distribution company La Rondelle in Senozan: **La Rondelle** (a blonde), **La Ronboise** (a raspberry beer) and **La Giboulée** (a bière de mars translating as 'April Showers').

For the Musée de la Bière in Stenay, it produces **Bière de Stenay** (very reminiscent of La Choulette Ambrée) and **Stenay Blonde** (which has a very similar character to La Choulette Blonde).

Brasserie De Clerck

- ✉ 42 rue Georges-Clémenceau, 80200 Péronne
- ☎ 03 22 84 30 94 Fax: 03 22 84 26 77
- 🕐 Mon-Fri: 0800-1200 & 1330-1700
- 🏨 Pre-arranged only. 28 days notice. In French & English. 10FF
- 🏪 Cases, bottles, glasses
- ⛟ 5,000hl (in 1997)
- ➔ Entering Péronne from St-Quentin, take any of the roads to the right. Rue Georges Clemenceau runs parallel with the main road. Alternatively, turn right at the traffic lights after the school then first right, the brewery is on the right after about 50 metres.

Although there is a history of brewing in the family going back to before the French revolution, 1774 to be precise, Brasserie De Clerck was not started until 1928. That was when Pierre and Gabriel De Clerck, two brothers, who were farmer brewers in the tiny village of Hondeghem just north of Hazebrouck sold the family farm in order to buy the current premises in Péronne. This had originally been a small local brewery and in 1928 only the large square building in the centre of the site existed. This included a small maltery upstairs and the very distinctive turret on top of it, which has become something of a local landmark. The brewing kit was considered too small so the brothers installed new boilers and fermentation vessels. All the buildings are a mixture of brick and concrete construction, though the administration office is currently in a portacabin in the yard. In 1932, Gabriel moved back near to Hazebrouck and bought another brewery so the De Clerck operation was run from two sites. It continued to operate from both breweries until 1985, nine years after Pierre died, when the Hazebrouck brewery, which had employed 50 people, was closed. The Péronne brewery had 38 employees at that time, down from its peak of 60 but far in excess of its current nine.

A lot of the business had originally been direct deliveries to outlying villages and properties, mostly with table beer. This still goes on to a certain extent with three or four trucks doing these runs but it is very much a dying service.

The brewery is now run by Michel, son of Gabriel, and his wife

Eliane. In the mid 1980s Michel had been considering the market for beer in general and theirs particularly and had decided that the best approach would be to brew artisanal beers, hence the creation of a new range which started with Colvert in 1988. The presentation of the beers, particularly the names and labels, is aimed at evoking visions of Picardie and rural life. Colvert and La Fanette benefit from two months fermentation. Twelve days primary and then seven weeks in storage vessels during which it continues to develop as a little yeast remains. Given the character of these beers it is surprising to discover that they are all bottom fermented.

La Belle Siska has a different rationale behind the name as it is intended to evoke memories of the Flemish origin of the De Clerck family rather than their current association with Picardie. Siska is the Flemish version of the French name Françoise.

In summer 1998, De Clerck introduced a new beer which was too late to be included in detail in this book. It is a white beer called **Bière Blanche de Péronne** and comes out at 4.1% alc/vol. It is a naturally cloudy beer available in 75cl bottles.

LA BELLE SISKA

7.2% alc/vol. 25cl crown corked & 75cl corked bottles.

APPEARANCE: Rich ruddy amber colour.

NOSE: JW: Rich fruity malt with a pungent hop just trying to get through. KR: Heady hoppiness at first then a strong fruity crystal malt, but ultimately quite dull.

PALATE: JW: Full fruity hoppy palate. A little red berry character to the fruit. An abundance of hop adds an extra element and plenty of depth. Bittersweet with a slight sharpness to the fruit. A touch tangy and very fruity. KR: Very sweet and red fruity with a typical red fruit sharpness. One dimensional fruity malt. Sharpness is subdued and separate from the sweet fruit.

FINISH: Lingering fruitiness. JW: Lots of berry and currant fruits with a gently tangy hop. KR: A citric sharpness comes through with a touch of red fruit.

OVERALL: JW: Immensely fruity beer with loads of berries and currants plus some full hop giving it depth. There is a slight tart edge to the fruit that further adds to the depth. Very satisfying. KR: A little over-sweet which unfortunately overpowers the other elements.

GENERAL: Try to drink as young an example as you can find, as the fruit dies away with age, leaving rich maltiness as the dominant character. Also labelled as **Pot Flamand** for the Flemish market and as **Reserve du Caveau** for a distributor.   JW: ☑☑☐ KR: ☑☑☐

BIÈRE DU PAYS DE SOMME

5% alc/vol. 25cl crown corked bottles.

APPEARANCE: JW: Light gold with a massive frothy head.

NOSE: Interesting light and artisanal green flowery hop aroma. Very like a Belgian Saison – very hoppy but with plenty of light orchard fruit and a spicy promise.

PALATE: A very light pale malt with an interesting hoppiness. JW: A spritzy character that threatens a tartness but never quite delivers. KR: Sweet quite sharply tart, lightly fruity but very, very full.

FINISH: Bittersweet light fruit with a gently dry citric hoppy bitterness.

OVERALL: Light, interesting and characterful beer very much like some of the saison beers from Wallonia. Fairly complex artisanal character with a good hoppiness. JW: A tartness is suggested but not actually there. KR: A cracking summer quaffer despite the intrusive fizz and tartness.

JW: ☑☑☐   KR: ☑☑☐

COLVERT

7% alc/vol. 25cl, 33cl crown corked & 75cl corked bottles.

APPEARANCE: Rich light golden colour.

NOSE: A light but fresh, pleasantly earthy hop aroma with a little sweetish pale malt supporting it. KR: Gives a sweet fruity promise with an apple touch.

PALATE: Full, sweet pale malt with a pleasant fruitiness. Fresh and lightly bitter, lightly lemony and satisfyingly refreshing. The pale malt develops with age but the hops and lemon are still there. Freshness reduces with age and the pale malt becomes more fruity and pronounced. A real mouthful of taste with multi-dimensional interest.

FINISH: Gently bitter light lemony hoppiness with a lingering fruitiness. As it ages the pale malt becomes stronger but there is still lemon and hops.

OVERALL: Excellent multi-dimensional beer which has a great depth and an unusual but very impressive balance – sweet, sharp and quite bitter. Pleasantly refreshing, lemony, light and hoppy with a gentle bitterness and a satisfying pale malt element that also contributes some sweetness.

GENERAL: First brewed in 1988. Colvert is French for Mallard.

JW: ☑☑☑   KR: ☑☑☐

LA FANETTE

6% alc/vol. 25cl crown corked and 75cl corked bottles.

APPEARANCE: Bright rich honey gold with a big rocky head and beautiful lacework.

NOSE: Exquisitely inviting artisanal aroma with oodles of fresh, earthy, slightly green, hop. A touch sweet yet also promising a sharpness. Behind all this is a mellow fruitiness. KR: Occasional wafts of tart red fruit.

PALATE: Wonderfully full tasting yet light and refreshing. Bags of citric hop, very lemony with a sharp lemon bite. Interestingly grainy once you get through the citric element. A few sweet notes are thrown in but do not really counter the lemon sharpness which makes it very refreshing. KR: Fizz burn almost masks the palate.

FINISH: Mouthdrying yet despite this, very satisfying and quenching with a lingering lemony acidity. Fairly subdued after the palate. KR: Lashings of leftover lemon and red fruit.

OVERALL: If you are looking for a satisfying and interesting thirst quencher there are few better than this gorgeously artisanal beer. This is supremely quenching with its very strong citric character well to the fore. However, if you look, there is plenty more going on including an interestingly grainy base, other (non-citric) hop characteristics and the odd sweet note can be found. It is only marred by the excessive fizz. It adds to the spritzy nature of the beer but makes it frothy in the mouth. Although no aged Fanettes have been sampled we expect the citric element will be overtaken by the malt after a while – these notes refer to a very young version from the brewery.

GENERAL: First brewed 1990. Faneur (or the female faneuse) translates into English as Haymaker, so logically a Fanette is a young, female haymaker.

JW: ☑☑☑   KR: ☑☑☑

BARS & CAFES RECOMMENDED BY THE BREWERY

HISTORIAL DE PÉRONNE, 80200 Péronne

LE MONIA, 2 rue Pasteur, 60870 Villers St-Paul

LES BONS ENFANTS, 23 rue d'Arras, 80600 Doullens

HOSTELLERIE DE BELLOY, 29 route Nationale, 80310 Belloy sur Somme

LE XVIème SIÈCLE, 53 rue Motte, 80000 Amiens

HET BLAÜWERSHÖF, 9 rue d'Eecke, 59270 Godewaersvelde

L'AUBERGE PICARDIE, place de la Gare, 80 Chepy

HOSTELLERIE DES REMPARTS, rue Beaubois, 80200 Péronne

BEER SHOPS RECOMMENDED BY THE BREWERY

J & C GIRARD, 5 avenue Général Leclerc, 80270 Airaines

CORBEILLE PAYSANNE, les Halles du Beffroi, Place M. Vaast, 80000 Amiens

SUPERMARCHÉ MATCH, 80000 Amiens

SUPERMARCHÉ MATCH, Beauvais

LE RELAIS DU CHÂTEAU, 24 rue d'Ulm, 60400 Compiègne

SUPERMARCHÉ MATCH, 80600 Doullens

EPICERIE GILLE, 24 Bd. Ste-Barbe, 59140 Dunkerque

LA CAVETTE À BIÈRES, 385 rue de la Mabonnerie, 60320 St-Sauveur

Brasserie des Deux Rivières

- ✉ 1 Place de la Madeleine, 29600 Morlaix,
- ☎ 02 98 63 41 92 Fax: 02 98 88 61 27
- 🕐 Contact brewery for opening times
- 👥 In summer only (Mon-Wed, 1030, 1400 & 1530). 15 days notice. In French & English. No charge
- 🛒 Cases only
- 🍺 4,000hl (in 1996)
- ➡ The brewery is above the town on top of the eastern valley slopes. We recommend asking for directions at the Office de Tourisme at the quayside in the town

Morlaix sits in a dramatic valley up a coastal inlet and its pretty docks and quaysides show its links to the sea. Still a fishing town, the population has grown to the point that the town has now expanded up and over the valley slopes. A dominant feature of the town is the colossal railway viaduct which takes trains high above on their way along the north Brittany coast. On the valley floor, the old town consists of narrow streets which has meant traffic (and especially parking) has become a major problem in high season.

The town is at the confluence of the rivers Jarlot and Queffleuth and it is from these that the brewery took its name. The original brewery of Deux Rivières was situated in the heart of the old town, but a gradual expansion through increased sales necessitated a move to larger premises. A suitable site was eventually found atop the steep valley slopes, and the unusual proportions give away the building's previous identity as a rope factory. It is quite narrow, but seems to go on forever through a series of different rooms.

There is a characterful brewery tap at the front of the building which has glass panels looking in on the mash tun and kettle – the ideal place to try your first hand-pumped draught Coreff beer. The owners, Christian Blanchard and Jean-François Malgorn, looked to British brewing consultant Peter Austin for advice and were trained by him at the Ringwood Brewery in Hampshire, UK, prior to going it alone in Morlaix in 1985. Much of the plant is secondhand British equipment which was also found and bought through Peter Austin – the mash tun, for instance, was originally at Archers Brewery, Swindon, UK.

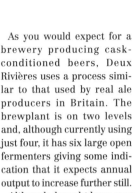

Inside the characterful old rope factory – one of the series of rooms which extend behind the brewery tap

As you would expect for a brewery producing cask-conditioned beers, Deux Rivières uses a process similar to that used by real ale producers in Britain. The brewplant is on two levels and, although currently using just four, it has six large open fermenters giving some indication that it expects annual output to increase further still.

Although draught beer accounts for the vast majority of their turnover, they also bottle their beers – but bottling a beer which normally conditions itself in the cask requires an extra process. This is done by refermenting the beer, this time in a sealed fermenter. Once enough CO_2 has been absorbed the beer is cooled to allow it to clear and is then pumped over to the bottling line. This process enables Deux Rivières to offer its bottled beer unfiltered and unpasteurised.

It is not often that you see handpumps in France, but any bar/cafe serving draught Deux Rivières beers is supplied them with the beer, along with bar towels, which gives many bars a British feel. Now available in around 150 outlets, the brewery should be applauded for re-introducing cask-conditioned beer to France. Although brewpubs like the Frog & Rosbif in Paris and Ardennaise in Charleville-Mézièrs also make and serve beer the same way, the original trail was blazed by Deux Rivières, whose 'real ale' has now been taken up as something of a pseudo-regional beer style and is widely available throughout Brittany where it is identified as a true Breton product.

Another commendable feature of Deux Rivières is that of successful marketing to bars and cafes in the face of the strict supplier ties which tend to hold back new breweries in terms of outlets. This has been achieved by obtaining an agreement to supply Coreff beers to newly-opened outlets prior to the owners negotiating brewery loans with one of the big brewing concerns.

Confusingly, its dark beer is sold as Etiquette Noir (Black Label) in bottles but is called Vin d'Orge (Barley Wine, which it isn't!) in its draught form. For its stock beer the name Coreff is used for bottled and draught versions. British real ale enthusiasts will find the easy-drinking beers of Deux Rivières very accessible – although we would recommend trying it on draught rather than in bottles.

COREFF

5% alc/vol. 50cl crown corked bottles & draught.

BREW DETAILS: Unfiltered. Unpasteurised. Top fermentation.

DECLARED INGREDIENTS: Saaz, Hallertau & Alsace hops; Pale, Crystal & Torrefied malts.

APPEARANCE: Deep chestnut with a big rocky head.

NOSE: Strongly fruity (redcurrant-like) with a light hop overlay.

PALATE: Extremely fruity with lots of red currants. Slightly sharp and tart but with a resiny bitterness.

FINISH: Slightly tart, very tangy, fruity bitterness.

OVERALL: A nice smooth texture and full red fruitiness offer much but the tartness detracts from the promised appeal. These notes relate to bottles that were approaching their sell-by dates and bears little resemblance to the hand-pumped draught version. On draught it was smooth and surprisingly quaffy for its strength with far less fruit than in the bottle and no tartness. On draught it gets two ticks.

GENERAL: First brewed 1985.

JW: ☑☐☐   KR: ☑☐☐

COREFF ÉTIQUETTE NOIRE

6.5% alc/vol.   50cl crown corked bottles & draught.

BREW DETAILS: Unfiltered. Unpasteurised. Top fermentation.

DECLARED INGREDIENTS: Saaz, Hallertau & Alsace hops; Pale, Crystal & Torrefied malts.

APPEARANCE: Deep burgundy black colour with an excellent, creamy, lasting head.

NOSE: Interesting, pleasant estery fruit notes plus a fair bit of dark malt are inviting but there is a slightly tart note which is off-putting. KR: A distant hoppy note and dark, stoutish suggestions.

PALATE: A fruity black malt character verges on being a stout but whilst being helped by a hoppy element it is dragged down by the tartness to the fruit.

FINISH: Fruity, slightly resiny bitterness and dark, almost burnt, malt. KR: Lingering tart fruit.

OVERALL: Fruity, malty, resiny, bitter, nearly tart ale that gets more tart with age. Quite complex. It gets two ticks on draught as it is very full and powerfully malty with a robust hop lifting the overall taste to become very easy to drink. Far less tart than the bottled version.

GENERAL: First brewed 1986. Known as **Vin d'Orge** on draught.

JW: ☑☐☐   KR: ☑☐☐

OTHER BEERS BREWED

Coreff de Noël (5.5% alc/vol.) – Draught only.

BARS & CAFES RECOMMENDED BY THE BREWERY

The brewery publishes a list of just over 100 bars which can be picked up at the brewery or some bars – here is a small selection. **Brest**: Le Bataclan Bar, La Casserole, Ducouedic, Les Fauvettes, Le Good Night, L'An Vie, Café de la Plage, Les Mouettes, Aux 4 Vents Bar, Tara Inn, Triskell Bar, Pub Victory, The World's End. **Quimper**: L'Eden. **Vannes**: Le Swansea Pub. **Rennes**: Le Barantic, La Cité D'Ys, Le Nabuchodonosor, Le Sablier, Le Trocadero. **Saint Malo**: O'Flahertys.

Micro-Brasserie des Diaouligs

✉ La Ville Échet, 22550 Saint Potan

☎ 02 96 83 74 61   Fax: 02 96 83 74 61

🕐 1500-1800. Every day in summer. Weekends only in winter

🏨 Always available. In French and English

🏪 Cases, bottles, glasses

🍺 Around 300hl (projected for 1998)

➡ From Plancoët and Pluduno, heading towards St-Potan on D994, the brewery is 2 miles (3.5 km) from Pluduno on the right-hand side of the road just before a sharp right-hand bend. Look out for the cream-coloured rendering and brown wood fascias

One of the new wave of French breweries, this is operated by a company called Breizh Traders but preferring to be known on the bottle labels as 'Fabrique de Bière des Diaouligs' (Makers of the Devil's Beer), and opened on New Year's Day in 1997. The word Breizh is Breton for Brittany and the name of its first product reflects the French penchant for giving everything a regional identity.

This very small-scale operation nestles in the rolling landscape of north-eastern Brittany, not far from Dinan. It is run from an industrial unit, but has the benefit of having a shop and tasting room with a good amount of parking and frontage onto a road which is popular with travelling holiday-makers.

The brewplant is old dairy equipment and looks a little lost in the huge, quite empty factory unit. Capacity of the plant is 500 litres per brew, and they currently make 1,000 bottles (75cl) per month from their fortnightly brews.

The owners, Bruno Desson and Jean Michel Jezegou, started hobby-brewing some years ago, and have always been keen visitors to Belgium on trips to various breweries. This eventually led to them trying their hand at commercial brewing and their maiden brew was in January 1997. Apparently the recipe chosen was an attempt to replicate one of their favourite Belgian brews. Madame Jezegou runs the shop at the brewery.

The beer is spiced, although the brewery did not disclose specific ingredients, and it undergoes two weeks of garde prior to its bottle refermentation.

There's certainly plenty of room to expand!

The owners chose a piratical identity for their beer because of the historical link with pirates along the northern Brittany coast, hence the skull and crossed swords and the sub-title 'Bière des Corsaires', literally 'Pirate Beer'. Along with yet another sub-title 'Maison de mauvaise réputation' ('House of ill-repute') you are left in no doubt that the identity has been well pushed!

In 1998 a new beer was introduced, called **La Diaoul** (a shortened version of Diaoulig) which was described to us as a 'chouchen' (mead) which presumably means it is honeyed.

OLDE BREIZH

7% alc/vol. 75cl corked bottles.

BREW DETAILS: Unfiltered. Unpasteurised. Top fermentation.

INGREDIENTS: Spalt Alsacian hops. Pilsener and Caramel malts.

APPEARANCE: Very dark – almost black – with a good, creamy, beige coloured head.

NOSE: A mellow aroma of fruity dark malt. JW: Laced with cocoa and milk chocolate. KR: Some light appleskin notes.

PALATE: JW: Dark, slightly roasted, malt with a subdued dark fruit and a sharp hop edge. The very full taste is enforced by cocoa and liquorice elements. KR: Instantly dry with some lacticity and strong black malt and liquorice which tend to overpower the taste.

FINISH: JW: Dry and bitter, fairly fruity, chocolatey, roasted dark malt. KR: A dark and harsh dryness with a lingering fruitiness.

OVERALL: An uncompromising beer which has a very strong stout taste with a full, fairly well-balanced, bone-dry, roasted chocolate character. Has been known to be a little inconsistent.

GENERAL: First brewed 1997. Described by the brewery as a light stout, but we would disagree with the 'light' epithet.

JW:☑☐☐ KR:☑☐☐

OTHER BEERS BREWED

La Diaoul – Breton for 'The Devil'. Introduced in 1998. Described by the brewery as a mead, so we presume it has honey amongst its ingredients.

Brasserie Duyck

✉ 113 Route Nationale, 59144 Jenlain

☎ 03 27 49 70 03   Fax: 03 27 49 74 81   www.duyck.com

🕐 Mon-Fri: 0900-1200 & 1400-1700

👥 Occasionally, pre-arranged only. 7 days notice. In French.

🔤 Cases, bottles, glasses

📊 75,000hl (in 1997)

➡ See article

If there is one beer that is generally accepted as the 'classic' bière de garde, it has to be Jenlain. This is also the beer that is popularly attributed with starting the revival of the French brewing industry. The beer has been around since 1925 but it was only in the late 1970s, when it acquired something of a cult status amongst the student population in Lille, that it became generally available and the brewery was able to expand to take advantage of this popularity.

Brasserie Duyck (pronounced *dweek*) is a commercially aware company which approaches its marketing very seriously. The extent to which this has paid off can be seen in the market position of its brand, the investment in the brewery and the presentation of its product. The most recent developments have been the updating of its imp logo and a redesign of all the packaging in 1997. This followed the launch, in March 1997, of Jenlain in 50cl cans – making it the first canned traditional beer. Not possessing pasteurisation and canning facilities the beer goes to Menken Drinks in the Netherlands for processing.

In spite of the investment and attention to marketing image, the brewery itself still portrays elements of its farm heritage. It dates from 1922 when Félix Duyck set up operations here in Jenlain. The family had been brewing since the turn of the century (at which time Félix's father Léon was brewing in the Dunkerque area), but the operation went far more commercial when Félix moved to Jenlain and produced his first matured beer. That beer would eventually become known simply as Jenlain.

Prior to this, Félix's son Robert took over the reins in 1960 initiating the first modernisation in 1975 and adding a new brew-house in 1985. The brewery now boasts the fourth generation of family control when, in 1990, Robert's son Raymond took over the senior role. Like his predecessors Raymond feels a strong sense of tradition and has been able to marry this to today's commercial realities of running a successful brewery.

With the exception of D.B. (a bottom fermenting pils) all the other products are top fermented with two different strains of yeast and are filtered but unpasteurised. Sebourg and Jenlain Noël use one yeast, Jenlain and Bière de Printemps the other. For Jenlain the fermentation takes place at 15–20°C (which lasts for five days) followed by a garding period of 40 days before final filtration and bottling.

Amongst other developments the brewery hopes to develop a bar concept with the opening of Jenlain Café in the centre of Lille – a superb building, well laid out on a number of floors, handily located next to a metro entrance and the only place to currently find Bière Fraîche, a draught, unfiltered version of Sebourg. Well worth trying.

Still on the bar front, Brasserie Duyck puts its name to the 'Jenlain Ambassadeur' scheme (run in conjunction with Gault-Millau), a little like a good pub guide for bars which sell Jenlain – and usually an indication that other good beer is available. In addition to being awarded the year-marked sticker the bar gets an entry in a little booklet available from the brewery and selected bars.

BIÈRE DE NOËL

6.8% alc/vol. 25cl crown corked & 75cl corked bottles and draught.

DECLARED INGREDIENTS: Alsace and Hallertau hops; Plaisant, Carambri and Prisma malts.

APPEARANCE: Deep copper amber colour with a massive head.

NOSE: Light aroma of earthy hop with a few herbal and spicy notes plus a little fruit over an interesting crystal malt.

PALATE: A powerful, slightly bitter, fruity malt with loads of powdery dry hops A gentle fruity spice and quite herbal. JW: A little alcohol warmth. KR: A slight metallic note.

FINISH: A lingering very dry and bitter fruit with a sharp hop briefly biting through. JW: A touch roasted with some alcohol notes. KR: Quite tannic.

OVERALL: Good full malty fruity palate well tempered by a powerful hop and encouraged by a slight spiciness. Plenty of character and easy to drink. Seems to improve a little with age but only a few months after which it deteriorates noticeably. JW: Has a good creamy texture. KR: Just as you would imagine – a Jenlain beefed up on the malt with some dark, herbal character bestowed on it for Christmas.

GENERAL: First brewed 1950. Available November & December.

JW:☑☐☐   KR:☑☐☐

BIÈRE DE PRINTEMPS

5.4% alc/vol. 25cl crown corked & 75cl corked bottles and draught.

DECLARED INGREDIENTS: Alsace and Hallertau hops; Prisma and Nevada malts.

APPEARANCE: Lightish golden colour with a good head which leaves a lovely lacework.

NOSE: Gentle flowery hops with a moderately citric lemon element over a gentle pale malt. JW: Some distinctive yeastiness.

PALATE: A moderate sweetness from plenty of gently fruity pale malt tempered by being quite citric and lightly bitter. JW: A little yeasty.

FINISH: Hoppily dry and gently bitter with lingering fruit and citric hints. It induces some mouthwatering but creates a sensation of a slight powdery coating on the roof of the mouth and back of the teeth. KR: A persistent malt sweetness.

OVERALL: A similar palate to Sebourg though a little narrower in taste. A good smooth creamy texture and a pleasant quaffability should give it a wide appeal. JW: Very characterful from a good blend of malt, hop and yeast tastes. KR: A little disappointing for a Bière de Mars – and perhaps a little misleading as it appears to be based on Sebourg rather than Jenlain.

GENERAL: First brewed 1992. The brewery's Bière de Mars renamed as a Spring beer to allow a longer selling season, now available February to May.

JW: ☑☑☐   KR: ☑☐☐

JENLAIN

6.5% alc/vol. 25cl crown corked, 75cl corked bottles, draught & 50cl cans.

BREW DETAILS: Filtered. Unpasteurised (except in 50cl cans). Top fermentation.

DECLARED INGREDIENTS: Flanders, Alsace and Hallertau hops; Plaisant Carambri and Prisma malts.

APPEARANCE: Deep dark amber with a good, but shortlived, fluffy head.

NOSE: Slightly sweet rich malt. JW: With a faint hop edge. KR: With a light spiciness.

PALATE: Full mouth of rich malt and dark fruit with a pleasant sharp hop edge and alcohol warmth. The hop bitterness builds gently into the finish. The sharpness nearly verges on sourness and prevents any tendency towards cloying. KR: A red fruit hint in the sharpness.

FINISH: Slightly roasted dry fruity malt with a little bitterness and astringency. JW: Quite mouthdrying.

OVERALL: Very good full tasting but easy drinking beer with a good fruitiness and a nice hop edge that tempers the sweetish malt. A good introduction to bières de garde due to its solid but innoffensive character. Scores highly in the taste department but leaves complexity at home. The tannic and metallic elements increase with age.

GENERAL: First brewed 1925.

JW: ☑☑☐   KR: ☑☑☐

CANNED VERSION: JW: Doesn't lose much by being pasteurised. Seems to have a creamier texture and a slightly mellower palate. It will make a good bière de garde more accessible to the general public which cannot be a bad thing. KR: Less rich and satisfying throughout and the hops seem to have lost all their distinctiveness. Also more watery with a harsher bitterness.

SEBOURG

6% alc/vol. 25cl crown corked & 75cl corked bottles and draught.

INGREDIENTS: Alsace and Hallertau hops; Prisma and Nevada malts; unmalted wheat.

APPEARANCE: Golden with a good head and nice lacework.

NOSE: Pleasantly aromatic with a perfumed quality over a lightly fruity solid pale malt. JW: Sweet, fragrant lemony hops. KR: Aroma fades to a citric/appley hop with wheaty wafts.

PALATE: The excellent, full mouth of taste based around a sweet pale malt and fresh lemony hop, recedes leaving a watery element prior to the finish. A tingling bitterness on the tongue turns peppery. KR: Distinctly zingy with a light perfumed quality.

FINISH: A citric mouthwatering quality and a slightly tangy fruity pale malt lead into a bitter resiny dryness. KR: A peppery hop underlies the lingering sweet fruitiness, also some leftover creamy and watery wheat notes.

OVERALL: Pleasant, easy drinking beer with a good lemony hop character and creamy texture which makes it an interesting session beer. Very sweet but the sweetness is tempered by the lemon. Some of the hop character disappears as the beer warms. KR: A very distinctive and highly original beer with a great quenching quality.

GENERAL: First brewed 1993. Named after the nearby village of Sebourg where there was a tradition of blonde bières de garde.

JW: ☑☑☐ KR: ☑☑☐

OTHER BEERS BREWED

Bière Fraîche (6% alc/vol.) – Draught only, currently solely at Jenlain Café, Lille. Unfiltered. Unpasteurised. Top fermentation. Essentially this is Sebourg which hasn't been filtered, and a rare treat. A slightly hazy gold colour with a wonderful, whipped cream head and a citric hop nose laced with a few wheaty hints. Excellent, full taste of pale malt and lemony hops with wheaty, creamy, milky elements and a yeasty, tangy hop finish with a lingering natural sweetness. Fuller and more mellow than the standard Sebourg, giving the impression that more of the senses are involved in the overall satisfyingly pleasant experience. Introduced by the brewery as a concession to be offered for sale only at Jenlain Café franchised bars.

D.B. (5% alc/vol.) – Draught only. Filtered. Unpasteurised. Bottom fermentation. Declared ingredients: Alsace and Hallertau hops; Plaisant and Prisma malts. First brewed 1946. D.B. has a double meaning as it stands for Duyck Bières and also the name of the division which liberated the village during the Second World War.

La 2004 (5.9% alc/vol.) – Made for Fichel Distribution.

BARS & CAFES RECOMMENDED BY THE BREWERY

Jenlain Café, 43 place Rihour, 59000 Lille
Le Bastringue, 168 rue de Solférino, 59000 Lille
Le Bouquet du Nord, 85 rue de Mauberge, 75010 Paris
Magique Pub, 1 rue Anfoss, 06700 Saint Laurent du Var
Pub St-Germain des Prés, 17 rue de l'Ancienne Comédie, 75006 Paris
Royal Concorde, 7 rue Royale, 75008 Paris

Entre-Temps

✉ 1 place de la Gare, 59306 Valenciennes

☎ 03 27 46 86 30

🕐 Phone brewpub for details

✗ Not appropriate.

🏪 On draught only

ℹ 40hl (projected for 1998)

Entre-Temps (literally 'in the meantime') is a station buffet with a difference; this is the first one in France to brew its own beer. It is on a small scale, but then it is essentially just the buffet restaurant in the moderately grand main station building in Valenciennes (on the left-hand side as you look at them from the square). It is a clean modern café offering meals and snacks including jacket potatoes with various fillings (not so common in France – but noticeably smaller than typical UK offerings) plus the added attraction of its own beer.

The brew-plant is behind the bar with a fermentation/maturation room just to one side. The plant is of 150 litres capacity though the tanks will hold 300 litres. They brew once a fortnight and the beer ferments for five days before 15 days of garde. It is served directly from the garding tanks.

Entre-Temps is owned by Buffet de Dijon S.A. who also own many other station buffets and, we were told, have plans to open similar brew-pubs in many other main-line stations throughout France. This one became active in December 1997.

BIÈRE DE LA MAISON

5.5% alc/vol.   Draught only.

BREW DETAILS: Filtered. Unpasteurised. Bottom fermentation.

DECLARED INGREDIENTS: Hallertau hop pellets.

APPEARANCE: Cloudy wheat with a short-lived creamy head.

NOSE: Very little aroma. Just a slight hop with a suggestion of wheat.

PALATE: Mellow, soft and creamy with a good hoppiness. Dry, with a strongish hop taste but only gently bitter.

FINISH: Dry, gently bitter and strongly hoppy. KR: A little too dry, quite harsh, but very quenching.

OVERALL: Served very cold to the detriment of the nose. Displays wheaty characteristics without being wheaty. Nicely soft and creamy. Very easy to drink but fairly bland in spite of the distinct hop element. Well suited for summer quaffing.   JW: ☑☐☐ KR: ☑☐☐

Brasseries Fischer & Adelshoffen

- ✉ 9 Route de Bischwiller, BP 48, 67301 Schiltigheim
- ☎ 03 88 33 82 00   Fax: 03 88 33 82 18
- 🕐 Phone for details of individual brewery opening hours
- Pre-arranged only. 4 days notice
- Cases, bottles, glasses
- 1,700,000hl (in 1996)
- ➔ See article

February 1996 could be looked back on as a sad time in French brewing history, when the combined Brasseries Fischer & Adelshoffen was taken over by Heineken. At the time of publication, however, it was still operating independently so we have opted to treat it as a separate entity.

These two old established breweries merged in 1921 when Fischer, celebrating its centenary, bought a controlling interest in its near neighbour. Fischer had been founded, originally as Brasserie de l'Ours Blanc, in rue du Jeu-des-Enfants in Strasbourg in 1821 by Jean Fischer but moved to its current location at 9 route de Bischwiller, Schiltigheim, in 1854, just ten years before the Ehrhardt brothers founded Adelshoffen up the road at number 87. Heineken's plant is conveniently situated halfway between them with the offices on route de Bischwiller though the main entrance to the brewery itself is at 4 rue Saint-Charles, a side street to the left. Interestingly, all three sites are on the left-hand side of the road (heading out of town). Schiltigheim is north-north-east of Strasbourg and if you follow signs to Schiltigheim centre you will see Brasserie Fischer in front of you as get onto route de Bischwiller.

After the large name sign on the seven-storey brick building your eyes will be drawn to the chimney-like maltings vents with their distinctive hoods. Built in 1912, the maltings still supplies the brewery today

In the past Fischer also operated under the name Pêcheur (fisher in French) to give it a more French-sounding identity in the times when a Germanic name would be a positive disadvantage. Whichever name it displays on the sign, the little boy is still one of the strongest visual identities in French brewing.

though with 1.7 million hectolitres of beer made per year extra malt has to be bought in to supplement its output. The beers can be sampled in the Fischerstub, a bar and restaurant next to the brewery.

The buildings of Brasserie Adelshoffen, covered mainly in beige-coloured render, look less characterful than those of Fischer – yet behind this exterior lies an interesting history. Within 20 years of being founded on the site of an old oil works, it was lost to the Germans in their occupation of Alsace. All was not lost though since the Ehrhardt brothers had seen what was coming and built another brewery at Bar-le-Duc, called Brasserie de la Meuse. In 1918 Alsace was back in the hands of the French (and its original owners) by which time it had merged with a German brewery to become Strassburger Münsterbräu. In 1922 it was bought by the Pêcheur de Schiltigheim group who, in 1938, made it into a separate company called Grande Brasserie Alsacienne d'Adelshoffen.

Over the years Fischer & Adelshoffen has acquired a reputation for being innovative in both its beer range and its marketing. In the 1980s a beer called 3615 Pêcheur was sold via Minitel (the French national text-based telecommunications system, rather like a precursor to the Internet) and was promoted as an aphrodisiac having ginseng among its ingredients. It also blazed the original trail in the flavouring of beers with spirit (Desperados and Kingston) and using whisky malt (the Adelscott range) – both of which innovations were successful enough to make other breweries bring out their own imitations soon after, to the point that it is now something of a national trend.

Many beer fans still find it hard to forgive Fischer for challenging the legitimacy of the *reinheitsgebot* (the Bavarian Purity Law) and winning a judgment in the European law courts in 1987. Fischer's President, Michel Debus, claimed that Germany's ban on the import of beers not conforming to its purity law was protectionist and not in the spirit of free trade. With the brewery being so close to the German border, it was a problem to be excluded from its beer market. It was also an inevitability that one brewery would eventually challenge the import ban at a time when the *reinheitsgebot* was being vaunted as a possible EC brewing standard – a standard which would also have seen the end to many classic British and Belgian beers.

At the beginning of 1998 Fischer and Adelshoffen were undergoing a rationalisation of their portfolios; but with no definitive information about which beers may be dropped and which brewery will produce which brand we have decided to cover the beers available in 1997.

The Beers of France

ADELSCOTT

6.6% alc/vol. 25cl crown corked bottles, 50cl cans and draught.

DECLARED INGREDIENTS: Whisky malt.

APPEARANCE: Pleasant amber colour with a good fluffy head.

NOSE: Slightly sweet, perfumey, whisky malt. KR: A dry, husky hop over a faintly smokey hint.

PALATE: Quite a strong whisky malt taste comes through a thick sweet candy sugar. JW: There is an element of alcohol sharpness around the edge of the tongue. Just a touch of hop noticeable. KR: Hop bitterness, though subdued, gives the whole a needed lift.

FINISH: JW: A little cloying with a growing strong whisky alcohol tang that lasts. KR: Sticky, sweet tang tempered by a lovely malt element.

OVERALL: A very accessible whisky style beer. KR: Excellent, strong whisky malt character but just too sweet. Seems to have acquired extra sweetness over the years. JW: ☑☑☐ KR: ☑☐☐

ADELSCOTT NOIRE

6.6% alc/vol. 25cl crown corked bottles.

APPEARANCE: Very dark. Very black.

NOSE: Smokey, JW: Peaty and very inviting with oak smoked dark candy malt and a touch of hops. KR: Woody, smoked malt with demerara hints and liquorice.

PALATE: Bags of peaty, smokey roasted malt with planty of fruit. Sweetish candy notes balance the inherent bitterness. JW: As dark and earthy as it led you to believe with hints of caramel and whisky. KR: A full, yet surprisingly mellow character.

FINISH: Mellow bitterness dominated by the fruity, smokey roast malt which develops a slight dryness. JW: Seems to go on forever.

OVERALL: JW: Very impressive rich, fruity, tasty, sipping beer. Great to see that the appearance and nose are justified by the palate. KR: Excellent characterful beer with a superb, creamy mouthfeel.

GENERAL: Can develop tartness with age. JW: ☑☑☑ KR: ☑☑☑

ADELSHOFFEN 8.8

8.8% alc/vol. 50cl cans.

APPEARANCE: Golden colour with a good but very short-lived head.

NOSE: A pronounced, fragrant husky hop with a quite rich malt fruitiness just poking through.

PALATE: There is a fair whack of alcohol which results in it being quite warming. JW: Plenty of sweet pale malt with a gentle fruitiness which is tempered by a little hop bitterness. KR: A husky dryness in the start is replaced as a sweet, fruity malt washes through with a creamy maltiness which eventually mellows out to a very full, warming taste.

FINISH: JW: Lingering warm gentle resiny, bitter tang. KR: Long lasting mellow bitterness with an understated dry and warming quality.

OVERALL: Excellent, full tasting, clean and fairly interesting lager which is frighteningly easy to drink for its strength. Even in a can it is surprisingly good.

JW: ☑☑☐   KR: ☑☑☐

ADELSHOFFEN BIÈRE DE L'ÉTÉ

5% alc/vol.   25cl crown corked bottles.

DECLARED INGREDIENTS: Lime.

APPEARANCE: Pale gold.

NOSE: Initially a strong lemon & lime aroma which becomes more of a lemon zest overlaying a little pilsener malt. Reminiscent of lemon sherbet.

PALATE: Initial massive hit of lime hides the mellow malt. Like drinking a lager and lime.

FINISH: Fairly neutral, just a little dry and tangy.

OVERALL: Very lager and lime with some lager and lots of lime.

JW: ☐☐☐   KR: ☐☐☐

ADELSHOFFEN BIÈRE DE MARS

5.5% alc/vol.   25cl crown corked bottles.

APPEARANCE: Orange gold colour.

NOSE: Distinctly smokey, moderately strong whisky malt degenerates into a thick sweet candied vanilla and caramel malt with smokey hints. KR: A cloying promise and a distinctly husky hop.

PALATE: A biscuit malt tinged with vanilla, and a hoppy bitter edge that grows into the finish. JW: Smokey. Candy caramel malt. KR: Oversweet and very tangy.

FINISH: Dry, bitter hop gives a husky bitterness to relieve the tangy candied taste. JW: Lingering caramel hints. KR: A few distant citric hints.

OVERALL: JW: An interesting and slightly unusual taste being smokey, thick, malty, biscuity and dry with a distinct vanilla flavour and a gentle hop adding some bitterness. KR: Over sweet beer spoiled by a strange malty tang and an unfortunate husky character.

JW: ☑☐☐   KR: ☑☐☐

ADELSHOFFEN BIÈRE DE NOËL

6% alc/vol.   25cl crown corked bottles.

APPEARANCE: Rich amber in colour.

NOSE: Full, sweetish, slightly biscuity malt with a hint of caramel. KR: Quite artificially citric with a limey note.

PALATE: Sweet and sugary with a slight hint of caramel and a touch of malt. Resiny bitter hoppy notes grow to generate a resinous tang. KR: Artificial sweetness with some lime.

FINISH: Drying with a gently resinous element and some sweet notes. KR: Artificial citric tang and very bitter.

OVERALL: Overdone sugary sweetness dominates what little malt and hop there is, though a darkish caramel malt does come through as does a resiny bitterness. KR: Very much a shandy character – and as such the opposite to what most would expect from a Noël.

JW: ☑☐☐ KR: ☐☐☐

ADELSHOFFEN EXPORT

4.5% alc/vol. 25cl crown corked bottles.

APPEARANCE: Golden colour with a good head.

NOSE: Massive husky hop aroma with a strong biscuity malt. KR: A light pale malt fruit.

PALATE: Bitingly strong bitterness and very dry. Generally a very strong husky hop character supported by a little pale malt with some soft cream notes.

FINISH: Dry lingering bitterness – very hop induced – vies with some pale malt sweetness.

OVERALL: Intense use of hops gives a very strong bitterness to this tasty beer with a refreshing character. There is a touch of pale malt behind the strongly bitter husky hop character. KR: Particularly soft beer with a good hop character, though a little too sweet.

JW: ☑☐☐ KR: ☑☐☐

ADELSHOFFEN MÉTHODE ARTISANALE

5% alc/vol. 75cl & 100cl crown corked bottles.

APPEARANCE: Bright pale gold with a fluffy head.

NOSE: An aromatic husky hop with a full pale malt behind.

PALATE: Light but full with a strong, lightly oily hop which has a slightly sharp note and a strong bitterness. Behind the hop is a touch of malt.

FINISH: Dry and long lasting with a strong, oily hop bitterness with some resiny elements.

OVERALL: Strongly hoppy beer with oiliness to the hop. Surprisingly light in both texture and taste, quite refreshing and easy to drink.

JW: ☑☐☐ KR: ☑☐☐

DESPERADOS

5.9% alc/vol. 33cl crown corked bottles, 50cl cans and draught.

DECLARED INGREDIENTS: Hop extracts and Pilsener malt. Spiced with Tequilla extract and lime juice.

APPEARANCE: JW: Pale gold. KR: Rich honey gold

NOSE: Sweet tequila with a twist of lime. JW: A bit lemonade like. KR: Very limey

PALATE: Sweet with a lot of lime and a little light malt with an interesting spirit based character. JW: A harsh warmth. KR: Almost like a soft drink until the spirit hits after a long delay.

FINISH: Sharp, spirit-like heat lingers on with some lime and a faint bitterness in the background. KR: Sweet lemonade.

OVERALL: Very little beer character but a really refreshing lime drink with a distinct spirit base. A great summer quencher which makes no pretence at being a serious beer. The English translation of the ingredients on the back even lists beer as one of the ingredients. KR: Excrutiatingly sweet alcopop character which eventually has a definite tequila taste.

GENERAL: First brewed 1993. Sold in garishly-coloured, screen printed bottles.

JW: ☑☑☐ KR: ☑☐☐

FISCHER BIÈRE DE MARS

5.5% alc/vol. 65cl ceramic stoppered bottles.

APPEARANCE: Old gold in colour.

NOSE: JW: An unusual vanilla-ish, biscuity pale malt with a little fruit. A fair bit of hop induced character, a touch perfumey. KR: Quite heady and quite flowery hop over a light pale malt base.

PALATE: JW: A full but unusual palate. A distinctive vanilla malt, quite sweet with an almost whisky smoked character. The character gives the impression of being hop induced. KR: Strange perfumed taste with a fruity/tannic fullness and some lactic touches. Quite sweet but has a good tannic bitterness. Malt gives an odd fruit and sweet biscuits taste, but it has good balance.

FINISH: JW: Both cloying and saliva-inducing with a lingering, tangy, resiny hop and malt. KR: Bittersweet malt with a lingering peppery, lightly dry hop. Disappointing after the fullness of the palate.

OVERALL: JW: A full but very unusual taste reminiscent of confectionery. KR: Impressively different. Full and interesting with a multitude of tastes rather than being particularly complex. Tends to become a little tangy as it warms up.

JW: ☑☐☐ KR: ☑☑☐

FISCHER BIÈRE DE NOËL

5.9% alc/vol. 65cl ceramic stoppered bottles.

APPEARANCE: Rich copper with a rocky head.

NOSE: Flowery hop over a gently fruity malt. JW: With a touch or caramel. KR: With a peppery hint to the hop and a quite biscuity malt base.

PALATE: Very sweet, thick and candied. Suggestions of lemonade come through occasionally. JW: Some caramel malt and cooked candy sugar hide a hint of fruit. KR: Initial dry hoppiness recedes before an artificially sweet pale malt comes through, followed by some overly-sweet and saccharin-laced notes.

FINISH: Unpleasant tangy sweetness with few hop notes. JW: Slight burnt candy tang lingers and grows. KR: Hoppy bitterness vies with an artificially sweet malt with the latter unfortunately winning the day.

OVERALL: The excess of candy plus the thick smooth mouthfeel make it like a brown tablebeer – sweet and sickly. It is very artificial and there are no clues that it is 6%.   JW: ☐☐☐   KR: ☐☐☐

FISCHER TERROIR

4.5 % alc/vol.   75cl crown corked bottles.

APPEARANCE: Light gold with a fluffy head.

NOSE: A pleasant citric, quite perfumed hop with a metallic pale malt.

PALATE: Harsh, metallic pale malt with a quite oily hop. Some wateriness and an unpleasantly sharp bitterness. Distinct strong sweetness to the start.

FINISH: Good lingering hop bitterness with some light citric notes once the malt dies away.

OVERALL: JW: Interesting, surprisingly light, beer which starts with a strong sweet element in addition to the pale malt. This is soon overtaken by the hops which totally dominate the finish. KR: Nasty, harsh and pretty thin.

GENERAL: Used to be (and may still be also) called **Fischer Export** sold in 25cl crown corked bottles.   JW: ☑☐☐   KR: ☐☐☐

FISCHER TRADITION

6% alc/vol.   25cl, 33cl crown cork & 65cl ceramic stoppered bottles, 50cl cans and draught.

DECLARED INGREDIENTS: Hop extracts and Pilsener malt.

APPEARANCE: Deep dark gold with a good head.

NOSE: JW: Pleasant floral, lemony, hop over a gentle biscuity pale malt. KR: Lovely soft malt with a dry, slightly peppery and bitter hop.

PALATE: Gently fruity dry malt and peppery hop with a pleasant bitterness that grows.

FINISH: Very dry lingering pale maltiness with a massive hop character which is moderately bitter and induces a tingling in the mouth.

OVERALL: The impressively full taste and good depth of character make this a lager worth seeking out.

GENERAL: First brewed 1983. Used to be 6.5% alc/vol. Called **Fischer Gold** when on draught.

JW: ☑☑☐ KR: ☑☑☐

KINGSTON

5.9% alc/vol. 25cl crown corked bottles.

APPEARANCE: Light golden colour.

NOSE: Rich, quite heady spirit with a rum essence on a different plane. Not very beery and with a distinct brown sugar note.

PALATE: Sweet with a demerara and molasses taste before a warming, unmistakeable, rum rushes through. Tastes more of a dark rather than a white rum. It is surprisingly mouthwatering and rummy.

FINISH: Lingering candy sugariness with hardly any beery character apart from a sweet, light, fruity malt just about detected in the background.

OVERALL: Best drunk very cold to avoid it becoming cloying. Not as bad as one might imagine but if you don't like rum you won't like this. Not much like a beer but warming and strong-tasting with a tendency to be over-sweet and too thick.

GENERAL: Until recently it was 6.9% alc/vol. KR: Seems to have developed a sweeter character with the drop in alcohol.

JW: ☑☐☐ KR: ☑☐☐

OTHER BEERS BREWED ———————————————————

Adelshoffen Brune (6.1% alc/vol.)

Adelshoffen Lite

Adelshoffen Tradition (5.5% alc/vol.) – Made with hop extracts and Pilsener malt.

Alsa

La Belle Brasseuse (4.5% alc/vol.) – Very similar in character to Fischer Terroir.

La Belle Strasbourgeoise – Another beer which is very similar to Fischer Terroir.

Bière d'Automne

Dry Lime (4.5% alc/vol.) – Beer with added lime.

Münsterbräu (4.5% alc/vol.)

Münsterhof Export (4.5% alc/vol.) – Pale lemon-coloured beer, sold in a can. The full, tangy, bitter hop takes off from the plentiful pilsener malt which gives it is sweet start. The tanginess lingers long in the finish.

Rhinberg (5.9% alc/vol.)

Rheingold (5.9% alc/vol.) – Has a rich, thick hop aroma over a lager malt on the nose. Starts out as a refreshing beer but has a strong, tangy bitterness which builds into the finish. Not a bad lager at all, with a good balance until the finish.

Ferme-Brasserie Garland

✉ Les Pesquies, 81470 Algans

☎ 05 63 75 74 68

🕐 Opening times vary. Best to phone first

🏨 By prior arrangement – please contact brewery

🍶 Bottles and cases

🏭 130hl (in 1997)

➜ See article.

The brewery/maltery in the old brickworks

Algans is a tiny village just off the D126 which runs from Toulouse to Puylaurens, and is just a collection of buildings (including a mairie and a church) and a widespread sprawl of rural houses. The area is quite hilly very locally and there are some good views to the Montagne Noir to the south-east.

As the owner of Brasserie Garland tends to flit between his house and the brewery, it is best we give directions to both (presuming you will be coming from the direction of the D126). For the brewery: go past the mairie and church in Algans then take the second right (towards Bertre) and you will find the brewery/maltery on the left-hand side of the road after 150 metres in the building with the large square brick chimney (the entrance to the brewery is at the far end of the building). For the house, go past the mairie and church in Algans then take the first right (signposted Lacroisille). A few metres past the cemetery turn right onto a gravel track. The house is at the end of the track a few hundred metres along and up a steep hill into the yard of the farmhouse.

The brewery building is an old brickworks which still contains a couple of old kilns – one of which looks like it is still in use, perhaps for kilning malt on a small scale. The brewplant is located in a small room at the newer end of the building and it all appears to be old dairy equipment with some modification.

It is run by the Garland family and they pride themselves on producing all the malt for their beer on their own farm – a unique and admirable practice for a modern artisanal brewery. The brewery started here in 1994.

Les Pesquies, the Garland family farm.

The one product brewed is all organic (biologique in French) and carries the recognition logo of Nature et Progrès. The beer is top fermenting and undergoes a three-week garding period prior to the bottle refermentation.

Around 90% of the output is sold direct to the public from the brewery, but a small amount is supplied to very local shops and bars. If there is no-one at the brewery or farm on your visit, there is a wine merchant in the nearby, pretty town of Puylaurens (on the right-hand side of the road just before leaving town) which normally stocks both sizes of bottle.

KARLAND AMBRÉE

6% alc/vol. 33cl & 75cl crown corked bottles.

BREW DETAILS: Unfiltered. Unpasteurised. Top fermentation. Bottle refermentation.

APPEARANCE: Orange colour with a tight creamy head.

NOSE: Mellow, light, fruity, crystal malt with a few gentle hop notes. KR: Strong yeasty aroma with a red fruitiness behind it. Acidic fruity promise.

PALATE: Fairly complex with a fair bit of crystal malt and a biting oily hop both contriving to hide the fruitiness. Has a gentle buttery quality. Good balance and excellent full taste. KR: Quite sweet, balanced by a thick, quite sticky malt.

FINISH: Lingering buttery notes and a little fruit enhance the dry, tangy crystal malt. KR: Lightly acidic with some sweet notes over.

OVERALL: An organic beer with a lovely soft creamy texture and interesting bitterness that is well balanced and very easy to drink. It has a great fullness in the mouth with a strong crystal malt and hop character enhanced by a light fruitiness. A satisfying and quite complex artisanal ale.

JW: ☑☑☐   KR: ☑☑☐

BARS & CAFES RECOMMENDED BY THE BREWERY

Le Dubliner, Toulouse

Les Brasseurs de Gayant

- ✉ 63 Faubourg de Paris, B.P. 89, 59502 Douai Cedex
- ☎ 03 27 93 26 22   Fax: 03 27 93 26 20
- 🕐 Not known
- 🏭 No information supplied
- 🏪 We believe the brewery does not normally sell direct, as we did not see a shop at the head office
- 📊 200,000hl (in 1997)

Douai is an old town, probably founded by the Romans, which was famous throughout late-medieval times for its fine textile production. More recently it was the administrative centre for the local coal mining industry. Both world wars left their mark, but the First World War especially left the town and its surroundings in ruins after years of German occupation very close to the front line.

It was in 1918 when, faced with the need to rebuild the local brewing industry and start the infrastructure of depots and transport all over again, that four smaller breweries (Caudrelier from Râches and three from Douai itself, Delfolie, Belle and Maronnier) chose to join forces to form Brasserie des Enfants de Gayant which started production in 1919.

Being well-placed for a good local trade in a highly-populated area, the brewery prospered in a very short time, producing many bocks, table beers and pilsener-type beers. After the Second World War it benefited from the large demand left unsupplied when other local breweries decided not to re-open or weren't in a position to start trading again.

In 1954 Jean-Pierre d'Aubreby and Emile Caudrelier bought the brewery which continued to trade under the same name as before. Around 1970 it took the bold step to launch Celta – its alcohol-free beer – which quickly became a leading national brand of its type.

There seemed to be a change of direction in 1982 when Bière du Démon was introduced into the world. This placed the brewery into the special beer market, a role it has been developing and building on ever since. Another adventurous product followed in 1986 with the launch of Bière du Désert, a paler-than-usual beer with plenty of flavour but which appears to have undergone many changes over the years to the point that it is now far less characterful.

The well-known St-Landelin 'abbey beer' range appears to have joined the Gayant portfolio in 1988. According to our research, there was a bottle-conditioned beer called Réserve Saint Landelin being made by Brasserie Rimaux before this date. The name is taken from a ruined abbey right on the Belgian border, north-east of Valenciennes near a village called Crespin (where Rimaux was based). Due to the lack of any response whatsoever from Gayant (to whom we sent many questionnaires and visited twice without even getting past the reception) we can do nothing but surmise that the brand name was bought or perhaps just taken over when Rimaux ceased trading.

Whatever happened, Gayant have made a great success of the St-Landelin range over the years, though we would question the claim on their labels that all of them are made 'in strict accordance with the method of the monks of the Crespin Abbey' (unless you believe that monks used rice in their beer). The range is not now bottle-conditioned and previously came in Blonde, Ambrée and Brune guises. Of late there had been a distinct absence of the Brune, but 1998 saw a 'Triple Brune' (8% alc/vol. instead of the old 6.2%) start to appear and may well have replaced the Brune altogether. With a Noël and a Mars version, these make up a major part of the company's portfolio.

Gayant's excellent mixed-grain Goudale became an instant hit when it was conceived in 1994 and is now widely available throughout the shops and bars of northern France. With its incredibly low price-tag it should be on every beer shopper's list.

1996 saw the brewery drop the 'Enfants' in its name to become simply 'Les Brasseurs de Gayant'.

After introducing a beer named after the devil, a range of so-called abbey beers and a mixed-grain beer, it would appear that Gayant is trying to offer the French home market a similar range to that available in Belgium. As if to complete this range, a white beer – called Amadeus but with wording paying homage to the monks of Crespin again – was launched in 1997.

AMADEUS

4.5% alc/vol.   75cl corked bottles.

APPEARANCE: Very pale lemony wheat with a good head.

NOSE: Sweet, wheaty and pungently floral. A little lactic, slightly citric and faintly spicy. KR: Quite hoppy becoming rich and lactic.

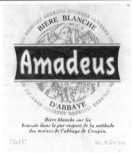

PALATE: Light, citric and lactic with a light tartness. A disturbing metallic note and a harsh husky hop add to its unpleasantness.

FINISH: Dry, spicy, lactic wheatiness with a tartness carried over from the palate. There is a peculiar sensation which lingers longer than you want.

OVERALL: JW: The tart lacticity detracts from the appeal of the citric wheatiness though it does enhance the thirst quenching qualities. KR: Poor white beer which has an over-lactic character, accentuated by its tartness. Also the husky hop gives a nasty bitterness.

GENERAL: Sold as a 'bière blanche d'abbaye' with reference to the abbey at Crespin, also referred to on the St-Landelin range.

JW:☐☐☐   KR:☐☐☐

BIÈRE DU DÉMON

12% alc/vol. 33cl crown corked bottles.

APPEARANCE: Golden colour.

NOSE: An initial, gently aromatic, light hop bitterness becomes a distinctly alcoholic pale malt with hints of ethanol. It seems to get even stronger as it warms.

PALATE: An immediate sledgehammer hit of ethanol and alcohol is not at all tempered by a lightly fruity pale malt. Once you are used to the alcohol it becomes more of a warm alcohol tang. Clean and dry. KR: Sweet and fruity start. Surprisingly light.

FINISH: A tangy pale malt and alcohol with a lingering warmth. KR: Lingering ethanol. A touch of lingering light fruitiness.

OVERALL: The first taste is the barrier which needs to be overcome. The alcohol comes over so intensely that it overpowers everything else to the detriment of a potentially interesting beer. However, once used to the alcohol it becomes disconcertingly easy to drink as it does not have much depth or fullness. Too strong and simple to be considered a classic.

GENERAL: Previously vaunted as the strongest pale beer in the world but now outdone by Jeanne d'Arc's 15% Belzebuth as certainly the strongest in France. Serve chilled. JW:☑☐☐ KR:☑☐☐

BIÈRE DU DÉSERT

7.5% alc/vol. 33cl crown corked & 75cl screw top bottles.

APPEARANCE: Lemon gold with a good head.

NOSE: Mellow aroma of light sweetish lemon hops over a pilsener malt. KR: Some alcohol notes and a sweet base

PALATE: Smooth full pale malt with a richness that is almost tangy. The hops supply a lemon note and a faint bitterness. A little alcohol is evident.

FINISH: An alcohol tang and warmth add to the generally tangy pale malt.

OVERALL: A good beer whose lightness of body is countered by the full pale malt and alcohol which are quite tangy.

GENERAL: The recipe seems to have changed during 1997. Previously it was a quite remarkable beer – amazingly light and refreshing yet with a very full (though light) palate and a good hop character with plenty of bitterness. The current tangy malt and alcohol warmth character prevents the beer living up to its name as it once did. Recently appearing in screen-printed bottles. JW:☑☑☐ KR:☑☑☐

BRUNE À CARACTÈRE ARTISANAL

6.4% alc/vol. 25cl crown corked bottles.

APPEARANCE: Dark ruby brown colour.

NOSE: Dark fruity malt. JW: A gentle hop. KR: A stale harsh hop.

PALATE: Full palate of dark malt and fruit with moderate bitterness and just a little hop character. A little mouth-watering. KR: Quite dry, and tannic, but chalky with a harsh drab fruitiness and chemical notes.

FINISH: Very dry with a lingering fruity bitterness. JW: Saliva inducing. KR: Watery, tannic and metallic.

OVERALL: Probably best summed up as a good fruitiness battling a watery texture. The strong bitterness certainly differentiates it from the normal brown but it does not have much artisanal character.

GENERAL: Its full name is 'Bière de Grande Classe à Caractère Artisanal' – a real mouthful which belies its very ordinary character.

JW: ☑☐☐   KR: ☐☐☐

GOUDALE

7.2% alc/vol.   75cl corked bottles.

APPEARANCE: Pale but bright gold.

NOSE: Excellent strong floral citric hop aroma with occasional wafts of pale malt. There is a slight damp mustiness to the hop. KR: A solid fruity base.

PALATE: Dominant, complex hop character which is floral, citric, bitter, quite sharp and very strong. Fighting through the hops are occasional wheaty notes. A slight alcohol note. JW: A gently sweet biscuity malt underpins the hops. KR: Very full wheat character.

FINISH: Builds to a bitter crescendo with lots of wonderfully acidic hops following in its wake.

OVERALL: Beautiful, immensely hoppy ale. Obviously a little one-sided but oozes quality and will appeal to Wallonian beer lovers. The hops reduce and a graininess takes over as the beer nears the end of its shelf-life.

GENERAL: Marketed as a wheat beer (not a white beer) due to the amount of wheat added to the mash. The brewery claims it is made to an ancient beer style. Comes in a distinctive screen-printed bottle (cream on brown glass). Surprisingly cheap and widely available, often sold in convenient boxes of six. Winner of our best value for money award. Don't let the low price put you off – this really is an exceptional beer.

JW: ☑☑☑   KR: ☑☑☑

LUTÈCE BIÈRE DE PARIS

6.4% alc/vol.   75cl corked and draught.

APPEARANCE: Rich dark amber colour with a pillowy head that is unfortunately short-lived.

NOSE: Pungent, rich, fruity malt lifted by a faint peppery hop.

PALATE: An instant mouthful of sweet, lightly fruited, caramelly malt. Wafts of hop bitterness with a sharp, citric, edge add to the interest. JW: Slight warming effect.

FINISH: A bittersweet, tangy fruitiness lingers over a caramel (JW) or toffee (KR) sweetish malt. Quite warming and just a touch metallic. JW: Slightly cloying.

OVERALL: Excellently full tasting, yet pleasantly lighter than the usual bières de garde, which makes it very easy to drink. Enough layers of taste to make you sit up and take notice though the hops do not exert their influence as strongly as might be expected.

GENERAL: Brewed for Brasseries Stella Artois apparently in a defunct style of the beer once made by many breweries in the Paris area (although evidence of any specific Parisien style is sadly lacking). Widely available throughout France.

JW: ☑☑☐ KR: ☑☑☐

SAINT LANDELIN AMBRÉE

6.1% alc/vol. 25cl crown corked bottles.

APPEARANCE: Amber colour.

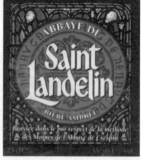

NOSE: Interesting flowery hop aroma. JW: Light fruity malt behind. Quite aromatic. KR: Hoppy with a rich red fruitiness from the malt.

PALATE: A sweet, thick, moderately fruity malt with a distinct hoppiness and growing bitterness. KR: Rich with an alcohol warmth and a fair complexity.

FINISH: JW: A lasting, dry, strong bitterness with a little sweetness persisting. Full. KR: Some sweet, some peppery dry and some creamy notes. Quite full and reasonably satisfying.

OVERALL: JW: A distinctive and very dry beer with a full taste. KR: A full taste – peppery hop, rich warming malt. Quaffable yet interesting enough to sip.

JW: ☑☐☐ KR: ☑☐☐

SAINT LANDELIN BIÈRE DE MARS

Alc/vol. Not specified. Sold only on draught

APPEARANCE: Lemon gold colour.

NOSE: Light citric lemon hop with a touch of pale malt (JW) or caramel (KR).

PALATE: Very sweet, slightly candied, pale malt punctuated by a sharp citric hop that is very distinctive but does not impart any benefit. Surprisingly watery character. After a while it develops a harsh bitter tang, almost artificial.

FINISH: A growing and lingering, tangy, bitter, drying, unpleasant experience though still citric and mouth watering. KR: A metal-like sensation at the back of the mouth and throat.

OVERALL: Lighter than expected with a good hoppy nose and palate seriously let down by the harsh and nasty finish. Not helped by the fact that the more you drink the more the finish intrudes into the palate.

JW: ☐☐☐ KR: ☐☐☐

SAINT LANDELIN BLONDE

5.9% alc/vol. 25cl & 33cl crown corked bottles.

APPEARANCE: Golden colour.

NOSE: Big fruity, perfumed, hop aroma. JW: A little lemon from the hops. KR: Spicy light fruit and some lacticity.

PALATE: Strong citric hop character with lots of lemon, a twist of lime, and some resiny notes over a rich pilsener malt. Quite sweet and fruity. KR: Almost wheaty, lactic notes.

FINISH: Suggests a powdery coating on roof of mouth. A few lemon notes remain. Causing some mouth-watering. JW: Dry, hoppy bitterness. KR: Creamy wheatiness with light lingering hop notes.

OVERALL: A moderate, very hoppy beer reminiscent of a Walloon blonde rather than an abbey beer. Interestingly, lemon (intense in places) comes through an otherwise unspectacular beer. KR: Odd creamy, lactic character.

JW: ☑☐☐   KR: ☑☐☐

SAINT LANDELIN SPÉCIALE NOËL

6.8% alc/vol. 25cl crown corked & 75cl corked bottles and draught.

APPEARANCE: Dark copper colour with a light fluffy head.

NOSE: Mellow but full farmyardy hop laced darkish malt with some not-so-pleasant vegetably/fruity notes.

PALATE: Fruity malt interlaced with a moderately bitter resiny hop. And an unfortunate slightly artificial candied element. KR: A rich metallic-laced fruit with a vegetable edge.

FINISH: Dry resiny and bitter yet with some sweet notes and a tangy malt. KR: Dark spice and vegetable notes

OVERALL: Oddly sweet yet strongly bitter at times, particularly in the finish. The sweetness is not particularly natural and overall it does not really work very well – a bit disjointed and tangy with a candied element.

JW: ☑☐☐   KR: ☑☐☐

SAINT LANDELIN TRIPLE BRUNE

8% alc/vol. 33cl crown corked bottles.

APPEARANCE: Deep reddish brown.

NOSE: Initially a pleasant, dark, lightly roasted malt with a hint of chocolate but eventually some hop character gets through. Quite earthy with a little alcohol.

PALATE: Full, dark, malty palate with a noticeable alcohol element adding warmth. Very sweet with a light bitterness trying to get through and some fruit and chocolate notes. KR: Sweet and fruity with a distinctly tangy fruit.

FINISH: Bitter dark chocolate malt lasts as the bitterness grows through the sweet fruitiness. JW: A little tangy. KR: Sticky and quite thick with a lingering fruit tang.

OVERALL: Full dark, slightly chocolatey malt is the main constituent of this beer along with its alcohol warmth. Although some alcohol and a hop element attempt to lift it, the whole does not quite gel. The palate grows tired of the strong fruit character after a while. KR: Quite impressively full, but ultimately many will find it just too fruity and tangy.

GENERAL: First brewed 1997. This may well be the replacement for the Saint Landelin Brune which became strangely absent from the supermarket shelves throughout 1998.

JW: ☐☐☐   KR: ☐☐☐

TEQUIEROS

5.9% alc/vol.   33cl crown corked bottles.

APPEARANCE: Honey gold with a fair creamy head.

NOSE: Very reminiscent of a lager and lime shandy. Citric, lemon and lime, with a light but aromatic hop and a distinct lemonade smell. JW: Faint malt base comes through. KR: More lemon than lime.

PALATE: Sweet and quite malty with a bitter hop trying hard to get through the shandy taste but just the bitterness makes it through. JW: A distinct, slightly artificial, tequila taste bites at the roof of the mouth. KR: There is a warmth that suggests added tequila but it defies actual detection until the finish.

FINISH: JW: Starts strongly bitter, an odd powdery dry bitterness, but this degenerates into a lingering tang from the bitter hop and the tequila. KR: Bitter with lingering sweet citric notes and a building hop dryness which doesn't quite make the mark.

OVERALL: JW: Has a nice texture but a very artificial character and is distinctly bitter and tangy, too much so for me. KR: Only in the finish does it get tequilla-like and that just seems to add to the bitterness. Thankfully not as sweet as other spirit beers.

GENERAL: Comes in a garishly-coloured, screen-printed bottle.

JW: ☐☐☐   KR: ☑☐☐

OTHER BEERS BREWED ──────────────────────────

Bière Bock Extra Blonde (3.8% alc/vol.)

Goldenburg (5.9% alc/vol.) – Pale gold with a bland pilsener maltiness and a touch of fruit on the nose. Sweet with a tingling, tangy, harsh bitter hop intruding on the washed-out pale malt and some metallic notes. The finish is fruity before a chalky, sharp hoppiness starts to dry the mouth.

Prima Saaz (4.8% alc/vol.)

Saaz Old Lager (5.2% alc/vol.) – A pale gold beer with a short-lived biscuity malt and hop aroma. Surprisingly sweet with a gentle pilsener malt dominated by a bitter resinous hop. Growing hop bitterness in the finish spoilt by a harsh powdery dryness in the mouth.

Brasserie de Granges-sur-Baume

- ✉ Au Village, 39210 Granges-sur-Baume
- ☎ 03 84 48 20 98
- ◷ Easter-August daily 1000-1900. December & January on request. Closed Monday
- 🏭 Pre-arranged only. 3 weeks notice. In French. No charge
- 🛒 Bottles and cases
- 📊 50hl (in 1997)
- ➡ 200m from church in centre of village

Granges-sur-Baume should be on every gourmet's 'must not miss' list – not only is it set in the stunning Jura countryside, well-known for its quality wines, but it also has a brewery which trebles up as a patisserie and chocolaterie. For many it could be considered heaven on earth – and thankfully the beer is pretty good as well.

Run by Pierre Lureau and Stéphanie Roy the brewery is in the centre of the tiny village which is perched on a hill-top overlooking the similar-sized and equally appealing village of Baume-les-Messieurs, complete with ancient abbey, nestling in the valley below. Neither village appears on many maps so the best way to find the brewery is to get to Lons-le-Saunier and take the D471 to Champagnole. About 8km out of Lons is the Cirque de Baume and the D70 to Voiteur. Take the D70 and the first village is Baume-les-Messieurs. A road, the D210, winds up the hill to the east, behind the abbey. Follow that to Granges-sur-Baume and go through the square, round the corner and the brewery is on the right.

It started on 3rd October 1995 and forms an equal part of the business along with the patisseries and the chocolates. Baking is done Tuesday, Thursday and Saturday, confectionery Wednesday and Friday with brewing on Monday – a very full week. Most of the brewing tends to be done in January and February when business is quiet since the majority of the trade is with tourists.

The main brewing equipment consists of two large gas-fired cooking pots which saw service in a previous life curing hams and other meats. They give a two-hectolitre capacity though usually only one hectolitre is brewed at a time. There is a three hour boil with half of that time at 56°C, the remainder at 65–68°C. The yeast used is, surprisingly, a dried yeast of English origin and this is used for a three-week primary and a three-week secondary fermentation. There then follows two to three months' maturation before sale.

The name and label are intended to evoke visions of a natural, ancient, cloudy beer with tradition behind it.

Currently only a blonde and amber are brewed. Previously there was also a brown but demand was not high enough to justify continuing with it (one theory for this is that brown beer is readily made by home-brewers so they do not need to go out and buy a brown beer). However, demand is good for the blonde. Pierre suggested that the local palate favours sweet, slightly malty and not too fizzy beers and that many people found his beers had too much flavour.

If demand does increase dramatically it will pose problems since the brewery has limited storage capacity and no delivery vehicles.

For those intested in sampling the food side of the operation, it offers a good range of speciality breads (with walnuts, hazelnuts, sesame seeds, currants, cheese or organic bread) as well the usual range of cakes. The chocolate they use is bought in from Belgium in large blocks which they turn into a wide variety of enticing individual chocolates.

He's not baking bread, and he's not making chocolates . . . so that means it must be Monday!

LA NÉBULEUSE AMBRÉE

6% alc/vol.   75cl crown corked bottles.

BREW DETAILS: Unfiltered. Unpasteurised. Top fermentation. Bottle refermentation.

DECLARED INGREDIENTS: Brewers Gold, Northern Brewer and Saaz hops. Prisma; 2-row Alexis and Caramel 110 malts.

APPEARANCE: Dark orangey brown with a good fluffy head.

NOSE: Mellow malt fruitiness with a strong but subdued hop and hints of grass. KR: The grassy hop has a citric note, but otherwise just a dull background malt.

PALATE: The hop character comes through strongly throughout and a sharp hop competes with a strong fruity malt to dominate the palate. The malt has a definite bite to it as well as adding to the fruitiness which has a faintly acidic edge to it. JW: Overall, these elements blend together to make it a fairly mellow taste, particularly when a little sediment is added. KR: Very hoppily bitter with a strong oily/resiny character. Sharply hoppy to the point of creating a tang.

FINISH: JW: Lingering hop bitterness with a gentle fruitiness and a tangy malt. KR: Very sharp hop bitterness (with a resiny bite) and a strong fruity tang from the malt.

OVERALL: JW: Lots of malt and lots of hop though there is a good balance between the two. The hop has a distinctly sharp bite to it and the malt is quite tangy. The tastes are strong and distinct, though well balanced, and mellow out considerably when a little sediment is added. KR: Has the balance the blonde lacks but it is let down by a complexity which feels like it should be there but isn't quite. Excellently artisanal, but lacking depth.

GENERAL: First brewed 1995. JW: ☑☑☐ KR: ☑☐☐

LA NÉBULEUSE BLONDE

6% alc/vol. 75cl crown corked bottles.

BREW DETAILS: Unfiltered. Unpasteurised. Top fermentation. Bottle refermentation.

DECLARED INGREDIENTS: Brewers Gold, Northern Brewer and Saaz hops; Prisma, 2-row Alexis, Caramel 110 and Chocolate malts

APPEARANCE: Golden with a large rocky head and some excellent lacework.

NOSE: Excellent, full, fresh, aromatic, citric hops with a sweetish pale background.

PALATE: Wonderfully fresh and refreshing hoppiness. Light but full with a refreshing citric quality and just a gentle yet persistent bitterness. This is supported by a light but solid pale malt base.

FINISH: Lingering hoppy taste with only a little bitterness.

OVERALL: Strongly hoppy blonde beer with plenty of character. Fresh and refreshing with a nice light pale malt behind. A good summer quencher with loads more to offer. When young it is uncompromisingly hoppy and brilliantly refreshing but as it ages the freshness dies down taking the edge off the hops. However, it remains a very satisfying hoppy beer.

GENERAL: First brewed 1995 JW: ☑☑☐ KR: ☑☑☐

BARS & CAFES RECOMMENDED BY THE BREWERY

Café de l'Hôtel de Ville, 39000 Lons-le-Saunier
Le Chalet la Frasse, 39000 Lamoura
Le Moulin de Brainans, B.P.45, 39800 Poligny

Brasseries Heineken

✉ HQ: 19 rue des Deux-Gares, 92565 Rueil-Malmaison Cedex

☎ 01 47 14 36 50   Fax: 01 47 14 36 51   www.heineken.nl

🕐 See article

🏭 See article

🏪 Bottles, cases and glasses

📊 5,300,000 hl (in 1996)

➡ See article

The modern buildings now at the Mons-en-Baroeul plant.

In 1996, around 30% of the French beer market was controlled by the Dutch-based multi-national which is also the second largest brewing company in the world. Heineken, founded in Amsterdam in 1864, first made an impression in France in 1972 when it bought its plant in Schiltigheim and recently expanded its French operation when, in 1996, it bought the Fischer and Adelshoffen breweries (but as these breweries operate somewhat independently, they appear as separate entries in this book).

Heineken has three production facilities in France, the largest of which, with an output of 3 million hectolitres, is the old Brasserie Pelforth at **Z.I. de la Pilaterie, Rue du Houblon, 59370 Mons-en-Baroeul (tel. 03 20 33 67 56)**. The old Brasserie de l'Esperance at **4 rue Saint-Charles, 67300 Schiltigheim (tel. 03 88 19 59 53)** produces 1.5 million hectolitres whilst the smallest of the three, making 1.1 million hectolitres, is **La Valentine, Av. Francois Chardigny, 13011 Marseilles (tel. 04 91 18 85 18)**. All of these are virtual beer factories and are relatively easy to find.

The Heineken plant at Schiltigheim.

The Schiltigheim plant came into the company in 1972 when Heineken bought the historic Brasserie de l'Esperance. Jean Hatt had founded the brewery in 1746 in rue des Veaux, Strasbourg, the site of the current Les Brasseurs brewpub. Jean was the grandson of Jerome Hatt who, in 1664, had founded what would become Kronenbourg – so the family left a major impression on the French beer industry as between them Heineken and Kronenbourg have 70% of the national market. In 1862 the brewery at Schiltigheim was constructed and the Esperance brewery moved there, benefiting particularly from the large cellars which improved the storage and maturing of the beer. The brewery continued to grow and was still controlled by the Hatt family for another century. Then came the major development which started in 1969 with the creation of l'Alsacienne de Brasserie (AlBra) group of breweries. Total production capability far exceeded what was being sold and rationalisation saw production concentrate on just two sites, l'Esperance and Mützig with the other breweries being closed down. In 1972 Heineken bought AlBra, although it didn't change its name to Heineken France until 1980.

The Mons-en-Barouel plant started life in 1921 as Brasserie du Pélican, which formed when two local breweries combined forces. In 1937 it developed the well-known Pelforth Brune (Pelforth being an Anglicised contraction of Pélican and forte, the latter meaning 'strong') which was a tremendous success and became synonymous with the brewery to such an extent it actually changed its name from Pélican to Pelforth in 1972. Over the next few years Pelforth fuelled its expansion by buying up other breweries and merging with Brasserie Carlier of Dunkerque before, in 1986, forming the Française de Brasserie group with Union de Brasseries and Heineken France. Two years later Heineken had acquired total control.

The Schiltigheim brewery welcomes visitors (around 28,000 a year) and the stunningly impressive brewing hall, dating from 1933, is probably the highlight of the 90-minute organised tour. Tours must be pre-booked and are available in English, French or German. They operate from Monday to Friday starting at 0900, 1000, 1400 and 1500 with additional starts at 1100 and 1600 in June, July and August.

"33" EXPORT

4.8% alc/vol. 25cl, 33cl, 75cl & 100cl bottles, 33cl cans and draught.

BREW DETAILS: Filtered. Pasteurised. Bottom fermentation.

APPEARANCE: Bright gold colour.

NOSE: An initially strong hoppiness becomes dull with a good background of light malt.

PALATE: Sweet kick in the start. A powerful hop bitterness overpowers the sweetness generated by an impressively full malt.

FINISH: Very bitter and quite oily hoppiness with a gradual tailing-off of the malt.

OVERALL: Strong, oily, resiny hoppiness throughout. Distinctly sweet pale malt, which is full in taste, forms a good base but the resiny bitterness dominates. Legend has it the name comes from the fact it was one of the first 33cl-bottled beers.

GENERAL: First brewed 1960. JW: ☑☐☐ KR: ☑☐☐

AMBERLEY

7.3% alc/vol. 25cl crown corked bottles & draught.

BREW DETAILS: Filtered. Pasteurised. Bottom fermentation.

APPEARANCE: Amber coloured.

NOSE: An immediate hit of sweet, lightly smoked malt mellows to a sweet, candied, malt with just a hint of butterscotch. JW: Faintly whiskied.

PALATE: Sweet, lightly smoked candy malt. JW: A little tangy, candied whisky with some alcohol warmth. KR: Very little hoppiness to offer balance.

FINISH: Candied and tangy with a gentle bitterness just poking through. JW: Slight whisky notes. KR: Alcohol hints and a lingering smokiness.

OVERALL: Too sweet and candied with just the lightly smoked malt to give it character. JW: Undoubtedly a French whisky beer – lots of artificial whisky taste, unfortunately. KR: Characterful but oversweet.

GENERAL: First brewed 1993. Exported to USA since 1995.

JW:☑☐☐ KR:☑☐☐

ANCRE

4.8% alc/vol. 75cl bottles.

APPEARANCE: Light gold with a fluffy head and nice lacework.

NOSE: Understated aromatic hop (apart from the citrus note) with a good fruity base. Pretty unusual.

PALATE: A persistent sweet note is dominant in the start, turning drier and slightly bitter as the hops take hold. Creamy and a touch wheaty. Quite full. Like the nose – pretty unusual and a welcome change.

FINISH: Dry and hoppily bitter. Citric notes linger, along with a wheaty creaminess. Quite interesting.

OVERALL: An amazingly soft and light texture complements the gentle hop character which builds into the finish where it really blossoms. A unique finish. Easy to drink with the dryness encouraging more drinking. Pleasantly different from the usual crop.

GENERAL: First brewed 1746.

JW:☑☐☐ KR:☑☐☐

BIÈRE DE MARS DE PELFORTH

5.3% alc/vol. Draught only.

BREW DETAILS: Filtered. Bottom fermentation.

APPEARANCE: Old gold in colour.

NOSE: Faint perfumed hop and amber malt.

PALATE: A mellow amber malt and a few hops overlay a balanced sweetness and bitterness. Some wateriness.

FINISH: A dry, tangy bitterness from a powder-like coating on the roof of the mouth, counteracted a mouthwatering quality.

OVERALL: With the major elements balancing each other out it becomes a relatively bland beer with a none too pleasant finish.

GENERAL: First brewed 1996.

JW:☐☐☐ KR:☐☐☐

BIÈRE DE NOËL DE PELFORTH

7.3% alc/vol. 25cl crown corked & draught.

BREW DETAILS: Filtered. Bottom fermentation.

APPEARANCE: Deep amber colour with a good tight, creamy, lasting head.

NOSE: Good hop note over a full, dark malt and a touch of alcohol. A warming, dark and spicy promise fades after a few minutes. JW: Some fruit and plenty of fruity esters. After quite a while it develops some cocoa hints.

PALATE: An instant mouthful of liquorice, treacle and dark spices coming through a fruity maltiness with a pronounced oily hoppiness adding to the spicy notes.

FINISH: Warming tangy bitterness. KR: A lingering dark character with all sorts of spices and herbs. Quite bitter but overtly sweet.

OVERALL: For a mass-market offering this is a great Christmas beer. Smooth, full, rich, fruity, malty and very warming with that 'special' taste that justifies the tag. JW: Excellent promise of the nose is almost delivered by the palate but the finish is disappointing.

JW: ☑☑☐ KR: ☑☑☐

GEORGE KILLIAN'S

6.5% alc/vol. 25cl, 33cl crown corked bottles and draught.

BREW DETAILS: Filtered. Pasteurised. Bottom fermentation.

APPEARANCE: Amber in colour.

NOSE: Sweet light, fruity malt with a little bland hop. JW: Some distinctive, possibly chicory, element over the top.

PALATE: A full palate of pleasant, slightly caramel, fruity malt with suggestions of light roastedness which develops into a harsh tang.

FINISH: Well balanced with a gentle bitter dryness and a tangy caramel malt.

OVERALL: An interesting beer with a distinctive French taste. KR: Not, as the label describes, in the traditional Irish style.

GENERAL: First brewed 1976. Brewed under licence in USA by Coors since 1980. Sold in the Netherlands as **Kylian**.

JW: ☑☐☐ KR: ☑☐☐

MÜTZIG

4.8% alc/vol. 25cl crown corked bottles.

APPEARANCE: Lightish gold in colour.

NOSE: Husky hoppiness with a touch of pale malt.

PALATE: A little, but quite bland, pale malt with a fair hop character imparting a gentle bitterness.

FINISH: Lingering, dry, bitter hoppiness.

The Beers of France

OVERALL: An unexceptional but quenching beer which majors on its strong husky hoppiness.

GENERAL: First brewed 1810. JW: ☑☐☐ KR: ☑☐☐

MÜTZIG OLD LAGER

7.3% alc/vol. 25cl crown corked bottles.

APPEARANCE: Classic golden pilsner colour.

NOSE: Sweet and thick pale malt with a distinct hop and a little vanilla.

PALATE: Initial sweet slightly fruity malt turns sharply bitter and hoppy with a pronounced hop bitterness, a little fruit and a gentle pepperiness.

FINISH: Very bitter and mouthdrying with a lingering tangy, dry hop. JW: Warming.

OVERALL: Full tasting beer with a strongly resiny, bitter hop character. JW: Gentle alcohol warmth. KR: Dangerously drinkable and surprisingly neutral for its strength. JW: ☑☐☐ KR: ☑☑☐

NiPS (or SPiN)

7.9% alc/vol. 33cl crown corked bottles.

BREW DETAILS: Filtered. Bottom fermentation.

APPEARANCE: Lemon gold colour with a good fluffy head.

NOSE: A solid but understated husky sweet pale malt with a distinctive dry hop. KR: A touch metallic.

PALATE: Full, sweet pale malt with a distinct alcohol edge and a resiny hop which imparts an instant bitterness. As it warms so the alcohol warmth in the beer increases.

FINISH: A fruity malt behind a strong bitter hop. JW: The bitterness lingers. KR: Fleeting sweet notes.

OVERALL: Excellent soft creamy texture and a full taste of pale malt with an edge of resiny hop and alcohol to give it some bite. Hardly complex but very full and tasty.

GENERAL: First brewed 1993. Very distinctive screen-printed clear bottle with its clever, palindromic name in black. JW: ☑☑☐ KR: ☑☐☐

PELFORTH BLONDE

5.8% alc/vol. 25cl crown corked & 65cl ceramic stoppered bottles bottles and draught.

BREW DETAILS: Filtered. Bottom fermentation.

APPEARANCE: Crisp, clean pale gold.

NOSE: A sweet mix of hop and pale malt.

PALATE: Full mouth of well balanced lightly citric hop and fruity malt. JW: Grows to be very tangy. KR: Starts sweet but quickly turns very bitter and dry.

FINISH: JW: Dry and very bitter with hints of slightly burnt candy. KR: Fades quickly to just a peppery dryness with bitter notes.

OVERALL: JW: An odd tangy light malt and hop jars after a while. KR: Easy drinking with a good balance. JW: ☐☐☐ KR: ☑☐☐

PELFORTH BRUNE

6.5% alc/vol. 25cl, 33cl crown corked bottles & draught (also 65cl ceramic stoppered bottles).

BREW DETAILS: Filtered. Bottom fermentation.

APPEARANCE: Reddish brown colour.

NOSE: Sweet, candy malt with a hint of caramel.

PALATE: Sweet, malty, caramelised candy.

FINISH: Tangy, leftover candy caramel.

OVERALL: Disappointing brown beer that does not taste its 6.5% and has just too much candy caramel malt throughout.

GENERAL: First brewed 1937.

JW:☐☐☐   KR:☐☐☐

PÉLICAN

4.8% alc/vol. 1 litre ceramic stoppered bottles.

APPEARANCE: Golden with a huge head.

NOSE: A pleasant, almost floral, waft of light hop with a gentle pale malt.

PALATE: Faintly citric hop with a solid pale/pilsener malt base. Instantly bitter and dry mouthful of taste but with a moderate malt sweetness coming through stronger.

FINISH: Dry, resiny hop with a balanced bitterness.

OVERALL: Surprisingly good, light, quaffing beer. Easy to drink, with a good hop character and a nice malt base. The bitter dry bite in the finish helps it achieve an impressive thirst slaking character.

GENERAL: First brewed 1921.

JW:☑☐☐   KR:☑☐☐

PORTER 39

7.1% alc/vol. 33cl crown corked bottles.

APPEARANCE: Deep ruby black.

NOSE: Rich and malty with wafts of nuts and raisins. JW: Lightly roasted with hints of chocolate. KR: Let down by metallic and saccharin hints.

PALATE: A full dark malt with a roasted start building into a vinous fruity malt. Warming alcohol and a hoppy bitterness add depth. Fleeting sweetness turns dry into the finish.

FINISH: Bitter and dry with a lingering roasted note and a strong, lingering tanginess. KR: A little saccharin disappoints.

OVERALL: A mellow, easy drinking evening beer with good balance, a full taste and lots of interest. Lingering tang detracts from its appeal.

GENERAL: First brewed 1929.

JW:☑☑☐   KR:☑☑☐

OTHER BEERS BREWED —————————————————

Heineken makes a variety of other beers (some of which are foreign beers brewed under licences) including: **Amstel, Amstel Legend, Dry de '33', Heineken, Record de '33'** and, **Sylver Christmas**

Brasserie Henry

✉ 6 rue Musard, 55170 Bazincourt-sur-Saulx

☎ 03 29 78 64 59   Fax: 03 29 78 66 15

🕐 Sat & Sun: 1400-1800

🏨 Pre-arranged only. 2 days notice. In French & English

🏭 Bottles and cases

📊 320hl (in 1997)

➡ In the village centre, ten metres from the café

Whilst Brasserie Henry is easy to find once you are in the pretty little village of Bazincourt-sur-Saulx the village itself certainly is not – unless you know where it is. The easiest route to find it without a detailed map is to take the N35 Bar-Le-Duc to St-Dizier road. Half-way between these towns the D997 crosses the N35, at the same point that the N35 crosses the River Saulx. Head southeast on the D997 following the river through Haironville and Rupt-aux-Nonains and you will come to Bazincourt. Follow your nose towards the centre and you should come to a T-junction with the village cafe on your right and the brewery diagonally opposite.

The tiny, sleepy village of Bazincourt in Lorraine is very attractive, and set in the valley of the River Saulx with the Fôret du Haut Juré to the north, Fôret de Trois-Fontaines to the west and Fôret du Ligny to the south-east. There is an obvious appeal to living in such a place and it was here that Englishman Ben Henry founded his microbrewery.

Having produced his first brew at the tender age of twelve it was perhaps inevitable that he would do it full-time one day. An interesting range of jobs, ending with a spell as a shop-fitter in London, did not discourage him from that idea and in 1991 he moved to France to a village in the area in which his wife, Frédérique, had grown up. Most of his time was spent rebuilding the house they bought and it was not until 6th December 1996 that the brewery actually started commercially, but even then it was more by nature than design.

Still home-brewing and always keen to try out new recipes, Ben decided to make use of the redcurrants that the area is renowned for by brewing two barrels of redcurrant beer which he planned to present to the village council for use at the local festival. It seems they didn't quite get the right idea – instead of accepting the beer and dispensing it at the festival they granted Ben a licence to sell beer from his house. So he opened his garage and sold the beer from there. Apparently it went very quickly and there were nearly some ugly scenes after it ran out. It was obviously time to take things more seriously.

The garage was turned into more of a commercial brewery and a small fermentation room was constructed which houses three fermenters. To supplement his home-brewing experience Ben went on a course run by Brewlab in Sunderland, UK, and to maintain his links with his homeland further he uses a London yeast in his beers.

The first commercial beer was La Bière du Père Fouettard which is a name that has great meaning in the area. The Lorraine, Alsace and northern France areas celebrate Christmas with Saint Nicholas rather than Father Christmas (Père Noël). Saint Nicholas is the patron saint of children and one of the more outrageous stories about him suggests that he restored to life three children who had been chopped up by a butcher and put in a brine tub. In 1552 the Spanish under Charles Quint (Charles V) laid siege to Metz, which finally ended around Christmas time. Saint Nicholas visited, followed by an effigy of Charles Quint whom they named Père Fouettard (Father Whipper). Because he was so disliked, local folklore has made him the one who beats the naughty children while Saint Nicholas gives sweets to the children who have been good. There are a number of representations of him but Ben's preferred version is the one he chose for his beer label.

If you want somewhere to stay whilst in Bazincourt try Bernard and Bernadette Herbillon (tel. 03 29 78 60 49) who run a pleasant farmhouse B&B, with evening meal if required.

LA BIÈRE DU PÈRE FOUETTARD

7% alc/vol. 33cl crown corked & 75cl corked bottles.

BREW DETAILS: Unfiltered. Unpasteurised. Top fermentation.

DECLARED INGREDIENTS: Kent Goldings hops. Pale and Crystal malts. Roasted barley.

APPEARANCE: Rich copper brown colour with a massive head.

NOSE: Rich and fruity crystal malt. KR: A heady, lifting hop note.

PALATE: JW: Roast malt and chicory. Quite fruity and moderately bitter. The initially strong sharp tangy bitterness mellows as you drink and it becomes more fruity, malty and tangy. KR: Sharply hoppy and resinous. Bitter with a good, solid crystal malt fruity background – gives the impression of top quality ingredients.

FINISH: Strongly bitter and dry. JW: A little astringent. KR: A strong residual resin from the hop.

OVERALL: JW: Initially strongly bitter with a sharp tangy bitterness but it mellows and takes on a character closer to its texture which is smooth and creamy with a little fizz lifting it. KR: Strongly bitter beer with a profoundly resinous hop, balanced by a full and fruity, crystal malt base. A quality beer.

GENERAL: First brewed 1996. The Kent Goldings used are new season hops for maximum aroma.

JW: ☑☑☐ KR: ☑☑☐

BLANCHE DE LA SAULX

5% alc/vol.   33cl crown corked & 75cl corked bottles and draught.

BREW DETAILS: Unfiltered. Unpasteurised. Top fermentation.

DECLARED INGREDIENTS: Aged Saaz and Bramling Cross hops; Winter barley and wheat.

APPEARANCE: Hazy wheat and a frothy head.

NOSE: Fruity (bananas and berries) with a pungent hop which quickly vents off. JW: With sediment added it is simply a strong lactic wheatiness. KR: A little musty with a fruity promise. Distinctly unwheaty, with a surprising cidery note.

PALATE: JW: Bags of wheat and quite lemony with a definite yeastiness. Good sweet/bitter balance with the sweet just on top. With sediment it is even more yeasty, lactic and wheaty. KR: Peculiar. Very citric with sharp red fruit notes masking a light wheaty character

FINISH: Lingering, very sharp citric notes. JW: A growing wheatiness with a building bitterness.

OVERALL: JW: A good attempt at a German style wheat beer though it becomes very lactic and yeasty when the sediment in included. KR: Very sharply citric and fruity masking most other elements, notably the wheat which never gets a hold. Very artisanal.

GENERAL: First brewed 1997.   JW: ☑☑☐   KR: ☑☐☐

GOLDING

5% alc/vol.   33cl crown corked & 75cl corked bottles and draught.

BREW DETAILS: Unfiltered. Unpasteurised. Top fermentation.

INGREDIENTS: Golding hops; Pale, Crystal and Chocolate malts.

APPEARANCE: Amber with a rocky head.

NOSE: Intensely estery and fruity with a fruity sweetness and a hint of hop.

PALATE: Strong hop character from the Goldings with the intense fruitiness of the nose continuing. Some malt sweetness but also a strongish bitterness which builds into the finish.

FINISH: Lingering sharp bitterness with a little fruity malt.

OVERALL: A full tasting beer in all departments.

GENERAL: First brewed 1997. Ben Henry says: "Golding gave his name to the most highly rated hop, my beer is homage to the man and his great hop".   JW: ☑☐☐   KR: ☑☐☐

LONDON PORTER ALE

7% alc/vol.   33cl crown corked & 75cl corked bottles.

BREW DETAILS: Unfiltered. Unpasteurised. Top fermentation.

DETAILS INGREDIENTS: Fuggles, Golding and Challenger hops; Pale, Crystal, Chocolate and Wheat malts. Roasted barley.

APPEARANCE: Deep, dark, red black.

NOSE: Gorgeous quite darkly spiced and very inviting. Excellent balance of full, lightly roast, fruity malt with a surprising level of hops and spice.

PALATE: Full strong palate of multi-layered dark tastes. Fairly complex with an interestingly strong spicy fruitiness. A good hop gives bitterness to counter the inherent sweetness. The roasted malt is quite light and works as the perfect foil for the unusual hoppiness. KR: A thick lactic note in the background.

LONDON PORTER ALE

Cinq malts différents sont utilisés pour obtenir cette bière complexe et foncée, brassée dans le style traditionnel de la ville de Londres.

75 cl
alc. 7% vol.

BRASSERIE HENRY
55110 BAZINCOURT/SAULX - FRANCE

FINISH: Lingering dark, malty complexity with a faint tartness and a lifting hoppiness. KR: Leftover dark spices giving dryness.

OVERALL: Excellent porter which, for such a light stout character, displays a surprising fullness, depth and complexity with a lovely smooth texture. Very accessible.

GENERAL: First brewed 1997.   JW: ☑☑☑   KR: ☑☑☑

LA SAULX

7% alc/vol.   33cl crown corked & 75cl corked bottles.

BREW DETAILS: Unfiltered. Unpasteurised. Top fermentation.

DECLARED INGREDIENTS: Fuggles, Golding & Challenger hops; Pale, Blond, Crystal, Chocolate and Wheat malts.

APPEARANCE: Deep dark red brown colour.

NOSE: Rich and vinous dark spiced fruity malt with a hint of liquorice.

PALATE: A well-blended range of subtle tastes give a full, complex palate, consisting principally of dark, fruity malt.

LA SAULX

BRUNE
BIÈRE SPECIALE

BIÈRE ARTISANALE À L'ANCIENNE
REFERMENTÉE EN BOUTEILLE SUR LEVURE
VERSER AVEC PRÉCAUTION À 10-12°C

e 75 cl

ALC.
7.0% VOL.

Beer
OG 10.70

MADE IN FRANCE

BRASSERIE HENRY - 55170 BAZINCOURT SUR SAULX - FRANCE

Spicy and herbal elements and a resiny hop counter the sweetness, making the overall taste quite bitter.

FINISH: Fruity, dark malt with a lingering resiny bitterness.

OVERALL: A distinctive, fruity, alcoholic, malty, late night beer which has a good level of complexity without being over-full.

GENERAL: First brewed 1997. La Saulx is the name of the locality and also the stream running through the village.

JW: ☑☑☐   KR: ☑☑☐

OTHER BEERS BREWED ─────────────

Bière de Mars (6% alc/vol.) – First brewed 1997.

BARS & CAFES RECOMMENDED BY THE BREWERY

La Renaissance, 55320 Sommedieue
Le Cent Sept, 107 rue le Roux, 55100 Ligny-en-Barrois
L'Estaminet, 45 rue Rouyers, 55000 Verdun

BEER SHOPS RECOMMENDED BY THE BREWERY

Les Jardins du Val de Lorraine, 41 rue de Metz, 54390 Frouard
K. Bière, 64 rue du Mont St-Denis, 75018 Paris

Institut Français des Boissons et de la Brasserie Malterie (IFBM)

- ✉ 7 rue du Bois de la Champelle, BP 267, 54512 Vandoeuvre
- ☎ 03 83 44 88 00   Fax: 03 83 44 12 90
- 🕐 Not applicable
- ♨ The Institute only offers tours to professionals in the industry
- 🏠 Not applicable
- 🍺 Approx. 2,000hl (projected for 1998)
- ➜ Vandoeuvre is on the south-west side of Nancy, and the IFBM is on the outskirts. From Junction 2 of the A33/E23 head towards Nancy, turning left into Les Hautes de Brabois and the Hippodrome. Opposite the entrance to the Hippodrome turn left into rue du Bois de la Champelle, the IFBM is on the left

The Institut Français des Boissons et de la Brasserie Malterie wins the prize for the longest name of any French brewery. It was founded in 1962 but could argue that it has a history nearly as long as its name. Back in 1895 l'École de Brasserie de Nancy came into being as a formal training centre for the brewing industry. This had a long and successful, though sometimes difficult, history and when it finally folded the role was taken over by the IFBM which is now the 'centre of excellence' for brewing education in France.

It has three principal functions – technical studies, research and the training of professional brewers, in addition to which it also possesses an impressive library of documentation relating to brewing.

In 1994 Qualtech was created. This is a sister company, based at the same site, which concentrates on the commercial aspects of the operation – selling the beers and running/marketing the laboratory services, principally sensory analysis or microbiological and chemical analysis.

The 'technical workshop' was built in 1981, covers 1200m² and contains a micro-maltery (just 16kg of grain); a micro-brewery (25 litres); a pilot maltery (2 x 600 kg); a pilot brewery (20hl) and a conditioning line including a 2,000 bottles/hour bottling line. All the beers produced are bottom fermenting.

In addition to training brewers this plant is also used for helping them get their breweries off the ground. A budding brewer may contact the Institute with a concept for a beer which can be developed and tested without the need to build an actual brewery. The IFBM can also assess the economic viability of the project by piloting it for a client until a sizeable marketing base has been established. Once the recipe is finalised and the market established it can provide support and assistance with the installation of the brewery.

Their own beers are marketed under the Qualtech banner but they have no distribution network so they are sold direct from the premises to clients or distributors. They hold four festivals a year at which they launch their seasonal beers.

BIÈRE DE MARS

6% alc/vol. 33cl crown corked bottles.

BREW DETAILS: Filtered. Bottom fermentation.

APPEARANCE: Orangey mid-brown colour.

NOSE: Faint sweetish fruity malt.

PALATE: JW: Fairly fruity malt with a distinctive, quite resiny, hop edge. KR: Light fruitiness with a tired, quite bitter hop. Coppery/metallic.

FINISH: Lashings of resiny hop with a little fruity malt behind.

OVERALL: When young a pleasant easy drinking beer with a good texture. Plenty of fruity malt is well tempered by a strongish resiny hop. Later in life the resiny hop starts to dominate leaving little else.

JW: ☑☐☐ KR: ☑☐☐

BIÈRE DE NOËL

7% alc/vol. 33cl crown corked bottles.

BREW DETAILS: Filtered. Bottom fermentation.

APPEARANCE: Chestnut brown with a good head and lacework.

NOSE: Mellow, lightly roasted, chocolatey, fruity malt with a gentle spicy hop. Inviting. KR: Hints of liquorice.

PALATE: Very fruity with a pleasantly fruity dark malt (with hints of roast and chocolate) and a distinct hop bite but not much bitterness. The hop is a little resiny and peppery with an almost spicy note and generates a distinct dryness to the bitter element.

FINISH: Dry, slightly spicy/peppery hoppiness, resiny bitterness and gentle roastedness take over from a fruity malt.

OVERALL: Fairly impressive example of a Christmas beer. Good dark malt, pleasantly fruity with a big hop element and even a suggestion of spice. Has the typical IFBM 'over-clean' taste but this recipe is strong enough to carry the character through.

JW: ☑☑☐ KR: ☑☑☐

BIÈRE SUR LIE

5.8% alc/vol. 75cl corked bottles.

BREW DETAILS: Bottom fermentation. Bottle refermentation.

APPEARANCE: Amber with a good pillowy head.

Nose: Mellow buttery amber malt. JW: A gentle earthy hoppiness. KR: Appley and a little citric hop.

Palate: After a sweetish start a strong bitter fruit builds to fill the mouth. JW: A yeastiness to the pale malt taste KR: Very fruity with a mouthwatering sharpness.

Finish: Dry and long lasting fruity bitterness.

Overall: Interesting and moderately complex beer with a growing bitter fruit character.

General: Beautiful label, quite unlike the other Institute own brands.

JW: ☑☐☐   KR: ☑☑☐

LA STAN'

5.2% alc/vol. 33cl crown corked bottles.

Brew Details: Filtered. Bottom fermentation.

Appearance: Pale gold colour with a bronze hint.

Nose: Unusual hop aroma. JW: Quite light with an odd chemical-like element. KR: Some metallic hints.

Palate: Surprisingly full for a light texture. Lashings of pale, slightly husky, malt is dominated by the hops which have a sharp bite and a citric note, adding some bitterness which grows towards the finish.

Finish: Drying bitter hoppiness. JW: A touch of biscuity malt. KR: The fullness of the malt lingers, with a bready note.

Overall: The unimpressive aroma belies what follows. For a light beer it has a surprisingly full palate with a powerful hop which almost hides the good quality malt base. Fuller and deeper in interest than many blonde beers but spoilt by an awful nose and an over-clinical note which gives occasional saccharin hints.

JW: ☑☐☐   KR: ☑☐☐

OTHER BEERS BREWED

Bière de l'Été

Bière de l'Automne

The IFBM also brews the following beers for other companies (some may be in development, others may be just for a distributor):

ROUGET DE LISLE (a distributor in Perrigny) – **La Rouget de Lisle** (5.8%), **Grand Rivière** (6%), **Fourche du Diable** (5.4%), **La Marseillaise** (6.4%).

LES TROIS ÉPIS in Paris – **L'Épi Rouge** (5.6%), **L'Épi Blanc** (5.6%), **L'Épi Noir** (5.6%).

CLAIR DE LORRAINE (a distributor in Void Vacon) – **Bière de Stanislas** (5.2%), **Bière du Chardon** (6%).

SOFABO (a distributor in the Ardêche) – **Combel** (6%) a chestnut beer and **Brimbel** (6%) a bilberry beer.

WARENGHEM in Brittany – **Bier Breizh** (6%) a whisky beer.

MOULIN DES MOINES (a flour mill near Strasbourg) – **Speltor** (4.8%) and **Spelty** (0%) organic beers

Brasserie Jeanne D'Arc

✉ 38 rue Anatole France, 59790 Ronchin

☎ 03 20 16 92 92   Fax: 03 20 88 26 01   www.orpal.tm.fr

🏰 By arrangement only. 21 days notice. In French & English. 30FF

🏪 From Oct '98 – Bottles, cases, glasses.

🍺 100,000hl (in 1997)

➜ See article

Brasserie Jeanne d'Arc celebrates its 100th anniversary in October 1998 and plans to substantially change its approach to visitors. Next to the brewery is a house previously occupied by the old director of the company (now in his nineties) who has now moved out, giving the brewery an opportunity to convert the house and gardens into a visitor centre complete with a museum, bar and shop – facilities currently unavailable at the brewery.

Although Ronchin is now very much a suburb of Lille, when the brewery was founded in 1898 Ronchin was a small town in its own right, with a population of 3,500 and five breweries. The owner of one of those original five, Henri Vandamme, wanted to build a new brewery to take advantage of the advances in industrial brewing techniques and, after going into partnership with Pierre Hovelaque, chose the location and founded what was to become Jeanne d'Arc on the current site in 1899, producing its first brew in June of that year.

After Henri's partner retired in 1902, he found a replacement in Désiré Desruelle – a local farmer whose land was well sought after by the developers of the expanding city of Lille. Trading his farmland for smaller, urban corner-plots Désiré gave the brewery the chance to own lucrative tied outlets at which to sell its beer – some of which are still a valuable part of its core business to this day.

In 1906 Henri handed the business over to Désiré at which point it became Brasserie Desruelle-Theetten (Theetten was his wife's maiden name). The last name change came in 1927 when Désiré's daughter married the son of a well-known brewing family and the company adopted the name Jeanne d'Arc (Joan of Arc) after a successful bock beer it had been producing since 1912.

In common with the other local breweries it closed during both world wars but was the only one to reopen after the Second World War and as such was able to take over all the local business. With this local monopoly it was able to expand quickly and took advantage of this resurgence of interest in beer in the post-war years by extending the premises and modernising the plant.

Expansion is no longer possible on their present site as they have successfully managed to fill it completely. From a modern distribution viewpoint it does not look like the best of locations – sited in an almost triangular plot of land hemmed in on two sides by railway lines. The other side is residential and the streets are fairly small. In fact it is not that easy to find, though it should be visible from the A1 heading south out of Lille. One way to find it is to take Junction 20 from the A1-E17 and head into Ronchin on the D916. Eventually you will go over a railway line with a station and sports park on your right. Take the first right, a one-way street called rue du General Leclerc. When you reach a crossroads (right goes under the railway) the brewery is in front of you to the left. Turn left and the entrance is around 100 metres along the road.

Today the brewery has dropped the old practice of home deliveries, mostly of the bock beers, and concentrated on developing its range of special beers. This paid off in 1996 when its flagship brand Grain d'Orge won a prestigious trophy in the USA.

AMBRE DES FLANDRES

6.4% alc/vol. 25cl crown corked, 75cl corked bottles & draught.

BREW DETAILS: Filtered. Bottom fermentation.

DECLARED INGREDIENTS: Saaz, Styrian and Brewers Gold hops.

APPEARANCE: Rich amber.

NOSE: Lashings of malt. JW: Good blend of malts including

a hint of roasted malt. KR: Fruity malt with a tannic background and a touch of damp hay. Surprisingly hoppy.

PALATE: An abundance of malt, predominantly a lightly roasted chocolate malt, with a hoppy edge. KR: Some odd plum-like red fruit and apple skin tastes give it a sharpish, garded character.

FINISH: JW: Just a gentle amber malt. KR: Malty and bitter with a good deal of leftover fruit and a tannic note at the very end.

OVERALL: Quite deep and interesting, moderately complex ale with an excellent smooth and creamy texture.

GENERAL: First brewed 1992.

JW: ☑☐☐   KR: ☑☑☐

BELZEBUTH

15% alc/vol. 25cl crown corked bottles.

BREW DETAILS: Filtered. Top fermentation.

DECLARED INGREDIENTS: Vienna malt.

APPEARANCE: Golden with a good head.

NOSE: Quite sweet, rich and tangy with an almost rasping edge and some alcohol.

PALATE: Very strong alcohol taste and its attendant burn dominates a strongly tangy amber malt. Has a distinct barley wine character.

FINISH: Masses of lingering warmth almost burns the roof of the mouth. Behind this is a slightly fruity tangy malt and hints of caramel.

OVERALL: Not surprisingly for a 15% beer it is dominated by the alcohol, but once you get through the burn there is a strong barley wine character and a full, very tangy, amber malt. KR: Perhaps a little gimmicky, but nevertheless an impressive, quality beer

GENERAL: First brewed 1997. Served in a 10cl flute which encourages sipping. Probably the best approach.

JW:☑☐☐   KR:☑☑☐

BIÈRE DE MARS

5.5% alc/vol. 75cl corked bottles.

BREW DETAILS: Filtered. Bottom fermentation.

APPEARANCE: Orange gold colour with an excellent creamy head.

NOSE: Strongly hoppy with distinctive perfumed earthy note. KR: Citric hints.

PALATE: Moderately bitter with a powerful hop character. A fruity malt and some citric notes take a back seat to the earthy hops.

FINISH: Masses of resiny hop bitterness lingers on and on over a gently fruity malt. KR: The hops feel like they are eating away at the inside of the mouth. A creamy bitterness.

OVERALL: A distinctive beer with a strong earthy character that makes it stand out from the other Bières de Mars. Has a good creamy texture in addition to the very strong hop character. A distinctly artisanal character.

GENERAL: First brewed 1975.

JW:☑☐☐   KR:☑☑☐

GOLD TRIUMPH

6% alc/vol. 25cl crown corked bottles & draught.

BREW DETAILS: Filtered. Bottom fermentation.

APPEARANCE: Palish gold colour.

NOSE: A dry citric hop. JW: Interesting biscuity malt. KR: A zesty lemon hint and a light metallic note.

PALATE: A sweet, biscuity pale malt and a lemony hop with a

good bitterness and just a dash of sweetness. KR: Light, spritzy and zesty.

FINISH: JW: Very dry, tangy bitterness. KR: A light zingy bitterness.

OVERALL: KR: Surprisingly good summer refresher. A little shallow in character perhaps but the impressively full taste is enough to carry it through.

GENERAL: First brewed 1984.

JW:☑☐☐   KR:☑☑☐

GRAIN D'ORGE

8% alc/vol. 25cl, 33cl crown corked, 75cl corked bottles & draught.

Brew Details: Filtered. Top fermentation.

Declared Ingredients: Brewers Gold, Styrian & Saaz hops; Caramel, Vienna & Flanders malts.

Appearance: Honey gold with a big creamy head and good lacework.

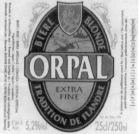

Nose: A gentle fruity pale malt with a light perfumed hop. KR: A light resiny hop and a strong alcohol note.

Palate: Very much a full tasting grainy malt and alcohol experience. Some fruit and a resiny hop bitterness with an underlying alcohol warmth. Alcohol element increases with age.

Finish: A warming, distinctive tangy malt bitterness. KR: Lingering tannic fruit.

Overall: A good malty beer that seems to be in the style of a Belgian Flemish amber ale. On older examples you need to get used to the alcohol before dicovering a quite deep and interesting character.

General: First brewed 1993. Won US Association of Brewers 1996 World Beer Cup for French-style bières de garde.

JW: ☑☑☐ KR: ☑☑☐

ORPAL

5.2% alc/vol. 65cl ceramic stopper & 25cl crown corked bottles & draught.

Brew Details: Filtered. Bottom fermentation.

Declared Ingredients: Brewers Gold and Flemish hops; Maize.

Appearance: Palish gold colour.

Nose: Hoppy with a creamy pale malt.

Palate: Rounded and soft creamy maltiness with some sweetness and a gentle, faintly citric hop character.

Finish: JW: Slightly astringent. Dry and bitter. KR: Gentle hop bitterness with some lingering sweetish malt notes.

Overall: Pretty good, inoffensive beer which will impress with its softness and roundness. Unfortunately not particularly exciting in spite of its hoppy character.

General: First brewed 1949.

JW: ☑☐☐ KR: ☑☐☐

SCOTCH TRIUMPH

6% alc/vol. 25cl crown corked bottles & draught.

Brew Details: Filtered. Bottom fermentation.

Appearance: Very dark red/brown.

Nose: JW: Very, very faint fruitiness. KR: A dull hop with a dark, dull fruity malt. Quite dry with a coffee note.

Palate: Sweet start with a subdued malt which is not as dark in character as you would expect from its appearance. Fruity and a little citric.

FINISH: JW: A little dry with a faint roast malt. KR: Lightly fruity with a metallic edge. Turns dry with some mouthwatering citric hop.

OVERALL: Though dark it is not really a true scotch and, thankfully, nothing like as sweet as many other versions. Doesn't quite deliver the expected fruity dark character.

JW: ☐☐☐   KR: ☑☐☐

SPÉCIALE NOËL

6.4% alc/vol. 25cl crown corked, 75cl corked bottles & draught.

BREW DETAILS: Filtered. Bottom fermentation.

DECLARED INGREDIENTS: Saaz, Styrian and Brewers Gold hops; Maize.

APPEARANCE: Dark amber in colour.

NOSE: JW: Odd and earthy. KR: A lightly metallic fruity malt with darker undertones and some hops which give a bitter promise.

PALATE: Sweet and malty. JW: Has an earthy hoppiness. KR: Full mouth of roasted malt with a fruity, quite sticky tang.

FINISH: Bitter. JW: Tangy, dry, and a little astringent. KR: Fruity and winey, though quite shallow.

OVERALL: Nicely textured but one dimensional beer. Not really special enough to be a Spéciale Noël.

GENERAL: First brewed 1975.

JW: ☐☐☐   KR: ☐☐☐

OTHER BEERS BREWED

The brewery is a prolific table beer and bock beer producer. From the little information obtained, we believe it makes the following brands, though some may be labelled versions of the same beer:

Alsatia (4.7% alc/vol.).

Alsatia Bock (3.7% alc/vol.).

Bière Bock (3.7% alc/vol.).

Bière Bock St-Jean (3.7% alc/vol) – Easy drinking, pale gold, bottom fermented beer with a distinctly sweet pale malt a tangy hoppiness but a disappointingly bland finish.

Bière de Table (2% alc/vol.).

Bière Luxe (4.7% alc/vol.).

Cristalor (4.7% alc/vol.).

Orpal Première (5.6% alc/vol.).

Pilsor (4.7% alc/vol) – Very dark, bottom fermenting beer with a particularly gentle, but watery, roasted character. Nothing to write home about.

Pilsor Luxe

Pilsorbock

Spécial Bock (3.7% alc/vol.).

Super Alsatia (4.7% alc/vol.).

Brasseries Kronenbourg

✉ 68 Route d'Oberhausbergen, 67200 Strasbourg

☎ 03 88 27 44 88   Fax: 03 88 27 42 06
www.brasseries.kronenbourg.fr

🕓 0900-1000, 1400-1500 winter, hour longer in summer

🏃 By prior arrangement. See article. In French & English

🏬 Bottles, cases and glasses.

📊 10,000,000hl (in 1997)

➡ See article

Cronenbourg – still an active brewery and the company's head office

The best known of all French breweries has to be Kronenbourg – and the most familiar of all brands has to be its premium beer, 1664, named after the year Jérôme Hatt made his first brew in Strasbourg, starting the long evolutionary road to today's brewing leviathan. Figures published for 1995 show the total French beer market being 22,750,000 hectolitres with Kronenbourg having a 42.7% share of that market, though that had slipped a little to 41.3% by 1997.

Getting to be France's largest brewery, and maintaining that position, has been helped greatly by it being part of the multi-national conglomerate Danone, though it was expanding rapidly in the 1960s before becoming part of the BSN Group (later Danone) in 1970. There are currently four breweries which make up Brasseries Kronenbourg – all of which are very large, but the daddy of them all is the plant at Obernai, capable of producing a colossal 6,000,000hl per year.

The Obernai facility became necessary when the Strasbourg plant was having difficulty keeping up with demand – the 1,000,000hl barrier was reached in 1961, but by 1968 the output had doubled. Built in 1969 on a 60-hectare site just south of Strasbourg at **Boulevard de l'Europe, 67210 Obernai**, in the northern outskirts of the town, it was the most up-to-date facility of its day and became known as K2 (the Strasbourg plant being K1).

The Strasbourg facility, which is also the company's head office, is located in the Cronenbourg area of the city and is still active, with an annual capacity of 1.5m hl. The other two sites are at **2 rue Gabriel Bour, 54250 Champigneulles** (just north of Nancy), with 3m hl and **138 rue Saint-Hélier, 35044 Rennes** with 500,000hl. These plants combined employ 2,100 people and annually consume 120,000 tonnes of grain. They provide beer to be sold in 127 countries worldwide.

Obernai – the 6m hl per annum beer factory

All the sites are relatively easy to find except Cronenbourg – the site most geared up to visits – which is best approached from the A35 motorway (take the Cronenbourg exit and head west in the direction of Oberhausbergen). It offers a free guided tour (over 40,000 people visited in 1996, mostly in organised groups) which, in addition to the usual sights, includes a visit to the well-preserved cellars. To arrange a tour telephone 03 88 27 41 59.

The history of Kronenbourg started when Jérôme Hatt bought Brasserie du Canon in Place du Carbeau, Strasbourg, in June 1664. It stayed in the family for many generations with little change until Frédéric Guillaume Hatt was in control. He expanded the business, buying Brasserie du Bas-Rhin in 1842, then in 1850 moved both businesses to the current site in Cronenbourg in a bid to avoid the regular floodings of the River Ill. The opening of the railways enabled wider distribution, leading to the brewery, by now called Brasserie Hatt, being awarded several gold medals in the 1867 Paris Universal Exhibition. In 1922 it took over Brasserie du Tigre and its Tigre Bock brand, making it the largest in Alsace with an output of 130,000 hectolitres. The next landmark was 1947 when it renamed Tigre Bock as Kronenbourg (using a K rather than a C to evoke the Alsacian origin of the beer). The prestige brand 1664 was launched in 1952 and in 1963 it introduced a new concept – the six-pack.

In 1970 Kronenbourg was swallowed up by the huge BSN group along with Brasserie de Champigneulles which a year later went on to introduce the almost-as-famous Kanterbrau beers. The final part of the story took place in 1987 when both breweries were merged by Danone to form the one entity known as Brasseries Kronenbourg.

Champigneulles has been around since 1897 and became part of the Société Européenne de Brasserie (SEB) in 1966 when it merged with another famous northern brewery, La Meuse. SEB was producing 6m hl of beer from 23 sites when it was taken over by BSN in 1970. The Kanterbrau marque was introduced in 1971 (named after one of Lorraine's famous brewing figures, Hans Kanter – the Maître Kanter), but as with most multi-plant breweries it is not clear which brands are now made where. Although mainly very modern and state-of-the-art, it still retains some of its old buildings and there is a small exhibition of historic items from the brewery just inside the office entrance. Amongst these items is the original ledger with entries for purchase of the materials required for brewing.

In addition to owning Kronenbourg, Groupe Danone is also a major player in the world brewing market. It wholly owns Alken-Maes in

Left: With such huge marketing clout it is perhaps not surprising that Kronenbourg is something of an innovator in advertising in France. The latest series of ads gives subliminal images of 1664, here in the flames.

1864. QUATRE CHIFFRES PLUS FORTS QUE TOUS LES MOTS.

Right: This series uses words with the letters "kro" (the affectionate name of the nation's favourite beer) to put over a strong image.

A[kro]BATE

KRO
LA BIÈRE

Belgium, has a controlling interest in San Miguel in Spain, and has large stakes in Mahou in Spain and Birra Peroni Industriale in Italy. With these interests it is not surprising it brews other beers in France, both from its sister breweries abroad and well-known international brands, under licence. These include Guinness, Carlsberg, Bud, Tuborg, Grimbergen, Kilkenny, Blanche de Bruges and Mort Subite.

One of Kronenbourg's other claims to fame is the role it played in the development of alcohol-free and low-alcohol beers, the most famous of which was introduced in 1964 (but originally made in 1839 as a summer beer by a long-defunct brewery) called **Tourtel**, now available in three guises. It also makes **Silver**, **Force 4** (a shandy, 'panaché' in French) and two fruit flavoured beers (in raspberry and peach but with little discernible beer character) called **Krony** – all of which are less than 1% alc/vol. It also makes X-Cider which is widely available throughout France on draught.

Now that Kronenbourg has been established as a national leader, the company appears to be trying to raise the profile of the Kanterbräu brand as shown by the national chain (49 to date) of up-market eating and drinking establishments called 'Les Tavernes de Maître Kanter' which have been opening regularly all over France.

All its own-brand beers are filtered, pasteurised and (Tradition Anglaise excepted) bottom fermenting – a shame really when it makes ales under license but chooses not to brew a quality ale of its own.

1664

6.3% alc/vol. 25cl, 33cl & 75cl bottles & mini-kegs and draught.

APPEARANCE: Bright gold with a good head.

NOSE: Light aromatic husky hop.

PALATE: Strong hop character with a sharp edge and a distinct huskiness. Quite bitter and the bitterness grows. A fullish pale malt base.

FINISH: Lasting strongly hoppy dry bitterness.

OVERALL: Immensely hoppy beer with a strongly husky and bitter hop. So strong that it hides almost completely the fairly full pale malt base. KR: Commendably clean for a beer of 6.4%.

GENERAL: First brewed 1952. 1664 is the year that Jérôme Hatt made his first brew in Strasbourg and this, like all Kronenbourg brand beers, carries the Hatt name on the crest. If you have to ask for it by name, ask for 'seize cents soixante-quatre'.

JW: ☑☐☐   KR: ☑☐☐

1664 BRUNE

6.9% alc/vol.   25cl crown corked bottles.

APPEARANCE: Deep ruby brown colour.

NOSE: Full, rich dark malt that is quite fruity and slightly sweet. JW: A hint of roast malt.

PALATE: Full and fruity, sweet dark malt. JW: A slight hop character helps dry out the sweetness and a gentle alcohol element adds a little warmth. KR: Sweet start turns very fruity and nutty with an artificial tang.

FINISH: Bitterness grows and increases the dryness. JW: Dark, almost roast malt. KR: An annoying candied tang lingers long.

OVERALL: Definitely more dark lager than brown ale. JW: Impressively dark and fruity sweet brown beer. A bit one-dimensional but it is easy to drink. KR: Very one-dimensional and that single dimension is a pretty uninteresting one.

GENERAL: First brewed in 1990. Like the 1664, sold as a 'spéciale'.

JW: ☑☑☐   KR: ☐☐☐

GOLD DE KANTERBRÄU

6.4% alc/vol.
25cl crown corked, 75cl bottles and draught.

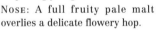

APPEARANCE: Not surprisingly … golden.

NOSE: A full fruity pale malt overlies a delicate flowery hop.

PALATE: Full, fruity, pale malt in abundance with a good balance achieved by a moderately bitter hop. A fair degree of alcohol warmth.

FINISH: Dry and bitter with an oily hop note. Full and lasting with an alcohol warmth.

OVERALL: Full, malty, lager with a good hop character and a surprising level of alcohol warmth. Clean and easily accessible in character but it is a full, long-lasting, well balanced, tasty lager.

GENERAL: First brewed 1979. Until recently marketed as the 'spéciale' Kanterbräu brand, but that was before the introduction of Maître Kanter Réserve.

JW: ☑☑☐   KR: ☑☐☐

K

4.7% alc/vol.   25cl crown corked bottles.
APPEARANCE: Bright pale gold.

NOSE: JW: Initially very strong floral hops with a sweet pale malt behind but the malt grows and the hops recede. KR: Very hoppy with a light but fruity malt.

PALATE: JW: Masses of light malt, balanced by gentle, citric, hops and just a touch of bitterness. Slightly astringent. KR: Quite sweet with a distinct fruity bite. Some hop bitterness with a lightly citric background.

FINISH: JW: Dry and gently bitter with a little astringency. KR: Quite full and lingering with a malty sweetness and a light bitterness.

OVERALL: JW: Very easy to drink light beer with an excellent soft texture and a good balance. KR: Original taste like a fruitier-than-usual lager – ale drinkers may prefer it to the usual French fare.

GENERAL: First brewed in 1995. There is a useful temperature indicator on the back label (a letter 'K') which turns dark blue when the beer is cool enough to be served.

JW: ☑☑☐ KR: ☑☐☐

KANTERBRÄU

4.7% alc/vol. 25cl crown corked, 75cl screwtop bottles and draught.

APPEARANCE: Lightish gold.

NOSE: Understated aromatic hop over a biscuity malt. JW: Slightly buttery.

PALATE: Pilsener malt forms the base for a strongish hop character. Quite bitter with a little oiliness to the abundant hop. Some sweetness from the malt. JW: Faintly metallic. KR: A zingy citric note.

FINISH: Very drying and quite bitter. JW: Distinctly hoppy with some metallic notes. KR: Disappointingly short-lived with fleeting sweeter fruity notes.

OVERALL: JW: Has that Strasbourg nose – biscuity, buttery, husky maltiness and very hoppy. Once through the nose it is almost all hop. Unfortunately also a little metallic. Very similar to Kronenpils. KR: Wonderful hop character for a mass-market luxe beer – full and well balanced. More Czech than French character.

GENERAL: First brewed 1971. 1.7m hl is produced annually, 63% of which is in kegs.

JW: ☑☐☐ KR: ☑☐☐

KANTERBRÄU BIÈRE DE MARS

Alc/vol. not declared Draught, perhaps also in bottles.

APPEARANCE: Reddish amber with excellent but short-lived creamy head.

NOSE: Minimal, just a faint hint of malt and a metallic hop note.

PALATE: Initially very hoppy which is resinous, but only slightly bitter. Once you become accustomed to this, a full, quite interesting, fairly sweet malt comes through to give a better balances to the hop.

FINISH: A refreshing dry bitterness.

OVERALL: A very good example of a Bière de Mars with a full quota of hops to give it a nice kick and avoid being overpowered by the sweetness.   JW: ☑☑☐   KR: ☑☑☐

KRONENBOURG

4.7% alc/vol.   25cl crown corked, 75cl bottles, mini-kegs and draught.

APPEARANCE: Lightish gold.

NOSE: An interesting hop aroma is rapidly replaced by a sort of biscuity pale malt. JW: Gently citric. KR: Flowery hop.

PALATE: Gently bitter hop sits well over a pilsener malt though it grows more bitter and resiny after a while. KR: Very clean and refreshing.

FINISH: Dry lingering hoppy bitterness. KR: Fleeting sweet notes.

OVERALL: Fairly nondescript lager though it has a pleasant hop character and fairly full taste. It is noticeably bitter and resiny and gets more so.

GENERAL: First brewed 1947. A staggering 4.5m hl is produced annually, 83% of it on draught. Comes with different labels depending on whether it is a multi-pack, etc. There is also a 5% alc/vol. **Kronenbourg International** which we believe is essentially the same beer made for the export market.   JW: ☑☐☐   KR: ☑☐☐

KRONENBOURG BIÈRE DE MARS

4.7% alc/vol.   Draught only.

APPEARANCE: Pale amber with a good head.

NOSE: Very neutral.

PALATE: Pretty malty with just a touch of hop bitterness. Also some caramel-tinged candy sugar notes.

FINISH: Tangy, candy caramel sugar and a little malt. KR: A lingering hoppy note.

OVERALL: Pretty false. Gives the impression of being very much a forced amber character which fails to impress.

GENERAL: Unlike most of the others in the range, the beer is flash-pasteurised.   JW: ☐☐☐   KR: ☐☐☐

KRONENBOURG BIÈRE DE NOËL

5% alc/vol.   25cl crown corked bottles & draught.

APPEARANCE: Golden reddish brown.

NOSE: Hop-tinged sweet caramel and malt.

PALATE: Very sweet with a full caramel sugar and malt. A resiny hop note grows gently towards the end.

FINISH: Still sweet with a distinctly resiny hop and lingering caramel sugar.

OVERALL: Very sweet and very caramelly with little else apart from a touch of hop.   JW: ☑☐☐   KR: ☐☐☐

KRONENBOURG TRADITION ALLEMANDE

4.7% alc/vol. 25cl crown corked bottles.

APPEARANCE: Honey-tinged gold.

NOSE: Light, flowery hops with a little lager malt. JW: Suggests sweetness. KR: Powerfully hoppy when first poured, but this soon fades leaving a harsh metallic note.

PALATE: Once over the initial big hit of bitterness you get a predominantly hoppy beer with some malt lurking behind which lends it a little sweetness. KR: Some light citric hints.

FINISH: Dry. JW: Tangy from lots of very resiny hops. KR: Lingering hop bitterness.

OVERALL: Quite an impressive full mouth of taste if a little one-sided on the hop front.

GENERAL: First brewed in 1993.

JW: ☑☐☐   KR: ☑☐☐

KRONENBOURG TRADITION ANGLAISE

4.7% alc/vol. 25cl crown corked bottles.

APPEARANCE: Amber colour.

NOSE: Quite a lot of fruity malt and sweet candy helped by a light hop. KR: Light peppery hop. Artificial.

PALATE: Sweet, candied, tangy, lightly fruity malt with a touch of bitterness. KR: A distinct caramel taste.

FINISH: Slightly fruity malt with some lingering bitterness. JW: Cloying with a resiny hop. KR: A distant peppery hop.

OVERALL: Kronenbourg obviously has an interesting idea of what an English beer should be! Seems to have a forced interest which does not suit it.

GENERAL: First brewed in 1993. The only Kronenbourg own-brand to be top fermented.

JW: ☐☐☐   KR: ☐☐☐

MAÎTRE KANTER BIÈRE DE NOËL

5% alc/vol. 25cl crown corked bottles.

APPEARANCE: Dark amber in colour.

NOSE: Pleasantly hoppy with a sweetish caramel malt background.

PALATE: Full malt with a candy sugar sweetness and some metallic notes. JW: Some bitter hops help balance the sweet malt. KR: Quite fruity.

FINISH: A drying, fruity, bitter tang.

OVERALL: Disappointingly sweet and candied beer which doesn't measure up to the Noël tag. A weak character, but a step in the right direction.

JW: ☐☐☐   KR: ☐☐☐

MAÎTRE KANTER, LA RÉSERVE

6.1% alc/vol. 65cl ceramic stoppered bottles.

APPEARANCE: Rich dark gold.

NOSE: Starts with a sharp, heady hop aroma over a full, sweetish fruity, buttery, pilsener malt which soon comes to the fore.

PALATE: An unusual strong, dry, tangy hop edge to a full, creamy, buttery, pilsener malt dominating the palate. The initial sweetness is balanced by a gentle bitterness as the hop comes through.

FINISH: Dry, bitter and astringent hop character lasts and lasts. KR: Good, but masked, solid maltiness.

OVERALL: A remarkably full tasting beer with a reasonable depth and a full body. Pilsener malt and hops are well balanced adding to an interesting alternating sweet and dry character.

GENERAL: First brewed 1996. JW: ☑☑☐ KR: ☑☑☐

OBERNAI

4.5% alc/vol. 75cl screw top bottles.

APPEARANCE: Pale gold.

NOSE: Immediately on opening you get a good strong Czech pilsner-like hoppy aroma but this quickly mellows to a gentle pilsener malt and hop and then fades to almost nothing. KR: Citric edge.

PALATE: Slightly bitter hop over a distant pilsener malt. KR: Lightly citric but disappointingly oversweet.

FINISH: Dry gentle hop bitterness which builds. KR: Lingering, sweet lemonade-like taste.

OVERALL: A light, fairly bland beer with just a hoppy, bitter, Czech pilsener character. KR: Shame about the sweetness throughout.

GENERAL: First brewed in 1978. Despite its bock-style presentation it is sold as a 'bière de luxe' and proudly states 'pure malt' on the foil neck wrapper. JW: ☐☐☐ KR: ☐☐☐

WEL SCOTCH

6.2% alc/vol. 25cl crown corked bottles and draught.

INGREDIENTS: Scottish whisky malt.

APPEARANCE: Rich, quite dark amber colour.

NOSE: Aromatic whisky malt with some alcohol. JW: Sweet, smokey whisky malt which becomes more malty with time. KR: Distinct lactic and buttery note.

PALATE: Sweet malt with a gentle

smokey whisky taste. JW: Thick and slightly syrupy with a gently bitter resiny hop that gives balance.

FINISH: Sweet, sticky and tangy with some slightly fruity smokey malt.

OVERALL: Ridiculously thick and sweet. The light smokey whisky character and gently fruity malt is ruined by the excessive sweetness.

GENERAL: First brewed 1993. Unusually, this beer is marketed separately from the rest under the trading name of Kanterbrau S.A.

JW: ☐☐☐　KR: ☐☐☐

WILFORT

6.9% alc/vol.　33cl crown corked bottles and draught.

APPEARANCE: Dark chestnut colour.

NOSE: Invitingly sweet, full and aromatic. Very rich and fruity with pear drop notes. JW: Very reminiscent of wine gums. KR: A dry and very dark promise.

PALATE: Full and very fruity with some warming pear drop notes and a hop induced bitter edge. JW: Moderately sweet dark malt with more fruit than malt. KR: Just a touch of sweetness then a full, dry and tannicly bitter fruitiness hits the mouth. A peppery hop tries unsuccessfully to get through.

FINISH: Warming with a very dry fruitiness which is relieved by the gently roasted malt. KR: A peppery hop dryness balances the fruit.

OVERALL: Excellent aroma and superb soft creamy texture lead you into a porter style beer which is full of flavour and overtly fruity. Possibly the pear drops are overdone a little. KR: An unfortunate chemical note present throughout.

GENERAL: First brewed in 1949. When tried on draught it lacked the depth of character noted above, being much sweeter with a gently roasted malt and an excess of burnt sugar. Listed by Kronenbourg as one of its 'spéciales'.

JW: ☑☑☐　KR: ☑☐☐

OTHER BEERS BREWED

Chicada (4.7% alc/vol.) – Sold exclusively on draught. A beer with added rum, mandarin and cinnamon. Supposed to evoke the taste of South America!

Ducasse (4.7% alc/vol.).

Koenigsbier.

Kronenbourg 2.6°.

Kronenbourg Ice (5.5% alc/vol.).

Kronenbourg Légère (3.1% alc/vol.).

Kronenpils (4.7% alc/vol.) – Light gold with a light aromatic husky note. Sweet maltiness supports a growing bitter hop going into a short-lived lightly bitter finish. JW: Fairly well balanced – a reasonable, basic lager. KR: Oversweet with a washed-out character. Sold in 100cl screw-top bottles.

Valstar (3.7% alc/vol.) – Golden-coloured with a husky, lightly fruity malt nose. Solid, slightly biscuity base with a sharp hoppiness giving a bitter edge to the taste and a dry but dull finish. KR: Some artificial sweet notes. JW: Easy drinking, light and quaffy beer. Sold in 100cl screw-top bottles.

Brasserie Lampée-Baumgartner

✉ Z.A. 17580 Le Bois-Plage-en-Ré, L'Ile de Ré

☎ 05 46 09 45 28   Fax: 05 46 09 33 20

🕐 April to September: 1000-1200 & 1600-2000

🏃 Pre-arranged only. 2 days notice

🏭 Bottles, cases & glasses

📊 300hl (in 1996)

➡ After the toll-bridge, keep to the D201 towards Le Bois-Plage. On the left-hand side you will eventually see the tower of the Cooperative Vinicole. Turn left here and pass to the left of the tower, after which you should keep straight on. The brewery is the last unit on the left.

It may seem a little strange that a brewer should choose a holiday island off the west coast of France to start making beer commercially – but it is even stranger that the beer he chose to make there is a great example of a German weizenbier (an unspiced wheat beer typically found in Bavaria).

The Ile de Ré is a very flat island which attracts thousands of holidaymakers each year who come to take advantage of the large number of quality sand beaches. The island is close enough for it to now be joined to the mainland by road, using one of the longest road bridges in Europe. The toll for using this bridge is 60FF for most of the year but rises to 110FF in July and August, presumably to discourage casual day visitors in high season; however, residents enjoy a subsidised rate of just 15FF all year by displaying their ID cards. Just south of where the road joins the mainland is the historic port of La Rochelle.

Gerhard Lampée-Baumgartner is Austrian by birth, but moved to the island in 1992 to find work in a holiday environment. A keen homebrewer, the quality of his weizenbier was well-known to his friends, and when work became scarce in 1996 he went commercial, producing his first brew in June of that year. Since then the business has grown to the point that his wife now works at the brewery which also provides islanders with rare local employment.

The operation is quite small scale, with a brew capacity of just 200 litres. Most of the equipment is stainless steel construction which once saw service in restaurants. The mash tun and brew kettle are huge bain-maries (cylindrical vats heated by a surrounding water jacket) – ideal for a brewery like Gerhard's. A 50/50 mixture of malted wheat and barley is used in the mash. Due to the high content of wheat, which tends to clog the straining mesh, the filtration process takes around four hours to complete. Cooling is done in three stages, via plastic vats with cooling elements and a sealed stainless steel tank – an effective system which cools the wort from 80° to 20°C very quickly. Fermentation takes place in a tall open fermenter before being bottled with krausening yeast after which it rests in crates on the brewery floor – as opposed to the usual warm room – for two to three days (although in winter it can take longer and can be shorter in summer). To complete the process, the bottles are stored in what looks like a refrigerated truck trailer to undergo their two-week cold room stint at 6°C.

The brewery enjoyed Presidential recognition in 1997 when an order was received for 10 bottles from a famous haut-cuisine restaurant in Bordeaux. The customer wanted the bottles that afternoon as Jacques Chirac and John Major (then British Prime Minister) were dining at the restaurant and they wanted to offer quality French produce. Gerhard drove there himself and watched the premières drinking his beer on national television that evening – John Major commenting that he preferred the beer to a fine Bordeaux wine.

The beers come in distinctive flip-top ceramic stoppered bottles which he imports from Germany (although they are actually made in Italy). The yeast he uses comes from Wienstefan (a yeast bank in Germany) which he likes to collect himself so he can familiarise himself with the real Bavarian hefe-weizenbier while he's there.

Despite the amount of sediment in the bottle, Gerhard prefers to drink the beer clear (like a crystal-weizen), but we would recommend drinking it clear for the first half, and cloudy for the second – thereby experiencing two totally different tastes and characters from just one bottle.

BLANCHE DE RÉ

5% alc/vol. 33cl & 50cl bottles.

DECLARED INGREDIENTS: Hallertau & Magnum hops; French malt; Wheat.

APPEARANCE: Hazy wheaty gold with a good head

NOSE: Pleasant mellow fragrant wheat aroma with a distinct vanillary banana element and a little hop. JW: A touch lactic.

La Blanche de Ré

Alcool. 5 % vol.
Bière blanche de fabrication artisanale
sans conservateur, ni colorant, ni additif,
refermentée en bouteille.

Brasserie Lampée-Baumgartner S.A.R.L. - 17580 Z.A Le Bois Plage en Ré

A consommer de préférence avant :

33 cl

PALATE: Sweet but full wheat, lots of wheat, with some vanilla and lemon notes. Quite lactic. JW: There is a spicy, peppery element. KR: Lashings of vanilla and fruit. The very full taste masks the strong lactic tartness that lurks within.

FINISH: Lingering lactic wheaty creaminess. KR: Some bananas, vanilla and fruit carry through to the end.

OVERALL: Excellent wheat beer that is more German than Belgian in style. Very flavoursome yet quenching beer with a superb creamy texture.

GENERAL: First brewed 1996.

JW: ☑☑☑   KR: ☑☑☑

OTHER BEERS BREWED

Bière de Noël – Introduced since our visit.

A special, very limited 7% alc/vol. version of Blanche de Ré was produced for its first birthday, which may be repeated in the future.

Brasserie Lancelot

- ✉ Au Manoir de Guermahia, 56120 St-Servant-sur-Oust
- ☎ 02 97 73 02 41   Fax: 02 97 73 02 39
- ⏱ Mon-Sat: 0900-1200 & 1400-1800
- 🏃 Always available (groups 8 days notice). In French & English. 10FF
- 🛒 Bottles, cases & glasses
- 📊 2,000hl (in 1996)
- → See article

With a name like Brasserie Lancelot, one could be forgiven for thinking that the brewery was named after the legendary Knight of the Round Table and that the name was exploiting his Breton origins along with (depending on which interpretation of the legends you follow) King Arthur himself. The truth is, however, that the owner is called Bernard Lancelot (pronounced 'lonselo') – apparently not such an uncommon surname in his native region of Anjou to the south.

The operation is run from a very tastefully converted outbuilding across the courtyard from a beautiful 15th century manor house which nestles in a stunning location off a single-track lane in the rural southern reaches of the Brittany peninsula, just west of Ploërmel. Although the postal address is given as St-Servant-sur-Oust, the brewery is closer to the village of Lizio. The best way to find it is to leave St-Servant in the direction of Lizio, keeping your eyes open for a right hand turn (signposted to the Manoir de Guermahia) which is a very long single-track road. Eventually on your left you will reach a short, tree-lined entrance to the courtyard bordered by low stone walls. The brewery and shop is on your right as you enter the courtyard.

Bernard started brewing commercially in 1990 following a training course at Ringwood Brewery (in Hampshire, UK) under the direction of brew consultant Peter Austin, the same man who taught the brewers of Deux Rivières at Morlaix. Since then he has expanded his plant to the current 20 hectolitre capacity per brew. Six people now work at the brewery at its busiest times, and he brews four times per week.

A keen long-time bee-keeper, it seemed only natural for Bernard to use honey to prime all his beers prior to their bottle refermentation, and many of his hives can be seen through the window looking out of the back of his shop. He says his original brew – Cervoise – is very true to the old Celtic brew once drunk by the Gauls, having a low hóp content in comparison to modern beers and is spiced with six herbs.

The Knights of the Round Table theme makes a strong marketing tool and the brewery has taken advantage of this with an attractive label/poster design of Sir Galahad by a Breton artist for the Cervoise and a sword for the Lancelot beer. Some of its products are also sold in 50cl stone bottles (at extra cost).

The Breton/Celtic connection is exploited through its Telenn Du beer, although this brought a swift reaction from Guinness attempting to preserve their harp logo (Telenn Du is Breton for Harpe Noir, or Black Harp). Before any pre-judgement, it should be pointed out that the buckwheat (sarassin) used is a Breton variety called 'Harpe'. Around 50% of the mash for Telenn Du is buckwheat, which makes for a very long brewing day due to the time it takes to filter the clogging grain.

Around 90% of Lancelot's production is sold around Brittany, but it has a presence nationally through Géant hypermarkets (and their smaller shops in the Casino chain) and exports to Quebec and Italy.

All its beers spend 14–16 days in the huge, closed fermenters which bubble away merrily (and noisily) in the salle de brassage after which they spend a week in the cold room (at 3–5°C), followed by bottling and kegging where they are primed with honey and spend 4–6 days in the warm room. All Lancelot's products are unfiltered, unpasteurised and undergo a bottle refermentation.

The yeasts are kept in the laboratory room in the corner of the brewery and three different types are used for the range (one for Blanche, one for Telenn Du and one for the others).

BLANCHE HERMINE

4% alc/vol.   75cl corked bottles.

DECLARED INGREDIENTS: Wheat.

APPEARANCE: Creamy orange gold with a good head.

NOSE: A pungently citric (lemon & lime), floral hop with just a faint suggestion of honey. JW: An earthy wheat aroma. KR: Honeyed. With sediment it is dulled greatly and left with just a little citric hop.

PALATE: Without sediment: Gorgeously full and interesting with a solid pale malt base supporting a strong hop character. Some lemon, honey and a cream soda/vanilla element. A resiny bitterness but also moderately sweet. With sediment: Becomes very muddied and less specific in taste. JW: Some lactic wheatiness.

FINISH: Without sediment: A lingering bitter honey with some citric notes and a strong wheatiness building. With sediment: Confusing and muddy. Full and mouthwatering but a little tangy with an unspecific citric note.

OVERALL: As a blanche one would expect to drink it with the sediment but this particular beer suffers if you do that. Without sediment it is a superb, multi-faceted experience with beautifully clean tastes. With the sediment it is still good but the clarity is lost and the elements blend into each other to the extent that many are lost.

GENERAL: First brewed 1997.   JW: ☑☑☐   KR: ☑☑☐

CERVOISE LANCELOT

6% alc/vol.   33cl crown corked, 50cl & 75cl corked bottles (also some stone bottles) and draught.

DECLARED INGREDIENTS: Spiced with six herbs (one of which is hop).

APPEARANCE: Copper brown colour.

NOSE: Exquisite honey-sweet herbal aroma with a good dark spice note. Gently fruity malt supports the herbs and spices. JW: A little powdered ginger grows with time.

PALATE: Full, spicy and herbal with some gentle dark malt and a little resiny hop just about evident, but the herbal tastes (on a variety of levels) overpower everything. JW: Some ginger. After quite a while it becomes more spicy than herbal.

FINISH: Lingeringly spicy, herbal, bitter and dry. The herbs last for ages with a multitude of fleeting tastes.

OVERALL: Intensely herbal beer with a gloriously complex, honeyed character. The malt and hop base is pushed into the background by the multitude of herb and spice tastes that come to the fore throughout an immensely enjoyable experience. It should be said that you need to be in the mood for a very complex beer to enjoy this to the full, as it has so much going on in the taste department it can simply be TOO complex.

GENERAL: First brewed 1990. Intended to be in the traditional Gauloise beer style.　　　JW: ☑☑☑　KR: ☑☑☑

DUCHESSE ANNE

6.5% alc/vol.　33cl crown corked, 50cl & 75cl corked bottles and draught.

APPEARANCE: Orangey honey gold with a good creamy head.

NOSE: A rich pale malt lurking behind a pungent, fresh, citric and flowery hop. Very inviting.

PALATE: Like the nose a full rich fruity malt supports a distinctly hoppy character. Strong hop flower taste with plenty of lemon and a gently tangy honey bitterness.

FINISH: Long lasting rich honey and hop bitterness.

OVERALL: Impressively hoppy blonde with all the right hop elements – floral fragarance, citric, bitterness from a pungent resiny hop. A solid malt supports the hops well though never threatens their domination. Adding interest is the use of honey. KR: In spite of being initially impressive it gets a bit sticky and tangily bitter.

GENERAL: First brewed 1996. Named after Anne of Brittany who married Charles VIII, bringing the principality under the Kingdom of France.　　　JW: ☑☐☐　KR: ☑☑☐

LANCELOT

6% alc/vol.　33cl crown corked and 75cl corked bottles.

APPEARANCE: Golden amber with a good creamy head.

NOSE: A pleasantly heady hop over a mellow, lightly fruity malt.

PALATE: Beautifully balanced hop and malt with a light fruit and some honey. JW: Both bitter and sweet with a tangy bite to the bitterness. KR: Fruitily bitter and slightly over-honeyed which creates a tanginess that could get a little much.

FINISH: Very much a strongly dry and tangily bitter finish. KR: The honey sticks out as the tanginess develops. Well balanced finish.

OVERALL: Excellent texture adds further to the appeal of this impressively balanced beer with a pronounced hop character and well defined use of honey. Easy to drink, though it benefits from sipping, and very satisfying. KR: May be a little too tangy for some palates.

GENERAL: First brewed 1996.   JW: ☑☑☑   KR: ☑☑☐

TELENN DU

4.5% alc/vol. 33cl crown corked, 50cl & 75cl corked bottles (also some stone bottles) and draught.

DECLARED INGREDIENTS: Includes 50/50 barley malt and sarrasin.

APPEARANCE: Black with a good but short-lived head.

NOSE: Very interesting, liquorice enhanced roasted dark malt with a strangely separate hop adding interest.

PALATE: Very dark, roasted malt with a little hop lifting the dark roasted nature. Quite bitter with fruity notes. JW: There is a slightly tangy sweetness reminiscent of honey and hints of liquorice.

FINISH: JW: Very strongly roasted, bitter, black malt with some liquorice to add a little interest. It lingers and mellows as it does so. KR: Drying and lightly bitter with some lightly tart elements.

OVERALL: Initially the roasted bitterness is close to overpowering, only being lifted by the hops and liquorice. Once used to this, it becomes apparent that there is more to the beer and a honeyed sweetness eventually becomes prominent giving it a deeper, more satisfying quality. It has many stout and porter characteristics.

GENERAL: First brewed 1993. The sarrasin used is a local Breton variety called Harpe and Telenn Du is Breton for Harpe Noir (Black Harp)

JW: ☑☑☐   KR: ☑☑☐

BARS & CAFES RECOMMENDED BY THE BREWERY

LE SWANSEA, Vannes
LE CEILI, Quimper
BAR DE LA TOUR, Ploërmel
BAR LA CITÉ, 44000 Nantes
LE ALZEY, Josselin

BEER SHOPS RECOMMENDED BY THE BREWERY

L'EPICERIE LE VERGER, Josselin,
LA TRINITAIRE, St-Philibert, near Carnac
LA TAPENADE, Vannes

Pub-Brasserie Malkehr

✉ 147 avenue Galliéni, 93170 Bagnolet, Paris
☎ 01 43 62 76 04
🕐 0830-1930 daily
🍺 120hl (in 1997)
🍴 Not known
➔ See article

Unfortunately, as is often the case in researching books like this, the brewpub was locked and shuttered on our visit (6.30pm on a Saturday in April!) so it was not possible to do a full review of either the premises or the beers. Subsequent phone calls and information offered by John White have enabled us to offer the following information.

It is quite straightforward to find. Bagnolet is just outside the periphique in Paris and avenue Gallieni runs parallel with it south from Bagnolet. From the Metro (the last stop on line 3) and bus station head south (turn right on exiting the Metro) and keep walking. Avenue Gallieni starts after a crossroads and Pub Malkehr is a further 100 metres or so on the left. The area appears to be fairly run down and the bar staff suggested they were not really in the best of locations. However, John was very enthusiastic about the bar itself, so don't let this put you off.

The frontage is glass panelled and protrudes onto the pavement, but behind the glass are roller shutters which were pulled down on our visit. When you can get inside the bar it is nicely decorated and the copper and mash tun are treated in a novel way as they are actually built into the bar itself (much like, but rather larger than, the brewplant at Chez Nino in Nice). Behind this are the fermenters and conditioning vessels.

The premises, which is actually more of restaurant than a pub, has a strong Alsace connection which is highlighted by the logo of a white stork on a nest in addition to the name, which is of Alsacian origin.

The company is in fact registered in the Alsace. It started brewing in 1994 and produces just two beers, both of which are bottom fermenting and unfiltered. The **Malkehr Blonde** (5% alc/vol) is uncompromisingly hoppy, whilst the **Malkehr Ambrée** (5.2%), though still hoppy, is softer in character.

The sign on the outside of the brew-pub displays its Alsacian connections.

Brasserie Meteor

- ✉ 6 rue du Général-Lebocq, 67270 Hochfelden
- ☎ 03 88 71 73 73   Fax: 03 88 91 79 82
- 🕐 1400 Mon & Thur
- 🏛 Tours sometimes possible by prior arrangement. 15 days notice. In French & English. No charge
- 🛒 Bottles, cases & glasses
- 🍺 450,000hl (in 1997)
- ➡ Easily found on the main road through the town

Meteor is another Alsace brewery with a long, interesting history, and is today particularly proud to be the largest (and staunchly independent), family-owned brewery in the region.

Brewing was originally started on this site, in the centre of the little town of Hochfelden, by Jean Klein in 1640 although it was not until 200 years later, in 1840, that the current family interest began. In that year the brewery, then known as Brasserie de la Couronne, was bought by Martin Metzger, a member of a Strasbourg brewing family. In 1898 the family dynasty which still runs the brewery was created when Marie-Louise Metzger (only daughter of Alfred, who succeeded his father Martin) married Louis Haag whose family owned a long-established brewery (founded 1795) in Ingwiller, around 20km north of Hochfelden. As was often the case in brewing family mergers, the Hochfelden brewery now took on the name of Metzger et Haag though it was also known as Grande Brasserie du Salvator. The adoption of the Meteor name and its distinctive logo came in 1925.

Perhaps the most interesting element of their history came in 1927. These days we think nothing of using the term Pils to describe a beer that should be of a very specific style but invariably is not, and has become over-used to the point that the difference between bière blonde and pils is impossible to tell. Things were not quite the same back in 1927 when Louis Haag developed a beer using a selection of Czech hops which he wanted to call Meteor Pils. Rather than just going ahead and assuming the term was impossible to protect, he approached the Czech authorities to seek official blessing to use the word Pils. He obtained the Czechs' permission (the only European brewery, according to Meteor, to have been given such official endorsement), and the beer is the finest example of a true Pilsner made in France and has contributed to the brewery's success in the intervening years.

Today it is still very much a family business with all three directors being part of the Haag family. The brewery comes under a parent company called Meteor Distribution which altogether employs 220 people and in addition to the beer it also produces 20,000hl of soft drinks. Eighteen per cent of its beer is exported.

Many breweries have a fond, often very loyal, following from the local inhabitants, but Meteor seems to have penetrated further into the local psyche than most. The people of Hochfelden are very enthusiastic and particularly proud of their town's beer to such a degree that it can become positively infectious.

The brewery frontage on the main road through Hochfelden is particularly impressive with a lovely view of brewing coppers behind glass panels across a cobbled courtyard framed by the wrought iron gates set in the wall. The main reception is actually down the first road to the left after passing this view (if travelling from the east).

ACKERLAND BIÈRE BRUNE SPÉCIALE

6.1% alc/vol. 25cl crown corked bottles and draught.

BREW DETAILS: Filtered. Pasteurised. Bottom fermentation.

DECLARED INGREDIENTS: Alsace hops.

APPEARANCE: Dark red brown colour.

NOSE: Candied malt with some faint hops but mainly a sticky-sweet promise from the malt. KR: Toffee-like with a light roasted character.

PALATE: Loads of darkish roasted malt with a fair bit of caramelly candy sugar. JW: An odd tangy bitterness. KR: Chicory and sultana notes in the heavily roasted taste.

FINISH: JW: Bitter, tangy, caramelly malt lasts long. KR: Dry and fruity with a bittersweet note and a chicory tang. Becomes very mouthdrying.

OVERALL: An unusual beer with an unusual taste. It has both ale and lager characteristics which adds to the interest.

GENERAL: First brewed 1977. Ackerland is the Hochfelden region which produces Alsace hops.

JW:☑☐☐   KR:☑☐☐

ACKERLAND BIÈRE SPÉCIALE

5.9% alc/vol. 25cl crown corked bottles and draught.

BREW DETAILS: Filtered. Pasteurised. Bottom fermentation.

APPEARANCE: Golden colour.

NOSE: JW: Full and aromatic biscuity and buttery nose that is fairly sweet with suggestions of toffee. KR: An aged hop with a light fruity malt.

PALATE: Full, sweet, fairly fruity, tangy, lager malt with a strongly evident dry, resiny hop. JW: Gentle buttery and toffee notes. KR: A slightly fruity, persistent tang.

FINISH: Dry hoppy and bitter with a sweetish fruity malt coming through in lingering waves. A good, balanced finish.

OVERALL: Good, interesting taste with an excellent finish. There are strong elements of distinctive hop and malt throughout with the added attraction of an unusual butteriness.

GENERAL: Ackerland is the Hochfelden region which produces Alsace hops.

JW: ☑☐☐   KR: ☑☐☐

BIÈRE DE MARS

5.1% alc/vol.   75cl crown corked bottles and draught.

BREW DETAILS: Filtered. Pasteurised. Bottom fermentation

APPEARANCE: Deep rich amber.

NOSE: Mellow but very deep sweet amber malt with a perfumey hop. JW: Buttery with suggestions of caramel. KR: Toffeeish, with a sweet and fruity character and a metallic note.

PALATE: Full and moderately complex. Mostly malt with toffee and caramel elements but also an interesting perfumey hop adding a lot of bitterness which is needed to balance the inherent malt sweetness.

FINISH: Strongly bitter and quite tangy with caramel and butterscotch hints.

OVERALL: A good texture and very full tasting toffee/caramel malt based beer with plenty of interest and a strange, distinctive perfumed hop quality which helps it stand out from the Bière de Mars crowd.

JW: ☑☐☐   KR: ☑☐☐

BIÈRE DE NOËL

5.8% alc/vol.   75cl crown corked bottles & draught.

DECLARED INGREDIENTS: Flavoured with orange (presumably peel).

APPEARANCE: Classic amber colour with a good fluffy head.

NOSE: A fruity malt with a touch of hop and a slight herbal element. KR: Some orange hints, but not intrusive.

PALATE: A full taste of fruity malt with a light, bitter, hoppiness with a few spicy, peppery notes generating a dryness.

FINISH: Bitter and slightly astringent with fruity overtones. Slightly warming. JW: Tangy with some initial orange hints. The bitterness is very long lasting.

OVERALL: Not really what you would expect from a Christmas beer however, it is certainly different, fairly full tasting and a pleasant drink. JW:☑☐☐ KR:☑☐☐

METEOR / METEOR EXPORT

4.6% alc/vol. 25cl, 33cl & 75cl crown corked bottles.

BREW DETAILS: Filtered. Pasteurised. Bottom fermentation

APPEARANCE: Rich gold with a good head.

NOSE: A distinctive aroma – full, pungent, fragrant, fruity and hoppy yet quite sweet with a malty base.

PALATE: Sweetish toffee, caramel malt with a resiny hop that gives plenty of bitterness. Quite tangy.

FINISH: Long lasting. Starts a bit sweet with some toffee malt but ends with a gentle resiny bitterness which lasts forever.

OVERALL: Amazing, unique aroma leads into an equally unusual palate. Strong hop characteristics and a tangy toffee malt dominate. The bitter finish lasts as long as anything anywhere. KR: One of the best buys of the widely-available hypermarket bière blondes.

GENERAL: Very similar to the red-labelled **Meteor Export** (4.5% alc/vol.), which is only available in the very local vicinity of the brewery, and which the brewery told us was unpasteurised, though it does not state this on the label. Our samples exuded a creamier, distinctly vanilla-ish character and greater depth than the yellow label. KR: Without the opportunity to do a comparison test, I am inclined to give the Export an extra tick. Meteor is also sold as **Zornbier** and relabelled as **Kochersberg** and **Kochersbier** for supermarkets. JW:☑☑☐ KR:☑☑☐

METEOR PILS

5% alc/vol. 25cl, 33cl & 75cl crown corked bottles, draught & 5ltr kegs.

BREW DETAILS: Filtered. Unpasteurised. Bottom fermentation.

DECLARED INGREDIENTS: Saaz hops.

APPEARANCE: Bright paleish gold with a fluffy head.

NOSE: A strong aroma full of biscuity malt and hop. Promises an interesting palate. JW: Wonderfully aromatic creamy, wheaty, hoppy and lightly citric. KR: A creamy fruity pilsener maltiness and a touch of light spice.

PALATE: A real mouthful of taste – fills every sensation on the tongue. Suitably complex with a distinctive malt and a strong, coarse hop balancing each other well. The pale malt supplies some sweetness and there is a strong but pleasant bitterness from the hop. Hints of caramel and toffee.

FINISH: Hops to the fore, you can taste them clearly and they impart a distinct dryness and bitterness. Hints of toffee. Full and satisfying. KR: A touch of hop spice.

OVERALL: Wonderful aroma leads you into an equally full and distinctive palate which continues into the finish. Beautiful balance with a good complexity but simple enough on the quaffing level to make it easily accessible. An excellent Pilsner which is on a very different plane to the other French attempts.

GENERAL: First brewed 1927. Surprisingly for a mass-market Pilsner it is unpasteurised. Like Meteor's other large bottles the crown cork is covered by a plastic cap that can be used to reseal the bottle once opened – an excellent idea.   JW: ☑☑☑   KR: ☑☑☑

MORTIMER

8% alc/vol.   25cl & 75cl screw top bottles and draught.

BREW DETAILS: Filtered. Pasteurised. Bottom fermentation.

DECLARED INGREDIENTS: 'Confidential', but it is a pure malt beer.

APPEARANCE: Copper brown in colour.

NOSE: Slightly sweet whisky malt with a light smokiness.

PALATE: A strong alcohol element is evident as a sharp warm sensation, not unlike whisky, which dominates the mouth. The rich, buttery malt is almost smoked and generates a real fullness in the mouth.

FINISH: A little dry and a touch cloying with a rich whisky malt tang. JW: A strongish alcohol burn. KR: A long-lasting tannic bitterness.

OVERALL: An excellent whisky malt beer which has a very strong and distinctive malt element. Warming and satisfying with a very rich, strongly alcoholic taste. KR: Not too complex, but the best of the whisky malt beers – avoiding the oversweetness of its competitors.

GENERAL: Presented in a miniture whisky bottle (or full size when 75cl). Sometimes served in a miniature whisky glass which holds just 15cl, enhancing this image further.   JW: ☑☑☑   KR: ☑☑☐

OTHER BEERS BREWED

Blanche de Meteor (5% alc/vol.) – A recently-introduced white beer initially only available on draught. The first, and currently only, top fermenting beer made by the brewery. Described by the brewery as being unfiltered with a slight lemon taste.

Pravda (4.5% alc/vol.) – A vodka-flavoured beer released at the end of 1997 and aimed at the night-club market.

Zorn Val (2.7% alc/vol.) – A low-alcohol beer, named after the river Zorn which runs through the region.

BARS & CAFES RECOMMENDED BY THE BREWERY

Schlosserstub, 67100 Strasbourg
Au Bureau, 31 place d'Armes, 59300 Valenciennes

Brasserie Métreau

✉ Grésille, B.P. 19, 17360 St-Aigulin

☎ 05 46 04 81 78   Fax: 05 46 04 85 20

🕐 Not applicable

🔬 Pre-arranged only. In afternoons. 28 days notice

🍺 Cans and 5-litre mini-kegs

🏭 40,000 (in 1996)

➡ From the centre of St-Aigulin, take the D30 in the direction of Montguyon. After crossing the railway, go straight over the crossroads and proceed up a slight hill. A few hundred metres up the hill the industrial estate Grésille is on the right. The brewery is in front of you to the left as you enter the estate

For a brewery with such a low profile, you may be surprised to find that Brasserie Métreau is the second largest producer of beer in the southern half of France – brewing 40,000 hectolitres per year.

Not only is the brewery on a low profile, so are the beers it produces. You probably won't have heard of the 'Brasserie L'Iloise' range or Aiguilinoise, Saint-Fort or even Saint-Aquilin – and most of the time you wouldn't even know when you are being served with it. This is because of the marketing strategy of the owner – the highly enterprising Michel Métreau – who, since starting up the brewery in 1993, has managed to find a way to sell vast quantities of his beer on a national level right under the noses of the 'Big Two' brewers. He has a way of gesticulating with his hands to explain how he operates: Heineken is on the left, Kronenbourg on the right and he snakes his way up the middle – hinting that the big boys leave odd niches which he has managed to plug. These niches include small, independent bars, hotels and restaurants (with no brewery loans, and hence no ties) which often sell his beers anonymously. Next time you are given a beer (usually the Blonde) from an unlabelled pump with a sweeter, fuller palate than the usual national French fare, it could well be that you are drinking Métreau beer.

It seems there are two problems usually encountered by independent breweries wanting to go national – distribution of the beers themselves and the fact that most bar furniture (pumps, etc.) is supplied and installed by one of the big brewers. The former never was a problem as Michel has a successful haulage business in the adjoining unit on the estate, where kegs are stacked almost to the ceiling prior to being despatched every Monday. To combat the other problem, the brewery now has a production line in another adjoining unit to re-condition old beer founts, chiller units, drainers, etc. – meaning he can offer proprietors, outside function organisers and clubs all the accoutrements necessary for professional beer dispensing.

The brewery itself is not as large as you might imagine, but it makes up for it with its highly industrious atmosphere. Mornings are spent brewing the new beers and afternoons cleaning and looking after the fermenters, garding tanks and the latter parts of the brewing process. At the back of the main brewing room are rows of conical fermenters, behind which is the chambre froid where the beers are garded in huge tanks. From there all the beers undergo filtration and pasteurisation on their way to the kegging room, which is conveniently adjoining the loading bays and racked storage of the despatch warehouse. Little of the equipment appears to be new, having seen a good deal of service in now-defunct breweries.

Métreau sells its beers in kegs, but it has recently joined the latest national trend for also selling 5-litre mini kegs and a small proportion of the Blonde (Export) is tankered to the Netherlands to be put into cans and sold as L'Iloise Export. It sells its beer all over France (usually through a network of local distributors) and does a healthy trade in northern Spain. It also makes a lemonade and a cola.

Although brewery trips (with tastings) are offered by appointment in the afternoons, we were at the brewery in the morning and were offered dégustation of all the beers in their 'fraîche' state (i.e. from

a pipe from the fermenters). For this reason it is difficult to be objective in our tastings, so we can only produce brief notes. All beers are bottom fermenting, filtered and pasteurised, are hopped with Hallertau and are unspiced.

BEERS BREWED

L'ILOISE EXPORT (5% alc/vol.) – Golden with a light bloom. Surprisingly full taste and a distinct sweetness. Growing light hop bitterness. A pleasant change from the norm. Sometimes sold as just 'Blonde'.

L'ILOISE SPÉCIALE

SAINT-FORT – Deep chestnut brown beer with a sweet, but quite bland, taste and a roasted dryness developing into the finish. A little washed-out. Sometimes sold as just 'Brune'.

SAINT-AQUILIN – Hazy, quite light, unspiced wheat beer with a full and refreshing character but little depth. Easy drinking. Sometimes sold as just 'Blanche'.

AIGULINOISE – The best of the Métreau range. Excellently balanced beer with a bright copper amber colour, a fruity malt and an ample hoppy bite going into the finish. Sometimes sold as just 'Ambrée' and **Export Spéciale Ambrée**.

Le Moulin à Bière

- ✉ Cité de l'Europe, 62231 Coquelles
- ☎ 03 21 85 30 02   Fax: 03 21 36 02 63
- 🕐 1000-2400 daily
- ✗ Tours not available
- 🛒 Bottles, 5 litre mini-kegs, glasses
- 📊 1,600hl (in 1997)
- ➔ In the Cité Gourmande area of the Cité de l'Europe

Cité de l'Europe is a large indoor shopping mall conveniently located next to the Eurotunnel entrance just off the A16 at junction 12. The western end of the complex is called Cité Gourmande where all the units – bars, restaurants and shops – are all food- or drink-related. Le Moulin à Bière is on the ground floor at the bottom of the stairs to the first floor in a spacious area where the frontages are allowed to extend to the full height of the building. What you see in the picture is essentially an indoor replica of a French village square complete with parasols, despite the fact that neither sun nor rain will ever penetrate the area. The whole effect is like a Christmas grotto.

The brewpub was opened in March 1995 by Bernard Happiette with S.A.Bars de France providing and installing the brew kit, making it the seventh such installation in the country. Bars de France also trained the Belgian brewer, supply the yeast, and provided the original recipes which have apparently been altered slightly by the current brewing team. It is, therefore, not surprising that there are many similarities between the beers here and those of Bars de France's own chain of brewpubs (Les 3 Brasseurs/O'Neil). Likewise, the beers are all unpasteurised, unfiltered and top fermenting.

The interior of the bar is pleasantly spacious since the ceiling is high and in the centre of the building is an old-style signpost pointing out the brewing area, fermentation room, storage cellar and the Channel tunnel, which it places at just 100 metres away.

The 8hl brewing kettles are almost in the bar serving area making it a very warm working environment when they are brewing. Behind this are the fermentation tanks with the storage tanks upstairs. When the beer has matured sufficiently it is pumped directly from these tanks to the fountains on the bar for serving.

Bernard Happiette's also owns Bernard's Farm, just two doors down – a smaller enterprise which sells the beers from Moulin a Bière via pipes from the same tanks as the brewpub!

AMBRÈE

5.5% alc/vol.   75cl bottles & draught.

APPEARANCE: Amber colour.

NOSE: Gentle crystal/amber malt with a faint hint of caramel.

PALATE: Quite sweet, almost fragrant, amber malt with a pleasant sharp bite to give it an edge.

FINISH: Very tangy bitter amber malt with hoppy overtones. Long lasting but not very pleasant.

OVERALL: Interestingly-used malts make the palate memorable but the very distinctive finish is unpleasant.   JW:☐☐☐   KR:☐☐☐

BLANCHE

5% alc/vol.   75cl bottles & draught.

INGREDIENTS: Wheat. Spiced with coriander.

APPEARANCE: Hazy lemon wheat colour with a good head.

NOSE: Lactic wheatiness.

PALATE: Distinctly wheaty and quite lactic with a milky hoppiness and a fair degree of yeast. Full but mellow.

FINISH: Lactic, tangy wheat, dry and a little astringent. It leaves a powdery coating sensation on the roof of the mouth.

OVERALL: Standard quaffing wheat beer – wheaty and lactic with a strong yeastiness.   JW:☑☐☐   KR:☑☐☐

BLONDE

4.7% alc/vol.   75cl bottles & draught.

APPEARANCE: Pale golden colour.

NOSE: Sweetish light lemony hop and pale malt.

PALATE: Strong hop character in a full pale malt. Very distinctive, slightly soapy, hoppy bitterness. Moderately sweet malt.

FINISH: Dry, tangy, lingering bitterness with a touch of lemon and a powdery coating to the roof of the mouth.

OVERALL: Fairly light and easy to drink yet full tasting. The odd powdery sensation in the mouth lets it down.   JW:☑☐☐   KR:☑☐☐

BRUNE

5.5% alc/vol.   75cl bottles & draught.

APPEARANCE: More black than brown.

NOSE: Dark roasted malt.

PALATE: Sackfuls of roast malt give it a full, dark undeniably roasted character. A gentle hop tries to add a little to the palate but struggles against the malt.

FINISH: Lingering burnt malt bitterness.

OVERALL: Very strong on the roast malt with a distinctly burnt character. A little too one-dimensional.   JW:☑☐☐   KR:☑☐☐

OTHER BEERS BREWED ─────────────

Bière de Mars (7% alc/vol.).

Bière de Noël (7.5% alc/vol.).

Brasserie des Naufrageurs

- ✉ Les Landes, 17190 St-Georges-d'Oléron
- ☎ 05 46 76 67 50
- 🕐 0900-1230, 1530-1930
- 🏛 Pre-arranged only. 2 days notice. In French. No charge
- 🏪 Bottles & cases.
- 🛢 70hl (in 1996)
- ➡ From the road bridge, keep on the main road (D734) and pass through St-Gilles. You will see a roadside sign before the turn-off to St-Georges which takes you up a gravel track. The brewery is on the right after 100m (use right-hand gate).

Just south of the Ile de Ré is the larger and heavily-wooded Ile d'Oléron which is far less known to tourists than its near neighbour. Like the former there is a link to the French mainland via a road bridge which is older and, as such, does not now rely on a toll to pay for its construction. There is, however, a 25FF toll on the road south from Rochefort across the huge expanse of the Charente tidal marshes. The road bridge to Oléron provides a great view over the shallow sandbanks and vast quantities of oyster beds ('parcs') at low tide.

Three-quarters of the way along the island's main road, there is a small gravel track leading to a collection of quaintly ramshackle stone farm buildings. Parking outside there are two gates, the left-hand one leads to the owner's home and the right-hand gate takes you into a grassed farmyard where the shop can be found on the right.

Jean Luc Metayer runs a company called 'Les Ruchers d'Oléron' (ruchers are apiaries) which specialises in all manner of honey products – royal jelly, pollen, beeswax, spiced honey cake and mead. He decided to expand his portfolio of sales by adding an excellent, and very adventurous, range of artisanal beers in July 1995.

From the courtyard you can't miss the brewery shop, you just have to follow the bees – there is a constant stream of them entering and leaving a pipe protruding from the outside wall which connects to a glass-panelled box inside the shop where you can see them working on their honeycombs. It is a beautiful location for a brewery and it gives you the feeling that you are buying a true farmhouse product.

The word 'naufrageurs' translates as shipwreckers and the labels on all the Bières des Naufrageurs range depict a goat with a lantern hanging round its neck showing the way unscrupulous locals would lure the ships onto the rocks on the treacherous coastline. The ships would then be looted and the cargo sold as booty.

The majority of the brewplant is old stainless steel dairy equipment. For such a tiny annual output it is surprising to find that the capacity is 1200 litres per brew.

Making beer so far south, even with the moderating coastal breezes, can cause problems for summer brewing. For this reason he only brews in the cooler months (usually once a fortnight), and concentrates on selling his wares in the summer when the island has many visitors from the French mainland and beyond.

All beers have the same label, but are marked in the bottom left-hand corner with a word or symbol – e.g. a picture of a fish for 'Spéciale Poisson' or the word 'Miel' for the honey beer. Essentially there are just three beers – Bière des Naufrageurs (which is described as a rousse and will have no marks on the label), Bière des Naufrageurs Blonde and Naufrageurs à la Bergamote) but the rousse is spiced to produce all the other beers. All are unfiltered, unpasteurised, top fermenting. The malt used is actually grown on Ile d'Oléron but it goes to the mainland to be malted.

BIÈRE DES NAUFRAGEURS

7.5% alc/vol. 33cl crown corked and 75cl corked bottles.

DECLARED INGREDIENTS: Strisselspalt hops; Pilsener & Munich malts.

APPEARANCE: Dark red brown with a creamy, tight head.

NOSE: Very fruity with a dark fruit and a dark malt. A few pear drop notes. KR: Strongly alcoholic.

PALATE: Impressively tasty palate with lashings of fruit and masses of darkish malt plus a strong tangy hop element and a few herbs. Some bitterness and a growing tangy fruitiness. KR: Warming fruit with an alcohol/pear drop bite. Strong caramel malt base with a tart note. Strangely little hop character.

FINISH: Lingering hop bitterness and distinctly tangy fruit with a gentle warming glow and a honeyish note.

OVERALL: Full dark tangy fruity beer that you would associate with winter firesides rather than a summer holiday island. A warming glow gives away the alcohol which is one of a good mix of elements that provide plenty of depth and interest. Possibly too tangy for its own good. KR: Quite strong on alcohol, but a unique character.

GENERAL: First brewed 1995.

JW: ☑☑☐   KR: ☑☑☐

BLONDE

6% alc/vol. 33cl crown corked and 75cl corked bottles.

DECLARED INGREDIENTS: Strisselspalt hops; Pilsener malt.

APPEARANCE: Deep gold with a good tight head.

NOSE: Complex and inviting with a lovely fresh, clean hop that is quite citric. A maltiness bolsters the whole aroma to make it full and impressive. KR: An orangey note.

PALATE: Sharply hoppy with a very full but not overly bitter character. Excellent depth of interest with wafts of wonderful tastes at all levels of the palate. JW: As it ages the alcohol grows to dominate the palate.

FINISH: A very strong but not overdone hoppiness imparts bitterness and a degree of oiliness. JW: Strong alcohol warmth lasts long.

OVERALL: Formidably hoppy with enough other interest to give an excellent, full, balanced taste. A true artisanal character yet clean and fresh. A wonderful example of what France can offer if you look hard enough.

GENERAL: First brewed 1997. JW: ☑☑☐ KR: ☑☑☑

MIEL

7.5% alc/vol. 33cl crown corked bottles.

APPEARANCE: Rich red-brown colour.

NOSE: Very inviting. Dark, rich, honeyed malt. JW: A sweet tanginess and some alcohol notes. KR: A little treacle.

PALATE: A good hop element and plenty of honey. JW: Warming with a good helping of malt and a distinct bittersweetness. KR: Quite sweet and treacly.

FINISH: A lingering honeyed bittersweet taste. JW: Dry. KR: A quite thick warmth.

OVERALL: A very impressive, full and very honeyed but still balanced beer. Fairly complex with a good depth and a gentle warmth. Should be one to inspire other French brewers, particularly in the area of Christmas beers. Simply excellent – if you get the chance try it out, it will not fail to impress. JW: ☑☑☑ KR: ☑☑☑

MÛRE

7.5% alc/vol. 75cl corked bottles.

DECLARED INGREDIENTS: Strisselspalt hops; Pilsener & Munich malts; flavoured with blackberries.

APPEARANCE: Reddish mid-brown colour with an excellent head – large, tight, creamy and lasting.

NOSE: Rich, complex and herbal with fruit, hops and alcohol notes. Definite blackberry aroma.

PALATE: Very full fruity and herbal with distinct blackberry taste. Very complex malt and herb tastes go through it all the time. Some alcohol and an interesting bitterness in addition to a full hop taste add to this impressive complexity.

FINISH: Surprisingly mouthdrying and quite bitter with fleeting sweetness. Lingering herbal tastes and an alcohol warmth.

OVERALL: Excellent, very full, complex beer with a superb texture and a strong blackberry fruitiness. There is good use of a rich malt and a hop that gives a full hoppy taste with a sharpish bite to the bitterness. Infiltrating all this is the alcohol which certainly helps increase its appeal as a winter warmer. JW: ☑☑☑ KR: ☑☑☐

NAUFRAGEURS À LA BERGAMOTE

7.5% alc/vol. 33cl crown corked bottles.

DECLARED INGREDIENTS: Strisselspalt hops; Pilsener malt; spiced with bergamot orange (see 'general' note).

APPEARANCE: Reddish mid-brown colour with a good head.

NOSE: JW: Wonderful orangey dark herbal aroma dominates a gentle sweetish dark fruit. KR: Very strongly herbal, like Earl Grey tea without the tea. Dark, herbal and very interesting.

PALATE: JW: Strong sweet herbal, floral taste dominates a bittersweet tangy fruity malt with full hop character and gentle bitterness. Some alcohol. KR: Bergamot gives a dark, quite tannic, almost overpowering herbal quality. Very hoppy background with a strong body of fruity malt.

FINISH: JW: Strong tangy herbal bittersweet fruity malt with some alcohol. KR; Very herbal, with a bitter and fruity aftertaste.

OVERALL: JW: Supremely herbal beer, the character of which seems to grow as the beer is drunk – possibly getting a little too strong. Superbly balanced malt and hop provide a good base. KR: Excellent quality beer with perhaps too much of the herbal character.

GENERAL: First brewed 1995. There is much confusion as to exactly what bergamot is – in the UK it is a common garden herb, but in France it can be either a pear or an orange. The latter is the particular one used for this beer and is also used in Earl Grey tea.

JW: ☑☑☐   KR: ☑☑☐

SPÉCIALE POISSON

7.5% alc/vol.   75cl corked bottles.

DECLARED INGREDIENTS: Strisselspalt hops; Pilsener & Munich malts; flavoured with herbs.

APPEARANCE: Reddish mid-brown colour with a good tight head.

NOSE: Intense root ginger aroma which fades a little to reveal a solid pale malt and a touch of fruit.

PALATE: A strong ginger pervades a full fruity crystal malt. Although there is no real hop taste there is a distinct resiny bitterness. A growing sweet tanginess suggests honey.

FINISH: Dry with a spicy ginger note and a tangy bitterness.

OVERALL: A very good artisanal beer with plenty of character and a strong ginger element. Lovely soft, creamy texture. Although the hop tastes are missing it is well balanced. An excellent evening beer.

GENERAL: Ile d'Oleron is very famous for its fish cuisine, so the brewer made a beer to be the perfect accompaniment for fish dishes garnished with herbes de Provence.

JW: ☑☑☐   KR: ☑☑☐

OTHER BEERS BREWED

The following beers were added to the range in late 1997 or early 1998 and are all based on the Bière des Naufrageurs (so are all 7.5% alc/vol.) but spiced with different ingredients:

Cannelle – Spiced with cinnamon.

Orange – Spiced with orange blossom, making a pleasant change from the usual orange peel.

Vanille – Spiced with vanilla.

BARS & CAFES RECOMMENDED BY THE BREWERY

Pizzeria Le Forum, 11 place Gambetta, 17310 St-Pierre-d'Oléron
l'Escale, 76 rue Hippocampes, 17190 St-Georges-d'Oléron
Novotel Thalassa Oléron, plage de Gatseau, 17370 St-Trojan.
Relais des Salines, Port des Salines, 17370 Grand Village Plage

BEER SHOPS RECOMMENDED BY THE BREWERY

La Sangria, 27 avenue de la Narne, 17100 Saintes
Gamm Vert, ZI, route Miranelles, 17310 St-Pierre-d'Oléron
Le Taste Vin, 98 rue de la Republique, 17310 St-Pierre-d'Oléron

Brasserie L'Olanier

- Olanier, 07110 Beaumont, nr. Aubenas
- 04 75 39 56 90
- Not applicable
- Not open to the public until perhaps 1999
- Bottles and cases
- Around 25hl (1997)
- From Joyeuse (24km SW of Aubenas on D104) take D203 towards Sablières. At Les-Deux-Aygues take D220, again towards Sablières (brewery is roughly halfway to Sablières). After 3–4km go past a turn to the right marked Beaumont (via hamlet of Issac), then past a fork to the right signposted Bazalet. 200–300m further on you will see a steep gravel track to a house below the road just before a sharp left-hand bend in the road – this is one of the two tracks to the brewery (the other one is just around the bend). Don't drive down the track unless you have four-wheel drive!

Anyone who has driven on the road which follows the dramatically beautiful Gorges de l'Ardeche between Pont-St-Esprit and Vallon-Pont-d'Arc will know of the breathtaking topography of the region – a vast area of rocky hills and deep, heavily-wooded river valleys. The pretty hill-town of Joyeuse, however, sits on a relatively flat basin (giving some relief from the constantly winding roads) and, although the brewery has named its beers after the town it is quite some distance away, near Beaumont. Those who like a challenge can try the pretty way via a 'Traverse Dificile' road (marked on Michelin maps as a red-striped road – a real rarity) up to Beaumont and down the other side, via the hamlet of Issac). Whichever way you go, you cannot fail to notice the endless tracts of chestnut trees which in late summer drop a carpet of their spiky-cased fruit onto the road.

André Robardet started operations in 1995 in his farmhouse on a steep slope near the bottom of a valley overlooking a bend in the river. Built of dark stone and roofed with local slate, the buildings are set in a U-shape around a small paved courtyard reached by some very rustic steps. He sells his current range of organic beers through the national network of organic fairs, specialist shops and markets. He brews two regular beers (Blonde and Ambrée) and a Brune which is his Bière de Noël, all of which are spiced with honey. He said he was experimenting with a couple of new recipes, one for a chestnut beer (not surprising given the liberal quantities of the 'chataignes' – a particular variety often used in French cuisine – in the surrounding trees) and an apple beer and was considering pears for a future project. André apparently chose the name La Joyeuse for his beers not only because of his proximity to the town, but also because he believes they fill the drinker with joy!

One of the benefits of living in a rural French farmhouse is that you will usually have outbuildings which can be converted to a multitude of different uses. The 150-litre capacity brewplant is presently in an annexe attached to his house but he is planning to convert the large, roofless shell of a building to the left side of his front door into a brewhouse and sampling room in the future but until that is done he won't be accepting public visits – not before summer 1999. Asked about the difficulty of finding his brewery and the lack of parking on the road above, he says he is also planning some off-road car parking space when he starts offering brewery visits.

All the beers made at l'Olanier are top fermented and undergo a 3-week garde. We have suspicions that the beers may be spiced, but André is keeping all the recipes very close to his chest! The organic certification comes from Ecocert and André's beers carry the 'Nature & Progrés' mark. All bottles have the same main label.

LA JOYEUSE AMBRÉE

7.5% alc/vol. 75cl corked bottles.

BREW DETAILS: Unfiltered. Unpasteurised. Top fermentation.

DECLARED INGREDIENTS: Honey

APPEARANCE: A muddy orange brown colour.

NOSE: Very light, just a touch of damp hay and a little fruity malt. JW: A hint of marzipan. KR: A light tropical fruit.

PALATE: Very sharp, lots of fruity malt with suggestions of melon, gooseberry, apple and pear adding to the tartness. There is a disjointed sweetness that attempts to stave off the tartness but it does not really work.

FINISH: Bittersweet fruit with a tooth-squealing dryness yet mouthwatering from the acidic fruitiness.

OVERALL: A disappointing hotch-potch of elements. Predominantly strongly tart and fruity but with some malt breaking it up.

GENERAL: Organic beer.

JW: ☑☐☐   KR: ☑☐☐

LA JOYEUSE BLONDE

7.5% alc/vol. 75cl corked bottles.

BREW DETAILS: Unfiltered. Unpasteurised. Top fermentation.

DECLARED INGREDIENTS: Honey.

APPEARANCE: Dark orange gold with the fastest disappearing head ever seen.

NOSE: JW: A perfumey aromatic fruitiness with hints of orange. KR: Lots of nose-tingling aromas with an intriguing fruitiness, including tropical fruit hints and sherbet notes.

PALATE: A full sharp bittersweet fruit with a bone dry background. JW: Apple skins, pears and gooseberries.

FINISH: Bone dry with a little fruit and a lingering mouthwatering acidity.

OVERALL: Very like a cross between a rough cider and a gueuze. Very, very dry, quite sharp and fruity. It is quite refreshing yet difficult to come to terms with. Probably best reserved for hot summer days and served straight from the fridge.

JW: ☑☐☐   KR: ☑☐☐

LA JOYEUSE BRUNE/BIÈRE DE NOËL

7.5% alc/vol. 75cl corked bottles.

BREW DETAILS: Unfiltered. Unpasteurised. Top fermentation.

DECLARED INGREDIENTS: Honey

APPEARANCE: Dark brown colour.

NOSE: Pronounced fragrant, flowery, herb and spice aroma with a slightly roasted fruity malt base. Gives a warming promise.

PALATE: Starts off watery with a sweet fruity malt but the herb builds from nothing to dominate the taste. A background tartness adds to the complexity.

FINISH: The herbiness builds into the finish and lasts for absolutely ages. A bitterness helps fend off the tartness and there is a tangy honeyed note. Mouthwatering.

OVERALL: It has the typical Olanier fruity tart character yet is very interesting and truly reminiscent of a well-made Christmas pudding.

GENERAL: Although the bottle carries a 'Brune' neck label separate from the 'Bière de Noël' label it is exclusively sold as the brewery's Christmas beer.

JW: ☑☑☐   KR: ☑☑☐

Paris Real Ale Brewery

- ✉ 116 rue St-Denis, 75002 Paris
- ☎ 01 42 36 34 73   Fax: 01 42 36 48 02
- 🕐 1200-0200 daily (except for 3 days around Christmas)
- 👥 Groups pre-arranged only. In English & French. Small charge
- 🏪 No shop facilty
- 🍺 1600hl at each pub (in 1997)
- ➔ See article

Conceived as a business college project, the Paris Real Ale Company has gone from strength to strength in its short life, and at the time of publication it was taking the next step towards becoming a true brew-pub chain with its involvement in the launching of a new operation in Toulouse.

Englishman Paul Chandler and Icelander Thor Gudmundsson both took a business course at a French college and chose the enterprising subject of running a brewpub for their course project. By the time they went out into the real world they had convinced themselves that their project could work and set about bringing it to reality, forming the Paris Real Ale Company in April 1993 at the above address.

Once the company was set up, all that was now needed was a name and a theme. Choosing an English pub theme was at that time a rela-tively new idea in France, and since then hundreds of English (and Irish) theme pubs have sprung up all over the country, showing just how good a concept it was. Taking the national slang term for the French in England and marrying it to the slang term for the English in France made it an instant conversation piece for drinkers and jour-nalists alike on both sides of the Channel.

It opened the Frog & Rosbif in October 1993, on a corner at the crossroads of rue St-Denis – a renowned red light district – and rue de Turbigo, brewing English-style real ales (served via handpumps) and offering such delicacies as bangers and mash to accompany them. To British eyes the Frog & Rosbif will look similar to the earlier pubs in the British 'Firkin' chain with its green and brown livery, bare floorboards, wooden tables and

The Frog & Rosbif – even the weather looks English!

The Frog & Princess – keep kissing those frogs!

chairs, piano and the functional-yet-lived-in feel. The walls are decorated with pub mirrors and rugby/cricket kit.

The pub is essentially a single room broken up by a few pillars and a central column which forms the staircase down to the brewery itself – a somewhat cramped affair, visible behind glass panels.

After the Frog & Rosbif had proved to be a winning formula it opened its second Frog, south of the river. In mid-1996 the Frog & Princess was born. This has a different feel to it with a lower roof yet a lighter, painted interior giving the impression of more space. Better planning in the design of it has left much more space for brewing. The brewplant is at the back of the bar, near the kitchen, with just a rail separating it from the bar area. The storage tanks are behind another rail, this one forming a drinking 'bar' with high stools on the left as you walk in. **The Frog & Princess, 9 rue Princesse, 75006 Paris (tel: 01 40 51 77 38)** is close to Boulevard St-Germain, just north of Jardin du Luxembourg. From the Mabillon metro station on Boulevard St-Germain head down rue du Four and you will find rue Princesse is the second left.

Both Frogs use the same brewer – the aptly named Englishman, Jan French – and the basic range is the same in both pubs though the Princess has Trente Wheat (a wheat beer) and Blonde Bombshell (a lager) which are not available at the Rosbif.

The pubs attract a sport-viewing clientele who come to watch the cricket, rugby and soccer on their large-screen TVs. They have curry nights on Mondays and seem to have a party night whenever there is no sport to watch. All the printed material, advertising, beer card, menus etc. is in English (or at least English first), and a prerequisite for all bar staff is that they speak English. To complete the theme, the Princess even attempts to educate the indigenous population in the finer points of pub culture by displaying signs (in French) telling them to go to the bar to get served!

Another **Frog & Rosbif** opened in April 1998 at **14 rue de l'Industrie, 31000 Toulouse** – which is only half-owned by the Paris Real Ale Brewery as there is a new partner in this latest venture. It will be on the same theme and Jan French has been overseeing the initial brews. No doubt if they can make a go of this one, especially being so far from its Paris base, we may well see Frogs all over France one day.

BLONDE BOMBSHELL

5.1% alc/vol. Draught only at the Frog & Princess.

BREW DETAILS: Unfiltered. Unpasteurised. Bottom fermentation.

APPEARANCE: Golden colour.

NOSE: A slightly musty yeasty aroma.

PALATE: Fairly full pale malt with an interesting bite on the tongue from a hop that imparts a gentle hop flower taste and only a little bitterness.

FINISH: Lingering tangy astringency with lots of fresh hop taste left in the mouth.

OVERALL: Full and interesting blonde with a very strong hop character. Not a bombshell but definitely different.

JW:☑☐☐   KR:☑☐☐

DARK DE TRIOMPHE

5 % alc/vol. Draught only.

BREW DETAILS: Unfiltered. Unpasteurised. Top fermentation.

APPEARANCE: Very, very deep brown with a good tight head.

NOSE: A light, roasted, chocolate malt.

PALATE: A very roasted chocolatey malt with hints of coffee. A slight wateriness.

FINISH: Long lasting, gently bitter but very dry roast malt.

OVERALL: Good example of a stout with a lovely smooth mouthfeel, lashings of chocolate and roasted tastes yet not too bitter.

JW:☑☐☐   KR:☑☐☐

FROG NATURAL BLONDE

4.2 % alc/vol. Draught only.

BREW DETAILS: Unfiltered. Unpasteurised. Top fermentation.

DECLARED INGREDIENTS: Mount Hood hops. Pilsener malt.

APPEARANCE: Golden colour.

NOSE: Very light hop over a pale malt.

PALATE: Well rounded mellow taste with a solid pale malt and a pleasant oily hop which imparts a strong flavour and hop taste after a while.

FINISH: Very dry and gently bitter with a lingering, almost fruity, malt and an oily hop.

A selection of some of the colourful labels used on the fermentation tanks.

PALATE: Good pale English ale with a good hop character. The hops generate a lot of taste but do not make it too bitter.

JW: ☑☑☐   KR: ☑☑☐

INSEINE

4.2 % alc/vol.   Draught only.

BREW DETAILS: Unfiltered. Unpasteurised. Top fermentation.

NOSE: Pleasant hoppy aroma. Distinct greenish hop flower notes come through strongly.

PALATE: Bags of hop character. The greenish hops from the nose are strongly evident and give a sharp bite to the creamy pale malt that supports it all.

FINISH: Again those green hop flowers making it strongly hoppy, yet lightly bitter, and long lasting.

OVERALL: An interesting beer with a powerful green hop flower character.

JW: ☑☐☐   KR: ☑☐☐

PARISLYTIC

5.2% alc/vol.   Draught only.

BREW DETAILS: Unfiltered. Unpasteurised. Top fermentation.

DECLARED INGREDIENTS: Bramley Cross, Styrian Golding hops; IPA, Crystal, Chocolate and Wheat malts.

APPEARANCE: Mid-brown colour.

NOSE: Lightly fruity malt.

PALATE: Moderately fruity malt with a very strong resiny hop dominating to the detriment of the palate.

FINISH: The very strong resiny hop continues, adding bitterness as well, and crowding out the fruity malt.

OVERALL: It promises to be a pleasant fruity English best bitter but gets hijacked by the strongly resiny hop which overpowers the fruity malt.

JW: ☑☐☐   KR: ☑☐☐

TRENTE WHEAT

5% alc/vol.   Draught only at the Frog & Princess.

BREW DETAILS: Unfiltered. Unpasteurised. Top fermentation.

DECLARED INGREDIENTS: Flavoured with orange zest.

APPEARANCE: Only slightly hazy lemon gold.

NOSE: Fairly neutral.

PALATE: A light grainy wheatiness with a distinct citric element making it appear quite sharp. It gives the impression of being lightly fruity but is mostly a lemon sharpness and a weird orangey taste.

FINISH: Lingering dry tangy wheat.

OVERALL: A very interesting but quite harsh taste counteracts the pleasant soft mouthfeel but it is ultimately not that satisfying.

JW: ☑☐☐   KR: ☑☐☐

OTHER BEERS BREWED

Paris Brown Ale (4.5% alc/vol.) – Brewed a couple of times a year.

Raspberet (5% alc/vol.) – A sweet raspberry beer brewed occasionally in the summer.

Rosbif Revenge (6.7% alc/vol.) – A winter ale, spiced with cinnamon, ginger & orange peel.

Brasserie Pietra

- ✉ route de la Marana, 20600 Furiani, Corse
- ☎ 04 95 30 14 70   Fax: 04 95 30 14 74
- 🕘 Mon-Fri: 0900-1200 & 1400-1700
- 🏃 Always possible. In French (English by arrangement). No charge
- 🏪 Cases, bottles and glasses
- 🍺 6,400hl in 1997 (10,000hl projected for 1998)
- ➔ On the N193 south of Bastia, below the village of Furiani

Corsica, the mountainous island south-east of Nice, is an official départe-ment of France (number 20, but often listed as 2A and 2B). It has problems with its local economy as its rocky topography makes large-scale farming impossible. It does, however, have plenty of chestnuts – in fact, one of its specialities is polenta made with chestnut flour (rather than the wheat used in Italy). It is appropriate, then, that Brasserie Pietra uses chestnut flour to make its Pietra beer – and probably helped to obtain funds from a Corsican development agency.

The idea for a brewery came at the time that work was being car-ried out to develop new ways to use the fruit from the island's 30,000 hectares of chestnut groves. Apparently highly fermentable and good for head retention, the chestnut flour is mixed with the barley malts at the mashing stage.

It opened in June 1996 with all-new equipment and quickly reached an output of 2,800hl in its first year. It didn't take long to become established on the French mainland where it is surprisingly easy to find, and now around 30% of its production is in draught form.

The name of the brewery (and the beer) comes from the village of Pietraserena, in Haut Corse, where the owner was born.

Many may find Pietra a little bland, despite its unusual ingredients, but it is an admirable choice for a conceptual product.

PIETRA

6% alc/vol.   25cl, 33cl crown corked & 75cl corked bottles and draught.

DECLARED INGREDIENTS: Hallertauer hops; a blend of malts; chestnut flour.

APPEARANCE: Amber with a good head.

NOSE: JW: Unusual nutty aroma over a light pale malt. KR: Grainy and fruity.

PALATE: JW: A strong hop, bitingly sharp at times, dominates the palate to such an extent that the floury maltiness is pushed

well to the back. KR: A clinically clean taste of a bitter fruitiness.

FINISH: JW: Dry, resiny hop imparts a strong bitterness to this long-lasting finish. KR: Tannic with a grainy dryness.

OVERALL: JW: A distinctive beer with an unusual element in the taste which is predominantly a strong resiny hop over a floury malt. The taste seems to generate a tingling sensation in the mouth. KR: Quite bland and clinical but has a unique grainy character which tends to grate in the mouth. Interesting but dull.   JW:☑☐☐   KR:☑☐☐

OTHER BEERS BREWED

La Serena (5% alc/vol.) – A blonde beer launched in 1998.

Brasserie Piste Rouge

✉ Les Granges, 24260 Mauzens

☎ 05 53 54 19 17

🕐 Phone brewery for details

⚒ By prior arrangement only

🛍 No information available

ℹ No information available

➡ From Les Eyzies, find the centre of Mauzens-Miremont (which is essentially the church), go past the church and take the second right turn (signposted Les Granges and Chambre d'Hôtes) and go up the hill. At the 90° left hand bend there is a dirt track signposted Sarazin. At the end of this track is the brewery building.

Some breweries can be difficult to find, but others (and this is one of them) are nigh on impossible. Just north of the Dordogne river and close to the Vezère valley (famous for its troglodytic remains and the prehistoric cave paintings at Lascaux) are the hamlets of Mauzens and Miremont which together make up a sprawl of rural dwellings. It is here that our sources had stated that a brewery existed called (depending on the source) either Piste Rouge or Clandestin.

Many knocks on doors later, we eventually tracked the brewery down to a small building in the middle of a field with a heavily-brackened track leading down to it.

It is owned and run by Damien Sarazin, and appears to operate on a part-time basis. By conversation on the telephone we have actually ascertained that it does exist and that it is called Piste Rouge. The confusion about the other name appears to be due to the fact that its beers are called Clandestin.

Unfortunately we were unable to obtain any Piste Rouge beers and subsequent, but unfulfilled, promises from the owners to send beer labels and a completed questionnaire back to us has meant that at the time of going to press we have no further information to pass on here. A scan of the above photograph, which we believe is the brewery, was also sent so that the owners could confirm that it is indeed their premises, but this has also gone unanswered.

Further details, when (and if) they are received, will be posted on our website.

Café de la Poste

✉ 16 place Général Leclerc, 62130 St-Pol-sur-Ternoise
☎ 03 21 03 35 87

The Café de la Poste is a corner café on the same square as the post office in St-Pol-sur-Ternoise. If you enter the town from the north on the D916 the bar is clearly visible on the right.

A pleasant enough locals' bar, it is small but clean, with a restaurant attached. The business part of the brewplant, the same as that installed in the Taverne de l'Ecu and Entre Temps (supplied by BBG Accompany, a Villeneuve-d'Ascq-based company which imports the equipment from Germany) is prominently on display at the end of the bar where it is easily seen through the windows facing onto the main road. Various pipes lead away from the coppers, but the fermenters and garding tanks are not on view, presumably due to lack of space.

One cannot help but feel that the incentive for installing the kit was to try to compete with the nearby Brasserie St-Poloise as there is not one but two brewpubs in this small town when they had existed happily without one until 1997. Unlike the other similarly-equipped brewpubs the beer here is not called Bière de la Maison – preferring to name it after the nickname of an inhabitant of St-Pol.

LA POLO POLITAINE

5.5% alc/vol. Draught only at the brew-pub.

BREW DETAILS: Unfiltered. Unpasteurised. Top fermentation.

APPEARANCE: Cloudy wheat colour.

NOSE: Yeasty with a little pale malt.

PALATE: A bit watery with a strong hop character generating a harsh bitterness. Some yeastiness and a touch of lemon.

FINISH: A sharp, tarty hop and a harsh dryness. Quite lemony. JW: Bitter and a little astringent. Long lasting.

OVERALL: Fairly light beer with a strong hop character producing some lemon notes but also a strong harsh bitterness.

GENERAL: First brewed 1997. La Polo Politaine is the name given to inhabitants of St-Pol.

JW: ☑☐☐   KR: ☑☐☐

OTHER BEERS BREWED

Ambrée – We have heard that an ambrée was introduced in 1998.

Brasserie Ste-Colombe

- ✉ La Landelle, 35134 Ste-Colombe
- ☎ 02 99 47 73 23 Fax: 02 99 47 73 23
- 🕐 Sat: 1000-1500
- 🔍 By arrangement only. 7 days notice. In French. 10FF charge
- 🏪 Bottles & cases
- 📊 140hl (in 1996)
- → Between Retiers and Baine-de-Bretagne take D47 from Coesmes to Ste-Colombe. Go past the first turn-off to Ste-Colombe then turn right onto the D46 in the direction of Janzé. After 2.5 km, turn right up a small lane. The brewery is in the yard of a house at the end of the lane.

Few breweries can boast a more tranquil, rural setting than Brasserie Ste-Colombe. Just inside the southern edge of Brittany, amid the undulating fields of this wide-open agricultural landscape near the village from which the brewery takes its name is an old farmhouse where Gonny Keizer (one of France's, indeed Europe's, few lady brewers) started brewing in an ancient outbuilding in July 1996.

With the help of husband Henri she renovated the outbuilding and brought in old dairy equipment which was converted to suit their needs. Their farmhouse home opposite is around 200 years old, but the brewery building is closer to 500 years old and is built of local traditional stone and soil. Originally a farmworker's dwelling, it was more recently used as a milking shed.

Gonny and Henri moved to France from Overijsel in northern Holland in 1992. Henri is a farmer by trade and soon started work on a local farm. For Gonny, who is a nurse, it was far more difficult to find local employment as the region is so rural. It was in this scenario that she decided to take up brewing to supplement their income and to keep herself busy.

The plant has a capacity of 400 litres per brew and she usually brews every fortnight. The brewhouse is tiled and spotlessly clean but has little room for further expansion. A future improvement will be to convert the attic room above to take a grist mill – at present the milled grain has to be carried from the house to the brewhouse by the sackful. The chambre chaud, however, will still be in the house.

All Gonny's beers are unfiltered, unpasteurised and undergo a bottle refermentation. One week in the open fermenter is followed by one week of garde (quite generous, given the small amount of space in the brewery). After priming for the bottle refermentation (using the same yeast as the primary fermentation), the bottles then spend one week in the chambre chaude, then finally a period of maturation in the cellar – the Bière de Froment for four weeks, her other beers for eight weeks.

The Ste-Colombe range is adventurous and untypical of normal French styles. The Bière de Froment is exactly what it says – it is not a 'white' beer, it is a wheat beer. It has little in common with Belgian or French whites, and is best described as a farmhouse version of a German weizenbier. The Ambrée is supposedly loosely in the style of the classic Antwerp beer De Koninck (Henri's favourite tipple), and her Bière d'Hiver is a dark and complex brew which boasts 14 different herbs in the ingredients – one of which is hop.

Gonny doesn't market her beers as necessarily Breton, unlike the other breweries in Brittany – she prefers to be considered simply as an artisanal brewery rather than be given a regional tag. This is probably a wise decision bearing in mind the brewery is only just inside the officially-recognised Breton region and she is just as likely to attract sales from the region of Anjou just to the south.

Unfortunately the Ste-Colombe beers can be very difficult to find in bars and cafes, as most of its products are sold direct or to shops and at fairs. Thankfully there has been much positive local press coverage and we hope that increased interest will eventually result in these excellent beers becoming more widely available.

AMBRÉE

6% alc/vol.   75cl corked bottles.

DECLARED INGREDIENTS: Saaz & Hallertau hops; Pilsener, Caramel & Roast malts; malted wheat.

APPEARANCE: Rich bright amber colour.

NOSE: Pleasantly mellow, gentle, rounded fruity malt.

PALATE: Starts sweet but turns into a rich caramel malt and fruit with a biscuity note. JW: A generous helping of hop imparts a slightly bitter, sharp edge to the palate. KR: Surprisingly light despite the full, malty palate.

FINISH: Very hoppily bitter with a dryness replacing all but the lingering caramel of the palate.

OVERALL: Interesting beer that has a sweet start followed by a fruity caramel malt then a tangy bitterness turning dry. All this yet still light and easy to drink.

GENERAL: First brewed 1996.   JW: ☑☑☐   KR: ☑☑☐

BIÈRE DE FROMENT

5.5% alc/vol. 75cl corked bottles.

DECLARED INGREDIENTS: Saaz hops; Pilsener malt; malted wheat.

APPEARANCE: Warm, honey-tinged, wheaty gold with a good fluffy head.

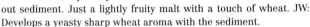

NOSE: Surprisingly neutral for a wheat beer, especially without sediment. Just a lightly fruity malt with a touch of wheat. JW: Develops a yeasty sharp wheat aroma with the sediment.

PALATE: Light tastes but a surprisingly full palate. Soft gentle wheatiness with a light citric sharpness and a faint lemon taste from some hops that also add bitterness. There are wafts of herbal notes without seeming to be spiced. JW: Yeasty notes are added with the sediment. KR: Quite sweet start.

FINISH: Gentle but lingering moderately bitter wheatiness. JW: Suggestions of spiciness when sediment added. KR: Some lingering fruity/citric notes.

OVERALL: Very good beer that is decidedly wheaty yet original. There is plenty of wheat throughout yet it is not allowed to dominate – it displays a wonderful balance. Excellent soft creamy texture. Good with or without sediment, just the citric element being reduced with sediment and the suggestions of spice being increased.

GENERAL: First brewed 1997.   JW: ☑☑☐ KR: ☑☑☐

BIÈRE D'HIVER

8% alc/vol. 75cl corked bottles.

DECLARED INGREDIENTS: Saaz & Hallertau hops; Pilsener, Caramel, Coffee & Roast malts; malted wheat; spiced with 14 herbs and honey.

APPEARANCE: Rich mid-brown colour.

NOSE: Gorgeously full, fruity, herbal and faintly spicy with

some alcohol. Rich and very inviting like a winter ale should be.

PALATE: Full and fruity with a gentle herbal spiciness, some dark malt and a touch of caramel. A good hop character adds some bitterness and there is an alcohol warmth. Sediment greatly increases spiciness. Fairly complex with a slight sweet tanginess from honey.

FINISH: Long lasting bitter, fruity, caramel malt with a persistent herbal spiciness. Warming, with a little honey tanginess.

OVERALL: Immensely impressive winter warmer with all the right characteristics – full palate, fruity, dark, spicy, warming, moderately complex. Superbly satisfying. Fairly full, thickish & sweet. A well rounded winter evening beer that is unusual for France. KR: A beer which benefits from a year or two's ageing, giving it extra depth.

GENERAL: First brewed 1996.   JW: ☑☑☑ KR: ☑☑☑

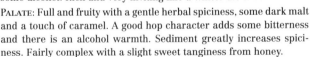

Brasserie Artisanale St-Martial

- ✉ 8 Place Denis-Dussoubs, 87000 Limoges
- ☎ 05 55 79 37 98   Fax: 05 55 79 38 33
- 🕐 Open every day
- 🍻 Telephone brewery to confirm
- 🏪 Bottles, glasses and bottle-packs
- 🍺 1,300hl
- ➡ Place Denis-Dussoubs is in the centre of Limoges

Place Denis-Dussoubs is an old and architecturally impressive square near the centre of the bustling town of Limoges, capital of the region of Limousin. Odd as it seems, Brasserie St-Martial has two bars on the square, a bar called Le Paris and the brewery tap which simply displays the Saint-Martial name. Both bars are very clean and efficiently run, but the brewery tap in particular has been fitted out with an impressive array of old and current brewing equipment.

The brewing kit was installed by S.A. Bars de France, the company which owns the 3 Brasseurs/O'Neil chain of brewpubs, and the format of its Blonde, Ambrée, Brune and Blanche range, along with the four-page newsheet-style menu and explanatory leaflet of the brewing process are all along the same lines. There are, however, some differences. For instance it sells all its beers in bottles and even offers two 'Grand Crus' – the Blonde and Ambrée which have undergone a bottle refermentation – a real bonus for beer-lovers and for which the brewery should be congratulated.

The brewery tap is on two levels, but the upstairs was not being used on our visit. Despite the narrow frontage, it is very deep and has a long bar down the left-hand side. At the end of the room is a small laboratory where it keeps and cultures its yeasts.

From the outside you can look through the glazed frontage at the beautiful beaten copper kettles with their brick surrounds which stand either side of a wood-panelled mash tun. All the brewplant is on a slightly raised platform which you must walk past to enter the bar itself. Behind the bar are the glass-panelled rooms where you can see the six fermenters and 12 garding tanks. There is also a 'chambre froid' for garding beer downstairs in the cellar, where they also do the kegging and bottling.

All the St-Martial beers are top-fermenting and are unfiltered and unpasteurised. Unlike the normal 3 Brasseurs/O'Neil beers, the products here appear to have had some tweaking from the Bars de France recipes – thankfully, mostly for the better. The Brune especially was different, displaying a more distinct stout character, but all of them were fuller and more characterful.

Le Paris only offers the standard versions of Blonde and Ambrée in bottles so you will have to visit the brewery tap to sample the Grand Cru versions. Both bars offer a good selection of snacks and meals – the brewery tap specialising in 'flammekeuches' (savoury pancakes with cheese and meat), but Le Paris has a greater range. Both sell individual pretzels and give tiny snack dishes with most orders of beer (we had some very interesting French black pudding with the order for our Ambrée).

The brewery tap has a 'happy hour' between 6.00 and 7.00 pm each evening, during which time 33cl glasses of all their beers are charged at the 25cl rate. A bell will ring at the beginning and end of the happy hour.

Overall, both bars have a friendly, lively atmosphere and attract a good, mixed clientele but best of all is the brewery tap where you can enjoy six pretty good quality beers in a cosmopolitan, city-centre environment.

AMBRÉE

5.5% alc/vol. 75cl corked bottles and draught.

BREW DETAILS: Unpasteurised. Top fermentation.

DECLARED INGREDIENTS: Kent hops.

APPEARANCE: Amber colour with a light to good, creamy head.

NOSE: Light, slightly stale hops over a fruity crystal malt.

PALATE: Great bitter fruit mouthful in the start with a strong bitter hop bite. The bitter fruit also has a sharpness to it although there are fleeting sweeter notes threading through the background. The strong, though muddy, hop that is present is overshadowed by the bitter fruit.

FINISH: Lingering hop bitterness with waves of bitter fruit and malt. The sharp hop bitterness tries to dry the inherent fruit sweetness and just about succeeds resulting in a slighty bittersweet element.

OVERALL: In spite of the very strong bitterness this is a well balanced beer though perhaps a little over-hoppy for most people's idea of an ambrée. An interesting beer with a strong bitter fruit throughout.

JW: ☑☐☐   KR: ☑☐☐

AMBRÉE GRAND CRU

7.5% alc/vol. 75cl corked bottles.

BREW DETAILS: Unpasteurised. Top fermentation. Bottle refermentation.

APPEARANCE: Amber in colour with a good, creamy, fluffy head.

NOSE: Lovely hoppy character with a very light fruity malt base, though a touch musty.

PALATE: Very bitter. Quite acidic with a distinctly tart red fruit and a mouth-drying trait. Very spritzy. Complex with a farmhouse/artisanal character if a little too sharp.

FINISH: JW: Tart, astringent, lingering, bittersweet fruit. KR: Deeply interesting. The crystal malt gives it its sharp fruity notes and the hops make it almost bone dry in the mouth despite the sharpness making the mouth water. Long lasting and deeply intriguing.

OVERALL: Has been found to be quite inconsistent – for this tasting we have averaged out the sampling of four bottles, each with a particularly different character. JW: Nice texture and an interesting artisanal quality, but the finish particularly is very difficult to live with. KR: Has great depth of character which displays a very bitter and sharp facet missing in the 'ordinaire', but the uninitiated may find it a little odd.

JW: ☑☐☐   KR: ☑☑☐

BLANCHE

4.4% alc/vol. 75cl corked bottles and draught.

BREW DETAILS: Unpasteurised. Top fermentation.

DECLARED INGREDIENTS: Styrian Goldings hops.

APPEARANCE: Cloudy wheat colour with a massive frothy head.

NOSE: A light aroma of wheat with distinct citric notes and some fruit. JW: A gently floral hop.

PALATE: Strongly wheaty with a distinct citric taste and a hoppy dryness. JW: Lemon. Quite lactic (creamy). KR: Orangey. Some oaty hints.

FINISH: Dry, mouthdrying and wheaty. KR: Fruity notes.

OVERALL: Unconventional but impressive blanche. Excellent creamy texture, full and interesting taste but still quenching. Fairly plain with a strong wheatiness throughout but no spiciness. On draught it can exude a sweeter palate.

GENERAL: Sold as **Blanche de Limoges** in the Le Paris bar. The brewery says it is based on an old recipe from Louvain (Leuven), Belgium.

JW: ☑☑☐   KR: ☑☑☐

BLONDE

4.5% alc/vol. 75cl corked bottles and draught.

BREW DETAILS: Unpasteurised. Top fermentation.

DECLARED INGREDIENTS: Saaz hops.

APPEARANCE: Paleish gold with a short-lived but initially massive rocky head.

NOSE: Gentle, slightly citric hop over a light pale malt. JW: Hint of lime.

PALATE: Full pale malt and a hop which gives a very flowery, citric character which gives some gentle bitterness and adds to the overall fruity sensation.

FINISH: Starts citric but becomes very bitter, slightly fruity and astringent. Very long lasting.

OVERALL: Quite tasty for a blonde and impressively full. Essentially, hoppy, citric and quite bitter with a dry finish. On draught we found it to be less full with a short-lived finish. JW: ☑☐☐ KR: ☑☑☐

BLONDE GRAND CRU

7% alc/vol. 75cl corked bottles.

BREW DETAILS: Unpasteurised. Top fermentation. Bottle refermentation.

APPEARANCE: Golden with a massive rocky head and good lacework.

NOSE: Initial light fragrant hoppiness soon mellows and it develops yeasty overtones. KR: Damp hay and woody notes.

PALATE: Strongly hoppy with a sharp lemon bite and a light white pepperiness. JW: Gently bitter. KR: Excellent – on the surface it has a clean and fresh character yet gives a deep complexity with a light pale malt fruitiness filling it out to produce a good mouthful of taste and interest.

FINISH: Dry, citric hop bitterness. Astringent and a little resiny. Very mouthdrying and long lasting.

OVERALL: A most distinctive beer though the character is almost entirely hoppy. Very like a hoppy Walloon blonde especially with the slight yeasty character which does not intrude too much yet adds another dimension. KR: A spritzy, quenching character but a deeper multi-layered facet if you're looking for it. JW: ☑☑☐ KR: ☑☑☑

BRUNE

6% alc/vol. 75cl corked bottles and draught.

BREW DETAILS: Unpasteurised. Top fermentation.

APPEARANCE: Very dark chestnut.

NOSE: A mellow roast malt with hints of coffee and cocoa. KR: Some unfortunate stale hop aromas.

PALATE: Bags of dark roast malt with a sharp hop bitterness. Hints of fruit as though it is trying to get out but cannot. On draught we found it to have a stoutish character and distinct chocolate notes.

FINISH: Dry, bitter, chocolatey roast malt lingers. KR: Some sweet fruit still trying to get through.

OVERALL: Very roasted for a Brune, more stout-like, Very full and surprisingly fairly well balanced with a light hop character. KR: A little over-sweet but has an impressive hoppiness throughout for a brune. JW: ☑☐☐ KR: ☑☐☐

Brasserie de St-Omer

✉ 9 rue Edouard Devaux, B.P.190, 62504 St-Omer CEDEX

☎ 03 21 98 76 00   Fax: 03 21 88 57 50

🕐 Contact brewery for details

⚒ By prior arrangement only

🏪 Contact brewery for details

🍺 1,420,000hl (in 1996)

➡ From the tourist office, just past the NE end of the public gardens, continue down Boulevard des Allies to the roundabout. Turn right, then right again into rue de Calais. Third left is rue Edouard Devaux.

One of the most prolific of France's contract brewers, with a major share of the cheap 'bière blonde' market is Brasserie de St-Omer. Although the name has only been around since 1985, it has many long-established brands in its portfolio – like Semeuse and Facon – which it acquired through a series of takeovers and mergers.

Brasserie Artésienne, founded in 1866, closed its doors in 1985 when its brewplant came to the end of its life and no money was available for such a major reinvestment. Later that year, a company called Caves St-Arnould – a wine merchants – took the gamble to buy it, build a new brewhouse and change its name to Brasserie St-Omer. Within a year it was successful enough to warrant expansion by buying the respected Brasserie Facon at Pont de Briques (near Boulogne), which came under the ownership of the Groupe St-Arnould.

By the end of 1987 the group had also acquired Brasseries Semeuse (in Lille), Brasserie de Solesmes and Brasserie de Denain – making it a major beer-making force in the region. Semeuse was the last of Lille's large breweries, based in the east of the city at Hellemmes – itself starting life as two breweries merged in 1922.

Despite some investment in its newly-owned sites, the decision was taken to rationalise the business by moving all production to the one site in St-Omer – Facon closing in 1991 and Semeuse a year later.

The site, which is on both sides of a surprisingly narrow street in an essentially residential area of town, is in two distinct parts on either side. On one flank stands a modern brick-built salle de brassage (with feature windows looking in on the brew kettles) next to its older, more characterful offices, and on the other side is the array of huge conditioning tanks and transport depot. The wording on the external wall says 1866–1986, referring to the foundation of Brasserie Artésienne and its rebirth as St-Omer.

An indication of its success can be gained by the fact that in 1986 the production was just 60,000hl (with 50 employees) and by 1996 output had reached 1,420,000hl (with 200 employees). Over 5% of its produce is exported to Belgium and the UK, though most will be sold quite anonymously through supermarket chains as contract beer.

The image on much of its publicity is of the tower of a monastery demolished in the days of the French revolution. Although it was finally destroyed in the Second World War, it became famous enough as a landmark in the region for the brewery to adopt as its logo.

St-Omer proudly states it has a brand portfolio of well over 100 different beers (although we suspect most are relabelled brews of the same recipe), so we have chosen to concentrate only on its major brands. The list in the 'other beers brewed' section is not meant to be comprehensive – it is a sample list of beers we regularly saw on supermarket shelves during our time researching the book.

L'ÉPI DE FACON

5.5% alc/vol. 25cl crown corked bottles.

APPEARANCE: Pale golden colour.

NOSE: Highly aromatic wheat-based nose with a touch of vanilla, hints of toffee and a little hop. JW: Quite caramelly.

PALATE: Loads of taste generated by the wheat and hops. A little lemon and a light resiny bitterness form the basis. JW: Some caramel and a touch of vanilla. KR: Lactic, lightly fruity with a spicy bite from the hops.

FINISH: Dry and bitter with a little hoppiness. KR: A little pepperiness and a watery creamy wheat.

OVERALL: An interesting full nose and palate that are difficult to describe and cause the beer to be difficult to categorise.

GENERAL: The label describes it as a 'special wheat beer' in French and a 'lager beer' in English! JW:☑☐☐ KR:☑☐☐

FACON BIÈRE DE NOËL

4.8% alc/vol. 25cl crown corked bottles.

APPEARANCE: Full amber colour with a good lacey head.

NOSE: Strong, sweetish, candy malt. KR: Quite fruity.

PALATE: A candy sweet start with some hop notes. JW: Rapidly develops a strong bitter

tangy taste with a dry slightly burnt candy and malt. KR: Full and quite creamy with some artificial sweet notes, candy and some bitter hops.

FINISH: JW: A little earthy and bitter with an odd tang. KR: Bitter with lingering saccharin.

OVERALL: JW: Disappointing. The ever-present tanginess is too much for me. KR: A tired bitter hoppiness.

JW:☐☐☐ KR:☐☐☐

FACON DE LUXE

4.6% alc/vol. 100cl screw top bottles.

APPEARANCE: Pale golden colour.

NOSE: Gentle pale malt with an unfortunate metallic element. A gentle dull hop is also evident.

PALATE: Very dry and bitter with fairly tangy sharp hops and some pale malt. JW: A metallic edge to the malt. KR: A sharp pale malt fruit and a creamy hint.

FINISH: Unpleasant. Uncompromisingly mouth-drying with a long lingering metallic hop tang.

OVERALL: What little promise there is in the distinctly dry and bitter hop character is destroyed by the unpleasant finish. Overall though it is bland and insipid.

JW:☐☐☐ KR:☐☐☐

LA MILLIONIÈME DE SAINT-OMER

9.2% alc/vol. 25cl crown corked bottles.

APPEARANCE: Golden colour.

NOSE: A lightly fruity alcohol with a touch of bitter hop and a little pale malt.

PALATE: Full, rich tangy, slightly fruity, pale malt with masses of alcohol. KR: A dry hop balances the sweet fruity alcohol.

FINISH: Lingering tangy slightly sweet pale malt with a gentle, dry, bitterness. Strongly alcoholic.

OVERALL: Very strong, sweetish, tangy, alcoholic beer that is easy to drink for its strength. The level of alcohol is a little excessive and gets to you in the end (literally).

JW:☑☐☐ KR:☑☐☐

NORDIK EXTRA LAGER

5.9% alc/vol. 25cl crown corked bottles.

APPEARANCE: Pale gold colour.

NOSE: Gentle but dull and metallic hop and pale malt.

PALATE: Sweet pale malt with a little hop. JW: A little watery and a touch metallic. KR: Extremely boring.

FINISH: JW: A strong tangy metallic bitterness that grows as you drink. KR: Leftover, slightly sweet, malt with a gently dry and bitter hop, turning metallic.

OVERALL: The disturbing metallic element is present throughout a fairly nondescript beer, though it must be said that drinking at 5.9% doesn't get much less demanding.

JW:☐☐☐ KR:☐☐☐

SAINT-OMER BLONDE DE LUXE

4.6% alc/vol. 25cl crown corked & 100cl screw top bottles and 33cl cans.

APPEARANCE: Pale golden in colour.

NOSE: Quite a heady hop over a gentle pale malt with an unfortunate metallic element.

PALATE: An interesting biscuity pale malt is the dominant taste though with a fair bit of hop character. The hops provide a slightly sharp, almost citric, edge and a gentle bitterness. KR: Sweet, fruity malt.

FINISH: Very dry and mouth-drying with a little citric hop and a strong tangy bitterness. KR: An unpleasant lingering sweet malt.

OVERALL: Lots of citric hop and a biscuity pale malt help lift this basic lager.

JW: ☐☐☐   KR: ☐☐☐

SEMEUSE

5.2% alc/vol. 25cl crown corked bottles.

APPEARANCE: Pale gold in colour.

NOSE: A dull subdued hop over a light pale malt with a subtle earthiness.

PALATE: Hoppy and instantly bitter with some citric lemon notes over a light maltiness. KR: Hoppiness pales against a bittersweet citric maltiness.

FINISH: Watery with a bitter and citric hop residue. KR: Sweet malt dies away quickly.

OVERALL: Earthier than a usual Pilsner but let down by a short-lived watery finish. The hops give an interesting promise that is not delivered. Easy to drink.

JW: ☑☐☐   KR: ☑☐☐

OTHER BEERS BREWED

Bière de Mars

Bière Spéciale de Noël Semeuse (6.4% alc/vol.)

Blondhellia (4.6% alc/vol.) – Typical French pilsener qualities with some added citric notes. JW: A strong hop character but very bitter and a little too metallic. KR: Very sweet, masking a good hoppiness.

Brandenberg (2.8% alc/vol.) – Almost characterless. A subdued malt and hop just about manages to deliver a horrible sweetness.

Helbrau (2.8% alc/vol.) – Another particularly dull brew which, once the earthiness in the nose vents off, leaves just an artificial taste.

La Reserve du Brasseur (6.5% alc/vol.) – An amber beer described by the brewery as a bière de garde.

Saint-Omer Bière Bock (3.7% alc/vol.) – Uncompromisingly resinous character from the hop though surprisingly dull. A disappointing, sweet pale malt struggles to impose itself.

Saint-Omer Bière Brune (4.6% alc/vol.) – A cheap and cheerful brown beer with enough interest to encourage drinking but essentially dull. Gently roasted character. KR: Quite nutty dryness.

Brasserie St-Poloise

- ✉ 2 rue de la Calandre, 62130 St-Pol-sur-Ternoise
- ☎ 03 21 41 91 00 Fax: 03 21 41 91 00
- 🕐 Bar hours
- ♨ Daily: 1000-2000. 7 days notice. In French & English. 20FF
- 🏠 Cases, bottles, glasses
- ⛏ 200hl (expected for 1998)
- ➔ See article

In an unusual step for a well-established brewery, Brasserie Castelain opened a brew-pub in June 1997 in the provincial village of St-Pol, which operates as a separate entity under the same umbrella as Castelain's many other activities.

The original St-Poloise beer was developed at the parent company's facility in Wingles where it has been on sale for some time (and still is) in its bottled form, joined later by the Grand Cru. Brasserie St-Poloise concentrates on making unfiltered versions of the beers to be sold at the brew-pub on draught, and has recently introduced two new brands of its own. The new facility has created an interesting role for Bertrand Castelain, son of Yves and the latest generation of the Castelain family to become a brewer.

The brew-pub is situated away from the main road through the village, directly opposite a school, in a converted ex-abbatoir which has been extended and enhanced in a particularly tasteful manner. There are two eating areas inside, the restaurant (which displays many of the building's original features but has had the addition of an impressive fireplace and chimney breast) and a basic brasserie-style area for simpler food such as flammekueches. There is also a large room adjoining the bar under a naturally-lit, glass-roofed area plus a very large function room at the back for weddings, conferences or similar occasions. In all there is table seating for about 200 people.

The bar itself displays half of an old brew kettle (salvaged from the now-defunct Brasserie Schneider from south-west France) and the main drinking area has various tables sporting the St-Poloise label designs on their tops. Gift packs (including Ch'ti) and souvenirs, such as bar towels and enamel signs, are also on sale in this area.

The brewkit is visible as soon as you walk through the front door. On the left is a glass-panelled room containing the mash tun, brew kettle and mill and immediately on your right are half of the conical fermentation and garding vessels (the rest being at the far end of the bar). The salle de brassage forms an excellent centrepiece, visible from three sides within the brew-pub and also from outside.

The brew capacity is 10 hectolitres and it is put to good use with Bertrand developing two additional beers – a blanche and an ambrée – within six months of opening, both of which are named after the local area famous for its seven valleys. All its beers are stored for a shorter period than their bottled equivalents before serving which, with the lack of filtration, gives them a totally different character.

The easiest way to find the bar is to enter St-Pol on the N41 from Béthune. Going past an Intermarché on your right you will then pass a small square on the right with Taverne de la Poste on the corner and another small square on the left. Just as you round the corner, and opposite the square to the left is a small right-hand turn – rue des Procureurs. Take this road and turn first left into rue de la Calandre, St-Poloise is on the right, opposite the school.

The salle de brassage viewed from one of the eating areas.

The bar and fermentation tanks as viewed on entering the building.

AMBRÉE DES 7 VALLÉES

5.9% alc/vol. Draught only at the brew-pub.

BREW DETAILS: Unfiltered. Unpasteurised. Top fermentation.

APPEARANCE: Darkish red amber.

NOSE: Strong aroma of crystal malt with a red fruit and a slight hop. JW: Roasted suggestions.

PALATE: Rich malt with a crystal bite and a growing caramel/roast element which becomes tangy. Some resiny hop tries to get through but just adds to the tanginess. Very full malty taste with a fair fruit element.

FINISH: Gentler than the palate suggests. Tangy caramel/roast malt. KR: A tangy hop resin.

OVERALL: Creamy full texture and very full taste but the tangy elements of both the malt and hop are turned up a bit too much.

GENERAL: First brewed 1998. A very new brew which may well change and/or develop over time.   JW:☑☐☐   KR:☑☐☐

BLANCHE DES 7 VALLÉES

4.5% alc/vol. Draught only at the brew-pub.

BREW DETAILS: Unfiltered. Unpasteurised. Top fermentation.

APPEARANCE: Cloudy wheat colour.

NOSE: Perfumed hop with a touch of spice. JW: Suggestions of marzipan. KR: A very strong hop.

PALATE: Over-strong sweet hop 'flakes' with a citric sharpness and waves of bitterness.

FINISH: Dry, lingering, hoppy wheat with a gentle bitterness. KR: Mouthwatering from the lingering acidity.

OVERALL: An unusual blanche which is very unlike anything else. Our tasting was done on the second-ever brew so it could well change or develop over time.

GENERAL: First brewed 1998. JW: ☑☐☐ KR: ☑☐☐

ST-POLOISE

6.5% alc/vol. Draught only at the brew-pub.

BREW DETAILS: Unfiltered. Unpasteurised. Bottom fermentation.

APPEARANCE: Lemon-tinged gold.

NOSE: Citric and exotic fruit aroma.

PALATE: Excellently complex with masses of interesting elements – malt, hops, exotic fruit and yeast – all working on various levels to create a constantly challenging taste.

FINISH: Dry, fruity, hoppy and moderately bitter with all the complex elements of the palate continuing to work.

OVERALL: An amazingly complex yet easy to drink beer with a quite unique exotic fruit element. More than enough interest to keep even Belgian beer fans happy. Easily accessible yet worthwhile character. KR: Some may consider the palate too sweet but the finish makes up for it.

GENERAL: First brewed in 1996. Developed and still brewed in its bottled guise by Castelain in Wingles. Also on sale in bottles at the brew-pub, so you can try both versions. JW: ☑☑☑ KR: ☑☑☑

ST-POLOISE GRAND CRU

7.5% alc/vol. Draught only at the brew-pub.

BREW DETAILS: Unfiltered. Unpasteurised. Bottom fermentation.

APPEARANCE: Golden colour with a light head.

NOSE: Pleasantly fragrant fresh hop and fresh pale malt.

PALATE: Sweet pale malt with a full fresh hop taste. A touch of bitterness helps offset the high level of sweetness which initially comes as a surprise before the other elements come through to balance it. Multi-layered and interesting character. KR: A touch of fruity tang.

FINISH: Still the sweetness comes through with a resiny hop almost matching it. The pale malt that forms the solid base is a little tangy.

OVERALL: The excellent soft creamy texture enhances this very full tasting beer which is multi-layered, wonderfully balanced and very satisfying. There is a massive malt and hop character throughout, though a surprisingly high level of sweetness.

GENERAL: First brewed 1997. Developed by Castelain in Wingles and the bottled version is still made there. JW: ☑☑☐ KR: ☑☑☐

Brasserie de St-Sylvestre

✉ 141 rue de la Chapelle, 59114 St-Sylvestre-Cappel, Steenvoorde

☎ 03 28 40 15 49   Fax: 03 28 40 13 44

🕐 Tue-Fri: 0800-1200 & 1400-1800. Sat: 0800-1200

🏃 Tours not encouraged.

🏪 Cases, bottles, glasses

🍺 290hl (in 1997)

➡ Turn off the main street opposite the church

Most will think of northern French Flanders as being relatively flat and featureless (which is true for much of its expanse), but there are three knolls which rise out of the otherwise rolling landscape between Dunkerque and Lille. Mont Cassel, a strategically important elevated position throughout history, is one of these, along with Mont des Recollets and Mont des Cats – the latter being a landmark from the Lille motorway with its huge radio mast. In the centre of these three hills lies the sleepy village of St-Sylvestre-Cappel, home to some of France's most characterful beers.

Records show that there was a brewery on the present site as long ago as 1500, although information is very sketchy. At the time of the First World War the brewery was in the hands of the Dehaene family and sold most of its production through the 35 locally-owned bars. In the aftermath of the war it changed hands when Marcel Bacquaert, a maltster until his business was destroyed, bought it in 1919. Soon after, the brewery was handed on to his nephew, Rémy Ricour, a peasant's son who had to sell some of the tied estate to raise capital to keep the business afloat. The installation of a bottling line in 1934 gave the brewery a wider market than before, and it supplied many of the former breweries in the area which ceased beer production to concentrate on being distributors following the Second World War.

Pierre Ricour took over operations from his father and undertook a modernisation programme which culminated in 1954 with the construction of new brewplant – including the revolutionary (for the time) conical fermenters. In 1964 production was limited to bottom fermented beers, following the European trends of the day.

The brewery took the brave step to produce a limited experimental brew of a 7% top-fermented Bière de Mars in 1984 which was well enough received for it to launch a major new brand the following year to coincide with Pierre's sons taking over the operation of the business. Named 3 Monts, after the surrounding hills, it took a little time to become established, but by the early 90s it was widely available throughout France and justifiably famous.

The established trilogy of top-fermented beers – 3 Monts, Bière de Noël and an evolved Bière de Mars (now bottle refermented, 8.5% and called Bière Nouvelle to extend its selling period) – were joined recently by Gavroche. This latest addition is a welcome new product which shows that St-Sylvestre has no intention of standing still. The brewery's other products, some of which are brewed to recipes introduced at the turn of the century, are all bottom-fermented.

The brewery itself is not the prettiest one by any means, evoking a true workmanlike character and the operation straddles both sides of a small road just off the main Cassel–Bailleul road.

Forget the aesthetics, this is a working brewery with some of France's best beer in its portfolio.

3 MONTS

8.5% alc/vol.   75cl corked bottles.

BREW DETAILS: Filtered. Unpasteurised. Top fermentation.

INGREDIENTS: Hallertau & Flemish Brewers Gold hops; Pale malt.

APPEARANCE: Golden colour with an impressively rocky head.

NOSE: A fruity pale malt with a gentle hop aroma that increases as the beer ages. A distinct yeasty note is present. KR: Hints of apple skins and a strong promise of alcohol.

PALATE: Full mouth of rich, slightly fruity, pale malt with a lot of sharpish alcohol generating considerable warmth. JW: A bit barley wine-like in the malt bite and the alcohol intensity. KR: Vinous, but hugely satisfying.

FINISH: JW: A strong warmth from the mouth-puckering alcohol is tempered by hints of tangy malt and the bitter hop. KR: A warm glow from the alcohol with a full, lingering, very rich apple and red fruit.

OVERALL: Good full bodied, full tasting, moderately complex ale with possibly a little too much alcohol character. KR: Immensely full bodied and complex ale which does a good job in showing that filtered beer doesn't necessarily mean bland and characterless.

GENERAL: First brewed 1984.   JW: ☑☑☐   KR: ☑☑☑

BIÈRE DE NOËL

8% alc/vol. 75cl corked bottles.

BREW DETAILS: Filtered. Unpasteurised. Top fermentation.

DECLARED INGREDIENTS: 50/50 Hallertau & Brewers Gold hops; Munich malt.

APPEARANCE: Dark chestnut amber with a massive head.

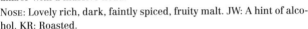

NOSE: Lovely rich, dark, faintly spiced, fruity malt. JW: A hint of alcohol. KR: Roasted.

PALATE: Very full, very Christmas-like. Complex with oodles of dark, rich, fruity malt tempered by a hop character that grows slowly imparting bitterness as it does so. JW: Some alcohol warmth. KR: Some chicory notes.

FINISH: Warming, rounded and well balanced with a tangy fruity malt offset by a slightly peppery hop bitterness. KR: An after dinner dark chocolate dryness.

OVERALL: Excellent Christmas beer. Moderately complex, suitably warming, rich and fruity with a slight spiciness. Just perfect for a winter evening by the fire.

GENERAL: First brewed 1988.   JW: ☑☑☑   KR: ☑☑☑

BIÈRE NOUVELLE

8% alc/vol. 75cl corked bottles.

BREW DETAILS: Filtered. Unpasteurised. Top fermentation.

DECLARED INGREDIENTS: Hallertau hops; Pale & Munich malts.

APPEARANCE: Orangey gold with a massive, pillowy head and great lacework.

NOSE: Gorgeous, big, flowery, hop aroma with citric hints that get stronger with addition of sediment. JW: A mellow vanilla is also present. KR: Beautiful appley/fruity malt.

PALATE: Strong full-mouthed hop character with a sharp citricity and tannic bitterness cutting through a light orchard fruit. JW: Pale malt present throughout. Quite warming. KR: Zingy and spritzy.

FINISH: Hoppy bitterness over a pale malt. JW: All hops – resiny, bitter, citric, slightly acidic and a little astringent. KR: A little tangy with a touch of red fruit.

OVERALL: Superb hoppy beer with a sharp, rather than mellow, hop character. Just what you would expect from a Bière de Mars which is supposed to represent the finest of ingredients. JW: It has a young 'upstart' character much like a Beaujolais Nouveau has. Without any sediment added the fizz makes it distinctly frothy.

GENERAL: First brewed 1984. The brewery's March beer. Was called Bière de Mars until 1995 when it was renamed to allow a longer selling season.

JW: ☑☑☐   KR: ☑☑☑

GAVROCHE

8.5% alc/vol. 33cl crown corked bottles.

APPEARANCE: Copper amber with a good head.

NOSE: Rich, pleasantly fruity malt. JW: Full deep crystal malt with faintest roast suggestions. KR: Promise of fruity malt, especially red fruit. Very strong aromatic hop.

PALATE: Full tasting fruity malt with the fruit displaying a red character. Rich. Starts turning dry and bitter with a little tang even before you swallow. Gentle alcohol glow. KR: Intense bitter fruit building into the finish. Strong alcohol note. Citric, peel-like, fruit quality.

FINISH: Lingering dry bitter gentle malty tang with some leftover red fruit and a bit of alcohol. Deep and interesting.

OVERALL: Impressive red fruit character never gives sweetness but it has a full palate and a good lingering, quite bitter finish. Lots going on in a very easily drinkable beer. Some may find it too richly fruity and bitter. KR: Could well get three ticks with more tasting.

GENERAL: Gavroche is French for 'street urchin' – like those in the Victor Hugo novel *Les Misérables*.

JW: ☑☑☐   KR: ☑☑☐

OTHER BEERS BREWED

Bière des Chênes – The name of the house beer at Brasserie St-Georges in Eecke. Could be something else relabelled.

Hoppeland Bier (3.6% alc/vol.) – Sold in 75cl corked and 100cl screw-top bottles. A pale lemon-coloured beer with a faint pale malt base on the nose and a distinctive hop quality. Sweetish start turning bitter with a resiny hop. Surprisingly uncompromising on the resins for such a weak beer. First brewed 1970. (Labelled as **Bock du Moulin** when sold in 25cl bottles.)

Hoppeland Light (2% alc/vol.) – As one would expect, a gentle character throughout, with a little soapy pale malt and some astringency. Seems to lose what taste it has the more your drink. First brewed 1900.

Luxe de Moulin (5% alc/vol.) – Sold in 75cl screw-top bottles. Gentle, dry, earthy hop aroma with an understated, surprisingly light, palate of pale malt and a touch of hop bitterness. Quite dull overall but for the sharp contrast between sweet malt and dry hop. First brewed 1970. (Labelled as **Ophelia** when sold in 25cl bottles.)

Bière des Flandres (5% alc/vol.).

A selection of labels, all of which appear in the 'other beers brewed' list – and all are bottom fermented.

Brasserie de Saverne

- ✉ 60 rue de Dettwiller, 67700 Saverne
- ☎ 03 88 02 19 99   Fax: 03 88 02 19 77
- 🕐 Mon-Fri: 0900-1700
- 🔀 Sometimes possible if pre-arranged. 15 days notice. In French & English. No charge
- 🏪 No direct sales
- 🍺 700,000hl (in 1997)
- ➔ See article

Brasserie Saverne is somewhat of an anomaly when it comes to its appearance in this book as you could argue that it is really a German brewery. It is in fact part of Karlsbräu France S.A. which is the French subsidiary of the Karlsberg Group based in Homburg not far over the border to the north, near Saarbrucken. Having its own brewery in France has helped Karlsbräu become the number one exporter of German beers to France. In addition to that it also influences the beers produced at Saverne.

The Germans bought into a good deal of local tradition as the brewery dates from 1845 when Henri Schweickhardt started a small artisanal brewery at 11 rue des Clés. By 1866 he had managed to develop to the extent that he was the largest producer of the dozen local breweries. Four years later it passed to the grandfather of Charles Gerber and would stay in the family for 102 years. It was the Gerber family that moved it to the current location on rue de Dettwiller in 1911 and constructed a modern brewery. The First World War got in the way of any further growth but by the 1920s it was expanding again, establishing outlets throughout the Alsace region.

The Second World War took its toll when the brewery was damaged in the conflict and later requisitioned by American troops. Ever resilient, it survived this and began to reconstruct the business. To achieve this Charles Gerber brought a businessman and a brewer into the company. Over the next 15 years they built the brewery up to become one of the region's major companies.

The business was still growing in 1972 when Charles decided it was time to retire. Having no children to whom he could leave his brewery he sold it to the Becker brothers of Brauerei Becker at Saint-

Ingbert, between Homburg and Saarbrucken in Germany. They created Becker France, based at Saverne. When the Beckers were taken over by Karlsberg in 1989 it became part of the large Karlsberg Group.

The Saverne site has seen many developments recently so that in addition to the original brewhouse, which is a pleasant traditional stone and render construction, it now has an angular, almost futuristic new brewhouse. The old brewhouse is no longer used and the intention is to turn it into a museum. A commendable idea since it contains a very impressive brewing hall.

The brewery is easy to find as rue de Dettwiller is just what is says, the road to Dettwiller. Entering Saverne from the A4 junction 45, head for the town centre and turn left at the first set of lights which is the D421 signposted Brumath and Haguenau.

BECKER'S 8.8%

8.8% alc/vol.   50cl cans & draught.

APPEARANCE: Rich deep gold with a good head.

NOSE: Rich tangy pale malt with some fruit and a few sherry notes.

PALATE: Rich, full, tangy pale malt with an excess of alcohol and a slightly sherried fruity note.

FINISH: Masses of alcohol warmth and a rich tangy malt with a touch of fruit.

OVERALL: The 8.8% makes itself very noticed both in the alcohol and warmth as well as the character it imparts on the other elements. For instance the fruitiness, partly generated by the alcohol, has a sherry note to it. Certainly a very full and rich beer.

GENERAL: First brewed in 1996.   JW:☑☐☐   KR:☑☐☐

BIÈRE DE LA LICORNE

4.8% alc/vol. 25cl crown corked and draught.

APPEARANCE: Bright light gold in colour.

NOSE: Very faint and rapidly reducing, just a light hop and a hint of fruity pale malt.

PALATE: Quite a sharp hop edge to a pale malt which suggests sweetness though the palate has a generally bitter character. KR: A pale malt fruitiness.

FINISH: JW: Bags of resiny hop bitterness that attacks the roof of the mouth. The bitterness subsides but lingers. KR: What character there was is short-lived and quite dull.

OVERALL: JW: Not particularly inspiring beer with a strong bitterness tempered by a sweet malt until the finish when the bitterness takes over completely. KR: A very clinical beer with a disappointingly bland character despite its wonderful unicorn identity.

GENERAL: First brewed in 1995.   JW:☑☐☐   KR:☐☐☐

BIÈRE DE MARS

4.8% alc/vol.   25cl crown corked bottles and draught.

APPEARANCE: Amber in colour with a fluffy head.

NOSE: Light fruity darkish malts waft through quite heady dry hop. JW: Hints of caramel.

PALATE: A perfumed hop almost overtaken by a crystal malt. JW: Suggestions of candy sugar. KR: A dark, liquoricey spice.

FINISH: A dry, resiny, bitter hop with some darker malt notes.

OVERALL: Lots of darkish candy malt throughout and a perfumed resiny hop that adds bitterness. Quite an interesting taste but very much a forced character which doesn't go further than the cosmetic front.

GENERAL: First brewed in 1993.   JW: ☐☐☐ KR: ☐☐☐

BIÈRE DE NOËL

5.8% alc/vol.   25cl crown corked bottles and draught.

APPEARANCE: Deep ruby brown colour with a short-lived fluffy head.

NOSE: Very faint dark fruity malt.

PALATE: Unusual, bittersweet fruity malt with light spicy hints. JW: Sharp, tangy hop elements. KR: Strange Christmas cakey hints.

FINISH: Drying, resiny bitterness lingers. KR: Spicy hop and leftover dark spices.

OVERALL: JW: An unusual beer throughout. It promises much but has unfortunate elements in the palate and finish that are not appealing. Very much like something that is being given an artificial character in the hope of making it interesting. KR: Strange beer which does a good job of being drinkable yet having a winter character; however, it remains an ordinary beer that has had a slight tweak.

GENERAL: First brewed in 1994.   JW: ☐☐☐ KR: ☑☐☐

OTHER BEERS BREWED

Amos (4.9% alc/vol.) – Brewed since 1868 according to the brewery. Relabelled for various distributors.

Bière Blonde (3.7% alc/vol.) – Bright golden lager with a biscuity malt nose and a husky, biscuity palate giving a light bitterness, turning dry in the finish. Undoubtedly aimed at the cheap end of the market.

Fritzbräu (4.9% alc/vol.) – Sold in 33cl cans. A dull, mellow nose with a similarly dull, moderately sweet pale malt palate with a gentle citric hop bitterness. The finish is marked by a strong, lingering bitter hop. Pretty inoffensive, but ultimately bland lager.

Mosbrau

Moselbier

Saverne Blonde (4.8% alc/vol.) – Sold on draught only.

BEERS BREWED BY KARLSBERG & DISTRIBUTED BY SAVERNE

Black Baron (4.8% alc/vol.).

Braugold (7% alc/vol.).

Burgbräu (4.5% alc/vol.).

Karlsbräu (5% alc/vol.).

Karlsbräu Ur-Pils (4.8% alc/vol.).

Schilbräu (4.9% alc/vol.).

Brasserie Schutzenberger

✉ 8 rue da la Patrie, BP 182, 67304 Schiltigheim CEDEX

☎ 03 88 18 61 00 or 03 88 33 14 67 or 03 88 33 14 88
   Fax: 03 88 83 18 14   www.strasbourg.com/schutz/

🅂🄷🄾🄿 Cases only

ℹ️ No information received

➔ See article

Brasserie Schutzenberger, affectionately known as Schutz, has two very notable features – firstly it is in Schiltigheim yet is not owned by Heineken, and secondly it is run by a woman, Rina Muller-Walter.

Schiltigheim really is a brewing phenomenon. It is a north-eastern suburb of Strasbourg and on one road, rue de Bischwiller, you have Fischer, Heineken and Adelshoffen all of which are owned by Heineken and on rue de la Patrie which runs parallel is Schutzenberger. Rue de Bischwiller is the main shopping road through the town whilst rue de la Patrie is more residential, and the construction of the Schutzenberger brewery happily fits in with the feel of the area. The main buildings are constructed of brick and smooth cream-painted render which contrasts nicely with the brickwork to make a feature of it. The overall effect is one of tradition and good taste.

This classy appearance is appropriate for a brewery once known as the Brasserie Royale, which supplied beer to the royal court. The Schutzenberger family originally came from Austria but were already living in Strasbourg by the time Jean-Daniel Schutzenberger decided to become an apprentice brewer in Germany. Returning to Strasbourg, he acquired the Brasserie Royale, in the Krutenau quarter, in 1740 after marrying the widow of the brewer. He was a dynamic owner and the brewery flourished as did his reputation, rising to be head of the Union of Brewers by the time of the Revolution. However, being in the middle of a people's revolution it was felt politically unwise to be known as the Brasserie Royale so in 1789 the name was changed to Grande Brasserie de la Patrie. This did the trick and the brewery continued to prosper before, in 1866, it moved to its current location in Schiltigheim, an area renowned for the quality of its water.

The brewery remained in the control of the Schutzenberger family until well into this century when it made the fortunate decision to employ Charles Walter as general counsel. Although his initial time in this post was short-lived when he spent the majority of the Second World War as a German prisoner in Russia, on his return in 1946 he went back to the brewery to work with the final member of the Schutzenberger family, Irene, in the role of general manager and commercial director. 1968 almost saw the end of the story when its competitors, who had somehow managed to become major shareholders, decided to close the brewery. This was perhaps Charles Walter's finest hour as he embarked upon a legal battle to win control of the brewery. He eventually succeeded in 1972, being appointed president and general manager the following year. In 1978 his daughter, Rina, joined the company and is now in charge herself. In addition to running the brewery she has added to her respect within the industry by being made president of the Syndicat de Brasseurs d'Alsace.

BIÈRE DE MARS

5.2% alc/vol. 25cl, 75cl crown corked bottles & draught.

APPEARANCE: Deep orange gold colour.

NOSE: Fairly aromatic amber malt with a slightly caramel candy.

PALATE: Full dark candy and malt with a strong hop that has a distinct bite to it and eventually generates a little bitterness.

FINISH: Resiny hop, gently bitter. Tangy and slightly caramelled.

OVERALL: Fairly artificial and forced character with a candied malt and strong resiny hop. JW:☑☐☐ KR:☑☐☐

BIÈRE DE NOËL

6% alc/vol. 25cl, 75cl crown corked bottles & draught.

APPEARANCE: Dark reddish brown.

NOSE: Fairly hoppy with the occasional citric hint over. JW: A full fruity dark malt. KR: An earthy (quite muddy) roast malt.

PALATE: JW: Full, smooth, dark fruity malt with a slight hop bite and citric hints. Hints of liquorice. Gently roasted. KR: A harsh fizz is the first sensation, then a dark, roast malt and a fruity dryness.

FINISH: Lingering resiny hop over a gently roasted fruity dark malt. KR: Liquorice and a good hop bitterness.

OVERALL: JW: Good beer with less sweetness than other Alsace Xmas beers. Nicely roasted fruity malt and surprisingly strong hop character. Excellent smooth creamy texture. KR: Not too inspiring with its essentially bland dark lager character but stands up well against others with its pleasant, surprisingly light roast elements.
JW:☑☑☐ KR:☑☐☐

COPPER

7.6% alc/vol. 25cl crown corked bottles & draught.

APPEARANCE: As the name would suggest – copper colour.

NOSE: Pleasant, slightly smokey, whisky malt with buttery overtones. Mellow and inviting. KR: A lovely lactic creaminess.

PALATE: Fairly thick, quite sweet malt with a whisky tang instantly filling the mouth. A hop bite adds interest and bitterness. Butter and caramel notes as well as occasional wafts of fruit. Quite complex.

FINISH: Fairly bitter, hoppy and moderately tangy with a lingering alcohol. Dry. KR: Warming, slightly sticky, fruity bitterness with a very bitter hop and fleeting sweet notes.

OVERALL: An excellent, distinctive beer with a very full, fairly complex taste based on tangy malt with a touch of whisky. The finish particularly gets quite bitter and is very long lasting.

GENERAL: First brewed in 1990 to celebrate the 250th anniversary of the brewery. Previously sold as **Cuivrée**. JW: ☑☑☐ KR: ☑☑☐

JUBILATOR

6.8% alc/vol. 25cl, 33cl crown corked bottles & draught.

APPEARANCE: Golden in colour.

NOSE: Aromatic mixture of hop and pale malt with a flowery tone to the hop and a buttery note. KR: A citric note.

PALATE: Strongly husky, tangy, pale malt with a sharp greenish hop bite. JW: A moderate fruitiness and the hop is quite oily and distinctly bitter.

FINISH: Tangy slightly fruity bitter pale malt with a generous oily hop bitterness which fills the mouth for ages.

OVERALL: Full tasting pale beer with a greenish oily hop character and a bitterness building into the finish. JW: ☑☐☐ KR: ☑☐☐

PATRIATOR

7% alc/vol. 33cl crown corked bottles & draught.

APPEARANCE: Very dark red brown, almost black, with a good beige head.

NOSE: Rich dark and full of fresh fruit with bags of dark malt and a hint of liquorice and alcohol. Very inviting.

PALATE: Liquorice, lots of it, permeating a lightly roasted dark malt that contains plenty of slightly vinous dark fruit. Gently bitter from some hops that are really struggling to get through. Just a little alcohol warmth.

FINISH: Lingering gently roasted dark malt and fruit with liquorice and a hop bitterness following through.

OVERALL: Excellent though hardly typical Scotch ale – very fruity, plenty of liquorice and a gentle hop bitterness. JW: ☑☑☐ KR: ☑☑☐

PILS

5.2% alc/vol. 75cl crown corked bottles & draught.

APPEARANCE: Light gold and a good head.

NOSE: Strongly husky hop with a mellow biscuit malt.

PALATE: Strongly husky with a good hop character adding an impressive bitterness and a faint citric note. In spite of the bitterness there is some pale malt sweetness giving a good balance.

FINISH: Dry and astringent with a lingering hoppy bitterness.

OVERALL: An impressive pils with a good balance and plenty of taste yet the finish is totally hop induced. Very tasty and satisfying with the bitterness making it refreshing as well. The draught version is very full on taste in the palate in spite of a very light nose but is let down by a metallic note in the finish.

JW: ☑☑☐ KR: ☑☐☐

TRADITION

5% alc/vol. 25cl, 33cl, 100cl crown corked bottles.

APPEARANCE: Pale golden colour with a good but short-lived head.

NOSE: Pilsener malt with a biscuity/husky note and a strongish distinctive hop over the top.

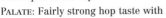

PALATE: Fairly strong hop taste with citric notes over a sweet full pale malt. KR: Light and watery.

FINISH: JW: Lingering, dry, moderately bitter hop character with a slight resiny note. KR: Gentle bitterness with a lingering sweetness.

OVERALL: JW: Fairly full tasting pilsner character with a creamy texture and plenty of hops which build gradually to dominate the finish with a lasting hoppiness. KR: Sweet, watery and only lightly bitter.

JW: ☑☐☐ KR: ☑☐☐

TÜTZ

4.8% alc/vol. 25cl, 33cl crown corked bottles & draught.

APPEARANCE: Watery lemon gold.

NOSE: Light but fragrant with an evenly mixed pale malt and hop. JW: A touch sweet.

PALATE: A distinctive taste – creamy pale malt with some fruity notes that stop just short of sweetness. Lightly bitter with the main characteristic being a tangy malt and a gentle resiny bitterness.

FINISH: A little cloying. Full fruity malt with suggestions of caramel and a little bitterness. JW: Quite astringent.

OVERALL: Quite full tasting for a beer under 5%. The maltiness is concentrated and there is some fruitiness but the hop comes through surprisingly lightly prior to the finish.

GENERAL: An ice beer. The whole bottle is covered in a distinctive, printed white plastic film.

JW: ☑☐☐ KR: ☑☐☐

OTHER BEERS BREWED ————————————

Boisson de l'Extrême. For export only.

Patria Brau (3.5% alc/vol.).

Schutz 2000 (6.5% alc/vol.) – Brewed in celebration of the bi-millenium of Strasbourg.

Brasserie de Séverac

- ✉ La Houssais, 44530 Séverac
- ☎ 02 40 88 71 77   Fax: 02 40 88 72 52
- 🕐 Jul & Aug: Tues-Sat. Rest of year: Sat midday.
- 🏭 Only by prior arrangement. 15 days notice. In French. 15FF
- 🛒 Cases & bottles.
- 📊 300hl in 1997 (375 projected for 1998)

Situated just off the D773 south of Redon, Brasserie de Séverac has given itself a very Breton identity – a factor considered very important to the owners. It was opened in 1996 by Claude Lebreton and his partner, both Bretons, who run it on a full-time basis with the help of family members. Although outside the four départements which most people associate or think of as Brittany, this part of Loire-Atlantique has many Bretons making up its population.

It is very close to the Parc Régional de Brière, a low-lying area of marshes famous for its sea salt production. This is shown on its beer labels (essentially the same, but the backgrounds are green for the brune and pink for the ambrée) which show the white mounds in salt pans ready for processing. The name chose for its beers is Gwenva, a Breton term for 'Celtic Paradise'.

Since its conception the brewery has been keeping a low profile (as have its beers) to the point that we missed the opportunity of a visit on our research trips, hence the lack of a photograph of the brewery here. Hopefully some of the speciality beer bars of France will pick up on the Séverac beers as they display a very good, very artisanal character and deserve to be sampled.

GWENVA AMBRÉE

5.5% alc/vol.   37.5cl & 75cl crown corked bottles.

BREW DETAILS: Unfiltered. Unpasteurised. Top fermentation.

DECLARED INGREDIENTS: Hallertau & Brewers Gold hops; Pilsener, Munich & Caramel malts.

APPEARANCE: Cloudy orange colour with a good, creamy head.

NOSE: Unusual nose based on a

pleasant fruity malt. There is a lactic element and a suggestion of tartness. Fragrant with hints of toffee.

PALATE: Unusual fruity element in the pale malt. The fruit is light and apple-like though there is also a definite lemon taste. There is a tart and lactic element that is surprisingly unobtrusive. A yeastiness adds further interest. A resiny hop is also lurking in there. Lots of unusual and interesting elements. A little sharp, almost acidic.

FINISH: Dry and lightly bitter with a citric sharpness.

OVERALL: Interesting but bizarre. Highly original beer that has a unique character. It threatens tartness but barely delivers. Could be an interesting summer quencher served straight from the fridge.

GENERAL: First brewed 1996. The Ambrée has a label with a pink background.

JW: ☑☐☐   KR: ☑☑☐

GWENVA BRUNE

7% alc/vol. 37.5cl & 75cl bottles.

BREW DETAILS: Unfiltered. Unpasteurised. Top fermentation.

DECLARED INGREDIENTS: Hallertau & Brewers Gold hops; Pilsener, Munich, Caramel & Black malts.

APPEARANCE: Deep dark brown with a colossal head.

NOSE: Interesting dark fruity aroma humming with esters.

PALATE: Very dark and fruity palate with a distinct, slightly sharp, red fruit lifting it and adding to the spritzy undertone. Over this is a lightly roasted dark malt. There is also a drying bitter hop with a citric bite. Full with lots of twiddly bits going on in the background. KR: Suggestions of apple-skins.

FINISH: A rich lightly roasted malt with fruity notes and a lingering hop quality. KR: An underlying long lingering citric hop note.

OVERALL: A very original beer that can be rewarding if you are looking for something interesting. A complex mixture of lightly roasted malt and fruit.

GENERAL: First brewed 1997. The Brune has a label with a green background.   JW:☑☑☐   KR:☑☑☑

BARS & CAFES RECOMMENDED BY THE BREWERY

Café du Port, Quartier du port, 35 Redon

BEER SHOPS RECOMMENDED BY THE BREWERY

Tout au Beurre, 16 rue St-Michel, 44 Guérande
Ar Blaz Mad, 40 rue St-Michel, 44 Guérande
Vergers du Littoral, 1a Gassun, 44 Herbignac
Le Cep de Vigne, route de St-Gildas, 44 Missillac
Ferme de Bellevue, Bellevue, 56 St-Jean la Poterie, near Redon

Spirit of Factory

- ✉ 14 rue de Bressigny, 49000 Angers
- ☎ 02 41 88 50 10
- 🕐 Evenings. Closed Sunday
- 🏃 Phone for availability
- 🍺 Beers available only on draught at the brewpub
- 📊 250-300hl (projected for 1998)
- ➔ In Angers city centre, close to the main station

A strange name for a brewpub, and we still haven't worked out why it was chosen. Strange, also, that Angers can lay claim to having two brewpubs when far bigger towns are struggling to offer even one decent speciality beer bar.

As is always the case in major towns, specific directions are very difficult to give, except to say that it is centrally located close to the main Angers railway station. It is up a narrow but particularly busy street with numerous other bars which seems to be in an area favoured by students. It is very easy to miss as it looks like any other bar and because it has half of its street frontage taken up by a friterie/ burger/sandwich outlet which sells its wares onto the street.

The general look of the bar is dominated by a shelving-system-look to everything, and there is a railway track hanging from the ceiling. Perhaps the first thing you will notice will be a large two-tone brown cow on top of the bar in front of the entrance. To the left (and half-obscured from the street by the food outlet) is the small collection of brewplant – an attractive copper kettle and an old, vastly over-sized grist mill (from Suffolk, UK) which has a 2-metre-plus worm screw to carry the crushed grain to the top of the mash tun. There are a couple of impressive-looking panels full of switches and lights nearby which we at first presumed was part of the operation, but which we later found out was for the bar lighting!

We chose to sit at the bar next to the brewplant, some of the chairs being old barber's chairs (or perhaps even dentist's chairs). The bar sells just two beers, both on draught only, and both are bottom fermented despite the fact that one is described as 'Type Anglaise'. The fermentation vessels are not on display in the bar – they are downstairs in the cellar along with the garding tanks (where the beers undergo a 2–3 week garde). Capacity of the brewplant is 800 litres and they brew in quantity and in type according to the requirements of the bar. They do not sell the beer to any other outlets.

We were offered no real explanation regarding the name of the brewery, but although much of the literature and signage around the bar sometimes stated the name as 'Spirit Factory' we were told the name had the word 'of' in it. We surmise that the name came from a wooden sign on the wall above the brewplant which shows a schematic of a distillery and the words spirit factory on it.

Snacks were on offer at the bar, and each order for beer was accompanied by a fistful of monkey nuts being left on the bar (not in a dish, but on the bar). The brewery's beer list looks full of different products, but most are for the two beers in different sizes of glass. The 'Dégustation du Brasseur' turned out to be a small glass of each beer with a glass of genever.

So, now you know why its beer is called 'Cow Beer'.

BIÈRE DE LA VACHE

4.5% alc/vol   Only available on draught at the brewpub.

APPEARANCE: Golden with a lively head which soon goes.

NOSE: Pleasantly hoppy and quite aromatic.

PALATE: A sweet sensation in the start with a reasonable balance of pale malt and hops following. Quite full with a citric edge.

FINISH: Dull, especially after the palate, turning dry and bitter with some lingering sugariness. Some saccharin hints.

OVERALL: Quite full-tasting Pilsener-type beer at first but a particularly dull, sugary finish. Smooth and easy drinking with a good creamy texture but a distinctly home-brew character.

GENERAL: The name comes from model cow which the taps are built into. Also called **Type Allemagne**.   JW:☐☐☐   KR:☐☐☐

LA SPIRIT

4% alc/vol   Only available on draught at the brewpub.

APPEARANCE: Amber, with a light, creamy head.

NOSE: Similar hop character to the Vache, but has a pronounced caramel note, almost like toffee.

PALATE: Light hoppiness, but dominated by a lightly fruity caramel character which gets more than a little tangy after a while. Soft and rounded, developing some hop bitterness.

FINISH: A lasting hop bitterness thankfully helping to balance the cloying caramel taste. Some fleeting fruity sensations now and then.

OVERALL: Too overtly caramelly for most. Tastes suspiciously like the Vache with added caramel. Easy drinking beer if you can cope with the cloyingness but, again, overtly home-brewy.

GENERAL: Also called **Type Anglaise**.   JW:☐☐☐   KR:☐☐☐

OTHER BEERS BREWED ─────────────────
Bière de Noël.
Bière de Mars.

Brasseries Stella Artois

✉ 14 Avenue P. Brossolette, BP9, 59426 Armentières Cedex

☎ Tel 03 20 48 30 30   Fax 03 20 48 31 97

Although it is not a brewery, Brasseries Stella Artois (the French outpost of the multi-national Interbrew and until recently called Interbrew France) is such a major player in the domestic beer market that we have chosen to include it in this section to explain the appearance of its beers, many of which are brewed exclusively for sale in France.

It operates from the old Motte-Cordonnier brewery in Armentières where it used to brew until September 1993. Today it is a huge distribution depot for Interbrew beers made in Belgium – mostly in Louvain (Leuven) – although a lesser activity involves the conditioning and bottling of certain beers, mainly Jupiler, Stella Artois and small runs of Leffe multi-packs. Such is the size of the operation that even this 'lesser' activity involves filling 800 barrels and 60,000 bottles per hour. From here the beer is distributed to a vast network of regional depots in order to service the whole country.

One interesting sideline which runs from here is a school for bar staff, to tutor them in all aspects of maintaining and serving good beer. With the growing number of concept bars Interbrew is pioneering throughout the country this training is obviously a good thing. It has had the Café Leffe concept for some time and there are now 35 such franchises. Interbrew does not own these businesses but it fits them out and decorates them, in return for which the owner is obliged to take Interbrew beer. Run along similar lines are the seven Brussel's Cafés and the three Le Hoegaardens, its latest venture.

Interbrew markets a very large portfolio of beers throughout France, including the Hoegaarden, Loburg, Leffe and McEwans brands but there are also those only available in France or which are considered to be French. Amongst these are **Stella Club**, **Stella Bière de Mars**, **Stella Bière de Noël**, **Jupiler Bière de Mars**, **La Bécasse Gueuze**, **La Bécasse Kriek**, **La Bécasse Framboise**, **Palten Brune** and the cheap, litre-bottled range of **Sernia** beers (**Bock**, **Brune** and **Pils**).

Two particularly well-known prestige beers handled by Brasseries Stella Artois (and labelled with its name) really are brewed in France but their production is contracted out. **Lutèce Bière de Paris** is brewed by Gayant and **Bière de Garde de Saint Léonard** is from Castelain.

La Taverne du Brasseur

✉ Bois de Coulange, Centre Thermal, BP 22, 57360 Amnéville

☎ 03 87 70 11 77

🕐 Sun-Thurs: 1000-2400. Fri-Sat: 1000-0200

🏭 Always available. 7 days notice. In French and English

🔠 Bottles, cases, glasses

🍺 1600hl (in 1996)

➡ Head in the general direction of Parc Walabi and Centre Touristique from the motorway and then follow the signs to Centre Touristique and Centre Thermal. The bar is signposted.

A thermal centre and tourist park is not the place you would expect to find a brewpub, but the Taverne du Brasseur has been brewing its beer here for around five years. It sells almost all its production on site although it does supply one other bar in the Strasbourg area.

Following the signs from anywhere around Amnéville you will eventually find yourself directed into a wooded area with a large wood and glass construction in the centre. Parking is available virtually outside, although limited, but just up the hill through the trees is a very large car park actually labelled 'Parking Taverne du Brasseur'.

The building itself fits fairly well into its surroundings and in addition to the large area of outdoor seating it has a good seating capacity inside. With so much glass in the walls and a very high ceiling it has an airy feel. The bar is located centrally within the generally round building and fronts the computer-controlled brewing vessels which came from Germany, not surprisingly really since that is also the home country of the master brewer, Christian Nuding. It also helps explain why all the beers are unfiltered, unpasteurised and bottom fermenting in classic German style. Brewing takes place 2–3 times a week.

The German theme goes far beyond the bottom fermentation. A beer name of Munichoise gives the game away. In addition to a German name and beer style it is served in a tall, thin, handled glass as frequently found in German bars.

The area in which the Taverne is located is one large pleasure park so there should be no shortage of passing trade, but it is too far from town to have a steady local clientele. The entire complex (called the Centre Touristique) including the Taverne is owned and run by the town of Amneville. The Taverne was set up in March 1993 as a company in its own right (like the swimming pool and ice rink amongst others) but nevertheless still gives rise to the somewhat incongruous situation of a brewery being run by civil servants.

As almost all the brewery is clearly visible once you are in the bar, the concept of a tour is pretty academic. You should be able to find somebody to show you round and talk to you provided you ask before about 8pm. From that point on they are tend to get very busy, first with food and then with general drinking.

It is possible to take beers home but, along with the beer, you have to buy the two litre bottle which is particularly expensive. If you are very ambitious they can supply you with kegs (30 or 50 litres) and the CO_2 which, again, is not cheap.

BIÈRE D'AMNEVILLE

4.8% alc/vol.   200cl bottles & draught.

DECLARED INGREDIENTS: Saaz hops; Munich, Pilsener, Carahell & Caraffa malts.

APPEARANCE: Gold with a bit of a chill haze.

NOSE: Fairly neutral, just a few faint hops. Develops more of a sweetness as it warms up.

PALATE: A good, quite strong Pilsener malt taste and a distinct hop. Clean tasting. Bitter but tempered by the sweetness of the malt.

FINISH: A fairly hoppy, lingering bitterness.

OVERALL: Full mouthed and reminiscent of an authentic well put together German lager.

GENERAL: First brewed 1993.

JW: ☑☑☐   KR: ☑☑☐

MUNICHOISE

5.1% alc/vol.   200cl bottles & draught.

DECLARED INGREDIENTS: Saaz hops; Munich malt.

APPEARANCE: Orangey mid-brown colour.

NOSE: Slightly sweet, caramel maltiness.

PALATE: A gentle caramel malt dominates the palate with just a touch of hop bitterness helping add some balance.

FINISH: Lingering, dry, almost tangy, hop bitterness with a little burnt malt sugar.

OVERALL: Very pleasant soft texture but uninspiring palate which is a little muddied, particularly when compared with the clean tastes of its blonde stablemate.

GENERAL: First brewed 1993. Sold simply as Brune in the bar.

JW: ☑☐☐   KR: ☑☐☐

OTHER BEERS BREWED ────────────

Bière de Mars (5.5% alc/vol.).

Bière de Noël (6.8% alc/vol.).

Salsa (4% alc/vol.) Draught only. A mix of pils, tequila & lemonade.

Taverne de l'Ecu

✉ 7 rue Esquermoise, 59000 Lille

☎ 03 20 57 55 66   Fax: 03 20 57 95 55

🕐 Tues-Sat: 1100-0200. Sun-Mon: 1100-2400

🍴 Always available. In French and English

🏼 300hl (projected for 1998)

The Taverne de l'Ecu is well situated, just off Place du Général de Gaulle (the main square) in the centre of Lille. It has two entrances, a very understated one at 7 rue Esquermoise which takes you down a mural-painted corridor before you reach the door to the bar, and a grander one in rue de Pas, within sight of the Palais de la Musique.

Once inside you cannot help but be struck by the grandeur and impressive scale of the building. It was once a renowned pornographic cinema and as such was originally one large very high-ceilinged room. When it was converted the owner wished to retain much of its original structure. This has been well achieved by the construction of a mezzanine floor which leaves those on the ground floor with a good appreciation of the height of the ceiling despite extensive use of wood in the construction and decoration.

The Taverne has a good reputation for food, specialising in regional dishes, and is laid out very much as a restaurant rather than a drinking bar. There is seating for 350 but not many stools near the bar. In addition to their own beer they have another 11 beer pumps plus 50 bottles from various countries and a beer of the month.

Along with its stock beer, **Bière de la Maison**, a 5.5% alc/vol. top fermenting unfiltered blonde, a **Bière de Mars** and a **Bière de Noël** are planned. The first brew was produced in June 1997 on the same 150-litre brew capacity plant as found at Entre-Temps and Taverne de la Poste. The brew plant is installed in the bar area and there is a glass plate in the floor that allows you to see down to the cellar.

At the time of our visit (Easter 1998) the brewery was experiencing a few problems and did not have any of its beer available. We feel, however, it is probably similar to that found at Entre-Temps.

Brasserie Terken

- ✉ 3 Quai d'Anvers, 59100 Roubaix
- ☎ 03 20 26 92 26   Fax: 03 20 36 75 05
- 🕐 Mon-Fri: 0900-1200
- 🏍 By prior arrangement (60 days notice). In French & English. No charge
- 🏪 No direct sales
- 🍺 600,000hl (in 1997)
- ➡ Leave the A22 at junction 11, direction Roubaix, Croix-Wasquehal and follow that road, the N356, in the direction of Roubaix and Tourcoing. The brewery will appear on your left.

After the major disruption of the First World War many breweries merged or re-formed as co-operatives, but over the years many have closed or made the transition into private ownership, leaving just Brasserie Terken as the surviving French brewing co-operative.

The brewery is situated on the bank of the Roubaix canal, at a place where the three towns of Roubaix, Tourcoing and Wattrelos have expanded and joined together to become one large urban sprawl.

It came into being in 1920 as the Grande Brasserie Moderne (GBM) under the guidance of Adolphe Briet, when three earlier breweries banded together. M. Briet remained in charge for many years guiding the business through the troubled times of the Second World War when brewing was suspended, starting up again in 1948. Following a gradual expansion of the business after the war a M. Teintenier took over the reins in 1955 by which time the brewery had become one of the major players in the region and a number of distribution depots were set up, three of which are still operating today.

In the 1980s GBM started to achieve some success in the export market, initially to Italy and Britain, a market which has since become a very important part of its trade. Specifically targeting supermarkets to produce their cheap own-brand French bières blonde (for instance Sainsbury in the UK) and distributors, it is now one of the leading exponents of the contract brewing scene, along with Brasserie St-Omer. In the last few years the brewery has been exporting its beer to Spain, Portugal, USA and even Russia.

In 1989 came the name change from GBM to Terken – apparently in an attempt to give the brewery a more international identity. The name GBM, however, is still used by the its distribution arm.

To find the brewery we advocate the route from the A22 as there is a link road which takes you straight to the brewery. It is quite a striking sight on the opposite side of the canal from the main road with its white-washed buildings along the waterfront.

Terken's beers are necessarily bland due to them being targeted at the value-for-money, supermarket sector and will not offer much to those looking for depth and complexity. All its products, including the bière de garde, are bottom fermenting.

BIÈRE DE MARS

5% alc/vol. Draught.

APPEARANCE: Golden amber in colour.

NOSE: A sweet sticky aroma with suggestions of JW: caramel fudge KR: candy sugar.

PALATE: Has a watery character throughout and is coarsely bitter with a fair degree of tangy hops. JW: Starts with a sweetish malt.

FINISH: Very mouthdrying with a lingering tangy candy taste.

OVERALL: A shortlived and disappointing experience with the overriding recollection being one of an unpleasant tangy bitterness left in the finish.　　　　JW:☐☐☐　KR:☐☐☐

BIÈRE DE PRINTEMPS

6.2% alc/vol. 25cl crown corked bottles.

APPEARANCE: Paleish gold.

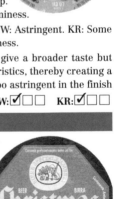

NOSE: Light citric hops with hints of wheat. JW: Initial pleasant flowery hop develops a chemically/soapy character. Fair bit of candy sugar and pilsener malt underlies the hop. KR: Pungent grainy nose.

PALATE: Full but undemanding pilsener malt with a satisfying bitterness and suggestions of sweetness, complement a slightly citric hop. JW: A hint of wheat. KR: Fruity, some creaminess.

FINISH: Dry with a distinct hop bitterness. JW: Astringent. KR: Some sweet malt notes and some creamy wheatiness.

OVERALL: The wheat has obviously helped give a broader taste but has not imparted the usual wheat characteristics, thereby creating a beer with a full but unexciting taste. JW: Too astringent in the finish for me.　　　　JW:☑☐☐　KR:☑☐☐

CHRISTMAS AMBRÉE

7.5% alc/vol. 25cl & 33cl crown corked bottles.

APPEARANCE: Amber.

NOSE: Initially a good, full, fruity hop but this soon disappears to leave an uninspiring thick sweet malt. KR: Dry, quite spicy hop with a darker, fruitier promise.

PALATE: Strong hop and malt tang, which is both bitter and sweet with a hint of alcohol. JW: Hints of caramel in the dark candy sugar. KR: Quite sweet with a red fruit character to the malt. Dryness builds in the finish.

FINISH: Lasting bitter tang. Cloying. KR: A drying, fruity character.

OVERALL: Starts pleasantly enough with its bittersweet hop character but develops a bitter tang.

GENERAL: First brewed 1950.　　JW: ☐☐☐　KR: ☐☐☐

ORLAND BLONDE

5.9% alc/vol. 25cl crown corked bottles & draught.

APPEARANCE: Golden with a minimal head.

NOSE: Initial citric hop whiffs soon disappear to be replaced with a dull aged hop. JW: A lager malt base. KR: Unpleasant metal note.

PALATE: A resiny hop astringency and bitterness. JW: Predominantly lager malt. KR: Lightly fruity.

FINISH: A building, mouthdrying, tangy hop bitterness. KR: Faint hint of malt.

OVERALL: JW: A pilsner-like character with a strong hop bitterness building into the finish. KR: A strong bitter hop creates a beer which is very quenching but very lacking in the taste department.

GENERAL: First brewed 1984.　　JW: ☐☐☐　KR: ☑☐☐

SEPTANTE CINQ

7.5% alc/vol. 25cl crown corked, 75cl corked bottles & draught.

APPEARANCE: Rich amber and a good head.

NOSE: Fruity hints penetrate an odd bittersweet hop and malt aroma.

PALATE: Full mouth of fruity malt with a tangy hop bitterness. JW: Some burnt candy sugar. KR: Starts sweet, turning bittersweet, then dry. An apple skin element.

FINISH: Lingering tangy dry bitterness with a little leftover fruit. JW: Hints of burnt sugar.

OVERALL: Trying hard to be a good beer. Quite fruity with a strong, resiny hop character.

GENERAL: First brewed in 1984. The name comes from its strength – septante-cinq is local patois for 75 (as opposed to soixante-quinze in the rest of France).　　JW: ☑☐☐　KR: ☑☐☐

OTHER BEERS BREWED

Beer & Brandy (6.5% alc/vol.) – First brewed 1998. As the name suggests, beer flavoured with brandy.

Bock (3.6% alc/vol.).

Breug (4.6% alc/vol.).

Garimperos (6% alc/vol.) – First brewed in 1998. Tequila flavoured.

Noordheim (4.6% alc/vol.).

Pils.

Stout Terken (5.2% alc/vol.).

Terken Blonde (5.9% alc/vol.).

Terken Brune (6.7% alc/vol.).

Ubald (4.6% alc/vol.).

Uberland (4.6% alc/vol.).

Upstaal (3% alc/vol.).

Upsthem (5% alc/vol.).

Brasserie Theillier

✉ 11 rue de la Chausée, Louvignies, 59570 Bavay

☎ 03 27 63 10 18   Fax: 03 27 63 10 18

🕐 Not applicable

🏭 Not available

🏪 No direct sales

🍺 3000hl (in 1996)

➡ See article

Some breweries like the high profile that comes with being successful, while others – like Brasserie Theillier – prefer to just keep on brewing their honest, wholesome beers with as little fuss as possible. We would ask readers to respect their wishes and not 'just pop in on the way past' or try to arrange a brewery tour.

Leaving Bavay on the D932 in the direction of Le Cateau you will pass the brewery on the left as you start down a hill following a bend in the road. There are actually some signposts in the town that direct you to the brewery but none at the brewery itself.

Theillier started up on this site in 1820 and the current brewer, Michel Theillier, is the seventh generation of the family to run the brewery. His father (Armand) was the brewer for 50 years and now, in semi-retirement, still works around the brewery, often running the local door-to-door beer distribution round which keeps customers stocked up with beer on a weekly basis within a 15 km radius of the brewery.

As you will see from the picture, the only tell-tale sign that this may be more than just another large house on an ordinary French street is the beer crates stacked high enough to be visible over the wall. Apart from that you are looking at a typical large 19th century house constructed of a number of materials but primarily in old red brick with contrasting pointing.

The brewery extends back from the house and across the yard are some buildings used for storage. Above the entrance to the brewery is an old carved stone crest of the village of Louvignies (dated 1670), the same crest which appears on all its beer labels. Louvignies has now been absorbed into Bavay but the Theillier family are proud to identify themselves with the village from which they originate.

Of the range of beers produced here, you will have great difficulty obtaining all but one – La Bavaisienne. This is one which Michel is particularly keen to promote as a product worthy of national distribution, preferring to keep his other beers for just local consumption. Of all the others, we feel it a shame that the Bière de Garde is not more widely available.

LA BAVAISIENNE

7% alc/vol. 25cl crown corked & 75cl corked bottles.

BREW DETAILS: Filtered. Unpasteurised. Top fermentation.

DECLARED INGREDIENTS: Alsace hops; Escourgeon malt.

APPEARANCE: A dark red amber colour.

NOSE: Good fruity malt with a dry aromatic hop. There is a gentle wine-like suggestion. Very inviting.

PALATE: Sweet, yet quite instantly bitter, fruity malt. It is a strong, vinous fruit with a pretty formidable bittersweet character engendered by some resiny hops.

FINISH: A long lasting rich bittersweet malt with some leftover resiny hop.

OVERALL: A very characterful, but not particularly complex beer that is reminiscent of a strong, well hopped, English winter ale. The hops and malt tend to contrast rather than blend, and add to the bittersweet character. Totally unpretentious but if you want a malty bière de garde, you can't do much better.

GENERAL: First brewed a long time ago – even the brewery is not sure exactly when.

JW: ☑☑☐   KR: ☑☑☐

OTHER BEERS BREWED

Bière Bock (3.3% alc/vol.) – A pale lemon gold coloured beer with a good floral hop and a strong pale malt character. Finishes with a gentle citric hop bitterness. Fuller and deeper than most typical bock beers.

Bière de Garde (4.6% alc/vol.) – A rich chestnut coloured beer with a great deal of fruity malt. JW: Slightly harsh, tart edge. KR: A little treacly and a touch spicy. The short-lived finish is mainly a bittersweet, fruity tang. A good example of an honest bière de garde.

Bière de Luxe (4.6% alc/vol.) – Strongly dry and quite resinous bitter quality with a tangy pale malt gives this a good full mouth of taste without being particularly challenging. The dry, oily and bitter hop finish ensures a good thirst-slaking character. Occasionally on draught in the local area.

Cuivrée de Noël (7% alc/vol.).

Pax Romana – Possibly a beer re-labelled for sale elsewhere.

BARS & CAFES RECOMMENDED BY THE BREWERY

Café, on junction of Rue de la Gare & Rue de la Chaussée, Bavay

BEER SHOPS RECOMMENDED BY THE BREWERY

Local supermarkets, such as Match and Auchan

Brasserie Thiriez

- 22 rue de Wormhout, 59470 Esquelbecq
- 03 28 62 88 44   Fax: 03 28 62 88 44
- Tues-Sat: 1000-1900
- Always available. 14 days notice. In French & English. 10FF
- Bottles, cases & glasses
- 700hl (in 1997)
- Entering the village from Wormhout (D17), about 200m before the village centre you will see a whitewashed farmhouse on the left side of the road. Limited parking in the side road alongside.

The extreme north-eastern corner of France, south of Dunkerque, is all too often passed over by travellers. To do this every time would mean missing some exceptional traditional Flemish bars such as Het Blauwershof at Godewaersvelde or, in Cassel, the superb T'Kasteel Hoff with its huge beer list. There are also historic towns like Bergues which has the estaminet Le Brueghel in a heavenly building dating from 1597. Against this background one would expect any brewery within the area to be of similar character and quality. Brasserie Thiriez does not disappoint.

Set in the village of Esquelbecq, half way between Bergues and Cassel, the brewery is in what appears to be an old whitewashed farmhouse which used to house Brasserie Poidevin, a farm-brewery which closed in 1945. The current owner, Daniel Thiriez, took on the property with the express intention of turning it into a brewery – something he achieved in December 1996.

Daniel used to work in the Human Resources department of the Auchan hypermarket chain but took the decision to give up the corporate life in favour of being an artisan brewer. The equipment came from Italy, but he had to go to Nancy for an IFBM brewing course followed by a spell in Brussels. The latter period was essential as his preference is for brewing Belgian-style beers.

On our first visit, March 1997, Daniel had his brewing area well organised with all the gleaming new equipment successfully installed and working well. It has a capacity of 600 litres and was being used once a month. Being of Belgian influence the beers complete their production cycle with two weeks in a warm room (22°C) to kick off the bottle refermentation. At this time Daniel was producing just the

Blonde d'Esquelbecq and sold most of his beer direct from the door. But by the end of that year the beers were available in supermarkets, a Noël had been added to the range and there was a contract to supply the house beer for another excellent local bar, l'Estaminet Flamand in Dunkerque.

Now there was a choice of beers for his visitors, he set about the refurbishment of a characterful tasting room large enough to double as a function room in the barn next to the brewery. The buildings are set around a grassed courtyard area (see picture) with the tasting room on the right, then the higher building which is the bottling and storage room, followed by the brewery (up some steps) in the corner.

L'AMBRÉE D'ESQUELBECQ

5.8% alc/vol. 75cl crown corked bottles.

APPEARANCE: Orange brown with a massive but often short-lived head.

NOSE: A good malt base with some hops and a quite strong oddly herbal/spicy aroma.

Quite complex. KR: A little tea-leaf-like. Can become very spicy with the sediment.

PALATE: Distinctive amber maltiness with a moderate bitterness. Strong taste with a good bite, faintly roasted and a touch fruity. There is a distinct, quite tannic herbal/spicy note. Full and satisfying.

FINISH: JW: Relatively mellow after the distinctive palate. Lingering amber malt, with a defined spiciness and a slight bitterness. KR: A lingering biting hop and a quenching spice.

OVERALL: Strongly malty beer. Not as complex as it could be but has an impressively malty character with an interesting hop element and quite a strong spiciness. KR: Tannic and very bitter – thankfully with quenching qualities.

GENERAL: First brewed 1997.   JW: ☑☑☐   KR: ☑☑☐

LA BLONDE D'ESQUELBECQ

6.5% alc/vol. 75cl corked bottles.

APPEARANCE: Hazy wheaty gold colour with an excellent rocky head and good lacework.

NOSE: Beautiful, flowery, citric lemon hops with a touch of yeast and a pale malt background. Very inviting. Yeast gives a slight farmyard quality.

PALATE: Quenching with a full pale malt and a sharply citric (lemon and lime) hop bitterness. JW: A touch of pepperiness. KR: Apple notes.

FINISH: A quenching and interesting lingering citric bitterness. KR: A few lactic notes.

OVERALL: Excellently refreshing and satisfying beer with good clean tastes. The citric quenching qualities make it superb on a hot summers day. Very far removed from the general clutch of French beers.

GENERAL: First brewed 1997.   JW: ☑☑☐   KR: ☑☑☐

L'ESTAM' BIER

6.2% alc/vol. 75cl crown corked bottles.

APPEARANCE: Hazy-red amber.

NOSE: Pleasant fragrant citric hop mellowed by a fruity malt.

PALATE: Full palate of fruity malt with a little caramel tempered by a lifting hop trying to deliver citric notes. Sweet overtones.

FINISH: A little tendency to cloy. Gets gently bitter and tangy with a strongish hop note.

OVERALL: Very like a 'rousse' in character with both the hop and malt playing strong roles.

GENERAL: First brewed 1997 for L'Estaminet Flamand in Dunkerque.

JW: ☑☑☐   KR: ☑☑☐

LA NOËL D'ESQUELBECQ

5.8% alc/vol. 75cl crown corked bottles.

APPEARANCE: Deep dark amber with a pillowy head.

NOSE: Inviting herbal, spicy, hoppy aroma with a pleasant mellow malt base. Trying to be citric but masked by the fruity herbal aroma.

PALATE: Strongly spiced and hoppy with a moderate darkish malt behind. There is also a little fruit. A bitter sharpish bite from the strong tasting resiny hops. It is a little unbalanced with the spice not sitting well with the other elements.

FINISH: Long lasting – spicy and a little bitter with an oily hop and a light fruity tang.

OVERALL: Great to find a French spiced beer, but the spices are a little overdone, overpowering (rather than complementing and enhancing) the other elements so it becomes somewhat dull after a while. Nevertheless a very interesting beer especially through the aroma, the wonderful creamy texture and unusual spritzy character.

GENERAL: First brewed 1997.   JW: ☑☑☐   KR: ☑☐☐

OTHER BEERS BREWED ————————————————————

La Bière des Tambours Majors (5.8% alc/vol.) – Produced (or maybe relabelled) for the Dunkerque carnival.

Pax Romana – Has been notified to us as a new beer for 1998, but no further details were available at press date.

BARS & CAFES RECOMMENDED BY THE BREWERY

La Taverne du Westhoek, 2 route de Wylder, 59380 Quaëdypre
Het Blaüwershöf, 9 rue d'Eecke, 59270 Godewaersvelde
Taverne Del-Yser, Grand Place, 59470 Esquelbecq
T'Kasteel Hoff, Mont Cassel (face au moulin), 59670 Cassel

BEER SHOPS RECOMMENDED BY THE BREWERY

T'Kasteel Hoff, Mont Cassel Face au Moulin, 59670 Cassel
Cadovino, Angle 2, rue Dampierre, 59140 Dunkerque
Crémerie Moderne, 67 rue Belle Rade, 59240 Dunkerque
La Mare Aux Bières, 16 bis, La Place, 59284 Pitgam

Brasserie de Ville-sur-Illon

✉ Route de Mirecourt, 88270 Ville-sur-Illon
☎ 03 29 36 53 18   Fax: 03 29 36 63 11
🕐 Tue-Sat: 1430-1800. Only open 15 June to 30 Sept
Beer is only sold for consumption on the premises
20hl (in 1997)
➜ See article

Of all the brewery museums of France, Musée Vosgien de la Brasserie de Ville-sur-Illon is the only one to produce its own beer, although it is available for sale in a somewhat limited manner and other brewers contribute to the production in order to satisfy the demand. In 1997 around 6,500 people visited the museum and drank 170hl of beer in the four months it was open.

It is based in a village where the D6 crosses the D4 just south of Dompaire and west of Épinal. If you can find the village, the museum is easy to find by following the signposts. Full details of the museum side of the operation appear in the Museums feature in this book.

The museum and the brewing are in the hands of the enthusiastic Bernard Saunier who produces two beers – **1627** and **La Vosgienne**, both of which are bottom fermented, unfiltered and unpasteurised.

1627 – named after the year in which the first brewer started up in the village – is the prime product, described as a Pilsner in the Bavarian style. It is 5.5% alc/vol. and served in 65cl swing-top bottles and was first brewed in 1994. It is an impressive, very full tasting brew with a fresh, lively, refreshing hoppiness.

La Vosgienne is 7% alc/vol. (served in more standard 75cl bottles) and although it uses the same hops as 1627 was much darker and

warming, with the malt not the hops dominating.

Both are brewed exclusively to be sold in the small bar you end up in after your museum tour, so we were not able to buy samples of the beers to take away in order to do objective tastings.

The label for La Vosgienne.

LATE ENTRANTS

The beer scene in France continues to flourish – new breweries open almost monthly and new beers with even greater regularity – making it impossible to be completely up to date by the time a book is available for sale. Since our detailed research visits, the following breweries have opened but have not been checked by the authors:

3 BRASSEURS, 8 rue du Château d'Isinghein, 59150 Lomme (Tel. 03 20 22 13 80). In western outskirts of Lille. Usual Bars de France range.

LES BRASSEURS DES ALPES, La Plagne 1800, 75210 Macot La Plagne (Tel. 04 79 09 04 47). *Beers:* Bière des Alpes (two blondes, one ambrée).

MICRO-BRASSERIE ALPHAND, Place du Village, 05290 Vallouise (Tel. 04 92 23 20 00). *Beers:* Ambrée, blonde, stout. SW of Briançon in the Hauts-Alpes Département.

BRITT BRASSERIE DE BRETAGNE KEROUEL, 29910 Tregunc (Tel 02 98 50 25 97. Fax. 02 98 97 77 70). *Beers:* Britt (rousse, blanche), Britt cuvée créperie. In the Finistère Département just SE of Concarneau.

BRASSERIE DU CANARDOU, 24230 Nastringues (Tel/Fax. 05 53 74 32 57). *Beers:* La Korlène (rousse 8%). In Dordogne Département.

BRASSERIE LA CHAPELLE, 76780 La Chapelle-St-Ouen (Tel. 02 35 09 21 54). *Beers:* Northmen (blonde, ambrée, rousse, brune) – plus a nettle beer project. In the Seine-Maritime Département.

BRASSERIE LA CORNUE, 79, av de la Grande Bégude, 13770 Venelles. *Beers:* La Cornue (blonde, brune, ambrée, blanche, asiatique, mexicaine). Just north of Aix-en-Provence. Rumours persist on this brewery despite it being checked out unsuccessfully in 1997.

LA FABRIQUE, 53, rue du Fg St-Antoine, 75011 Paris (Tel 01 43 07 67 07. Fax. 01 43 07 69 00). *Beers:* Bière du fabricant (blonde, ambrée).

THE FREEDOM & FIRKIN, rue De Berri, 75008 Paris (Tel. 01 40 47 60 33). Opened August 1998, the first Allied Domecq (UK) Firkin-branded brewpub to open in France. The first Firkin pub, The Financier and Firkin, 15 rue De Depart, 75014 Paris (Tel. 01 40 47 60 33) opened July 1998 with beer originally supplied by the Fiddler & Firkin in Den Haag, Netherlands. The Floozy & Firkin, 54 rue St-Denis, 75001 Paris, opened August 1998. The Financier and Floozy will now be supplied with beer by the Freedom. Annual output is expected to be 1000hl.

BRASSERIE ARTISANALE DES GRANDS COLS, 5, avenue du Dauphiné, 05100 Briançon (Tel. 04 92 21 31 49). *Beers:* La Tourmente (blonde). One of two in the Briançon area of the Haute-Alpes Département.

RESTAURANT-BRASSERIE LAUTH, 82 rue Principale, 67310 Scharrach-bergheim (Tel. 03 88 50 66 05. Fax. 03 88 50 60 76). *Beers:* La bière de Scharrach (ambrée), Blonde de l'Été, Bière des Vendanges, Bière de Noël, Bière de Mars. In the Bas-Rhin Département.

BRASSERIE NANTAISE, 23, bd de Chantenay, 44100 Nantes (Tel/Fax. 02 40 95 15 71). *Beers:* La Liger (blonde 7%, ambrée 8%).

NEZ ROUGE CAFÉ, 12, rue des Dames, 35000 Rennes (Tel. 02 23 40 05 00). *Beers:* Blonde, blanche, ambrée, noire, spécial événement.

NINKASI ALE HOUSE, 267 rue Marcel Mérieux, 69007 Lyon (Tel. 04 72 76 89 00). Large brewpub which opened in August 1997 just east of the confluence of the Saône and the Rhône. *Beers:* Ninkasi (blanche, blonde (rye), ambrée, stout, rouge, blonde (pilsener).

BRASSERIE OC'ALE, St-Simon, 82130 Lafrançaise (Tel. 05 63 65 91 73. Fax. 05 63 65 93 48). *Beers:* Oc'ale (blanche). In the Tarn-et-Garonne Département, NW of Montauban.

BRASSERIE D'OLT, 28, rue Sannié, 12130 St-Geniez-d'Olt (Tel/Fax. 05 65 52 75 03). *Beers:* La bière de la Marmotte (blonde, 6%). In the Aveyron Département between Rodez and Mende.

BRASSERIE ARTISANALE DE TRÉGOR, ZA Kerfolie, 22220 Minihy-Tréguier. Tel/Fax. 02 96 92 43 66). *Beers:* La Dremmwell (Blonde 5%, rousse 8%, dorée 7%, brune 7%, noire 5%). In the Côtes-d'Armor Département – Tréguier is east of Lannion, Minihy is a hamlet just south.

See The Artisan Press website (www.artisanpress.com.) for latest details

Low & No Alcohol Beers

A list of the more common alcoholically-challenged brews

B eer without alcohol, or with minute amounts of it, is something that appears to be here to stay. They were developed in response to the modern drink/drive laws and for those concerned about health risks associated with alcohol. Some are actually marketed with slogans stating 'beer you drink without moderation'.

Most countries now have a selection of alcohol-free beers but France probably has the widest choice of all. For the purposes of this book we were not considering alcohol-free beers as meriting inclusion in the tasting notes or even in the brewery sections. However, during our research we came across so many of them (hardly surprising when almost every good-sized brewery produces at least one) that we felt obliged to at least list those we came across. Please note – this is not a definitive list, as we were not looking for these beers.

One type of beer which appears frequently is 'panaché' – the French equivalent of shandy – a bottled mixture of beer and lemonade.

Brewery	Beer (alc/vol. if known)	Comments
Fischer & Adelshoffen	Alsator (0.5%)	
	Fink Bräu (0.5%)	Brewed/labelled for Lidl.
	Schouss Panaché (0.5%)	
	Shil Panaché (0.6%)	
Gayant	Celta Blonde	
	Celta Brune	
Heineken	Buckler (0.9%)	First brewed 1988.
	Monaco de Panach	
	Panach'	
Institut Français des Boissons (IFBM)	Spelty	Organic alcohol-free beer made with épeautre (spelt) for Moulin des Moines.
Kronenbourg	Chopp Panaché (0.6%)	
	Force 4 (1%)	First brewed 1981.
	Force 4 Lemon (1%)	
	Kronenbourg Légère	
	Krony Framboise	
	Krony Pêche	
	Silver (0.6%)	First brewed 1991.
	Tourtel Ambrée (1%)	First brewed 1990.
	Tourtel Blonde (1%)	First brewed 1964.
	Tourtel Brune (1%)	First brewed 1989.
Meteor	Klint (0.5%)	
	Panaché (1%)	
Saverne	Panaché de l'Ami Fritz	
Schutzenberger	Capt'n (0.5%)	
	Limousse	
	Sant'or (0%)	
Stella Artois	Jupiler N.A.	Brewed in Belgium.
	N.A. (0.5%)	Brewed in Belgium.
Terken	Elsoner sans Alcool (0%)	
	Panaché Elsoner (0.5%)	

RECOMMENDED OUTLETS

The recommended outlets are split into two sections – bars/cafes and shops – and represent possible sources of specific breweries' products or French beer in general. Many French bars consider 'special' beer to equate with Belgian beers. Therefore, it is easy to find bars with a good selection of quality beers but not so easy to find bars stocking French special beers. This section should point you towards some of them.

The intention is that bars recommended by breweries should stock that particular brewery's beers whilst those recommended by John White, Simon van Tromp or the authors will have a wider range of quality French beers.

Those recommended by specific breweries also appear against that brewery's entry elsewhere in the book. This is the complete list sorted by town/village with the Département number in brackets after it. The source of the recommendation follows the entry, in italics. A few entries show the source as *(Authors – but not tried personally)* these have come from a variety of sources and appear to be worth trying. We have included these in order to provide a greater choice.

BARS/CAFES

Aix-les-Bains (73)	**Murphy's Pub,** rue Haldihan, 73100 Aix-les-Bains. Tel. 04 79 35 16 16. Jenlain Ambassadeur *(Duyck)*
Amettes (62)	**Le Relais,** rue Principle, 62 Amettes. *(Castelain)*
Amiens (80)	**Le Penalty,** 39 place Alphonse Fiquet, 80000 Amiens. Limited range but best of bars by station. *(Authors)*
	Le XVIème Siècle, 53 rue Motte, 80000 Amiens. Tel. 03 22 92 41 65. Should stock Colvert but little else of note. Great building. *(De Clerck)*
	Pub Chez Marius, 9 rue Ernest Cauvin, 80000 Amiens. 8 draught (some French) 18 bottled French plus more than 100 others. *(Authors)*
	There are many bars around Place Parmentier which is the liveliest part of town. *(Authors)*
Annecy (74)	**Captain Pub,** 11 rue du Pont-Morens, 74000 Annecy. Tel. 04 50 45 79 80. Jenlain Ambassadeur. *(Duyck)*
Annœullin (59)	**Tiphany's,** place du Marché, 59112 Annœullin. *(Annœullin)*
Arras (62)	**l'Estaminet des Arcades,** place des Héros, 62000 Arras. L'Atrébate on draught. *(Bécu)*
	La Taverne du Ch'ti, place des Héros, 62000 Arras. *(Castelain)*
	OK Pub, 8 place de la Vacquerie, 62000 Arras. 300 beers but watch the sell by dates. Quite expensive. Range seems to be reducing. *(Authors)*
Avignon (84)	**Gambrinus,** 62 rue Carréterie, 84000 Avignon. Tel. 04 90 86 12 32. Jenlain Ambassadeur. *(Duyck)*
	Le Regina, rue de la République, 84000 Avignon. Over 50 beers including fairly standard French special beers. *(Authors)*
Bavay (59)	**Café,** Junction rue de la Gare & rue de la Chaussée, 59 Bavay. Has Bière de Luxe on draught. *(Theillier)*
Bayonne (64)	**Le P'tit Pub,** 6 rue des Tonneliers, 64 Petit Bayonne. A good typical pub of the area with over 20 beers. Petit Bayonne is bristling with lively bars. *(Authors)*
Belloy-sur-Somme (80)	**Hostellerie de Belloy,** 29 route Nationale, 80310 Belloy-sur-Somme. Tel. 03 22 51 41 05. *(De Clerck)*

Biarritz (64)	**Le Mannequin Pis,** place du Casino Municipal, 64200 Biarritz. Tel. 05 59 24 14 85. Beside Casino Municipal, up hill from Grande Plage. Over 80 beers, about 10 of which are French special beers. *(Authors)*
Boeschepe (59)	**Estaminet de Vierpot,** 125 rue du Moulin, 59299 Boeschepe. Tel. 03 28 49 46 37. Mostly Belgian beers but nicely situated bar. *(van Tromp)*
Caen (14)	**Welcome Pub'Club,** 22 rue de Falaise, 14000 Caen. Tel. 02 31 84 24 87. Jenlain Ambassadeur. *(Duyck)*
Cantin (59)	**Cave à Bière,** On N43, 59 Cantin. *(Cambier)*
Carvin (62)	**Café Bellevue,** n'guillomet, Grand Place, 62 Carvin. *(Annœullin)*
	Café de Paris, Grand Place, 62 Carvin. Do a beer flambée *(Authors – but not tried personally)*
Cassel (59)	**T'Kasteel Hoff,** Mont Cassel (face au moulin), 59670 Cassel. Tel. 03 28 40 59 29. Small and popular bar with extensive range of French artisanal beers (two on draught, 44 bottled). Excellent shop downstairs with beers and regional produce. Only thing letting it down is shortage of accommodation in Cassel. *(Authors, Thiriez, van Tromp, John White)*
Cavron-St-Martin (62)	**l'Estaminet Chés 2 Agaches,** 62 Cavron-St-Martin. Sells regional beers but no spirits. *(Authors – but not tried personally)*
Charleville-Mézières (08)	**Le Mawhot,** Quai Charcot, 08000 Charleville-Mézières. On a characterful barge, moored up-river close to the Ardennaise brewery. *(Ardennaise, Authors)*
Charmes (88)	**Bar le Zinc Bleu,** 88130 Charmes. *(La Cabane)*
Chepy (80)	**L'Auberge Picardie,** place de la Gare, 80 Chepy. Tel. 03 22 26 20 78. *(De Clerck)*
Cherbourg (50)	**La Renaissance,** rue Anglais, Cherbourg. Tel. 02 33 43 23 93. *(Alauna)*
	Le Bar Eldorado, 52 rue Françoise la Vieille, Cherbourg. Tel. 02 33 53 08 68. *(Alauna)*
	Le Freedom Café, 9 rue Charles Blondeau, Cherbourg. Tel. 02 33 94 08 88. *(Alauna)*
	Le Vertigo, 7 pass Digard, Cherbourg. Tel. 02 33 94 11 14. *(Alauna)*
Clermont-Ferrand (63)	**Bar La Perdrix,** 14 rue Terrasse, 63000 Clermont Ferrand. Tel. 04 73 91 21 35. Good selection of beers and some bizarre beer cocktails. *(Authors)*
	Le Palais de la Bière, 3 rue de la Michodière, 63000 Clermont-Ferrand. Tel. 04 73 37 15 51. 50+ bottled beers mostly French, Belgian & Canadian. Open 1900–0100 Mon–Sat. Jenlain Ambassadeur. *(Authors)*
Combronde (63)	**Nosferatu,** 63460 Combronde. Draught Volcans. *(Cerf)*
Coudekerke (59)	**Quarant Bières,** 59 Coudekerke. *(John White)*
Dijon (21)	**Beer Country,** 2 place du 30-Octobre, 21000 Dijon. Tel. 03 80 66 26 90. Jenlain Ambassadeur. *(Duyck)*
Dole (39)	**Pub Northwich,** place Grévy, 39 Dole. Pleasant bar with good Belgian selection but limited French choice. *(Authors)*
Doullens (80)	**Les Bons Enfants,** 23 rue d'Arras, 80600 Doullens. Tel. 03 22 77 16 58. Logis de France restaurant. *(De Clerck)*
Dunkerque (59)	**L'Estaminet Flamand,** 6 rue des Fusiliers Marins, 59140 Dunkerque. Tel. 03 28 66 98 35. Excellent beer list and food. House beer brewed by Thiriez. Gayant beers on draught. Closed on Mondays plus Sat/Sun lunchtimes. Booking ahead recommended if you want to eat. *(Authors, van Tromp, John White)*
	Le Tormore, 11 place Charles Valentin, 59140 Dunkerque. Tel. 03 28 63 15 95. A locals bar with a good range of Gayant beers. *(Authors)*

Eecke (59)	**Brasserie Saint Georges,** 5 rue de Castre, 59114 Eecke. Tel. 03 28 40 13 71. 100 beers on card, five on tap. House beer is La Bière des Chênes brewed by St-Sylvestre. Open Fri, Sat & Sun evenings but not early. *(van Tromp)*
Eleudit Leauwette (62)	**Le Domaine des Pinchonvalles,** rue Gabriel Péri, 62 Eleudit Leauwette. *(Castelain)*
Esquelbecq (59)	**Taverne Del-Yser,** Grand Place, 59470 Esquelbecq. *(Thiriez)*
Godewærsvelde (59)	**Het Blaüwershöf,** 9 rue d'Eecke, 59270 Godewærsvelde. Tel. 03 28 49 45 11. Wonderful, typical old Flemish bar with a good selection of French beers and some very interesting Flemish games. *(Authors, De Clerck, Thiriez, van Tromp)*
Grand Village Plage (17)	**Relais des Salines,** Port des Salines, 17370 Grand Village Plage. On the Ile d'Oléron. Tel. 05 46 75 82 42. *(Naufrageurs)*
Honfleur (14)	**La Cidrerie,** 26 place Hémelin, 14600 Honfleur. Tel. 02 31 89 59 85. Characterful crêperie which sells the Chant du Loup range of beers and many local ciders. *(Authors, John White)*
Josselin (56)	**Le Alzey,** 56 Josselin. *(Lancelot)*
Lamoura (39)	**Le Chalet la Frasse,** 39000 Lamoura. Tel. 03 84 41 24 81. *(Granges-sur-Baume)*
Le Havre (76)	**La Datcha,** 23 rue Racine, 76600 Le Havre. A few interesting French beers plus regular Belgian beers. *(John White)*
Le Mans (72)	**Le Dikken's,** 3 rue des Minimes, 72000 Le Mans. Tel. 02 43 24 14 98. Jenlain Ambassadeur. *(Duyck)*
Lens (62)	**La Taverne des Ch'tis,** Route de Lille, 62300 Lens. *(Castelain)*
Liévin (62)	**L'Hacienda,** rue Victor Hugo, 62 Liévin. Tex/Mex restaurant. *(Castelain)*
Ligny-en-Barrois (55)	**Le Cent Sept,** 107 rue le Roux, 55100 Ligny-en-Barrois. Tel. 03 29 77 03 32. *(Henry)*
Lille (59)	**Au Bureau,** 36/38 place de la Gare, 59800 Lille. Good selection of French beers reasonably priced. *(Authors)*
	Café la Taverne Flamande, 15 place de la Gare, 59800 Lille. Big beer list with reasonable number of French beers. Odd pricing with some very expensive. Seat covers leave a lot to be desired. *(Authors, van Tromp, John White)*
	Jenlain Café, 43 place Rihour, 59000 Lille. Tel. 03 20 15 14 55. Opposite Metro entrance. Sells the full range of Duyck's beers. The only place you can get the unfiltered Sebourg (called bière fraîche). *(Authors, Duyck)*
	Le Bastringue, 168 rue de Solférino, 59000 Lille. Tel. 03 20 57 60 22. Eight draught beers including three from Duyck. Lively student bar. *(Authors, Duyck)*
	Le Hochepot, 6 rue de Nouveau Siècle, 59000 Lille. Tel. 03 20 54 17 59. A restaurant that specialises in food and beer from French Flanders. *(John White)*
	Le Pub Mac Ewans, 8 place Sébastopol, 59800 Lille. Tel. 03 20 42 04 42. Superb beer list and enthusiastic owner. Clean and well presented locals bar. *(Authors)*
	Les Garçons, 26 rue de Paris, 59000 Lille. Tel. 03 20 57 38 38. *(Bécu)*
	Taverne du Ch'ti, 253 rue Nationale, 59800 Lille. A Castelain owned bar. *(Castelain, van Tromp)*
Lons-le-Saunier (39)	**Bières et Compagnie,** 26 rue du Commerce, 39000 Lons-le-Saunier. Tel. 03 84 47 63 10. *(Rouget de Lisle)*
	Café de la Mairie, 5 place Philbert de Chalon, 39000 Lons-le-Saunier. Tel. 03 84 24 05 33. *(Rouget de Lisle)*

	Le Bierstub, 6 rue Emile Marrot, 39000 Lons-le-Saunier. Tel. 03 84 47 41 23. *(Rouget de Lisle)*
	Café de l'Hôtel de Ville, 39000 Lons-le-Saunier. *(Granges-sur-Baume)*
Lyon (69)	**Le Palais de la Bière,** 1 rue Terme, 69001 Lyon. Over 150 beers including 13 on tap. Small range of snacks. Shame about the dazzling bar lighting. Open Mon–Thur 1700–0200, Fri–Sat 1700–0300. *(Authors)*
	Rue Ste-Catherine is an area popular with students and has many lively bars including the Barrel House Irish Pub which, until recently, was a brew-pub.
Missillac (44)	**Le Cep de Vigne,** route de St-Gildas, 44 Missillac. Tel. 02 40 88 38 59. *(Séverac)*
Mulhouse (68)	**Cave de Gambrinus,** 5 rue des Franciscains, 68100 Mulhouse. Tel. 03 89 66 18 65. House beers from Belgian brewery Lefèbvre. Extensive beer list including about 30 French. Good food. *(Authors)*
	Restaurant du Musée de l'Automobile, 192 avenue de Colmar, 68100 Mulhouse. Tel. 03 89 42 22 48. *(Les Caves de la Brasserie)*
	Restaurant du Musée du Chemin de Fer, 2 rue Alfred de Glehn, 68200 Mulhouse. Tel. 03 89 43 44 20. *(Les Caves de la Brasserie)*
	Restaurant Tour de l'Europe, 3 boulevard de l'Europe, 68100 Mulhouse. Tel. 03 89 45 12 14. *(Les Caves de la Brasserie)*
Nantes (44)	**Bar la Cité,** 44000 Nantes. *(Lancelot)*
	Le Graslin, 1 rue Racine, 44000 Nantes. Tel. 02 40 69 81 79. Jenlain Ambassadeur. *(Duyck)*
Olivert (Orléans) (45)	**l'Absinthe,** Olivert, 45 Orléans. Over 100 beers, but mostly Belgian. Series of small rooms which gives a slightly cramped feel to the place. *(Authors)*
Paris (75)	**Au Général la Fayette,** 52 rue La Fayette, 75009 Paris. Tel. 01 47 70 59 08. Pleasant small traditional Paris street corner bar. Good food. Good beer list including 15 French. *(Authors, John White)*
	La Taverne de St-Germain des Prés, 155 boulevard St-Germain, 75006 Paris. *(John White)*
	Le Bouquet du Nord, 85 rue de Mauberge, 75010 Paris. Tel. 01 48 78 29 97. Full range of Duyck beers. *(Duyck)*
	Le Falstaff, 42 rue du Montparnasse, 75014 Paris. Tel. 01 43 35 38 29. Jenlain Ambassadeur. *(Duyck)*
	Le Falstaff (II), 15 rue de Dunkerque, 75010 Paris. Tel. 01 42 85 12 93. Jenlain Ambassadeur. *(Duyck)*
	Le Sous-Bock Taverne, 49 rue St-Honoré, 75001 Paris. *(John White)*
	Le Tango du Chat, 6 rue St-Séverin, 75005 Paris. Small old bar in Latin Quarter. 15 French amongst good beer list. Good atmosphere. *(Authors)*
	Pub St-Germain des Prés, 17 rue de l'Ancienne Comédie, 75006 Paris. Tel. 01 43 29 38 70. Massive beer list in deceptively large bar. Describes itself as 'The Best Pub In France'. *(Authors, Duyck, John White)*
	Royal Concorde, 7 rue Royale, 75008 Paris. Tel. 01 42 65 91 77. Near Maxim's. *(Duyck)*
	Taverne de Nesle, 32 rue Dauphine, 75006 Paris. Tel. 01 43 26 38 36. Best beer choice authors found in Paris. 59 French, 66 Belgian, 31 others. Has the Trois Épis beers as house beers. Open daily but not until 9pm then through to 4am (5am on Fri & Sat) *(Authors, Cerf, John White)*

Périgueux (24)	**Les Toqués de Bière,** 38 rue Pierre Sémard, 24000 Périgueux. Tel. 05 53 08 13 39. Spotless, professionally kept by knowledgeable owner. Loads of beeriana. Over 100 beers but mostly Belgian. An excellent bar in a beer desert. Open daily from 6pm. *(Authors)*
Péronne (80)	**Hostellerie des Remparts,** rue Beaubois, 80200 Péronne. A restaurant. *(De Clerck)*
	Historial de Péronne, 80200 Péronne. Tel. 03 22 83 14 18. A First World War museum. *(De Clerck)*
Ploërmel (56)	**Bar de la Tour,** 56 Ploërmel. *(Lancelot)*
Poligny (39)	**Le Moulin de Brainans,** B.P.45, 39800 Poligny. Tel. 03 84 37 56 15. *(Granges-sur-Baume)*
Quaëdypre (59)	**La Taverne du Westhoek,** 2 route de Wylder, 59380 Quaëdypre. Tel. 03 28 68 68 14. Open Fri/Sat evenings, Sunday lunch. Owners work during week. Good Flemish food. Limited beer list – ask for any not listed. Lovely renovation of old Flemish tavern complete with old games. *(Authors, Thiriez)*
Quimper (29)	**Le Ceili,** Quimper. *(Lancelot)*
Redon (35)	**Café du Port,** Quartier du port, 35 Redon. Tel. 02 99 72 44 29. *(Séverac)*
Rennes (35)	**Le Barantic,** 4 rue St-Michel, 35000 Rennes. Tel. 02 99 79 29 24. Lancelot beers and Coreff on draught, 50 bottled beers. *(Quentin)*
Ribeauville (68)	**Pub le St-Ulrich,** 3 place de la République, 68150 Ribeauville. Tel. 03 89 73 74 38. *(Authors, Les Caves de la Brasserie)*
Schiltigheim (67)	**Au Cheval Blanc,** 25 rue Principale, 67300 Schiltigheim. Tel. 03 88 62 06 66. Normally nine beers from local breweries in C15th building. *(Authors)*
Sedan (08)	**Au Roy de la Bière,** 19 place de la Halle, 08200 Sedan. Characterful locals bar with a few French beers. *(Authors)*
	Caraïbes, 37 avenue Philippoteaux, 08200 Sedan. Tel. 03 24 26 48 31. Clean but fairly soul-less modern bar supplied by Bières de la Monde. *(Ardennaise, Authors)*
Sens (89)	**Café de la Gare,** place de la Gare, 89100 Sens. *(Champs)*
	Café de la Ville 'Aux 100 Bières', 3 place de la République, 89100 Sens. Tel. 03 86 64 38 37. In spite of the name there is only 57 on the list but it is a good selection. In square opposite the cathedral. *(Authors)*
Sommedieue (55)	**La Renaissance,** 55320 Sommedieue. *(Henry)*
St-Georges-d'Oléron (17)	**l'Escale,** 76 rue Hippocampes, 17190 St-Georges-d'Oléron. Tel. 05 46 47 39 78. *(Naufrageurs)*
St-Laurent-du-Var (06)	**Magique Pub,** 1 rue Anfoss, 06700 St-Laurent-du-Var. Tel. 04 93 31 13 68. *(Duyck)*
St-Malo (35)	**L'Aviso.** In the old town. *(Authors)*
St-Pierre-d'Oléron (17)	**Pizzeria Le Forum,** 11 place Gambetta, 17310 St-Pierre-d'Oléron. Tel. 05 46 47 19 25. *(Naufrageurs)*
St-Quentin (02)	**l'Éclipse,** 10 rue de Lyon, 02100 St-Quentin. Tel. 03 23 67 36 43. Nine draught beers from Kronenbourg, about 45 bottled, mostly Belgian. *(Authors)*
	Le Richelieu, 02100 St-Quentin. *(Bernoville)*
	Le Rond d'Alembert, 02100 St-Quentin. *(Bernoville)*
	Pub English, rue de Vesoul, 02100 St-Quentin. Eight draught beers from Kronenbourg, a few decent bottled French beers. Plenty of entertainment – five pool tables, 1 snooker table, darts, dance floor. *(Authors)*
St-Sylvestre-Cappel (59)	**Étoile du Jour,** 13 place de l'Église, 59114 St-Sylvestre-Cappel. Tel. 03 28 40 12 74. A classic. The large front room of owner's house. Unofficial tasting cafe for St-Sylvestre. *(van Tromp)*

St-Trojan (17)	**Novotel Thalassa Oléron,** plage de Gatseau, 17370 St-Trojan. Tel. 05 46 76 02 46. *(Naufrageurs)*
Ste-Marie-Cappel (59)	**Le Petit Bruxelles,** route Nationale, 59670 Ste-Marie-Cappel. Tel. 03 28 42 44 64. Excellent beer cuisine restaurant with 3 Monts available. *(van Tromp)*
Strasbourg (67)	**Aux 12 Apôtres,** 7 rue Mercières, 67100 Strasbourg. Tel. 03 88 32 08 24. Specialist beer drinking bar with good list. Around Christmas & Easter you can only get the seasonal beers. *(Authors)*
	Hôtel le Plaza, place de la Gare, 67100 Strasbourg. Tel. 03 88 15 17 17. *(Fischer & Adelshoffen)*
	L'Académie de la Bière, 17 rue Seyboth, 67100 Strasbourg. Tel. 03 88 32 61 08. Apparently has 75 beers with eight on draught. *(Authors – but not tried personally)*
	Le Pilote, 6 rue des Bouchers, 67100 Strasbourg. Tel. 03 88 36 22 70. Apparently has 100 beers with 14 on draught. *(Authors – but not tried personally)*
	Quai des Bières, rue du Vieux Marché aux Poissons, 67100 Strasbourg. Tel. 03 88 23 28 10. Apparently has big selection of beers. *(Authors – but not tried personally)*
	Schlosserstub, 67100 Strasbourg. *(Meteor)*
Toulouse (31)	**Le Dubliner,** 31 Toulouse. *(Garland)*
Tours (37)	**l'Académie de la Bière,** 43 rue Lavoisier, 37000 Tours. Tel. 02 47 66 63 83. 152 beers, some well-chosen French examples, though largely Belgian. Good bottle collection and selection of posters. *(Authors)*
	Le Gambrinus, 69 bis rue Blaise Pascal, 37000 Tours. Tel. 02 47 05 17 00. Only Belgian beer but lots of it in a well run bar with a very knowledgeable owner. Closed Friday. *(Authors)*
Tousson (77)	**La Tête des Trains,** 6 rue de la Mairie, 77123 Tousson. *(Bécu)*
Valenciennes (59)	**Au Bureau,** 31 place d'Armes, 59300 Valenciennes. *(Meteor)*
	Le Paradis de la Bière, 6–8 avenue de Lattre de Tassigny, 59300 Valenciennes. Tel. 03 27 33 30 33. 100 beers from around the world. Gayant beers on tap. *(Authors)*
Vannes (56)	**Le Swansea,** 56 Vannes. *(Lancelot)*
Verdun (55)	**L'Estaminet,** 45 rue Rouyers, 55000 Verdun. Tel. 03 29 86 07 86. *(Henry)*
Vervins (02)	**Le Cheval Noir,** 02 Vervins. *(Bernoville)*
Villers-St-Paul (60)	**Le Monia,** 2 rue Pasteur, 60870 Villers-St-Paul. Tel. 03 44 71 17 32. A restaurant that was one of the first customers to take Colvert, and still does. *(De Clerck)*

BEER SHOPS

The following beer shops are suggested as sources of French beer. If the recommendation is from a brewery it is likely to stock its beer, if it is from the authors the shop should have a well-stocked, wide selection of French beers. The source of recommendation follows the entry, in italics.

Airaines (80)	**J & C Girard,** 5 avenue Général Leclerc, 80270 Airaines. Tel. 03 22 29 41 17. *(De Clerck)*
Amiens (80)	**Corbeille Paysanne,** les Halles du Beffroi, Place M.Vaast, 80000 Amiens. Tel. 03 22 91 70 45. Specialise in regional products. *(De Clerck)*
	Supermarché Match, 80000 Amiens. *(De Clerck)*
Annœullin (59)	**Aux Caves d'Annœullin,** 1 Grand Place, 59112 Annœullin. Tel. 03 20 85 75 31. All the Annœullin

beers plus a good range of other artisanal beers. *(Annœullin)*

Arras (62)	**Colas Jacqueline**, 31 place des Héros, 62000 Arras. Tel. 03 2 12 32 03 87. Local artisanal products. *(Bécu)*
	Le Cellier des Bières, 8 rue de la Taillerie, 62000 Arras. Tel. 03 21 51 34 94. Sells many artisanal beers from many countries. *(Bécu)*
Beauvais	**Supermarché Match**, Beauvais. *(De Clerck)*
Berck-sur-Mer (62)	**Continent**, Z.I. de la Vigogne, 62600 Berck-sur-Mer. *(Bécu)*
Carvin (62)	**Le Palais des Terroirs**, 161 rue Florent Evrard, 62220 Carvin. Tel. 03 21 37 57 42. *(Bécu)*
Cassel (59)	**T'Kasteel Hoff**, Mont Cassel (face au moulin), 59670 Cassel. Tel. 03 28 40 59 29. Exclusively local products, with a good range of artisanal beers. *(Authors, Thiriez)*
Clermont-Ferrand (63)	**E. Leclerc**, 63 La Pardieu, *(Cerf)*
Compiègne (60)	**Le Relais du Château**, 24 rue d'Ulm, 60400 Compiègne. Tel. 03 44 40 03 45. Specialises in regional products. *(De Clerck)*
Dinan (22)	**Bières sans Frontières**, 14 rue Ste-Claire, 22100 Dinan. Tel. 02 96 87 00 20. Small but very interesting range of artisanal French beers. *(Authors)*
Douai (59)	**Le Monde des Bières**, 32 rue St-Christophe, 59500 Douai. *(Authors – but not tried personally)*
Doullens (80)	**Supermarché Match**, 80600 Doullens, *(De Clerck)*
Dunkerque (59)	**Cadovino**, Angle 2, rue Dampierre, 59140 Dunkerque. Tel. 03 28 21 00 99. *(Thiriez)*
	Crémerie Moderne, 67 rue Belle Rade, 59240 Dunkerque. Tel. 03 28 63 18 68. *(Thiriez)*
	Epicerie Gille, 24 Bd. Ste-Barbe, 59140 Dunkerque. Tel. 03 28 63 66 20. *(De Clerck)*
Frouard (54)	**Les Jardins du Val de Lorraine**, 41 rue de Metz, 54390 Frouard. Tel. 03 83 24 27 77. *(Henry)*
Godewærsvelde (59)	**Le Roi du Potje Vleesch**, 31 rue du Monts des Cats, 59 Godewærsvelde. Tel. 03 28 42 52 56. A charcuterie but a good selection of local beers. *(Authors, John White)*
Guérande (44)	**Tout au Beurre**, 16 rue St-Michel, 44 Guérande. Tel. 02 40 24 93 69. *(Séverac)*
	Ar Blaz Mad, 40 rue St-Michel, 44 Guérande. Tel. 02 40 15 63 70. *(Séverac)*
Herbignac (44)	**Vergers du Littoral**, 1a Gassun, 44 Herbignac. Tel. 02 40 88 90 59. *(Séverac)*
Josselin (56)	**L'Epicerie le Verger**, 56 Josselin. *(Lancelot)*
Kayserberg (68)	**S'Bierladl Boutique**, 50b rue du Général-de-Gaulle, 68240 Kayserberg. Tel. 03 89 78 13 92. *(Authors)*
Lille (59)	**Chez Rohart**, 59800 Lille. *(Authors – but not tried personally)*
	l'Art des Vines, 59800 Lille. *(Authors – but not tried personally)*
	Trogneux, 67 rue Nationale, 59000 Lille. Tel. 03 20 54 74 42. An artisan chocolate maker who makes chocolates with beer. *(Bécu)*
	Vinothèque Rohart, 66 rue Faidherbe, 59000 Lille. Tel. 03 20 06 29 92. *(Bécu)*
Missillac (44)	**Le Cep de Vigne**, route de St-Gildas, 44 Missillac. Tel. 02 40 88 38 59. *(Séverac)*
Mulhouse (68)	**Gambrinus**, 68 Mulhouse. *(Authors)*
Obernai (67)	**Planète Bière**, 67 Obernai. *(Authors – but not tried personally)*
Paris (75)	**Bootlegger**, 82 rue de l'Ouest, 75014 Paris. Tel. 01 43 27 94 02. *(John White)*

	K. Bière, 64 rue du Mont St-Denis, 75018 Paris. *(Henry)*
Pitgam (59)	**La Mare Aux Bières,** 16 bis, La Place, 59284 Pitgam. Tel. 03 28 62 18 83. Specialises in having a very good range of beers and wines. *(Thiriez)*
Redon (35)	**Ferme de Bellevue,** Bellevue, 56 St-Jean la Poterie, Near Redon. Tel. 02 99 71 24 88. *(Séverac)*
Ribeauville (68)	**S'Bierladl Boutique,** 68 Grand Rue, 68150 Ribeauville.
Riom (63)	**Intermarché,** Riom. *(Cerf)*
Roncq (59)	**Le Tire-Bouchon,** 59223 Roncq. *(Authors – but not tried personally)*
Saintes (17)	**La Sangria,** 27 avenue de la Narne, 17100 Saintes. Tel. 05 46 92 99 21. 350 beers. *(Naufrageurs)*
Sélestat (67)	**Village de la Bière,** 67 Sélestat. More than 350 beers *(Authors – but not tried personally)*
St-Philibert (56)	**La Trinitaire,** 56 St-Philibert, near Carnac. *(Lancelot)*
St-Pierre-d'Oléron (17)	**Gamm Vert,** Zone Industrielle, route Miranelles, 17310 St-Pierre-d'Oléron. Tel. 05 46 47 16 46. *(Naufrageurs)*
	Le Taste Vin, 98 rue de la République, 17310 St-Pierre-d'Oléron. Tel. 05 46 47 08 30. *(Naufrageurs)*
St-Sauveur (60)	**La Cavette à Bières,** 385 rue de la Mabonnerie, 60320 St-Sauveur. Tel. 03 44 40 50 99. *(De Clerck)*
St-Amand (59)	**E.Leclerc,** 59230 St-Amand. *(Amis Réunis)*
Strasbourg (67)	**Village de la Bière,** 67100 Strasbourg. Apparently more than 350 beers. *(Authors – but not tried personally)*
Thiers (63)	**Continent,** 63 Thiers. *(Cerf)*
Vannes (56)	**La Tapenade,** 56 Vannes. *(Lancelot)*

In addition to the above, the following breweries suggested supermarkets in their local area as sources of their beer:

Les Amis Réunis – Auchan, Carrefour.

Chant du Loup – Carrefour, E.Leclerc & Continent in Rouen and district.

Theillier – Local supermarkets, such as Match and Auchan.

Bécu – Supermarché P.G. and perhaps others in Pas-de-Calais.

TELL US AND WE WILL TELL EVERYBODY ELSE

DO YOU KNOW OF ANY BARS/CAFES OR BEER SHOPS WHICH SHOULD BE IN THIS LIST?

We are always keen to hear from anyone who can recommend a bar/cafe or beer shop. The main criteria is obviously a good selection of beer – preferably French beer – and a professional service. Occasionally we list outlets with a smaller choice which can still be recommended for other reasons, such as having a very traditional interior or being of great architectural interest.

To process all the relevant information we need the following:
- Name and address of establishment
- Telephone and fax numbers
- Opening times
- A résumé of the beer list (or preferably a photocopy of the list itself) and any comments (e.g. mainly Belgian, small but well-chosen, etc.) along with sample prices and the number of French beers
- A brief description of the bar itself, its overall atmosphere and its usual clientele (e.g. locals, students, etc.)
- If the owner is one of the reasons for its recommendation (e.g. knowledgeable, characterful, etc.) we will need their name

If requested we will publish the name of the person who recommends the establishment and, if possible, we will inspect it ourselves

BEER INDEX

This is an alphabetical index to the beers of France which appear in this book. Alternative names for existing brands appear in italics and the page number will refer you to the original beer, where we give alternative names in the general comments section of the beer notes.

Beer	Brewery	Page
Telenn Du	Lancelot	184
Tequieros	Gayant	148
Terken Blonde	Terken	244
Terken Brune	Terken	244
Thomas Becket	Champs	107
Tour d'Ostrevant, La	La Choulette	117
Tourmente, La	Grands Cols	251
Tourtel Ambrée	Kronenbourg	172, 252
Tourtel Blonde	Kronenbourg	172, 252
Tourtel Brune	Kronenbourg	172, 252
Tradition	Schutzenberger	233
Tradition (Adelshoffen)	Fischer & Adelshoffen	139
Tradition (Fischer)	Fischer & Adelshoffen	138
Tradition Allemande	Kronenbourg	176
Tradition Anglaise	Kronenbourg	176
Trente Wheat	Paris Real Ale Brewery	205
Tütz	Schutzenberger	233
Type Allemagne	Spirit Of Factory	237
Type Anglais	Spirit Of Factory	237
Ubald	Terken	244
Uberland	Terken	244
Upstaal	Terken	244
Upsthem	Terken	244
Valstar	Kronenbourg	178
Vanille	Naufrageurs	198
Viking Wolf	Chant du Loup	111
Vin d'Orge	Deux-Rivières	124
Vita-Pils	Annœullin	67
Volcan Xmas	Cerf	104
Vosgienne, La	Musée de Ville sur Illon	250
Wel Scotch	Kronenbourg	177
Wilfort	Kronenbourg	178
Winter Warmer	Café Chantecler	112
X-Cider	Kronenbourg	172
Zorn Val	Meteor	190
Zornbier	Meteor	189

BEERS OFTEN ON SALE ON FRENCH BEER LISTS – BUT WHICH ARE NOT ACTUALLY FRENCH

We are not saying the following beers shouldn't be sampled (in fact we would advise everyone to try the Unibroue range) but we feel we should point out that they aren't actually French beers – even though they are often sold as such on beer lists.

Abbaye des Dunes, L' (6.5%)	Brewed by Huyghe (Belgium)
Bière de la Grande Armée, La (7%)	Brewed by Engel Brauerei (Germany)
Blauwers Bier (6%)	Brewed by Watou (Belgium) for Het Blauwershof bar.
Cave des Pères, La	Brewed by Sterkens (Belgium)
Cervoise des Ancêtres, La	Brewed by Engel Brauerei (Germany). Sold in a stone bottle
Claeyssens, La, Bière au Genièvre Vieux Malt (7%)	Brewed by Brunehaut (Belgium) for La Distillerie de Genièvre Claeyssens in Wambrechies
Coq Hardi Spéciale (5.5%)	Brewed by Haacht (Belgium)
Eau Bénite (7.7%)	Brewed by Unibroue (Canada)
El Loco St-Tropez	Brewed by Huyghe (Belgium)
Fin Du Monde, La (9%)	Brewed by Unibroue (Canada)
Maudite (8%)	Brewed by Unibroue (Canada)
Raftman (5.5%)	Brewed by Unibroue (Canada)
Trois Pistoles (9%)	Brewed by Unibroue (Canada)
Trompe la Mort (7%)	Brewed by Engel Brauerei (Germany)
Valenciennoise, La (4.5%)	Brewed by De Smedt (Belgium). Appears on beer lists particularly often in the Valenciennes area